Islands and International Politics in the Persian Gulf

The position of the Persian Gulf as a main highway between East and West has long given this region special significance both within the Middle East and in global affairs more generally. This book examines the history of international relations in the Gulf since the 1820s as Great Powers and regional powers have vied for supremacy over this geopolitically vital region. It focuses on the struggle for control over the islands of the Gulf, in particular the three islands of Abu Musa, Greater Tunb and Lesser Tunb – an issue that remains contentious today. It describes how for 170 years Britain eroded Iranian influence in the Persian Gulf, both directly, by trying to assert colonial rule over Iranian islands and port districts, and indirectly, by claiming Iranian islands for their protégés on the Arab littoral. It shows how, after Britain's withdrawal, these islands became pawns amid the animosity and competition that, at one time, pitted Arab radicals and nationalists against monarchical Iran and, later, the conservative-moderate Arab camp against Islamic Iran. It goes on to explore the impact of the rise of American power in the Gulf since 1991, the US policy of containment of Iran, and how this has provided encouragement to the ambitions of the Persian Gulf Arab littoral states, especially the UAE, towards the islands of the Gulf.

Kourosh Ahmadi is a diplomat with 28 years of experience in the region and in international organizations. The research for this book was supported by the Center for Strategic Research – Tehran.*

> * The views, opinions, and/or findings in this book are those of the author, and should not be construed as necessarily reflecting the views of the staff, officers or Board of Overseers of the Center.

Durham Modern Middle East and Islamic World Series
Series Editor: Anoushiravan Ehteshami
University of Durham

1. **Economic Development in Saudi Arabia**
   Rodney Wilson, with Abdullah Al-Salamah, Monica Malik and Ahmed Al-Rajhi

2. **Islam Encountering Globalisation**
   Edited by Ali Mohammadi

3. **China's Relations with Arabia and the Gulf, 1949–1999**
   Mohamed Bin Huwaidin

4. **Good Governance in the Middle East Oil Monarchies**
   Edited by Tom Pierre Najem and Martin Hetherington

5. **The Middle East's Relations with Asia and Russia**
   Edited by Hannah Carter and Anoushiravan Ehteshami

6. **Israeli Politics and the Middle East Peace Process, 1988–2002**
   Hassan A. Barari

7. **The Communist Movement in the Arab World**
   Tareq Y. Ismael

8. **Oman – The Islamic Democratic Tradition**
   Hussein Ghubash

9. **The Secret Israeli–Palestinian Negotiations in Oslo**
   Their success and why the process ultimately failed
   Sven Behrendt

10. **Globalization and Geopolitics in the Middle East**
    Old games, new rules
    Anoushiravan Ehteshami

11. **Iran–Europe Relations**
    Challenges and opportunities
    Seyyed Hossein Mousavian

12. **Islands and International Politics in the Persian Gulf**
    Abu Musa and the Tunbs in strategic perspective
    Kourosh Ahmadi

Islands and International Politics in the Persian Gulf

Abu Musa and the Tunbs in strategic perspective

Kourosh Ahmadi

LONDON AND NEW YORK

First published 2008
by Routledge
2 Park Square, Milton Park, Abingdon, Oxon, OX14 4RN

Simultaneously published in the USA and Canada
by Routledge
270 Madison Avenue, New York, NY 10016

Routledge is an imprint of the Taylor & Francis Group, an informa business

© 2008 Kourosh Ahmadi

Typeset in Times New Roman by Prepress Projects Ltd, Perth, UK
Printed and bound in Great Britain by Biddles Ltd, Kings Lynn

All rights reserved. No part of this book may be reprinted or reproduced or utilised in any form or by any electronic, mechanical, or other means, now known or hereafter invented, including photocopying and recording, or in any information storage or retrieval system, without permission in writing from the publishers.

British Library Cataloguing in Publication Data
A catalogue record for this book is available from the British Library

Library of Congress Cataloging in Publication Data
A catalog record for this book has been requested

ISBN 10: 0-415-45933-8 (hbk)
ISBN 10: 0-203-92871-7 (ebk)

ISBN 13: 978-0-415-45933-4 (hbk)
ISBN 13: 978-0-203-92871-4 (ebk)

Contents

	Acknowledgements	vi
	Foreword	vii
	Maps	ix
	Introduction	1
1	Pax Britannica in the Persian Gulf	5
2	The Curzon strategy	31
3	The restoration of Persian Gulf autonomy and the issue of the three islands	73
4	Transitional period	115
5	Confrontational phase	144
	Conclusion: from containment to containment	179
	Notes	186
	Bibliography	209
	Index	213

Acknowledgements

In carrying out this research, I have profited from the assistance and counsel of many individuals whose services no words of appreciation can adequately measure. Especial acknowledgement is due to Dr Hossein Mousavian, the former Deputy-Director for International Studies, the Center for Strategic Research, whose enthusiastic interest in the project contributed greatly to its realization.

I owe a debt of gratitude to Professor Djamshid Momtaz, who patiently read the manuscript and provided me with his valuable specialist knowledge and advice at all times.

Also, I am grateful to Anoushirvan Ehteshami, the editor of the Durham Modern Middle East and Islamic World Series, and to the editors with whom I have worked during the preparation of the book – Peter Sowden, Tom Bates, Suzanne Peake, Andrew R. Davidson and Emma Davis. Their patience, professional skill and ability to provide expert viewpoints have been a vital asset in publishing this book.

I should not let this opportunity go without expressing my gratitude to my wife, Dr Tahereh Miremadi, for advice and encouragement. Nonetheless, the usual caveat applies that any remaining errors are solely my own responsibility.

Kourosh Ahmadi

Foreword

This study is an account of Irano-British encounters in the Persian Gulf from the time in the 1820s when Britain succeeded in sidelining its European rivals and establishing its ascendancy in the area. It shows how Britain's efforts aimed at enhancing its presence and entrenching its position in the Persian Gulf brought it into conflict with Iran, the major regional power.

It is a case study that focuses mainly on the Persian Gulf's islands and the importance that Britain, as a global maritime power, attached to them in its quest to control the area as a defensive outpost with which to secure the approaches to the crown jewel of its empire, the Indian subcontinent. Treaty arrangements regulated Britain's relationships with and dominance of the Arab sheikhs on the lower coast during the informal protectorate regime of the late nineteenth and early twentieth centuries. But, as this book will explain, British access to and control of the Iranian islands, especially those lining the north shores of the Persian Gulf or dominating the sealanes through the Strait of Hormuz, were a *sine qua non* for strengthening this protectorate regime, providing for the British flotilla and, at the same time, keeping European rivals out of those waters.

This study depicts the history of unrelenting struggle that accompanied the British presence for more than 150 years, with the control of these Iranian islands at stake. In the course of this long-lasting struggle between the pre-eminent global power and the major regional power, numerous individual disputes broke out, and almost every Iranian island in the Persian Gulf was the subject of dispute during one period or another. Although in the cases of most islands – including Kishm, Henjam, Hormuz, Larak, Kharg and Sirri – the British, after exhausting all avenues, gave up and grudgingly acknowledged Iranian sovereignty, they did not abandon efforts to establish or maintain their *de facto* control over those islands in one way or another.

This book explains how Britain became especially inflexible with regard to the islands of Abu Musa, Greater Tunb and Lesser Tunb, sovereignty over which it claimed for its Arab protégés, after it lost its bid to control the Iranian islands lining the north shores of the Strait of Hormuz. The expediency and self-interested strategic calculation with which the British approached the issue of the islands, and their efforts to work out an agreement among the regional players on the eve of their withdrawal from the Persian Gulf, are other important themes that the author covers thoroughly.

The issue of sovereignty over these three islands is important also as it is the only unresolved issue to have survived the British withdrawal. Chapter 3, in part, as well as Chapters 4 and 5, focus on the stages of the issue in the post-British periods. The author sheds light on developments in the issue under different circumstances and discusses regional and global interests that have affected it and tried to keep it alive. The description of the roles of the Arab radicals, who picked up the banner of claiming the islands for the Arab sheikhdoms against imperial Iran, on the one hand, and the Arab conservative-moderate camp who sided against Islamic Iran, on the other, is of great interest. The discussion of the impact of the enhanced US military presence in the Persian Gulf in the 1990s on the issue of the islands is also of great interest. These later developments are especially important, as the autonomy of the Persian Gulf from global powers, achieved after the British withdrawal in 1971, was again put in jeopardy.

Whereas almost all studies carried out so far on the islands issue have reviewed it from a legal point of view, what we are presented with here is a comprehensive study of a different nature. Although Kourosh Ahmadi assesses briefly the main legal arguments that the concerned parties have invoked, he does not attempt to offer a detailed legal review. Instead, he tries to place the issue in its strategic and political contexts. It is an interesting new look, in the sense that the struggle over the sovereignty of these islands is shown to be a manifestation of conflicting strategic and political interests in the region, as opposed to a simple territorial dispute pitting two countries against each other over a piece of land.

As the Persian Gulf remains today the strategic vortex of international politics, it is important that its problems be well understood. The need to revisit and discuss the issues that are of importance to the riparian states, and thus to the entire world, and indeed to examine the issues that in one way or another affect the area, can never be exhausted. And as today's problems can be understood only in the light of past developments, this study is a relevant and interesting contribution to the inexhaustible debates on the issues under discussion.

The material used in this study is drawn primarily from declassified documents published by the British Public Records Office and available in different compilations. Historic records made available by the Iranian government are reviewed too, as are UN and US documents, and local and regional leaders' statements and papers. Works by scholars and writers on subjects relating to the islands issue and to British imperial policies have also been consulted, albeit critically, and verified by other evidence. Thus, although the islands and politics of the Persian Gulf are reviewed from an Iranian perspective, Kourosh Ahmadi has done his utmost to maintain a high level of objectivity and impartiality.

For all of these reasons, this study deserves careful review.

Professor Djamshid Momtaz
School of Law and Political Science, University of Tehran, and
two-term member of the International Law Commission

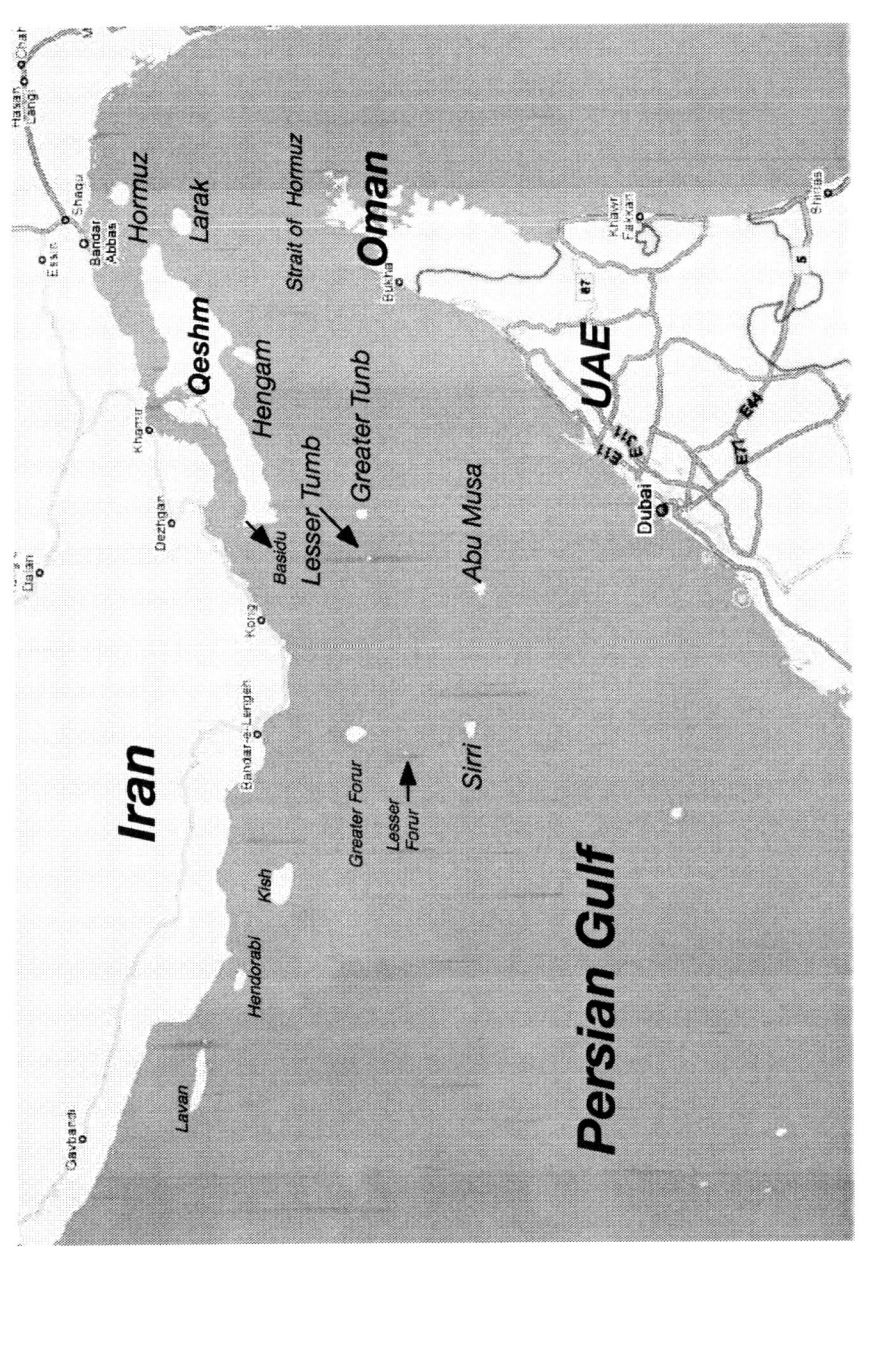

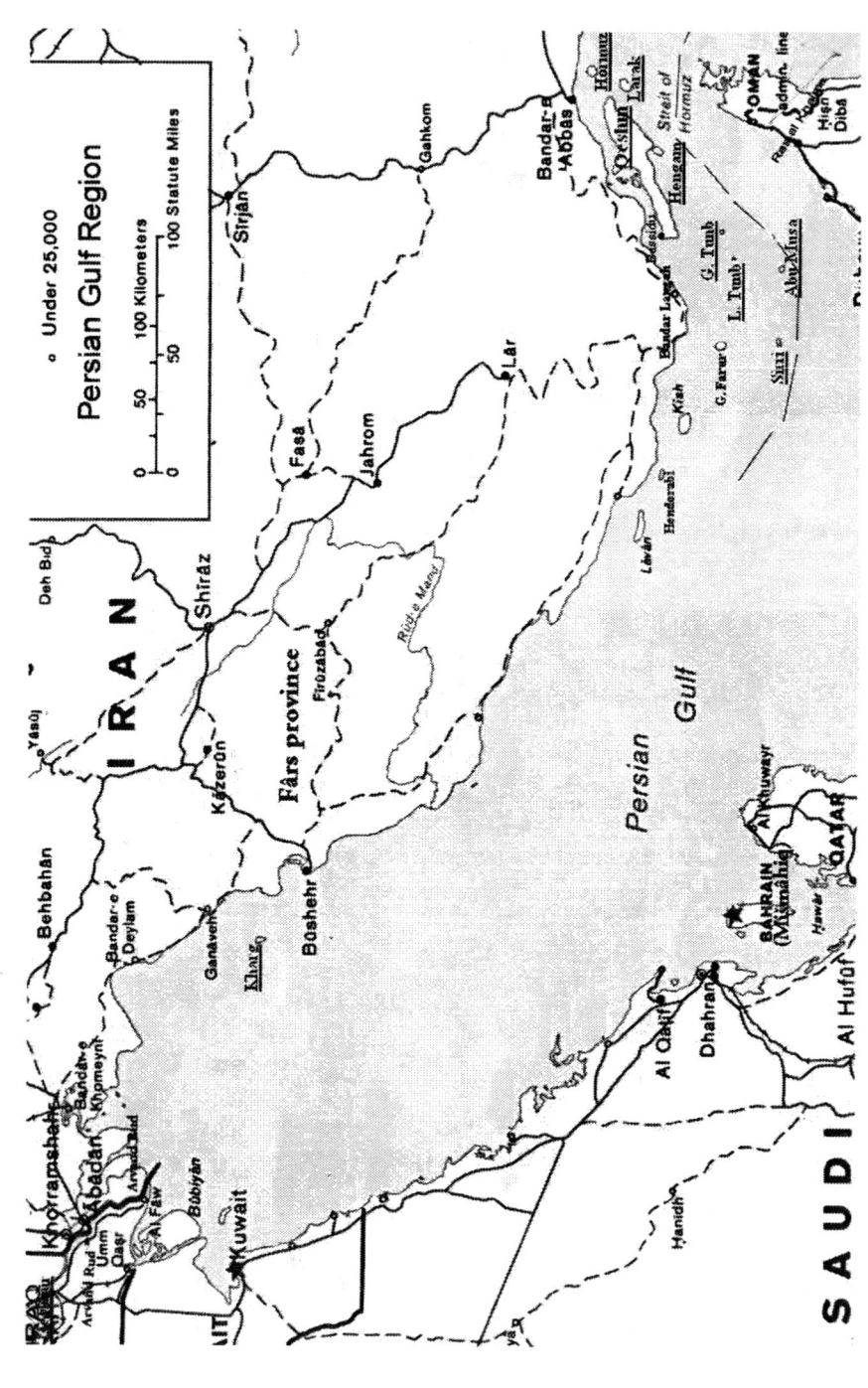

Introduction

The central position of the Persian Gulf as one of the main highways between East and West has long invested it with special importance. Portuguese explorers in the sixteenth century and British, French and Dutch trading companies in the seventeenth and eighteenth centuries sought to establish exclusive trading monopolies in its waters. Although all of the major Western maritime powers of the seventeenth and eighteenth centuries set their sights on maritime supremacy in the Persian Gulf, it was the British that won the race and eventually subordinated the Persian Gulf sheikhdoms.

The importance of the Persian Gulf as an outlet to the Indian subcontinent, and the other high stakes involved, accorded the area a very high priority on the British agenda for more than a century and a half. The colonial power's feckless tinkering with the map of the region, driven solely by self-interested strategic calculations throughout its rule, gave rise to unsettled borders and territorial disputes and turned out to be the main source of instability in the post-colonial era. Numerous past and current conflicts in the wider Middle East and elsewhere are direct outcomes of British colonial involvement and Britain's efforts to tinker with borders and territories.

It is noteworthy that Jack Straw, the former British Foreign Secretary, while reviewing current border and territorial conflicts and disputes in Asia and the Middle East, explicitly admitted in an interview that '[a] lot of the problems we are having to deal with now, I have to deal with now, are a consequence of our colonial past.'[1] In drawing up a list of British historical errors, he mentioned Kashmir, Palestine, Afghanistan, the Iraqi borders and Africa. Omitted by Jack Straw – maybe because it seems a minor issue compared to those others – is the issue of the three islands of Abu Musa, Greater Tunb and Lesser Tunb. This issue, the only one remaining out of numerous disputes that once pitted Iran and Britain against each other in the Persian Gulf, figures notably among the consequences of Britain's colonial past in the Gulf, and, thus, understanding its nature and development requires that it be put into the context of the tumultuous Anglo-Iranian relationship since the early nineteenth century.

Although the main legal evidence offered by the parties is briefly reviewed in Chapter 2, a detailed review and weighing of the purely legal evidence that Iran and the Arabs use in support of their claims to the three islands is beyond the scope of this study. Such legal arguments have already been the subject of numerous studies that describe, from a neutral or partisan standpoint, the perceptions and assessments of the two sides of the issue and different observers.

As the issue of the three islands cannot be understood in a vacuum, this author proposes to discuss it in a broader historical and strategic context and to look into the regional and international circumstances under which the issue took on relevance. This is especially important because the cycles of dormancy and activity that have characterized the sovereignty issue in the past are only explicable in light of the broader regional and global context. Nor could these islands be discussed in isolation from other Persian Gulf islands, all of which have been and continue to be important in terms of their international status and strategic location, as well as in terms of their involvement in successive imperial intrigues and their influential role in the relationship between Iran and foreign powers in the area. The Persian Gulf islands were vital for British policy in the region because of their importance for naval bases, coaling stations, navigation, trade, telegraphic lines, landing grounds and fuel-storage dumps along the Imperial Air Route and so on.

This research confines itself mostly to the interplay between Iran, as the main regional power on the Persian Gulf, and the main intervening global power in each period examined – the United Kingdom in the past and the United States at the present – and to the impact of these relations on creating and reviving the issue of the three islands. In its drive to strengthen its position against rivals, whether regional or global powers, the dominant power seeks to expand its direct or indirect control at the expense of the major regional power. The ups and downs of such relationships, which, except for a brief period in the 1970s, have generally been tense and fraught with constant competition and intrigues, have decided the main course of events in the Persian Gulf.

Under such circumstances, the issue of the three islands is not a standard border or territorial controversy analogous to those that pit so many countries against each other in the region and beyond; it is essentially a side effect of efforts undertaken by competing global powers, which in the course of their efforts to spread their influence in the Persian Gulf came into conflict with the major regional power. What has been and continues to be at stake is the autonomy of the Persian Gulf as a geopolitical unit. Whereas the major local power seeks always to uphold the autonomy of the Gulf region from outside powers, the dominance of a foreign power has generally tended to cost it its autonomy. Accordingly, the issue of the three islands has served as one of numerous instruments used by the dominating foreign power to facilitate its drive to advance its interests, which include controlling more territory and denying the regional power its natural latitude in the area. As a result, the three islands have only been a controversial issue when a foreign power is, or seeks to be, dominant in the Persian Gulf through taking advantage of small political entities.

This research also entertains the question as to why a host of different players, ranging from the British to Arab radicals to Arab moderates, became actively

Introduction 3

involved in different historical phases of the islands issue and why they took or refused to take the side of the sheikhs of the lower Persian Gulf.

Thus, the purpose of this research is fivefold:

- To show how the issue of the three islands is a side effect of the quest by a foreign global power to dominate the Persian Gulf.
- To depict the policy of Britain, as a global intervening power that aimed for about 170 years to contain and restrain Iran, as the main regional power, and to situate British policy on the three islands within the context of its general policy in the wider region. British policy consisted of undermining Iran's grip over its possessions in the Persian Gulf, mainly through claiming Iranian islands for British protégés on the Arab littoral, beginning with the island of Kishm in the 1820s, and then steadily annexing parts of Iran's eastern and south-western border areas in favour of their vassals.
- To demonstrate how the issue of the three islands is, in the final analysis, an outgrowth of strategic competitions among regional and transregional rival players, and how British self-interest lay at its origin. And how, after Britain's withdrawal, the islands became pawns amid the competition and conflict that pitted, at one time, Arab radicals and nationalists against monarchical Iran, and, at another, the conservative-moderate Arab camp against Islamic Iran. And, finally, to what extent the issue became influenced by the Cold War and the West's regional policy of containing the Islamic Republic of Iran, and excluding it from security initiatives in the Persian Gulf.
- To review the stance of the United Arab Emirates (UAE), and to demonstrate how it avoided initiating any dispute over the islands up to 1992 and adopted a different policy following the Kuwait crisis in 1991 and the extensive US military presence in the region.
- To illuminate the cyclical nature of the islands issue and the fact that real and perceived changes in the balance of power in the Persian Gulf have affected the courses of action of the UAE and other actors, thus inducing shifts between periods of dormancy and periods of activity on the issue.

Accordingly, this book is divided into five chapters:

- While trying to place the British policy on the three islands in the wider context of the British colonial approach, Chapters 1 and 2 discuss briefly the British interests, mainly imperial and strategic, that motivated Britain's protracted presence in the Persian Gulf, and the phases through which the British progressed in establishing and sustaining this presence. Both chapters attempt to explain how Britain, as a global power, came into a conflict of interest with Iran, as the major regional sovereign power, and to describe British efforts to undermine regional autonomy in the Persian Gulf and chip away at Iran's sovereignty. They further elaborate on the incremental encroachment of the British on Iranian territory through the method of claiming parts of

4   *Introduction*

Iran for the Arab chiefs under their protection, and address British assertion of supremacy on the seas by directly or indirectly controlling Iranian islands and port districts in the Persian Gulf. While the first chapter depicts British strategic behaviour up to the 1890s, the second chapter focuses on the new strategy that Lord Curzon, the Viceroy of India, promoted at the turn of the twentieth century, which, among other things, led to the claiming of the three islands for British protégés on the Arab littoral.

- Events leading to and following the British withdrawal from 'east of Suez' are discussed in Chapter 3. With Britain unable to remain in the Persian Gulf and the United States unwilling and unable to replace it, for the first time since the early nineteenth century the major Western global powers had no choice but to leave the region to its own devices. The removal of the main obstacle to the restoration of Iranian sovereignty over the three islands came in tandem with a period of regional autonomy. This chapter also focuses on the role of radical pan-Arabism in highlighting the islands issue, placing it on the agenda of the UN Security Council and dominating its subsequent developments. Arab radicalism gave rise to a several-month phase of activity on the islands issue before it returned to a period of dormancy for eight years. The subsidiary and mostly passive role of the newly constituted UAE, and its being dragged into the issue by the powerful Arab radicals, are discussed in this chapter as well.

- Chapter 4 reviews the development of the issue of the three islands in the transitional period that followed the Islamic Revolution in Iran, which drastically altered the geopolitics of the Persian Gulf and the course of developments therein. Although the United States endeavoured in this period to fill the vacuum left by the Shah and to contain revolutionary Iran, it would take it a decade for this global player to muster enough power to tacitly claim a status analogous to that of Britain before 1971. Thus, only the period immediately following the Revolution saw a brief round of activity on the islands issue, provoked almost exclusively by Iraq in 1979, before the issue fell back into a twelve-year phase of deep dormancy. The continued relative supremacy of Iran in the Persian Gulf in the 1980s, coupled with the abandonment of the pursuit of the issue of the three islands by Arab radicals, who had for the most part aligned themselves with revolutionary Iran, thwarted any serious challenges to Iran's position on the islands.

- Chapter 5 examines the extended phase of activity related to the three islands by the UAE and its allies since 1992, following the emergence of a totally new situation in the region in the aftermath of Iraq's humiliating defeat in the war over Kuwait, the loss of the status of Palestinians as a result of the perception that they sided with Saddam Hussein, and the collapse of communism. This chapter further elaborates on the drastic qualitative expansion of the US military presence in the Persian Gulf and the US containment policy against both Iran and Iraq, which provided unprecedented leeway to the Persian Gulf Arab littoral states, especially the UAE, and encouragement to them to embark on a path.

1 Pax Britannica in the Persian Gulf

The Persian Gulf constitutes a main highway between East and West and has been on the periphery of empires through the ages. As such, it acquired increasing importance for the British Empire in the eighteenth century and beyond, as Britain endeavoured to secure the approaches to its Indian colonial dominion, which was of paramount importance for the status of Britain in the world.

As George N. Curzon, who served as the Viceroy of India from 1899 to 1905, noted, 'the future of Great Britain . . . will be decided, not in Europe, not even upon the seas and oceans which are swept by her flag, or in the Greater Britain but in the continent whence our emigrant stock first came, and to which as conquerors their descendants have returned. Without India the British Empire could not exist. The Possession of India is the inalienable badge of sovereignty in the eastern hemisphere.'[2] Sir Percy Sykes, commander of South Persia[3] Rifles, a unit put together to secure British interests in southern Iran during the First World War, emphasized 'the importance of the Persian Gulf, the control of which is almost equivalent to the domination of the Middle East.[4]

The quest of external powers for involvement in the Persian Gulf has generally arisen from one or more of three principal motivations: trade, political rivalry and imperial security. Trade required penetrating or protecting long trading routes crossing or arising in the Persian Gulf, and the protection of local or regional trading. Political rivalry has motivated several countries to secure control over the Persian Gulf; the Portuguese dominated the Gulf in the sixteenth century and Britain dominated it in the nineteenth and most of the twentieth centuries. In other periods the Persian Gulf experienced either a bipolar balance of power or the more fluid conditions of multilateral control.

In British strategic logic, the defense of India against European challenges required the incessant extension of British zones of influence beyond the Indian frontiers. Thus, over time Britain attached greater importance to spreading its influence and supremacy to the regions surrounding India, including the Persian Gulf. The British involvement in Afghanistan was also mainly a product of this impulse.

The British rising star

The British, competing with the Portuguese and the Dutch throughout the sixteenth to eighteenth centuries, finally rose to prominence and superseded their rivals as hegemon in the Persian Gulf in the early nineteenth century. The furthering of commercial interests was what the British had initially sought in the area, but as the importance of Gulf trade diminished in the eighteenth century, new emerging political and imperial interests, including the imperative of neutralizing France and Russia, warranted a continued British presence in the area.

Relying on their supremacy at sea, and determined to preserve and enhance it, the British concluded, in the early nineteenth century, that their control of the Persian Gulf and the Strait of Hormuz was essential for the security of their possessions in the Indian subcontinent and beyond. This determination led the British to deploy their war flotilla in the Persian Gulf and to seek to subordinate local authorities – a move that was necessary to secure both their presence and secure access and facilities for their warships. They began by taking on the weakest points in the Persian Gulf, which consisted of autonomous tribes on its lower shores. Soon these tribal entities on the lower Gulf became major footholds for the British in the area.

The main goals Britain pursued during its long domination of the Persian Gulf – from the early nineteenth century until its withdrawal from the area in 1971 – can be summarized as follows:

- dominating local tribes as bases from which to carry out other goals;
- keeping European rivals, as well as Ottoman Empire, out of this body of water and off its shores;
- curtailing the presence and influence of the major regional power – Iran.

Britain's main concerns at first were to have a share in trade, ensure the freedom of communication between its centre and its colonies, and ward off rivals. Thus, the agreement between the East India Company and Muscat in 1798, known as Kowlnama, sought only to exclude the French and enlist the Sultan of Oman on the Company's side.

Later, motivated by imperial security and momentum, Britain sought to incorporate the Persian Gulf into its imperial domain, or its sphere of influence, in order to defend its colonial possessions in the East. As the Persian Gulf is located on what has been periphery of empires through the ages, and as the Middle East constitutes a strategic land bridge between three continents, the most enduring aspect of this motivation seems to have been that of establishing and protecting imperial lines of communication.[5]

Donald Hawley, the British Political Agent in Dubai from 1958 to 1961, mentions three specific factors that drew the British into relations with the people of the area in the early nineteenth century:

- 'First, wars arising from trade rivalry and tribal factions were endemic among Arab tribes on both shores of the Persian Gulf';

- second, 'the Wahabees, under the Al Saud family, occupied most of eastern Arabia and their fanaticism spreading to the Qawasim [drove] them to attack even those who were not their personal enemies';
- third, 'Napoleon's ambition for a vast eastern empire had increased both [British] sensitivity to potential dangers to their communications with India and their willingness to respond.'[6]

As an illustration of how conflicts in the colonies were often outgrowths of colonial powers' home rivalries in Europe, the Napoleonic invasion of Egypt in 1798, coupled with French activities in the Persian Gulf, aroused British suspicions of French designs on India through the Gulf and alerted the British to the geopolitical importance of the area.

This occurred at a time when each of the main powers on the shores of the Persian Gulf, Iran and the Ottoman Empire, although in competition with one another, lacked a navy powerful enough to establish order in its waters. Towards the end of the eighteenth and the beginning of the nineteenth centuries, then, there was no dominant power in the Persian Gulf, and as a result it was a place where piracy and anarchy reigned and the stage was set for competition among foreign rivals to play out fully.

French attempts to develop ties with Muscat in the early years of the nineteenth century, which included the posting of a commercial agent there, and the signing of the Treaty of Finckenstein with the Persian court of the Qajar, further highlighted for the British the threats to their possessions in the subcontinent and the need to secure the approaches to it.[7]

At the same time, impressed by the victory of Napoleon in Egypt, Fath Ali Shah of Iran sought to build a relationship with France. He was encouraged when the French sent a delegation to Iran in 1800, offering French support to Iran in its constant difficulties with the Russians and the British. Reinforced in his conviction by numerous very friendly diplomatic correspondences exchanged with Napoleon, Fath Ali Shah hoped to obtain assistance from France that would enable him to establish peace and order in Iran's remote maritime possessions in the Persian Gulf.[8] Despite Tehran's rejection of the French request for concessions over the islands of Kharg and Hormuz, the Treaty of Finckenstein was finally signed in May 1807.[9]

The change in French policy in the wake of the signing of the Treaty of Tilsit in July 1807, however, allowed Britain to enjoy a wider margin of manoeuvre and a freer hand in the Persian Gulf. Emerging successful at having subdued effective threats from European rivals, the British tried to dominate all maritime activities, strengthen their position and defuse regional threats to their supremacy, which came in several phases. They approached the Persian court, seeking unsuccessfully to acquire, among other things, concessions over some of the Iranian islands. And, at the same time, they embarked on a parallel path that led to the subjugation of Arab sheikhs on the lower Persian Gulf.

Subjugating Arab sheikhs

The chaos reigning in the Persian Gulf in the late eighteenth and early nineteenth centuries resulted in increasingly frequent attacks on British and British-protected vessels patrolling its waters. The combination of lack of political authority and depressed economic conditions on the lower Gulf led to what the British termed 'piracy', which provided Britain with a convenient pretext for advancing its scheme of dominating the area and entrenching its presence. The activities of certain Arabs of the area, known as Qawasim (Qasimi in singular) or Joasmis,[10] were regarded by the British in such a light and their territory was labelled 'the Pirate Coast.'

The principal British response to this 'piracy' came in the form of punitive expeditions launched against Qasimi ports. In a string of battles starting in 1808 and culminating in 1820, the Qawasim were finally subdued and their population centres either surrendered or set ablaze. The British left a small garrison behind when the fleet withdrew.

British aims included imposing their presence incontrovertibly in the Persian Gulf, securing the ability of unfettered movement, and deterring the activities of other powers, and these aims could be achieved, *inter alia*, by neutralizing and subordinating the tribes of 'the Pirate Coast'. The British did not move to establish military bases or colonies on Arab land, as they saw no benefit in entanglements with chaotic tribal politics, and did not consider it to be cost-effective. Instead, as discussed later, the British looked to Iran's maritime possessions, on or off the Persian shores, dominating the lower coast and the Persian Gulf entrance, as potential sites for a military base – a protracted preference that lingered for more than a century.

Following the British attack on the Qawasim in 1820 and the destruction of all piratical vessels and naval and military assets in Ras al-Khaimah, and the shelling of that city, some boats at the port of Lingeh and some other small Persian ports were also taken and destroyed, for which compensation had later to be paid, as the British could produce no definite proof of piracy by the people of these places.[11]

To prevent any misunderstanding on the part of the Persian government of the object of the expedition, the British took a series of measures, including sending a special emissary with a letter from the Governor of India to the Governor-General of Fars and the Governor of Bushehr, and sending a letter to the Persian government through the British chargé d'affaires in Tehran. The Shah, however, was not appeased, and the Prince of Shiraz wrote a letter to General Keir, the British commander, requesting him to refrain from further interference at any of his ports, especially Lingeh. Keir, therefore, thought it inadvisable to land any troops on Persian soil.[12]

Treaty-based relations with Arab tribes

The first steps in the establishment of a durable system amenable to British long-term interests in the Persian Gulf were taken in the aftermath of the 1820 battle.

These steps allowed Britain wide latitude to make the necessary arrangements for its lasting presence in the area.

A wide variety of formal treaties, agreements, and arrangements that Britain entered into in the nineteenth century with the rulers of the Arab coast dealt with topics ranging from peace and war to piracy, slave trafficking, and, most importantly, setting down restrictions on the capacity of Arab rulers to enter into treaties or other international relationships, or to permit any type of concession to foreign powers. In return for the cession of responsibilities for defense and foreign relations to the British, the local sheikhs were recognized by Britain as legitimate rulers.

The General Treaty of 1820

The General Treaty of 1820 was concluded between the British government and the 'Arab Tribes', and a number of sheikhs, including those of Abu Dhabi, Dubai, Ajman, Umm al-Qaiwain and Sharjah (then dominating Ras al-Khaimah), signed it. This agreement forbade piracy and plundering by sea, and distinguished between such actions and an acknowledged war. As defined in the agreement, piracy also included the slaughter of captives; in fact, the British interpreted the term 'piracy' in so broad a manner as to cover all acts of aggression. The real purpose of the 1820 treaty was the 'pacification of the Persian Gulf' for British vessels under the pretext of controlling piracy.[13] This purpose was made apparent in Articles 6 and 10, which authorized the British Residency in the Persian Gulf to act as a maritime police force.[14]

The General Treaty of 1820 was not meant to prevent the traffic in slaves; accordingly in 1838, 1839, 1847 and 1856, it was supplemented by further treaties that granted the right of search and confiscation to British vessels and prohibited the export of slaves from Arab ports. Needless to say, these agreements banning slave traffic also enhanced the British margin of manoeuvre in the Persian Gulf.[15]

The Perpetual Maritime Truce of 1853

One limitation of the 1820 treaty was its failure to regulate the conduct of warfare at sea among the Arab tribes, which tended to disrupt British vessel movements and the fishing and pearling seasons with some regularity. This omission was remedied by a maritime truce in 1835.

In 1835, the British persuaded the Arab rulers to bind themselves by a maritime truce for a period of six months, which was then extended year after year. It became permanent in 1853 by virtue of the Perpetual Maritime Truce of 1853, which recognized the benefits of the maritime truce and the mediation of the British Political Resident[16] and proclaimed a perpetual peace at sea. It further provided that the signatories would not retaliate against any breach of the truce but would inform the British authorities, who 'will forthwith take the necessary steps . . . for reparation.' Finally, it provided that the British government would 'watch over the maintenance of the peace which had been concluded, and take steps to ensure observance of the Articles'. It therefore denied the rulers the right of self-defence even against acts of aggression. Its effect was simply to deprive the rulers of their essential sovereign power and thus impose British maritime hegemony in the Gulf. Bahrain, for the reason later discussed, accepted these terms in 1861.[17]

After the Perpetual Maritime Truce of 1853, with which the *Pax Britannica* truly began, the British took control of the sealanes of the Persian Gulf. Even the presence of the Ottomans in Qatar and Saudi Arabia, and their close relations with Kuwait, did not have much maritime effect. With the agreement in force, the British opted to use the terms 'the Trucial Coast' and 'Trucial states' instead of 'the Piratical Coast'.

As Lord Curzon stated, 'The truce has not prevented, it was neither designed nor expected to prevent, warfare by land. These petty tribes exist for little else but internecine squabble, blood-feuds, puny forays, and isolated acts of courage or revenge. With their internal relations, Great Britain, who claims no suzerainty over Arabia, would have been foolish to interfere. All that she took upon herself to do was to secure the maritime peace of the Gulf'.[18]

The treaties were enforced at first from the short-lived base on Kishm Island. Regular Bombay Marine patrols, introduced to the Persian Gulf shortly thereafter, were able to deal effectively with the occasional attacks perpetrated over the next few decades.[19]

The exclusive agreements of 1892

In 1892, Britain concluded agreements with Bahrain and the Trucial states in which they surrendered the following rights of sovereignty to the British government:

- to establish diplomatic or consular relations with foreign powers other than Britain;
- to allow an agent of another government to reside within their territories;
- to sell, cede, mortgage or otherwise provide for occupation any part of their territory, except to the British government;
- to grant mineral or oil concessions to foreign governments or their subjects without the consent of Britain.

In return, the British undertook to protect them against foreign aggression, to look after their international political and economic interests and to extend its protection to their nationals abroad.[20]

These were comprehensive and definitive 'exclusive treaties'. It is worth noting that the term 'foreign power' was general and could be construed as covering regional as well as European powers. As one may surmise, the intent of these treaties was to insulate the tribal entities from the outside world, except through the mediation of Britain.

In 1899, at his own request, Sheikh Mubarak of Kuwait entered into a secret agreement with Britain to secure British protection and exclude foreigners. This was done despite the fact that Britain regarded Kuwait before 1899 as being under the suzerainty of the Ottomans. The British later had recourse to this 1899 agreement in warning Kuwait against negotiations with Germany on building the Baghdad railway without British approval. In 1913 the British government let it be known for the first time that Kuwait was 'an independent Government under British protection.'[21]

Given the Turkish claim to Qatar, it was only in 1916 – after the beginning of the Ottoman Empire's decline – that an Exclusive Agreement was concluded between Qatar and Britain.[22]

The Exclusive Agreements and the practice confirm that the Arab littoral states did not enjoy an international profile and were instead protectorates or protected states. All of these agreements had one central purpose in mind, that of pacification of the sheikhdoms and the establishment of British maritime supremacy in the Persian Gulf.

Thus, the formal structure of the exclusive treaties cast Britain in the role of arbiter and peacekeeper, and effectively excluded foreign powers from the lands of the signatories. They made it illegal for the Trucial states to consider external relations; that realm of action was firmly in the hands of the protecting power. These treaties enforced the so-called *Pax Britannica*, and, moreover, insulated the Arab territories of the region for more than a century from developments in the Middle East and from the two world wars.

In this way, the foundation was laid for Britain's legal and formal hegemony in the Persian Gulf. As permanent influence entails permanent supervision, official British representatives gradually were stationed around the Persian Gulf. In its final form, the British administration there constituted one part of the Government of India's far-flung residency system, with a Political Resident in the Persian Gulf (PRPG) headquartered at Bushehr on the Persian coast until 1947 and thereafter at Manamah, Bahrain. The Resident's subordinates were stationed in different population centres on the Persian Gulf's shores.[23]

Apart from foreign relations, Britain also assumed the defense of the tribal entities under its protection. To this end, an administrative structure developed with a headquarters in Bahrain, coordinating and directing the navy, army and air force. An officer was at the head of this organization as commander-in-chief, in close liaison with the Political Resident.[24]

Only on land was the situation less defined. While imposing British rule on the waters of the Persian Gulf, the *Pax Britannica* refrained from interfering in domestic affairs of the tribes before the First World War, thus leaving for long time the rulers and tribes to their own devices. The rationale for this state of affairs was twofold: the lack of any wealth worth exploiting on tribal lands, and the intense tribal rivalries, which would have threatened to entangle British resources. As we will see later, the discovery of oil and the advance of technology changed this situation.

Under *Pax Britannica*, there were no foreign representatives, apart from British agents and two American consulates at Dhahran and Kuwait, until 1961.

Journalists were unwelcome, as the British tried to keep the Persian Gulf out of the news. This policy, coupled with the inability of Tehran to maintain its traditional relations with the sheikhs, contributed to the maintenance of the status quo. As Sir Denis Wright, who served as British ambassador to Tehran from 1963 to 1971, put it, 'The British position in the Persian Gulf would not have remained so intact for so long had not the Iranian government been weak throughout the nineteenth century.'[25]

British policy towards Iran

A strained relationship

Britain's drive for supremacy in the Persian Gulf and its needs for reliable docking facilities and access brought it very soon into a conflict of interest with Iran, as the only major sovereign power on the shores of the Persian Gulf. As such, Iran's control over its possessions in the area placed considerable constraints on British movements there and on the entrenchment of British presence and the spread of British influence. Soon it became clear that the British presence in the regions adjoining India, and more importantly in the Persian Gulf and along the eastern Iranian border, could only be expanded at the expense of the Persian sovereignty.

As a result, Britain adopted the policy of undermining the Persian influence already in force on the subcontinent[26] and curtailing Iran's sovereignty along its eastern and southern borders, and pursued this policy vigorously throughout the era of British presence in the area. In 1902, the British Under-Secretary for Foreign Affairs elucidated his government's long-standing policy towards Iran when he declared that '[i]t would be impossible for us to abandon what we looked upon as our rights and position, not only in the Persian Gulf, but also in those provinces of Persia which border on the Indian Empire.'[27]

When the British started, in the early nineteenth century, to turn tribes on the Arab littoral into protectorate states, Iran found itself confused. When Britain signed treaties with those tribes, Iran's reaction was one of perplexity and reservation. As described in Chapter 2, Tehran never recognized the special relationship between Britain and the Trucial sheikhdoms, and refused to recognize their treaty relationship with Britain and their sovereignty through the mid-twentieth century.

Later, when Britain tried to gain direct control of Iranian islands, or control them indirectly by claiming them for the Trucial chiefs, Tehran firmly resisted. During Britain's ascendancy in the Persian Gulf, its decision-makers were haunted by two spectres: the social and political movement in nineteenth-century Iran that opposed both despotic monarchy and foreign interference, and the danger of the Iranian court allying itself with European powers hostile to Britain.

The reasons for British unease with regard to Persia throughout its presence in the Indian subcontinent and the Persian Gulf can be summarized as follows:

- Iran was the only major independent regional power in the wider area that adjoined territories under British dominion. The Persian state enjoyed the

attributes of a major regional power, including age-old imperial glory, a great ancient civilization, unrivalled state continuity based on 3,000 years of recorded history, a homogeneous national identity rooted in both the land and a functioning central government, a large population and a vast territory.[28]
- In the early decades of the nineteenth century, the Qajar Shahs of Persia, far from submitting to foreign powers, endeavoured to move in the footsteps of the Safavid dynasty by trying to revive the Persian Empire and extend its perimeters to where they had stood at the time of Shah Abbas in the seventeenth century. The three empires surrounding Iran – British, Russian and Ottoman – at first tried to contain the Qajars' efforts to expand their sovereignty over neighbouring territories, detached from Iran in the chaotic periods since the great Safavid Shahs, and then they began to encroach upon its territory proper.
- Iranian nationalism was vivid and active in the nineteenth century, preoccupied with reclaiming Iran's glorious heritage and preserving its national borders. Iranian nationalists, feeling nostalgic for ancient glory, focused mainly on land and keeping foreigners' hands off of land borders. Iran's defeat in the Russo-Persian War of 1813 ignited a spirited discourse that advocated political reform and patriotism, and in large part advocated the containment of foreign encroachment and influence in the country.[29] A report prepared by the British Foreign Office in October 1928 for the British Cabinet pointed out that 'Persian history during the last twenty years has been greatly influenced by the development of national feeling. . . . The quickening of dry bones in Persia preceded the similar movement in Turkey and furnished example and encouragement to the Young Turks of 1907–08. . . . Popular resentment against the granting of valuable concessions to foreigners by the Shah and the gathering force for constitutional liberty had become visible to the world by 1905.'[30] The report also states that 'Russian action, too, had caused Persian hatred to be directed not only against Russia and Russians, but almost equally against Great Britain and her nationals.'[31] Iranian nationalist zeal in opposing the British would reawaken a few decades later in the vigorous struggle for the nationalization of Iranian oil.
- Religious discourse greatly influenced the state of affairs after the Russo-Persian wars, during which the *ulama* sanctioned the *jihad* in defence of the lands of Islam. The aim of defending physical as well as political and economic perimeters of the state led to the formation of an alliance between religious and secular politicians, which found vivid expression in social and political movements in the nineteenth and the twentieth centuries.
- Protest against the influx of foreign goods and competition was another theme in Iran's vociferous nationalist discourse. It culminated in the 'tobacco protest' against granting to a British national, J. B. Reuters, a monopoly on the production and trade of tobacco. The tobacco concession brought far more protest than others because it dealt with a sphere that profited Iranian landlords, businessmen, and many large and small merchants. The widespread protest and a tobacco boycott by religious leaders forced the Shah

to repeal the concession in 1892. Nineteen years earlier another concession granted to the same British national to construct railways, irrigation systems and other works throughout the country for a period of 70 years had been vociferously denounced by the people, leading to the dismissal of the Iranian prime minister and the rescission of this concession as well. Lord Curzon attributed this loss to a 'hostile array of all the reactionary, or fanatical, or, as a Persian might say, patriotic forces in the country.'[32]

- Believing that India's front line of defence lay in Persia and the Persian Gulf, the intensification of Russian influence over the Qajar court, in the context of a Russian push from the north, was another threat perceived by the British. The Russians annexed Iranian territory in the Caucasus in the 1810s and 1820s, and the Russian-officered Cossack Brigade established in Tehran before and after the Constitutional Revolution in Russia further alarmed the British. They feared a breakthrough in favour of the Russians, enabling them to get to the shores of the Persian Gulf as a first stop on their way towards India. The control of Iranian possessions in the Persian Gulf was, therefore, sought by the British as a way, among other things, to dispel the danger of European rivals turning the islands into bridgeheads for the expansion of their presence in the area and undermining their Indian defense. Beginning with John Malcolm, the British envoy in the early eighteenth century, British officials believed that 'the establishment of a Russian ascendancy at Tehran would have an unsettling effect upon British rule in India.'[33] At several points during the 1838–42 occupation of the island of Kharg, British officials even discussed among themselves the retention of the island or adjacent city of Bushehr or both 'as being strategically and commercially desirable.'[34]
- Active popular resentment in Iran and competition from the Russians impeded British attempts to further their interests, and early in the nineteenth century Britain concluded that it would not be able to subjugate the Iranian body politic in a reliable and consistent way, as it did other political entities throughout the wider region. This decision was reinforced by the influential role the Russians played in the Qajar court, where they enjoyed a privileged status as the guarantors of the continuity of the reign of the Qajar family by virtue of the Treaty of Turkmanchai, concluded at the end of the second Russo-Persian war. Making use of their privileges, the Russians often outfoxed and outgunned the British in the course of their jockeying for a position of influence in Tehran.

In view of the above, the British adopted a policy that leaned towards containing and weakening Iran in the Persian Gulf and along its eastern land borders, as well as chipping away at its control in those areas. A dispatch from the British Government of India, written in 1870 and entirely approved by the Duke of Argyll, Secretary of State for India, reflects the general course of policy the British maintained throughout their colonial presence in the Persian Gulf and in the Indian subcontinent. This document states that 'the present is not when we can encourage the revival of old and unfounded claims such as those which Persia now puts forward.' It continues:

Even if the political engagements which we have contracted admitted of such a course, and Persia were possessed of an adequate naval force, it would be almost impossible and certainly impolitic to commit to her the guardianship of these vast and varied interests.[35]

While prohibiting the Trucial states, plus Qatar, Bahrain and Kuwait, from parting with any portion of their territory in favour of any power without British authorization,[36] Britain sought incessantly to bring maritime territory under its direct or indirect control. Consequently, the Persian Gulf islands, which were and continue to be, to some extent, exceptionally important in terms of their international status, strategic location and economic relevance, were deeply involved in successive imperial intrigues and played a very influential role in Anglo-Iranian relations.[37]

To strengthen its control in the Persian Gulf, Britain applied its established colonial policy of cultivating notables in charge of small political entities, as opposed to engaging regional powers, since smaller entities were much more amenable to adaptation to British wishes. It is said of Lord Curzon that his ideal was 'the creation of a chain of vassal states stretching from the Mediterranean to the Pamirs.'[38] This well describes British dealings with those found on the margins of their colonies and within independent states, including the Trucial Arab units.

In the early nineteenth century the British made clear for the first time that they had designs on a number of Iranian islands and port facilities in the Persian Gulf. They pursued this policy either by claiming certain Iranian islands for their vassals on the Arab littoral, by seeking them as concessions (as described later), or by making formal offers to the Persian government to lease or purchase them.

Securing the outer perimeters of India at the expense of Iran

In the aftermath of defeating the Qawassim (Joasmis) in 1820, the British toyed with different ideas for enhancing their presence in the Persian Gulf. These ideas ranged from establishing a base on an Iranian island in a commanding position near the Strait of Hormuz to enhancing and extending the power of the ruler of Muscat, Saiyid Sa'id, to promoting the Trucial sheikhs. The British began by supporting the claim of Saiyid Sa'id to the Iranian islands of Kishm and Bahrain, established a short-lived naval base on Kishm in 1820, and finally settled on the promotion of tribal sheikhs, thus establishing the main policy they pursued for the remainder of their presence in the Persian Gulf, until their withdrawal in 1971.

The policy of slowly but steadily separating Bahrain from Iran, the dispute over the islands lining the north shores of the Strait of Hormuz and the periodic occupation of the island of Kharg were the three major developments throughout the nineteenth century, guided by the overall British strategy in the east of Suez. The controversy over the islands lying at the centre of the Persian Gulf arose during the last quarter of the nineteenth century and culminated in the early twentieth century. In 1880 Britain considered proposing that Muscat purchase the island of Tunb.[39] The whole issue became a heated one following the British reaction to the action by Persia of hoisting its flag on Sirri in 1887.

A British base on an Iranian island – Kishm, Henjam or Kharg

With their increasing presence in the Persian Gulf, the British soon found themselves in growing need of access and docking facilities for their heavy and powerful flotilla. The idea of a base in the Persian Gulf to protect commercial interests had been broached in the eighteenth century, but the scheme advanced in the nineteenth century derived mainly from political and strategic considerations. A military presence on, for example, the Iranian islands of Kharg or Kishm, it was argued, would not only offer protection against pirates but also serve to counter Persian and French designs in the area.[40]

The islands of Kishm, Henjam and Kharg were the first Iranian possessions in the Persian Gulf on which the British set their sights. This came about in 1819 and after the general agreement in Bombay on future policy in the Persian Gulf and the need for a permanent British base to prevent a resurgence of piracy. Such a base, it was considered, should preferably be located on an island commanding the Strait of Hormuz.[41] British designs on the control of Iranian possessions in the Persian Gulf first came to light when Sir John Malcolm, the British envoy in 1800–01, tried unsuccessfully to persuade the Shah to cede or lease either Kishm or Henjam.[42] As Lord Curzon recorded, 'the land-locked bay between Henjam and Qishm was recommended by Sir J. Malcolm in 1800, as [a] naval station, having an easy entrance and excellent anchorage. But it was never occupied.'[43]

Later, in 1808, Malcolm switched his attention to Kharg and advocated its acquisition by force, if necessary. A year later the commanders of the first expedition against the Qawassim, who had been instructed to report on the suitability of Kishm and other islands near the entrance to the Persian Gulf as sites for a base, reported in favour of Henjam Island.[44]

During Malcolm's negotiations with the Persian court in Tehran, he requested concession of Kishm, Henjam, and Kharg islands. After the change in the French policy with regard to Persia, Sir Harford Jones arrived in Tehran in 1809 as the British ambassador and pursued further negotiations with Iranian officials. He offered naval assistance and an understanding against Russia in exchange for the expulsion of the French and the concession of a number of islands and port facilities in the Persian Gulf.[45]

At some point, the French and the British competition to control one Iranian island became spectacular. According to Lord Curzon, the island of Kharg 'was surrendered or was about to be surrendered to France during the short burst of Napoleonic ascendancy in 1807–08, but with the expulsion of the French Embassy from Persia in 1809, this second cession shared the fate of its predecessor. Sir John Malcolm was then instructed to occupy the island[46] in defense of British interests in the Persian Gulf; but this design was not executed.'[47]

The issue of establishing a British base on an Iranian island became dormant for more than a decade following the Iranian authorities' refusal to go along with the British offer on their maritime territories and a British disagreement among themselves on the wisdom of establishing a permanent base in the Persian Gulf. After the second expedition against the Qawassim in 1819, the idea of a base was revived. At this point, British forces occupied Kishm Island in order to remain in a position to control the lower Persian Gulf, and British officials approached the Imam of Muscat to sanction the occupation of the island, thus recognizing him as the authority owning the island. The British did this despite the fact that they had, earlier in the 1800s, approached the Iranian court to request cession of the same island to Britain, thus recognizing Iranian sovereignty over it.

The Government of Bombay, in a communication dated 28 October 1819, addressed to Sir William Keir, the British Commander in the Persian Gulf, sought his opinion on a number of issues. The document reads in part:

> As a measure the most effectually conducive to the permanent suppression of piracy on the Persian Gulf, the occupation by the British Government of a central and commanding situation appears to be indispensable; nor is the Governor in Council aware of a more eligible station than the island of Kishm for that purpose, upon which, however, your opinion is desired.

The dispatch continues:

> It is understood that the Island of Kishm, as well as Angar[48] ... belongs in full sovereignty to Sayyid Sa'id, the Imam of Maskat, and should the reports that may be received from you and the other persons to whom the consideration of this important subject has been confided be favourable to the measure now suggested, the necessary negotiation will be opened for obtaining possession of the spot that may be fixed upon for forming the establishment.[49]

Sir William Keir in his reply dated 1 April 1820 states:

> I have already most strongly recommended that the eventual removal [of British troops from Ras al-Khaimah] should be to the Island of Kishm, all that I have learnt since offering that recommendation, has tended to confirm my opinion of that island being the most favourable situation in every respect.[50]

Despite the fact that Sir John Malcolm had earlier requested the concession over Kishm from the Persian court, thus recognizing Persian sovereignty over the island, this time the British approached the Imam of Muscat, and in May 1820 requested his consent to the use of the same island. This was an important development because it marked the first time that the British attempted to gain control of a Persian possession in the Gulf by claiming it for a ruler in the Arab littoral. Captain Thomson, commander of the British troops in Ras al-Khaimah, reported to Bombay on 29 May 1820 that he had received 'the full consent of the Imam' in writing.[51]

The Imam's letter to the Governor of Bombay reads in part:

> With regard to the observation made by you, connected with the removal of the troops from Ras ul-Khima, God knows that the island in question and all

other territories appertaining to me, and subject to my authority, appertain also to the Honourable Company, and that I do not reckon these dominions as appertaining to me, but as appertaining to the Honourable Company.[52]

At the same time, Sir Henry Willock, the British chargé d'affaires in Tehran, approached the court to secure Persian consent to the British presence on Kishm too, and warned the Persian government of the consequences should they refuse. In the event, the takeover of the island of Kishm by the British set in motion a series of bitter Persian protests, which resulted in Britain disengaging from the island at a later date. Willock reported in a dispatch dated 10 May 1820 that:

The Persian Government were not very pleased with the British proceedings in the Persian Gulf and by no means welcomed the idea of the British occupation of Kishm or any other island on the Gulf.[53]

As Lorimer put it,

The occupation of Qishm provoked, as seems to have been foreseen, extreme resentment on the part of the Persian Government, who absolutely denied the title of the Sultan of Oman to independent sovereignty over Qishm ... No argument which the British representative in Tehran could adduce had any effect on the mind of the Shah or his ministers; and they continued to demand, as they had done from the outset, the withdrawal of the British detachment.[54]

The Persian government presented to the British chargé d'affaires a *note verbale*, dated 9 December 1820, strongly remonstrating against the British proceedings, noting in part that:

His Majesty's Chargé d'Affaires likewise stated ... that the Imam of Maskat (who on [sic] that part of Persia is the Governor of Bander Abbas and its dependencies[55]) was willing to allow of a British Settlement on the Island of Kishm or Henjam; to this was answered, that first Maskat is a dependency of Persia, and as the Imam has not the power of permitting the residence of British troops at Maskat, much less can he grant a permission at Kishm and Henjam which are dependencies of Bandar Abbas.

The same note goes on to question the wisdom of stationing a British detachment in the Persian Gulf, 'now that the Joasmis are subdued' and suggests that:

The Prince of Fars will use its utmost endeavours in preserving the security of the Persian Gulf, and if ships of war are necessary for that purpose, orders will be given for their outfit. We do not know on what account the troops from India have settled in the Persian Gulf. In short, orders will be issued to ... the Prince of Fars to send a person to the troops on Kishm desiring them immediately to leave it and we now request His Majesty's Chargé d'Affaires to direct the officer commanding at Kishm to return to India with his troops and ... in future to avoid such acts which are contrary to the spirit of the Treaty between our two States.[56]

From the minute recorded by Sir Monstuart Elphinstone, the Governor of Bombay, on the Iranian note, the following is of interest:

> The King of Persia's claim to Kishm does not appear to be strengthened by his present arguments, but on the contrary to be weakened by His Majesty's Minister making it in part depend on his sovereignty over Maskat, a pretension which seems to be entirely untenable.

He continues nonetheless:

> The King of Persia's alarm at our occupation of Kishm appears, however, to be serious and unfeigning and on this ground the Honourable the Governor would be disposed to give up the measure if it were not one of urgent necessity ... It is believed also that the British Government has in some measure countenanced the claim of the King of Persia to Kishm by requesting from His Majesty in the year of 1799 the cession of that island.[57]

British correspondence even reveals that at the time the British considered it probable that the Prince of Fars would attack British troops on Kishm, and directed their representative 'to point out the power the British Government possesses of avenging on Persia any unprovoked attack which may be made on our troops in the Gulf.'[58] A letter from the Government of Bombay to the Government of India indicates that the British, while under intense pressure by Tehran to withdraw from Kishm, were entertaining the idea of recommending to the Imam of Muscat that he retain his claim to Kishm, as this island 'was probably beyond the reach of [the Persian] Monarch's power.'[59]

The British thinking on Kishm becomes more evident through Bombay's harsh reaction against the Treaty of Shiraz that William Bruce, British Political Resident at Bushehr, entered into with the Prince of Fars. Letter No. 1491, dated 1 November 1822 and addressed to Bruce by the Secretary to the Government of Bombay, admonished him and disavowed the treaty, reading in part:

> [The Treaty] admits the claim of the King of Persia contrary to all history, to the protections of His Highness the Imam of Maskat, and to repeated declarations of this Government. It thereby admits the occupation of the [Kishm] island without the King of Persia's consent to have been an unjust aggression, and it agrees to admit a Persian force into Kishm, and to make over to the Persian the island we received from the Imam.[60]

Thus, Britain initially ignored the Persian protest against the British military presence on Kishm in favour of the pretensions of Sayyid Sa'id to the island. It was not long, however, before there were new problems with the Persians. Other difficulties on the ground, including inclement weather and diseases, coupled with the reassessment of the real need for a base, led to a discussion in British circles on the wisdom of maintaining a permanent base in the region. As a result, they decided to set aside the idea of establishing a base in favour of relying on a patrolling cruiser squadron, that is, a 'scheme of maritime control',[61] and on contractual arrangements with the sheikhs.

As Lorimer points out, eventually the British authorities in India arrived at the conclusion that it would be better to evacuate the island than to be constantly at issue with Persia in regard to it. But a sudden rupture of relation between the Monarch of Persia and the British representative at Tehran, which occurred in the spring 1822, made it inexpedient to appear to comply with the wishes of the Persian government until the end of that year or the beginning of 1823.[62]

Consequently, on 20 November 1822 the British Senior Officer in the Persian Gulf received instructions 'to bring down the garrison and the whole of the British establishment from the Island of Kishm to Bombay . . . [I]t has been expedient to make the port of Muscat the general rendezvous for the Honourable Company's cruisers accordingly.'[63]

After the British evacuated Kishm in 1823, they established a coaling depôt at Basidu, located at the northwestern extremity of the island. Lord Curzon maintained that Kishm was during a part of the nineteenth century a British military or naval station. A cantonment of English and Indian troops, several hundred strong, was established in 1820 to overawe the Qawassims. After being displaced on the island several times because of an inclement climate, the troops finally settled down at Basidu. In Curzon's view, the danger of malarial fever and the diminution of need for their services in the area led to their withdrawal three years later.[64]

Although rumours circulated for close to a century that Fath Ali Shah issued a *firman* (royal decree) formally ceding Basidu to the British, and some authors surmised that this might have happened through a covert accord between the Persian government and the British in 1822,[65] it became clear in the 1920s that this had not been the case. Declassified Iranian documents dating from 1925 to 1935 clarify that no document to this effect ever existed. Following the advent of Reza Shah, as Britian and Iran engaged in intense negotiations with a view to the settlement of numerous outstanding issues, the Iranian side thoroughly searched various national and local archives, looking for any document that might substantiate any possible acquisition of British rights to Basidu. Failing to find one, the Iranian Foreign Ministry recommended approaching the British and asking them to submit documents that they might hold that would 'clarify the extent of their concession' in Basidu, and, should no such documents be forthcoming, 'formally requesting them to evacuate the place.'[66] The Iranian government acted on this recommendation, but to no avail.

In respect to this issue, Iran's foreign minister Bagher Kazimi, in his letter No. 19803 dated 12 Aban 1312 (3 October 1933) to the British chargé d'affaires in Tehran, stated that, as 'any claim should be based on evidence, unfortunately, despite the fact that the Imperial Foreign Ministry has requested on numerous occasions leading to the latest one, dated 10 Khordad 1305 (31 May 1927), that the HMG of Britain present its evidence substantiating its claims to Bassidu, no answer has so far been given to the Imperial Government.'[67]

Differences between the two countries finally led to letter No. 37321, dated 13 Day 1312 (3 January 1934), from Kazimi to the British chargé d'affaires in Tehran, in which he confidently stated that 'the Iranian Government has never recognized any right whatsoever for the British at Bassidu and will never do in the future.'[68]

It should be noted that, although the British recognized Iran's title to the whole of Kishm for the best part of the nineteenth century, at the same time, they never fully gave up their claim to it for Muscat. An official British memorandum, dated 12 February 1908, still maintained that 'upon one of the Persian islands, *viz.*, Kishm, Great Britain possesses a piece of land by virtue of an original grant from the Imam of Muscat, to whom the island once belonged.'[69] The same memorandum claims that '[t]he British occupation [of Basidu] appears to have begun in 1820, under a verbal grant from Sultan Syed Saeed of Muscat, who then exercised jurisdiction over the island [Kishm]. This was confirmed by Agreement with his son and successor, Sultan Thoweymee, in 1864'.[70]

The Kishm episode was significant in the sense that it was the first time that the British actually claimed an Iranian island for a small local entity or a protégé of theirs from the lower Persian Gulf or motivated such an entity to advance such a claim, thereby expanding and establishing control. The fact that the British demonstrated for the first time their eagerness to control Persian Gulf islands, especially those located at its entrance, was significant too. That was a policy the British pursued for many decades, which culminated during the first years of the twentieth century in the case of islands such as Abu Musa, Sirri and the Tunbs.

Meanwhile, the decisions by Britain to abandon the idea of establishing a base and to discontinue the attempt to reach a deal with Tehran on Kishm helped move them towards adopting the policy of cultivating relationships with tribal Arab sheikhs through binding contractual arrangements, as discussed earlier, and containing Iran to their own advantage. Likewise, the unsuccessful British efforts in the 1800s and 1810s to induce the Persian government to allow them access to Persia's possessions in the Gulf was also important, as it led London and Bombay to adopt the policy of strengthening individual rulers on the Arab littoral and along common eastern borders at the expense of Persia. This new policy was pursued vigorously in the case of Bahrain.

Claiming Bahrain for an Arab littoral sheikh

The British policy of the pushing the Iranian government off the island of Bahrain, initiated in 1817–20, was another case in point where the British attempted rather successfully to divest Iran of its possessions in favour of the Arab sheikhs under their protection. In this period, the sheikhs of Bahrain (Sheikh Abdullah and Sheikh Salman), while reaffirming their submission to the Persian court and declaring loyalty to the provincial government of Fars, refrained from regularly sending the due tributes to the Fars Treasury. It is believed that advice by Lieutenant Bruce, Political Resident in the Persian Gulf, encouraged the sheikhs in this decision.

Iranian title to Bahrain was not in dispute at the time. It rested on Iranian sovereignty over the island for several centuries and at least since 1622 when the sheikh of Bahrain acknowledged himself a vassal of Persia, and on the fact that a substantial proportion of its inhabitants were Shia of Iranian descent or were immigrants from the Persian side of the Persian Gulf. As the authoritative scholar J. B. Kelly recognizes, at the beginning the Al-Khalifa ruling family did not deny Persian title to the island and they paid an annual tribute to Shiraz.[71]

In the confidential 'Memorandum on the Separate Claims of Turkey and Persia to Sovereignty over the Island of Bahrain', dated 25 March 1874 and written by E. Hertslet, a Foreign Office official, it is stated that 'Bahrein was occupied by the Portuguese in the sixteenth century, but in 1622 they were expelled by the Persians, who appeared to have held possession of the island till about the year 1782 or 1783.' A footnote to this statement reads: 'the "Imperial Gazetteer" states that the Persians withdrew from the island in 1790.'[72]

According to the same report, Willock, the British Minister in Tehran, described how in April 1817 the Imam of Muscat arrived in Tehran and requested that the Shah assist him with a body of troops in order that he might take 'possession of the island [of Bahrain] in the name of his Majesty.' He also reported on 6 April 1817 that an agent of the Sheikh of Bahrain was also at Tehran, and that a letter, of which he was the bearer, stated that 'as the inhabitants of the island were of the same sect as the natives of Persia, they had always looked up to the Persian Monarch as their protector and head, they therefore hoped for His Majesty's assistance to cloak them from the oppression of the Wahabees.' Willock's later report indicates that 'a *firman* was in consequence issued by the Shah to the Imaum of Muscat, granting the military assistance he solicited.'[73]

While recognizing at this time Iranian sovereignty over Bahrain, the British maintained that any act of coercion could be dangerous for the general peace in the Persian Gulf and for commercial British interests. At the same time in the early 1820s, seeking to flatter the Shah by securing from the Al-Khalifa the reiteration of titular recognition of his sovereignty over Bahrain at no real cost to their independence, the British hoped that he might be better disposed to agree to the cession of an island off his coast, preferably Kishm, for use as a base.[74]

Thus, Britain demonstrated itself to be in favour of the status quo and of nonintervention, that is, in favour of the maintenance of Persian sovereignty over Bahrain, exercised, as in the past, by the Al-Khalifa family, on the condition of paying tribute to Tehran. The Governor of Bombay, in a dispatch of 15 December 1819 addressed to the British chargé d'affaires in Tehran, wrote:

> We intend to avoid any intervention in the affairs of Bahrain; there is all reason to think that the Sheikhs of Bahrain will accept to pay tribute to the

Persian government, if it consents to leave them enjoy [autonomy]. With this objective, the mediation by the British would be readily offered.'[75]

Under the above instruction, Willock wrote to the Persian government that 'according to the arrangement, the Sheikh of Bahrain will pay the tribute to Persia, and the Shah will refrain from intervening in Bahrain's domestic affairs.'[76] Willock's follow-up reports pointed out that the promised military assistance was never granted, and E. Hertslet later admitted that the opposition of the British government to a Persian expedition against Bahrain prevented it from occurring.[77]

In the Treaty of Shiraz, concluded in 1822 between Captain Bruce, the British Political Resident, and the Governor of Shiraz, the British officially and clearly recognized 'the title of Persia to possession of Bahrain.'[78] The British Government of India opposed the treaty for different reasons, including for the recognition of Iranian sovereignty over Bahrain. F. Warden, the Secretary of the Government of Bombay, in a letter addressed to J. Farish, analysed the treaty, especially Article 2 concerning Bahrain, and wrote: 'the recognition of the Iranian sovereignty over Bahrain, there is no proof thereof, it is in contradiction of the pretensions of our friends, the Imam of Muscat, as well as the independence of the Utubis who are linked with us by a treaty of friendship.'[79]

Failing to strike a deal with the Shah on Persian islands and before opting to encourage the Sheikhs of Bahrain to claim independence from Iran, the British toyed for a while with the idea of placing the lower shores of the Persian Gulf under the authority of Sayyid Sa'id and investing him with possession of Bahrain and requiring him to contribute to the cost of a British military base.[80]

Sayyid Sa'id had claimed title to Bahrain and attacked the island in 1811, and then extracted a promise from the Sheikhs of Bahrain to pay him tribute. He made a renewed attack on Bahrain in 1828, at a time when the British had already made their mind up to pave the way for the independence of the island. Sayyid Sa'id's new attack in 1828 led finally nowhere, and an agreement signed by the belligerents committed Sayyid Sa'id to abandon his claim to tribute from Bahrain.[81]

Finally, the British officials concluded that Sayyid Sa'id was weak and restless, and wholly unsuitable as a chief to whom a sort of general supremacy in the Persian Gulf could be given. This conclusion turned out to be important as far as the future of Bahrain was concerned. The British later let it be understood that the accession of the Al Khalifah to the General Treaty of Peace in February 1820[82] implied the recognition by their government of the independent status of Bahrain and that the Al Khalifah should be assured that the British government had no intention of helping the Persians to subdue them, and that the Shah, for his part, should be told that any move by him to enforce his claim to the island that disturbed the peace of the Persian Gulf and disrupted trade would be viewed with regret in India.[83]

Based on India Office documents, 'in 1825, the Persians laid claim to the sovereignty of the island, and . . . the British Government refused to recognize the claim.'[84] Later, after the Persian prime minister reiterated Iran's claim to Bahrain while discussing the issue with Colonel Sheil, the British Minister in Tehran, 'the

British Resident in the Persian Gulf . . . was instructed by the Governor of India to resist by force any attempt of the Persian Government to establish troops on the Island of Bahrein.' Colonel Sheil was instructed by communication No. 23 of 21 August 1844 to inform the Persian government that 'unless the right of Persia to interfere in the matter [of Bahrain] was beyond dispute, any interference on her part might lead to unpleasant discussion with England.[85]

According to Hertslet's report, one of the proofs indicating Iran's right to the sovereignty of Bahrain forwarded by the Persian government was 'a gold coin which had been struck at Bahrein, in 1817, in the name of Fath Ali Shah, and Colonel Sheil admitted his belief in the genuineness of the coin'. In response colonel Sheil was instructed

> to employ the arguments adduced in a Foreign Office Memorandum (which was enclosed) to show generally the grounds on which Her Majesty's Government were unable to recognize as valid the claims advanced by Persia to the sovereignty of Bahrain; and he was further directed to state that the British Government would very much disapprove of any attempts on the part of Persia to interfere in the affairs of the Island, and thus disturb the peace of the Gulf and afford an opening to Piracy.[86]

The intervention of the British authorities in the quarrels between the sheikhs of Bahrain and Iran in the 1840s, marking the first serious British denial of Iranian rights in Bahrain, drew energetic protest on the part of the Iranian government. For example, Hadji Mirza Aghassi, then the Persian prime minister, wrote in a letter dated 15 March 1845 to the British chargé d'affaires in Tehran that:

> In the first place, the sentiments of all states, near or remote, are in agreement with those of Persia that the Persian Gulf, from the Shatt al-Arab to the Muscat, belongs to Persia, and that all islands in this sea, with no exception and without any association with any other government, fully belong to Persia, as you call this sea in your language, 'Persian Gulf'.[87]

In response to Persian objections against British interference in the affairs of Bahrain in 1848, Colonel Farrant was instructed on 2 May to inform Persian officials that 'the British Government were unable to recognize as valid the claims advanced by Persia to the Sovereignty of Bahrain.' And finally in 1851, in response to Turkish moves on Bahrain, the British announced that 'the Government of British India had relations with Bahrein as an independent State, and had concluded with it certain Treaties, namely in 1820, for the suppression of Piracy, and one in 1847 for the prohibition of the exportation of slaves, and that the British Government must object to any arrangement which could transfer Bahrein to the dominion or protectionship of any other Power.'[88]

In December 1860, the Bombay Government forwarded to the India Office a resolution that it had drawn up in which the opinion was expressed that 'Bahrein should be regarded as independent, and as subject neither to Turkey nor Persia';

these views coincided with those of the India Office and the Foreign Office as well.[89]

E. Hertslet concluded that 'in 1861, an understanding was to come between the Indian Government and the Foreign and India Offices, that Bahrein should be regarded as independent, and as subject neither to Turkey nor to Persia'.[90]

Another document, titled 'Foreign Office's Memorandum respecting the island of Bahrein' and subtitled 'British Declarations to the Persian Government respecting their claim to sovereignty over Bahrein', dated September 1908, discusses the issue since 1822.[91]

Another Foreign Office memorandum, dated February 1908, stated that, up to the year 1907, 'His Majesty's Government have repudiated the Persian claim to sovereignty over Bahrain nine times – 1822, 1825, 1844, 1848, 1861, 1862, 1869, 1906 and 1907.'[92]

Having secured their control over Bahrain through a friendly Arab chief, the British focused, in the latter part of the nineteenth century and in conjunction with the assertive Curzon strategy, on the Persian islands lining the north shores of the Strait of Hormuz – mainly Kishm and Henjam – and those immediately outside the Strait – namely, Sirri, Abu Musa, Greater Tunb and Lesser Tunb, which are discussed in Chapter 2.

British encroachment on eastern Iranian borders

The policy that Britain pursued during its colonial rule along the borders separating Iran from Afghanistan and the British dominions in the Indian subcontinent bore similarity to the one it pursued in the Persian Gulf – and this policy gave rise to similar troubles for Iran. There, too, the British endeavoured to contain and constrain Iran in favour of their friendly vassal entities in the region. As discussed later, the British also extended the same policy to the Iranian Khuzistan province in southwestern Iran, where they supported a local Arab sheikh, namely Sheikh Khaz'al, against Iran.

HERAT: ANGLO-PERSIAN ALL-OUT WAR

In the nineteenth century, the Iranian eagerness to recover the territories lost in the chaotic period following the death of Nadir Shah in 1747 became mired in British imperial policy in the region. The British worried that the exercise of Persian sovereignty over its eastern territory would mean the loss of their own influence and control, as well as Russian proximity to India. Fearful of an invasion of India, they speculated about routes by which a Russian army might approach Indian borders, and came to believe that one feasible route was through Persia, Herat, and Kandahar. As far as Herat is concerned, Iran's efforts to restore its sovereignty over the city took place in three phases.

In 1835 the British found it '[u]nsatisfactory to know . . . that the Shah . . . has very extended schemes of conquest in the direction of Afghanistan, and, in common with all his subjects, conceives that the right of sovereignty over Herat and

Kandahar is as complete now as in the reign of the Saffavean dynasty.'[93] Henry Ellis, the British ambassador, cautioned that 'I feel quite assured that the British Government cannot permit the extension of the Persian Monarchy in the direction of Afghanistan, with a due regard to the internal tranquility of India; that extension will, at once, bring Russian influence to the very threshold of our empire.'[94] The British opposition did not deter the Shah's government. In 1837, Iranian forces surrounded the city, but their grand hopes quickly dissipated as the British sent reinforcements from the Persian Gulf to reverse early Iranian victories – an effective manoeuvre that thwarted Persia's expansion towards the east.

After a final warning to the Shah that Britain would not tolerate the siege of Herat any longer, the expeditionary force from Bombay dropped anchor close to Bushehr in June 1838 and troops were put ashore on Kharg Island, a move that combined with other pressures on the Shah led him to abandon the siege and retreat to the west.[95] Despite the ending of the siege, the British refused to evacuate Kharg. They contemplated several options, including permanent occupation, proposing to buy it from the Shah, and returning it to nominal Iranian sovereignty but keeping effective control.[96]

In 1841, for instance, the British Resident proposed that the island should be purchased from Persia with a view to relocating the Residency there instead of at Bushehr, and a permanent settlement and coal depôt established. London considered this proposal carefully, but in the end decided that to acquire Kharg by purchase would give Russia an opportunity of obtaining the cession of part of the Gilan province.[97]

Under pressure from Tehran and Moscow, the British finally withdrew their forces from Kharg in March 1842, more than four years after the Iranian retreat from Herat.[98] As a result of the crisis of 1837–42 and the coercion employed against Iran, Anglo-Persian relations never resumed an even course. The experience affected the bilateral relationship in a deep and far-reaching way until the withdrawal of the British from the Persian Gulf in 1971. Lord Curzon described the British policy towards Persia throughout the nineteenth century as being afflicted by 'spasms of solicitude and torpor', and the period after 1842 as 'exaggerated languor'.[99]

In 1852, Nasir al-Din Shah embarked on renewed efforts to conquer Herat, limiting his ambition only to the city, contrary to his predecessors' attempts that extended well beyond it. British intervention and threats to occupy the island of Kharg in the Persian Gulf, however, quickly forced the Shah into renouncing his position and promising 'not to send troops on any account to the territory of Herat.' The agreement on 1853 further restricted Iran from 'all interference whatsoever in the internal affairs of Herat.'[100]

As relations between Iran and Britain worsened, the Iranians again renewed their efforts to take Herat. Following a dispute with the British over the sanctuary given by them to a rebellious Qajar prince, the Shah's troops finally entered Herat in 1856.

The British reaction was harsh and disproportionate. The rupture of diplomatic relations between the two countries followed the British declaring an all-out war on Iran. Nasir al-Din Shah met the British bellicosity by mobilizing troops across the country and proclaiming a *jihad* in January 1857 against the 'Christian invader, who already despoiled India and were now about to assert dominion over Persia.'[101] The British disembarked forces on Kharg and in Bushehr and engaged Persian troops. Another British force comprising close to 5,000 men sailed from Bushehr and attacked the city of Muhammarah (present-day Khorramshahr) on the northwestern shore of the Persian Gulf, and captured the city after a five-day battle. They also threatened to advance towards Shiraz from Bushehr, and from Muhammarah a reconnaissance force made its way up the Karun River to Ahwaz.

Ten days after the fall of Muhammarah, the Iranians engaged in negotiations with the British in Paris, where they eventually accepted the British terms and signed the Treaty of Paris in April 1857. As a result, Iran evacuated Herat and renounced all pretensions to the city.[102]

As a consequence of this full-scale war, Persian suspicions of British intentions ran deeper, and the eventual fate of Herat only turned the Persians' distrust to bitterness. A fear of piecemeal annexation, on the pattern of the British conquest of India, haunted the minds of Iranians throughout the nineteenth and part of the twentieth centuries. The same fear had been responsible for the repeated refusal, ever since John Malcolm first broached the subject in 1801, to cede or lease an island off the Persian coast to the British government.

SEISTAN

Learning from the Herat fiasco and bound by the Paris treaty, a decade later Iran agreed to submit to arbitration the half of Seistan Province that Iran claimed but did not control. A commission led by General Frederic Goldsmid, British Assistant Commissioner in Sind, was formed to address the Seistan boundary.

The decision rendered by the Goldsmid Commission entailed the partitioning of Seistan into two portions, which it called, respectively, Seistan Proper and Outer Seistan. Seistan Proper would go to Persia and outer Seistan to Afghanistan. As Curzon notes, the Persians 'professed themselves extremely dissatisfied with the result, and looked upon the partition as an attempt to enrich an English vassal state, Afghanistan, at their expense.'[103]

BALUCHISTAN AND MAKRAN

The particular British interest in Baluchistan and Makran in the 1860s occurred in the context of their general apprehension of stable Persian authority over its eastern frontiers and of any eastward expansion. These fears for the security of India resulted in the seceding of more Iranian territory in favour of British vassals in the area.

At the same time, the British were contemplating construction of a telegraphic line between England and India, with a portion to be laid along the Persian coast in the direction of Karachi. A major decision was whether or not to approach Tehran for permission to run the line through those districts over which Iran claimed suzerainty. In accordance with their general colonial policy, here too Britain supported the sovereignty claims of local rulers, in this case the Baluchi chieftains and the Sultan of Muscat who had leased a stretch of the coast from Tehran.

The Iranian government reminded British officials in Tehran that the continuation of the line was subject to the Shah's prior approval, and not that of the Sultan of Muscat, who had merely leased a part of the coast, nor that of Baluchi khans, whose territories were dependencies of Iran's Kirman Province. The British decided that something should be done about the Persian claims. In May 1863 the British Minister in Tehran requested that the Iranian government refrain from actions in Makran that might disturb Anglo-Persian relations. This drew from the Iranian foreign minister the reply that these places formed a part of the Makran territory belonging to Kirman Province. In response, the British claimed that 'for generations past the Persian Government has not possessed or exercised any rights whatever from Gwadur eastwards.' They further claimed that Gwadur had been a gift in perpetuity to Muscat from the Khan of Kalat, and that Chahbar, which had been acquired by conquest in the same period, belonged to the Sultan of Muscat. They claimed that Iranian actual jurisdiction in Baluchistan and Makran, as late as 1861, was almost exclusively confined to the interior, and therefore rejected the Iranian authority over the coast.[104]

The negotiations that ensued led to the agreement in 1870, through a mixed British–Persian–Kalat commission, of a frontier that began on the coast near the head of Gwadur Bay, about 50 miles west of Gwadur, and ran roughly northwards from there, resulting in the separation of Gwadur from Iran.[105]

KHUZISTAN

The accumulated effects of several developments on the eve of the First World War allowed Britain to include in its agenda the expansion of its control into southwestern Iran as well. These developments were:

- the accelerated decline of the Ottoman Empire;
- the weakening of the Qajars, which afforded tribal chiefs more opportunity to pursue their hopes of territorial autonomy through the steadfast support of the British Empire;
- the growing importance of the province of Khuzistan due to the discovery and export of oil.

These developments facilitated the British drive and enabled Sheikh Khazal, a tribal chief, to benefit from British support and encouragement to claim an autonomous fiefdom. In 1914, the Military Secretary of India Office advocated a campaign in Mesopotamia to defend the British position in the Persian Gulf and specifically to 'confirm the Sheikhs of Muhammarah and Kuwait in their allegiance.'[106]

The British had in the past given the sheikh numerous pledges supporting 'the

Continuance of the state of autonomy' that he enjoyed.[107] Though Tehran considered Khazal an Iranian subject, the British believed that '[i]t is many years since the Government at Tehran has exercised effective authority over him, or indeed over the other nominally Persian territories (Luristan, Bakhtiari-land, Kashgai-land, etc.) that border on his dominions.'[108]

An effort on the part of the Iranian central government to exercise jurisdiction over Khuzistan customs office in March 1900 through Belgian customs administrators ran into opposition by Sheikh Khazal. In December 1902, Khazal was told by the British that, provided he remained 'friendly', British influence would be used 'to maintain you and your tribes in the enjoyment of your hereditary rights and customs, and to dissuade the Government of Tehran from any endeavour to diminish or interfere with them.' Britain also committed itself with regard to intervention on the part of other powers: 'we shall protect Mohammerah against naval attack by a foreign Power, whatever pretext for such an action may be alleged'. The Persian government was given the essence of the commitment at the same time.[109] Nonetheless, Khazal was not entirely satisfied. He preferred a virtually independent position; the wish to avoid driving Iran into Russian arms by carving off sections of Persian territory outright was the only factor that made the British resist the sheikh's aims.

British interests in the area, though, had disturbed the delicate balance in favour of Sheikh Khazal. The British commercial presence in the area, already of long standing, grew after the 1901 oil concession to a British national, which led to the creation of the Anglo-Persian Oil Company. As specified in a formal memorandum by the Foreign Office:

> The discovery and the working of the oil-field outside the northern boundary of Muhammerah by the Anglo-Persian Oil Company, and the construction of a pipe-line from the oil-field to the Shatt al-Arab, across the territory of Mohammerah, led His Majesty's Government to extend their protection to the Sheikh. In 1910 he received an assurance that His Majesty's Government would safeguard him to the best of their ability against unprovoked attack or encroachment by a foreign power, and would support him to the extent of obtaining a satisfactory solution in the event of encroachment by the Persian Government on his jurisdiction and recognized rights, or on his property in Persia.

The memorandum goes on to state that in 1914, after Sheikh Khazal sided with the British in the First World War and helped them to capture Basra, 'His Majesty's Government renewed the 1910 assurance to him, and extended it to include his heirs and successors.'[110]

As nationalists encouraged Reza Khan in his efforts to put down local chiefs who threatened Iran's territorial integrity, Khuzistan proved a stubborn battlefield. Supported by the British, Sheikh Khazal struggled to preserve his autonomous province. Despite British efforts to deter the central government from enforcing the submission of the sheikh to Persian authority, military operations threatened by Reza Khan in 1924 forced him to render submission in November. But Reza Khan demanded that it should be unconditional. Eventually, in April 1925, the sheikh was arrested by Persian troops and removed to Tehran, where he was kept under house arrest for life.

2 The Curzon strategy

The growing importance of the Persian Gulf and new challenges

The British takeover of the three islands of Abu Musa, Greater Tunb and Lesser Tunb in the name of their Arab vassals in 1903–04 and 1908 can be considered one of the outcomes of the new British strategy[1] in the Persian Gulf. Devised by Viceroy Curzon and implemented in the early years of the twentieth century, the new strategy aimed to strengthen British control over the Persian Gulf and preserve it as a 'British lake' in the commercial as well as the political and military spheres by eliminating the growing threats perceived from Germany, Russia, France, the Ottoman Empire and Persia to Britain's omnipotence there.

Available documents underline the growing international importance assumed by the Persian Gulf islands during the 1890s, the 1900s and later in British strategic planning. In this period, Britain's policy towards the waters and islands of the Gulf was dominated by a fear of, and a strong determination to resist, rival regional and imperial penetration of her interests there. As such, disputes over Persian Gulf islands often had a more pronounced international flavor than in the previous century. A German mining firm was ejected from Abu Musa in late 1907. Fears that Russia might establish a naval base on or off Persian shores resulted in Britain's establishment of a telegraph station on the Henjam Island, later to be supplemented by a coaling station for ships of the Admiralty and the Royal Indian Marine.

The same anxieties underlay the placing of British flags on two small islands nestled in the channels surrounding the Musandam Peninsula. The Anglo-Ottoman dispute over the status of Zakhnuniyah Island, lying off the Hasa coast southwest of Bahrain, arose essentially as the two sides tried to reach an understanding on what exactly was the extent of Ottoman jurisdiction along the lower and western coast. And Britain's eagerness to support the sheikh of Kuwait's territorial claims over the islands of Warba and Bubiyan had been fostered in no small part by a desire to ensure that the proposed Berlin to Baghdad Railway did not have a terminal in Ottoman territory in the northwest corner of the Persian Gulf.[2]

The new strategy required coping with three important developments: the high point of 'the age of imperialism,' the Persian Gulf's transformation into a vital communication hub and Persian adoption of a newly assertive posture. Moreover, the growing threat to the regional lucrative trade, dominated by the British,[3] was also to be dealt with.

The high point of 'the age of imperialism'

The 1890s were the climax of 'the age of imperialism.' Between 1875 and 1885 most Western powers and Russia annexed vast areas of the non-Western world. With increasingly less room to expand, frictions among the Great Powers rose. As rival claims and pretensions collided, buffer areas that once separated the respective spheres of the modern powers evaporated. By this time the Persian Gulf was fully included among the contested territories, and the imperial clashes that occurred on the Gulf's shores and waters were part of a larger pattern of confrontation. In the early years of the twentieth century, correspondence from British agents in the Persian Gulf was abundant, and it recorded frequent calls by Russian warships on local ports and the possibility that the Russians sought to establish a naval base.[4]

As a consequence, Britain's grip began to tighten in the region and the local effects of its dominance grew more and more pronounced during the late nineteenth century. The chief cause for the British involvement in Gulf politics – the need to enhance imperial and Indian security – took on even greater weight. Thus, Iran's Persian Gulf ports and islands turned soon into one of the spheres of rivalry among the four great Western powers.

As a result, Persia became more entangled in the Anglo-Russian rivalry. Russia's position in Iran was perceived by the British to be more menacing than ever and Britain was fearful of the Russians expanding their influence in northern Iran and establishing themselves on the Persian Gulf through Iran, placing them in a position to mount either a land or a sea attack on India. The perceived Russian drive toward the Persian Gulf picked up momentum during the years 1899–1903, when Britain was preoccupied with the great imperial and international crisis caused by the Boer War in South Africa.

The British believed that the Russians undertook, in 1900 through 1903, a decisive move in the direction of the Persian Gulf and sought to expand their influence there and in Iran using a range of methods open to them, including:

- loans, financial manipulation and restrictive trade practices, through which they attempted to take over the economy of northern Iran;
- the stationing of Russian-led Persian Cossacks in Isfahan;
- 'scientific expeditions' that surveyed transport routes;
- the obstruction of overland trade between Iran and India by a quarantine service of Russian doctors, backed by Cossacks;
- regular warship visits to Persian Gulf ports;
- the establishment of a subsidized shipping line between Odessa and Persian Gulf ports, allegedly for political reasons rather than commercial;

- the opening of consulates, in Bushehr, Bandar Abbas, Seistan, Muhammarah and Baghdad, as well as an unsuccessful attempt to open a consulate in Muscat.[5]

France too undertook renewed efforts to gain footing on the Persian Gulf. The French established a consulate at Muscat in 1894, which signalled their plans to expand their influence and involvement in the area. They also actively sought to establish a coaling station there in 1899. The Franco-Russian alliance in 1894, other French advances (in Madagascar and Siam) and relative détente in French relations with Germany made the British more fearful of French designs on the Persian Gulf.[6]

Germany was another power showing interest in Persian Gulf affairs during the 1890s, at which time it directed strong German economic probes toward the Ottoman Empire, with an eye on Iran. Land penetration into many previously inaccessible parts of the Middle East through a Berlin–Baghdad–Kuwait railway figured high on the German agenda. At the same time, the Germans were actively establishing firms and consulates on the Persian Gulf and German businessmen and steamships were active in the area.[7]

The Persian Gulf as a vital communication hub

Moreover, with the Persian Gulf becoming a vital communication route between London and British possessions in the East, telegraph line being laid down through the Gulf and the prospect for oil exploration growing, the Gulf had never been so important to the British interests. A submarine-and-coastal telegraph cable was laid along the Persian Gulf in 1864 and provided an essential service until undercut by wireless competition in the 1920s.

These new developments, coupled with their need to secure the outer perimeters of India, prompted Lord Curzon to categorize British interests in the Persian Gulf at the turn of the century as being commercial, political, strategical and telegraphic.[8] Therefore, the entry of the British policy into a new phase was in the offing.

Assertive Iranian posture in the Persian Gulf

In parallel with these developments in the region, increasing pressure was brought to bear from within Iranian society on the central government to counter encroachment on Iran's sovereignty and territorial integrity, including in the Persian Gulf. A new period began in 1887–88, a year that was remarkable for attempts by the Persian government to pursue an assertive policy in the Persian Gulf and to try to assert Persian supremacy to the detriment of the British preponderance there. Amin-us-Sultan, who held the reins of government at Tehran, Malek-ut-Tujar, a wealthy Persian merchant at Bushehr who had held responsibility for the customs and government of Persian ports for some time, and Sartip (Brigadier-General) Haji Ahmad Khan were among those who were associated with this movement.[9]

Sartip Ahmad Khan, who was at the time the *daryabegi* (Lord Admiral) of the Persian Gulf, was described by British officials as 'a needy adventurer anxious to advertise himself and carry out what he understand to be the Sadr Azam's policy at that time, [who] went about the Gulf trying to assert Persian claims to control and jurisdiction over Bahrein and Pirate Coast, and the islands between that coast and the coast of Fars.'[10]

The new policy consisted of trying to strengthen Iran's control over its territory, creating a modern naval force, redistricting administrative areas and carrying out an active policy with regard to the political and tribal entities around the Persian Gulf.

Strengthening Tehran's control over Iran's territory

On 11 September 1887, Sartip Ahmad Khan, implementing the Persian government's decision, terminated the tenure of the Qasimi governors of Lingah and incorporated Lingah and its dependencies into the newly created 26th Iranian province, the Ports and Islands Province.[11] The Qasimi Governor of Lingah, Sheikh Katib bin Rashid, who in 1885 had murdered his predecessor and relative, Sheikh Yusuf-bin-Mohamed, was arrested and taken in chains to Tehran where he died. For many years afterward, the sheikhs of Lingah, as governors or deputy-governors, were under the power of the Persian government and acknowledged themselves Persian subjects, paying tribute to the Governor-General of Fars.[12] Tehran adopted the policy of increasing direct involvement in the affairs of Lingah and appointed a governor, under the governor-general of the 26th Province, to administer this district.[13]

In the same month, and immediately after the deposition of Sheikh Katib, Sartip Ahmad Khan sent a detachment of Iranian troops led by the Governor of Kishm Island to reassert Iran's sovereignty over the island of Sirri, located in the east-central part of the Persian Gulf, by hoisting the Iranian flag. Rejecting the remonstrance by the British chargé d'affaires in Tehran, the Iranian foreign minister stated that 'the Governors of Lingah had always held possession of the place and exacted taxes from its people and exercised jurisdiction over it.'[14]

The following communication, dated 19 August 1888, from Colonel Ross, the British Resident, to the British Minister in Tehran, indicates that what the British sought in essence was control, which was also the case with other Persian Gulf islands throughout the British presence. The communication states that,

> I would not wish to press unnecessarily hard on the Persians in this matter. But it is of some importance to us to maintain the right of control we have actually exercised at Sirri . . . and I think it necessary to uphold the Arab claim, which is just in view of preventing hostilities between the Arabs and Persians which might lead to serious results. My view is that we should insist on Persia withdrawing her flag from Sirri and reverting to the status quo ante, that is that a Joasimi governor should administer the island from Lingah . . . [T]he Persian Government would probably not consent to admit our right to interfere at Sirri for repression of maritime offences . . .[15]

Discussion on the subject culminated in August 1888, 'when it was postponed by the British Legation' in Tehran in order to facilitate conclusion of the Hastadan boundary negotiation, which was then in progress.[16]

A British Foreign Office memo, dated October 1928, referring to the islands of the Tunbs, Abu Musa and Sirri, states that '[t]he history and status of these islands is identical.' It adds that '[w]hile, however, the Trucial Sheikh of Shargah on the Arab coast still controls Tamb and Abu Musa, on which he flies his flag, His Majesty's Government, and the Sheikh under protest, have since 1887 tacitly acquiesced in Persian occupation of Sirri.'[17]

The British revisited the issue from time to time, aiming mostly to use it as means of pressure over Iran and a bargaining chip to have their way in relation to other contentious issues between the two countries. The exercise of Persian jurisdiction over Sirri was raised again in 1894 in relation to the Sheikh of Dubai's complaint about several fugitives taking refuge in Sirri. The point was referred to the British Legation in Tehran by the Viceroy of India in a telegram with the observation: 'Persian claim still untenable by removal of the Joasimi Sheikhs from office at Lingah and I trust you will press for removal of Persian flag.'[18]

A démarche from the British Minister, C. Greene, was greeted with a response from the Persian Prime Minister, dated 6 November 1894, setting forth Iran's arguments in support of its title to Sirri, and concluding that: 'I need not point out to you that the Persian Government will never remove their flag from the island in question.' These communications led to a memorandum of May 1895 by F. A. Wilson, Political Resident in the Persian Gulf, in which the essence of Britain's arguments in support of the Arab claims to Sirri was put forward.[19] These arguments, which are based on the Joasmis' alleged double capacity as both Persian officials and members of their tribes, are noteworthy in terms of their similarity with those put forward by Britain in support of Arab claims to the Tunbs and Abu Musa. We will review these documents later.

In another important move at about the same time, the Iranian government, deciding to enforce its sovereignty over its possessions in the Persian Gulf more vigorously, set up customs offices in several Iranian ports and islands in the Gulf, including Lingah, Kishm, Kung, Henjam, and Kish in 1901–03. The involvement of a Belgian national in setting up customs offices further alarmed the British. In 1898, the Iranian government hired Joseph Naus, a Belgian administrator, to reorganize the customs offices, which had for many years been farmed out and neglected by the government. In 1900 and 1902, Iran obtained large loans from Russia, and customs revenue served as collateral. Hence, the Russians became directly interested in tariffs and customs management and, through the Belgian officer, monitored the revenue.

Naus was suspected of leaning towards Russia both by the Iranian merchants and the British. Lord Curzon believed that the Belgians were 'almost uniformly Russian agents in disguise.'[20] Britain did not want a Russian protégé to establish his offices in the Persian Gulf islands and thus gain a foothold closer to India. In other words, the British did not want to see the islands fall into 'insecure hands.'[21]

Sir Percy Sykes, the British Resident, later noted that the new tariff, worked out by Naus, was received with enthusiasm in Russia and with consternation by British merchants. It was framed entirely in the interests of Russia and against those of Britain.[22]

An Iranian navy in the Persian Gulf

The Iranian decision to create a naval force in the 1880s troubled the British, as they had always suppressed the emergence of any rival naval force in the Persian Gulf. The lack of credible Iranian naval force had made Iranian possessions vulnerable and was one of the factors inviting encroachment on Iranian sovereignty in the area.

The British reacted adversely and did not spare any efforts to scuttle the plan. As Lord Curzon indicates, about the year 1865, the Shah had proposed the idea of a Persian naval flotilla in the Gulf to consist of two or three steamers manned by Indian or Arab crews and commanded by an English naval officer. Despite the modesty of the plan, Curzon records that '[t]he idea was discountenanced by the British Government; to whom it was known that the project really concealed aggressive designs upon the independence of the island and pearl fisheries of Bahrain.' As a result, the scheme died for some time but it was revived in 1883 'in a more innocent shape . . . which consisted of the proud total of one vessel, designated the *Persepolis*,' a steamship of 600 tons, armed with four 7.5-centimetre Krupp guns, bought from Germany, sent to Iran in 1885, and dispatched with German officers and German crew. And a steamer of thirty horsepower was also received, called the *Susa*.[23]

British officials did not fear, of course, that the nascent Iranian naval force would threaten their naval ascendancy in the area. What they tried to preclude was any increase in capability that might enable Iran to enforce its sovereignty over its maritime possessions, and which thereby might result in the British, sooner or later, losing their unlimited territorial engineering ability in the Persian Gulf.

Establishing closer ties with the Arab littoral

The third step taken by the Iranian government to reclaim its status in the Persian Gulf consisted of trying to forge closer ties with the Trucial Arab sheikhs. The visit by Sartip Haji Ahmad Khan, as Tehran's special envoy, to Dubai and Abu Dhabi aboard the *Persepolis* in August 1887 is a case in point. The envoy, who negotiated with the sheikhs of the places he visited, was closely watched by English officers. British communications maintain that the precise nature of Haji Ahmad's visits to the Arab sheikhs was not ascertained at the time, the Haji having obtained promises that his objectives would not be divulged to the British authorities. The Sheikh of Dubai, however, although adhering to his promise literally, considered himself free to inform the Sultan of Muscat of Haji Ahmad's proposals, which were framed with a view to the establishment of close political relations between the sheikhs of the Arab coast and the Persian government, to the exclusion of present preponderance of British influence.[24]

In January 1888, Sartip Haji Ahmad proceeded once again in an Iranian vessel to a place on the Cape of Masandim, but was warned off, according to British documents. Later, accompanied by the sheikh of Kishm and some armed men, he visited Umm-ul-Kowain, 'causing much excitement amongst the Arabs of that coast.' According to British communications, the responsible Persian minister, questioned by the British chargé d'affaires in Tehran, disavowed all knowledge of the Sartip's proceedings. In addition to issuing a diplomatic démarche in Tehran, the British dispatched a warship, the *Osprey*, to the area for the purpose. Sartip Haji Ahmad was subsequently presented with a sword of honor by order of the Persian minister.[25]

Undoubtedly, those who formulated this policy sought to undermine Britain's supremacy and enhance Iran's status on the shores and islands of the Persian Gulf. Considering this undertaking by the Persian authorities to be 'an attempt to establish a footing in the Trucial States,'[26] the British set a process in motion that led to the signing by the Arab sheikhs of the Exclusive Agreements of 1892, discussed earlier, which contained assurances to the British government that they would not negotiate, correspond, or form engagements with any other foreign governments.

In 1900 the Iranians were believed to have renewed their attempts, this time with regard to the sheikh of Abu Dhabi. In his letter No. 120 of 5 May 1900, Captain Kemball, Political Resident in the Persian Gulf, referred to 'the action of the Chief of Abu Dhabi in exchanging presents with *Darya Begi* and accepting and reading in Durbar a *firman* purporting to be addressed to him by the Persian Government.' He considered these actions to be in contravention of the Exclusive Treaty the sheikh had entered into in 1892. He reported further that recently certain subjects of the Sheikh of Abu Dhabi had presented directly to *Darya Begi* a claim that they had against a Persian subject and that 'the action of the Chief of Abu Dhabi appears to have excited the attention of other Trucial Chiefs.'[27]

In a previous communication, No. 19 dated 22 March 1900, Kemball had explained that the *firman* was 'a bond of friendship between the Persian Government and the Chief.'[28] As Donald Hawley has pointed out, 'The Sheikh was therefore taken to task, and direct dealings with the Persians ceased.'[29]

In search of a new strategy

The combination of developments in the Persian Gulf and the wider region convinced many in Britain that France, Germany and Russia were conspiring against British supremacy in the Persian Gulf and sought advantage from the British plight resulting from the Boer War in South Africa. At the same time, the new Iranian policy ran the risk of exacerbating the situation, and the British believed that it required an appropriate response.

By the end of 1890s, a full debate had emerged between the Government of India on the one hand, arguing that Britain must seize control of additional buffers of territory in order to safeguard India, and London, on the other, countering that the Empire could not support unending expansion and that influence and indirect control were preferable to conquest and direct administration.[30]

Lord Salisbury, the prime minister, believing that India faced an overland attack by Russia, did not see the Persian Gulf as a shield for India and instead recommended force concentration in Baluchistan to thwart any rivals' designs on the subcontinent. George Hamilton, the Secretary of State for India, considered Seistan and the eastern Persian Gulf ports absolutely essential for India's protection and warned against claiming more than Britain could defend; he disagreed with trying to maintain predominance over the entire Persian Gulf.

In contrast, Lord Curzon, who assumed office as the Viceroy of India in 1899, had been urging Britain since 1892 to strengthen its Indian defences. Regarding the Persian Gulf and Iran as especially vulnerable parts of India's buffer zone, he believed that imperialist encroachments by Britain's great rivals onto those regions should be resisted.[31] He believed that the retention of Britain's monopoly in the region was absolutely necessary for the safeguarding of India's security. He claimed that the only way to meet the Russian challenge was to 'fight Russia all along the line,' even to the point of dispatching Indian troops to the Persian Gulf. Curzon thought of the Gulf as a whole and acted according to what he believed were British interests there as a whole. He clearly identified a British interest in preserving the security of the Persian Gulf.[32]

As a student of Curzon's diplomacy has remarked, in carrying out his vision, 'always he had dreamt of creating a chain of vassal states stretching from the Mediterranean to the Pamirs and protecting, not the Indian frontiers merely, but our communications with our further Empire.'[33]

Lord Balfour replaced Salisbury as prime minister in July 1902. He displayed considerable interest in Asian affairs, and he shared Curzon's distrust of Russia. As the war in South Africa drew to a close in 1903, the stage was set for the British government to move towards Curzon's point of view to the extent of establishing a British 'Monroe Doctrine' over the Persian Gulf. Lord Lansdowne, the Foreign Secretary, set the British general policy over the area on 5 May 1903 when he stated the following in the House of the Lords:

> We should regard the establishment of a naval base, or of a fortified port, in the Persian Gulf by any Power as a very grave menace to British interests, and we should certainly resist it with all the means at our disposal.[34]

A formal memorandum by the Foreign Office, dated 12 February 1908, states that 'Lord Lansdowne's declaration of May 1903 was made primarily as warning to Russia, who was then suspected of harbouring designs upon Charbar. It was also intended . . . to prevent the construction of a fortified terminus of the Bagdad Railway.'[35]

With Curzon finally winning the debate, the British government made the direct or indirect control of more territories a part of British policy in the Persian Gulf. In short, after the adoption of the Curzon strategy things were never the same again. It was a turning point according higher priority to efforts aimed, in part, at undermining Iranian sovereignty and depriving Iran of its possessions in the Persian Gulf in favour of entities that the British could control. With this new assertive policy in place and the reins of action firmly in the hands of the protecting power, the British took the liberty of asserting their own interests in the ways they considered fit.

At around the same time, the discovery of oil in the region and the grant of an Iranian oil concession to a British subject in 1901 introduced a new dimension into British thinking about the Persian Gulf, and the first discovery of oil in Khuzistan in 1908 and the first shipment of oil from Abadan in 1913 increasingly affected regional politics. (Beginning in the 1930s the same trend, influenced by oil and advances in technology, also affected the lower Persian Gulf shores, as the rulers, including those of the Trucial states, granted oil concessions to Western companies, as discussed later.)

Escorted by an impressive naval flotilla, Viceroy Curzon's tour in the Persian Gulf in November 1903 was the ultimate expression of the new British policy for the region, and was designed, as Sir Denis Wright later put it, 'to demonstrate the commanding position that Britain enjoyed there.'[36] During this tour, the tension in Irano-British relations surfaced when Curzon angrily abandoned a planned visit to Bushehr when the Shah's representative there insisted that the Viceroy must pay the first courtesy call.[37]

In his address to the sheikhs of the Arab coast during his stay in the area, Curzon warned that '[t]he exclusive agreement bound the sheikhs not to, inter alia, part with any portion of their territory.' He also reminded the Trucial chiefs that 'out of the relations that were thus created ... the British Government became your overlords and protectors, and you have relations with no other Power.'[38]

Giving an account of his tour in a report No. 47 dated 17 December 1903, he described the most important policies that Britain pursued in the area. He reiterated that his 'main object' in undertaking the visit to the Persian Gulf was 'to visit the Arab Shaikhs who are in treaty relation with the British Government, and show by my presence the intention of the H. M.'s Government to maintain their political and commercial ascendancy in those waters.' He also describes his 'separate and perhaps even more important task,' carried out in conjunction with Admiral Atkinson-Willes, the naval commander-in-chief, to be 'to make a close study on the spot of the question of naval ports, bases, coaling stations, and anchorages in the Persian Gulf, which has been so much under discussion in recent years'.[39]

Following the Curzon tour, seven of the highest-ranking officials of the Foreign Department, Government of India, described to the Secretary of State for India, in communication No. 16 of 21 January 1904, 'the subjects under examination' by the British officials at the time as follows:

(i) The selection of suitable naval bases or coaling stations at the entrance to the Gulf.
(ii) The Choice of a telegraphic station either at Henjam or Bassidore.
(iii) The features and potentialities of the various khors or maritime inlets at the upper end of the Gulf, to which it seems likely that trans-Turkish or trans-Persian railways may be taken at some future date.[40]

Consolidation of the British position in the Persian Gulf

As the British endeavoured to tighten their control over the Persian Gulf, especially its entrance, they mainly focused on two groups of islands: first, the islands of Kishm, Henjam Hormuz and Larak, and second, the three islands of Abu Musa, Greater Tunb and Lesser Tunb, along with on-and-off attempts to revive the controversy over the island of Sirri as a bargaining chip. These two groups of islands were perceived as more or less dominating the sealanes of communication that entered and exited the Persian Gulf at the Strait of Hormuz.

These efforts indicated that the Persian Gulf had already transformed from an area where the British simply were busy with securing trade and communications and trying to exclude foreigners into an area regarded as a geopolitical whole and a special entity for political and military planning. The same efforts led to growing tension between Iran and Britain, as a result of the latter adopting an aggressive policy against the former – a tension that was exacerbated due to the dispute between the two sides over the three islands of Abu Musa and the Tunbs for several decades to come.

Unsuccessful attempts to control Kishm

Perceived threatening activities on the part of the Russians and other powers in the Persian Gulf, coupled with the new Iranian assertiveness, led the British to try to strengthen their position on the islands lining the north shores of the Strait of Hormuz and to develop contingencies should Russia or others unexpectedly seize a naval station in the area. These efforts included the quest for a suitable island on which to establish a naval base. British communications at the turn of century clearly show the British preoccupation with 'the question of the position to be assumed by them at the entrance of the Persian Gulf either in the event of hostilities with a foreign Power or . . . with a view to preventing the acquisition of coaling stations or harbours by such Powers in the time of peace.'[41]

There is much evidence of Britain's quest to strengthen its position at the entrance of the Persian Gulf prior to its claiming the three islands of Abu Musa and the Tunbs for the Trucial chiefs. A Foreign Office memorandum of 12 February 1908 stated that '[t]he importance of Bunder Abbas, with the adjacent Islands of Kism, Henjam, and Hormuz, as a naval station, was the subject of much official correspondence between 1900 and 1905, and was emphasized by an Inter-Departmental Committee which met in October 1907.'[42] The committee reiterated that 'such steps as His Majesty's Government might consider feasible should be taken to consolidate our positions at the entrance to the Persian Gulf, including Kishm.'[43]

As an earlier Foreign Department memorandum had noted in February 1901, 'it is unlikely that [Russia] would attempt to occupy any of these islands (Hormuz, Qishm, etc.) . . . if, however, she were to occupy Bunder Abbas, we should no doubt have to reply by seizing the islands.'[44]

Viceroy Curzon's answer of 2 May 1901, to an inquiry dated 30 November

1900, from Lord George Hamilton, Secretary of State for India, 'regarding the selection of a British naval base in the Persian Gulf,' indicates that Britain had focused since then on the Iranian islands lining the north shores of the Strait of Hormuz. In this dispatch, Curzon reiterates that

> We are strongly of opinion that, in the event of the Russians occupying Bunder Abbas or any other Persian harbour near the entrance of the Gulf, or acquiring political or naval privilege there . . . , our Naval Officer Commanding in the Gulf should have instructions at once to plant the British flag upon the three islands of Hormuz, Henjam and Kishm.[45]

In a minute dated 6 October 1902, Lord Curzon also expresses alarm over the possibility that either France or Russia

> might in time of trouble desire to take possession of a port or coaling station at some point at this projection on the Arabian coast. Still more might they contemplate such a proceeding, if we had been driven by Russian action or Russian intrigue to occupy the islands on the opposite or northern shore of the Persian Gulf – *viz.*, Hormuz, Kishm and Henjam.[46]

Among other possibilities, they looked at the Kishm Island, on which they had already occupied the small area of Basidu since 1820. A report written by Rear-Admiral Bosanquet, attached to an Admiralty letter dated 21 March 1902, states that 'Kishm is, in my opinion, the most strategical position in the Persian Gulf, from a naval point of view, and its possession would be very important to us as a port for our mercantile marine and a coaling station for our ships of war.'[47]

On 19 November 1902, a conference of delegates from relevant British departments was held at the Foreign Office, and 'amongst other recommendations as to the methods in which the extension of British influence could be most successfully prosecuted, and to the best advantage for general purposes,' it was advised that 'we should reassert our claims at Bassidu.'[48]

As the prospect of inducing the Persian government into any deal concerning its islands in the Strait of Hormuz was never promising, the British considered for a while the possibility of finding a local independent sheikh or notable on the islands in whose name they could claim an island. In his telegram No. 66, dated 2 May 1901 and addressed to Secretary of State for India Lord George Hamilton, Viceroy Curzon lamented that

> There are no independent local chiefs or authorities in the islands [of Hormuz, Henjam and Kishm] with whom we could enter into relations. With the exception of the track in our possession at Bassidore, the islands are under Persian authority, and since Lieutenant Hunt's visit, the Kalantar of Kishm, Sheikh Hasan, is said to have been superseded at the instance of the Director-General of Customs in Southern Persia by another official.[49]

This communication is important as it demonstrates that the British tried to apply their method of creating 'a chain of vassal states from the Mediterranean to the Pamirs' to Kishm as well, endeavouring to 'enter into relations' with local chiefs, in order to turn them into their protégés and claim territory in their names. It also shows the Persians' alertness at the time, which led to the sacking of the local official with whom the British had 'entered into relations.'

Setting sights on Henjam

The Iranian island of Henjam was another specific spot at the entrance to the Persian Gulf upon which the British focused. Numerous communications by British officials, military and civil alike, indicate the strategic importance they attached to Henjam. They found that '[i]ts position off the Persian coast at a point where the Persian Gulf is so narrow that the Arabian coast is ordinarily visible gives it considerable strategic importance.'[50]

In letter No. 16 of 21 January 1904, referred to earlier, seven officials of the Foreign Department, Government of India, told the Secretary of State for India that the British needed Henjam

> to provide for our ships a place of telegraphic call and signal station at no great distance from the entrance [of the Persian Gulf], and to strengthen our hold upon the island of Kishm, where we already possess a British settlement at the western extremity . . . while Bassadore is rather out of the way and difficult of access except to small vessels, ships of any size can anchor temporarily off Henjam.[51]

Consequently, the international status of Henjam formed the subject of considerable discussion. At one point, the application of the scheme of creating 'a system of vassal states from the Mediterranean to the Pamirs' to Henjam was contemplated too. The British leaned towards the idea that '[c]areful examination of the available evidence suggests that the claims of Muscat [to the island] are substantial', but finally they found it 'impracticable for His Majesty's Government, in view of their persistent recognition of Persian sovereignty over the last 60 years, to take any action at this stage to challenge the position of Persia.'[52]

To gain control of Henjam, it is striking that the British even considered a method analogous to the one they applied around the same time to the Tunbs and Abu Musa. In letter No. 16, one of the methods proposed is explained in the following way:

> The Malik-ul-Tajar [of Persia] . . . erected a flag-pole on this foundation [on Henjam] some 12 years ago; but it does not appear that a flag was ever hoisted upon it, nor are there any representatives of the Persian Government now upon the island. In fact, so far as the Viceroy was able to ascertain, connections are maintained by the inhabitants [of Henjam] with the opposite or Arab coast of the Gulf that might almost entitle Henjam to be described as a derelict, upon which no trace of Persian sovereignty is now in existence.

After referring to a few incidents in relations between Persia and Britain, the letter continues:

> and the general tone of unfriendliness that has characterized their recent communications, undoubtedly justify the adoption of a firm attitude, and will probably not have predisposed His Majesty's Government to any unnecessary display of courtesy.[53]

Declassified Iranian documents relate that the Iranian government was aware of the strategic importance of the island and was sensitive to British activities there. A report sent from the Governorate of Persian Gulf ports, dated 17 Azar 1302 (8 December 1924), to the Iranian Foreign Ministry emphasized 'the political and military importance of Henjam' and noted that

> while the British had only received permission from the Persian Government for constructing a telegraph office, they turned the island into a support base for their military operations in Mesopotamia where they frequently sent warships at the beginning of the World War I, and established a water and coaling stations and stationed a number of soldiers in the island.[54]

At some points in time and especially at the local level, the British actually claimed the island for the Sheikh of Muscat. A letter, dated 18 April 1906, from the Iranian Ministry of Customs and Post to the Iranian Ministry of Foreign Affairs reported that the British warship *Fox* actively supported a group of armed Arabs who had tried to prevent a group of Iranian workers from constructing a building to be used as the customs office. According to this letter, the commander of the British warship prevented the Iranian soldiers from disembarking, 'saying that the Island of Henjam appertained to the Sheikh of Muscat who is under the British protection.'[55]

In the end and in view of 'the persistent recognition of Persian sovereignty over the last 60 years' over Henjam, the British limited themselves to trying to resist the exercise of sovereignty by Iran over the island. As Sir Arthur Hardinge, the British Minister in Tehran, reported to the Marquess of Lansdowne, the Foreign Secretary, the Iranian Under-Secretary of State for Foreign Affairs summoned him and read to him a telegram from the Governor of the Gulf Ports 'reporting that the Indo-European Telegraph Department's officials at Henjam had removed the Persian flag and hoisted the British flag over the ruins of the old telegraph station reoccupied by them.' As Sir Arthur Hardinge reports, the Persian official regarded the proceedings 'as having, in connection with the recent incident respecting Tamb and Abumusa, some possible political significance.'

In the same telegram, Hardinge recalls the Government of India's opposition to 'disturbing the status quo [on Henjam] by the introduction of Persian officials, and [recalls] Major Percy Cox, in reporting a rumour that the Customs Department intended to place a post there,' and suggests that 'we might object to their doing so, but, though it would no doubt be preferable to keep Persian officials out of Henjam, where their appearance may be resented by Arabs, we can hardly claim a right to insist on this'.[56]

Nonetheless, the Secretary to the Government of India, in Foreign Department telegram No. 2164 dated 6 July 1904 to Hardinge, expressed his objection to the establishment of a Persian customs post on Henjam, and gave four reasons: first, the need to maintain 'the status quo'; second, the Persian coast was 'already adequately protected by customs posts against contraband importation from Henjam and local trade on the island would not warrant the establishment of a post there'; third, 'it might lead to regrettable friction with the telegraph officials'; and last, the 'Arab Sheikh [of Henjam] threatened resistance to attempts to enforce Persian authority over them.' The telegram ended by observing that 'we have already admitted Persian sovereignty, so that a post is not necessary to establish this.'[57]

Having failed to deter the Persian officials from establishing a customs office and placing a customs officer on the island, the British resorted to harassment tactics against the Persian customs officer and tried to incite the local Arabs against him. A telegram by Major Percy Cox, No. 59 dated 2 June 1905, records Cox's attempt to meet with the Arab sheikh on the island and the stoppage of the water supply to the Persian customs post.[58]

Similar efforts are also referred to in British records: Major Cox telegraphed on 7 December 1905 about the Sultan of Muscat's trip to Henjam and his protest against the Arabs of Henjam being 'subjected to any form of Persian jurisdiction.'[59] Captain Trevor, Assistant Political Resident, forwarded a letter on 28 October 1905 to the Government of India giving an account of a private interview between himself and the Sheikh of Arabs on Henjam on the extension of British protection to them.[60]

Contrary to the approach of the British officials in the Persian Gulf and Bombay, Hardinge in Tehran recommended a moderate course of action. His letter, No. 39 dated 28 June 1905, to Major Cox, reads in part:

> Persian sovereignty being unquestionable at Henjam, our wisest plan appears to be to recognize it, with all its consequences, in an ungrudging spirit. Some of these consequences, such as the presence of the Customs Mirza, may be disagreeable and inconvenient, but I do not believe that we shall render them less so by such measures as trying to starve the Mirza out by cutting off his water supply, or displaying resentment at the presence of Persian flags, or encouraging the Arab villagers to believe that we sympathize with their dislike of Persian authority.[61]

It is also significant to note that the measures adopted by Iran on Henjam were aimed in part, as reported by Major Cox, 'to prevent Englishmen from claiming the island later on.'[62]

The Persian persistence led the British to adopt a new approach, namely, to create 'a British enclave on a Persian island', as suggested by Viceroy Curzon in a telegram dated 27 September 1905 and sent to Grant Duff, the British Minister in Tehran, 'by having the Persians remove their flags and buildings from British demarcated area, and opposition to the sending of Persian troops to the islands.'[63] Grant Duff replied on 28 September 1905 that 'if His Majesty's Government is prepared to threaten dispatch of Indian guard to Henjam, probably Persian Government would consent to an arrangement on lines suggested, but mere diplomatic pressure would fail on account of the Shah's and Grand Vizier's suspicions of our doings in south Persia.'[64]

Finally, on 20 February 1906, the British Minister in Tehran formally informed the Persian foreign minister Mushir-ed-Dowleh that until the limits of the British telegraphic station at Henjam were satisfactorily settled, Britain 'must object to any coercive action against the Arab residents on Henjam,' and in such a case Britain 'will be compelled to send a ship of war to the island.' This mention of the settlement of the British station's limits was an allusion to the persistent British demand to appropriate a tract of land on the island of not less than 3 square miles. Grant Duff's telegram No. 169, dated 19 April 1906, indicates that the Persian foreign minister informed him that his government 'cannot give the land claimed by His Majesty's Government, as this would lead to Russia making similar demands in the north.'[65]

Iran's resistance to Britain's designs on the Iranian islands in the Strait of Hormuz brought the British to set sights on several other islands of strategic importance, located to the east of the Strait.

Abu Musa and the Tunbs: a long-lasting dispute between Iran and Britain

Abu Musa and Greater Tunb

After initially focusing on the Iranian islands lining the north shores of the Strait of Hormuz and failing to make any tangible headway there, the British widened their attention to encompass the three islands of Abu Musa and the Tunbs. These islands, located to the east of the Strait, were of strategic importance, as they commanded the sealanes entering and exiting the Persian Gulf. In addition, they were taking on a certain commercial significance as well.

The Russian and Iranian domestic predicaments in the years 1903–06 made the British job easier and provided them with wider latitude to pursue and implement the Curzon strategy in the Persian Gulf as far as the three islands were concerned; Russia and Iran were both increasingly submerged in periods of revolutionary uproar. The Russian government, moreover, was facing hostility on its far eastern frontiers and the Russo-Japanese war was in the offing.

As British records reveal, the suggestion made in January 1903 by C. A. Kemball, Political Resident in the Persian Gulf, set in motion a new round of dispute between Iran and Britain, this time over the island of Abu Musa and later over Greater Tunb. This disagreement lasted through Britain's withdrawal from the Persian Gulf in 1971. In his communication No. 3, dated 12 January 1903, Colonel Kemball contended that trade was being diverted from Lingah to the opposite coast because of the new Iranian customs policy. He further observed that he had been informed that some of the merchants of Lingah were trying to arrange with the Bombay and Persia Steam Navigation Company for steamers to make Abu Musa a port of call. He added that

> my reason for mentioning this matter now, is that I consider it to be within the range of possibility that if steamers call at Abu Musa, the Persians may proceed to claim this island as Persian, in the same way as they asserted their claim to the island of Sirri where the Persian flag has been hoisted. The Joasmis do not fly a flag on the island and it is a question for consideration whether I should not advise the Chief of Shargah to keep his flag flying on the island as a sign of ownership. If the government of India approves I will ascertain the view of the Shargah Chief on the matter.[66]

This letter is of great importance for the following reasons:

- It is the move that initiated the assertion of the Arab claim to Abu Musa, and later to the Tunbs.
- It shows that the British did not take action in order to act as protectors of an Arab chief nor on the basis of a request or a complaint made by one of their protégés, but that they initiated the move on the basis of well-considered self-interest and induced the Arab chief to follow through. All British communications of the time attest to this.
- It shows also that, although they were willing to initiate the move, the British were not aware of the chief of Sharjah's view, since in the letter Kemball proposed to ascertain it, if so authorized to do. Later British records further support this point.

On the last point, numerous examples from the British hegemonic period in the area indicate that what the British referred to as the rights of Arab chiefs under their protection usually served as a convenient justification for claiming control over territories. For instance, in his letter dated 11 June 1904, Sir Percy Cox suggested that in relation to the island of Sirri, 'we should press the matter again on the Persian Government on a request to be made by the Chief of Shargah.'[67]

Replying to an inquiry on this issue by the Government of India, Arthur Hardinge states in his letter No. 34, dated 22 July 1904, to the Government of India that he will be receptive if His Majesty's Government or the Government of India deem it desirable 'to reopen the question of Sirri . . . without the necessity of a reference to the Sheikh of Shargah.' He warns, however, that 'I would not wish to revive any hopes which the latter Chief may entertain of recovering Sirri, in the loss of which he has long *de facto* acquiesced, in case we should find it convenient to drop the question.'[68]

On the initiative being taken by Britain on Abu Musa and the Tunbs, a Foreign Office Memorandum dated October 1928 plainly states that, '[a]part from the fact that [the Trucial chiefs'] claim to the islands has consistently been upheld by His Majesty's Government, it was on the initiative of His Majesty's Government that

Jowasimi Sheikh of Shargah and Ras al-Khaima hoisted his flag on Tamb and Abu Musa in 1903.'[69] On this issue, the harsh way in which the British dealt with the Sheikh of Ras al-Khaimah, who renounced the ownership of the Tunbs and removed his flag therefrom in 1935, is of great significance. It will be referred to later.

Replying to Kemball's letter, the Secretary to the Government of India states in his letter No. 488, dated 10 March 1903, that

> [t]he island is in no way dependent on the Persian Government, and the Government of India agrees that it is desirable to take precautions to meet the advance of claims similar to those put forward in the case of the island of Sirri. I am therefore to request that, if the Shaikh of Shargah is willing to take action, you will arrange for him to hoist his flag at Abu Musa. It is also for consideration whether the Shaikh of Ras al-Khymah should be advised to hoist his flag at Tamb which apparently belongs to his section of the Joasmi tribe and over which, so far as is known here, Persia has never asserted sovereignty.[70]

Having travelled to Sharjah and spoken to 'the Chief of that place' about Abu Musa, Kenball reported back to L. W. Dane, the Secretary to the Government of India, on 30 April 1903 (telegram No. 71) that the chief 'at once expressed his willingness to take the suggested action and the following day when he came to see me again, he informed me that he had already sent orders to have his flag hoisted on the island.' Regarding Tunb, Kemball stated in the same letter that 'there is no representative of the Deputy Governor of Lingah on the island and so far as I am aware, Persia has never asserted sovereignty over it.' He then refers to the letters 'from former Arab Chiefs of Lingah, admitting the claim of the Joasmis of the Arab Coast to the island as against the claim of the Joasmis of Lingah.'[71] He then concludes that 'I think that we, in view of our relations with the Trucial Chiefs, would be bound to maintain the rights of Shargah to this island as against the Persians.' He goes on to add that, in case the Persians react to the hoisting of the Joasmis' flag on Tunb, 'we should have to take forcible measures to assert the rights of the Shargah Chief.'[72]

Almost a year later in April 1904, and upon instruction from the Iranian government, an Iranian mission, led by the Director of Customs in the south, which was visiting Abu Musa and the Tunbs in April 1904 to implement the government decision to set up a customs office on the island, apparently unexpectedly came across a raised Arab flag, hauled it down and hoisted the Iranian flag in its stead. As discussed later in more detail, the British considered this to be 'a proceeding initiated by the Persian Minister for Foreign Affairs, possibly at Russian instigation.'[73]

The Government of India reported to the India Office on 13 April 1904 the information that it had received from the Resident in the Persian Gulf on the removal of the Arab flag from the island of Tunb, the erection of a new flagstaff flying a Persian flag and the placement of two Persian guards there by the Director-General of Customs touring in the Persian Gulf on board a Persian government ship. The same telegram (No. 130) indicated that the Persian flag was hoisted on Abu Musa and similar guards appointed on that island too. It further stated that it 'is important that the Persian flag should be taken down and Arab flag reinstated, and that removal of guards should be effected at once' and proposed 'to send gun-boat to the islands, with representative of the Shaikh of Shargah on board, to haul down Persian flag and reinstate Arab flag, and to remove guards to Persian territory'[74] – a proposal that came from Viceroy Curzon himself.

While the British Government of India recommended a swift and decisive counter-action and resort to the ships of war, the British Minister in Tehran counselled to first try to gain the same result through the diplomatic path. A. Hardinge, whose view had been sought by the Foreign Office on the Viceroy's proposal, recalled in his telegram, No. 165 dated 20 April 1904, that, '[h]owever, [Tunb and Abu Musa] are coloured Persian in India Survey Map of 1897 and Viceroy's unofficial Map of 1892.' He adds that 'it is clear that the rights acquired by Shaikh of Sharga must be supported; but before the Persian flag is hauled down it would be courteous to give Persian Government chance of themselves removing it.'[75]

Foreign Secretary the Marquess of Lansdowne concurred in the view expressed by A. Hardinge;[76] Viceroy Curzon found the proposal agreeable on the condition that 'it should be made clear to the Persian Government that, if they delay in complying with the request for the removal of the Persian flag from the islands, His Majesty's Government will have no alternative but to send a gun-boat to replace the flag of the sheikh of Shargah.'[77]

It was finally decided[78] to give the Persian government the opportunity to withdraw from the position they had taken up. Representation at the Court of Tehran on this occasion brought about a temporary way out. Faced with Britain's military might and the consequences of the Anglo-Iranian War of 1857 still fresh in their collective memory, the Iranian authorities were left with no other choice but leave the islands to British control and limit themselves to continued diplomatic protest.

On 24 May, the Iranian foreign minister told the British Minister in Tehran that they had telegraphed orders to Bushehr to remove the flags and guards from Abu Musa and Tunb, while reserving their right to discuss with Britain the respective claims to the islands.[79]

Later, Foreign Minister Mushir al-Dowleh sent a note, dated 14 June 1904, to the British Embassy in Tehran 'with reference to the islands of Tamb and Abu Musa', which stated that

> the Persian Government considers these two islands as its own property, and the measures taken by the Customs authorities in those two places have been on this account; but, . . . the Royal Command has been issued that, for the present, the measures taken by the Customs authorities in the above-mentioned places should be given up and neither party hoist flags in the two places pending the settlement of the question.[80]

In his reply dated 15 June 1904, Hardinge rejected the suggestion that 'this Trucial Chief should not be permitted to replace his flag pulled down by the Persian Customs officials'. In the meantime, he promised to 'transfer to the Government of India any proofs with which you may favour me that the claims of the Persian Government to the ownership of these islands outweigh those of the Sheikh of Shargah.'[81]

Accordingly, Sir Arthur Hardinge described the mentality of the Persian establishment on the dispute over the islands and his approach to it in the account of his meeting with the Ain-ed-Dowleh, the Persian Prime Minister, on the subject of establishing a telegraph station in Bandar Abbas. His dispatch, No. 111 dated 20 June 1904, to the Marquess of Lansdowne reads in part:

> [I]n the course of our conversation, the Ain-ed-Dowleh referred to our insistence upon the removal of the Persian flag from Tamb and Abu Musa as a discouraging indication that we, on our side, were not as considerate to Persia as he could wish, or to her interest in the Gulf, and seemed, indeed, to attach more importance to the interests of a petty Arab Shaikh than to the friendship of the Shah. He suggested that, pending the discussion and the decision of the question of ownership, the Arab flags should not be rehoisted on the islands... I explained the impossibility of complying with his highness's last suggestion about the flags... I reminded him that any controversy on this subject might open the question of the ownership of Sirri, whose occupation by the Persians had only been tacitly and never formally recognized by ourselves.[82]

Following the Persian agreement to remove their flags from Tunb and Abu Musa, Major Cox sent an important and interesting letter, No. 64 of 11 June 1904, to Sheikh Suggar, the ruler of Sharjah, informing him of 'recent proceedings'. He went on to say 'I accordingly request you to take the necessary measures for... hoisting the special Jowasmi flag described in the Treaty.' He also inform him that

> His Majesty's ship *Sphinx* is now proceeding to your coast in this connection, and you should make most careful arrangements in regard to all matters affecting these two islands, and should station two men on each of them, whose duty it will be to see to the hoisting and guarding of the flags permanently.

He continues that 'you can send [the men] by the ship *Sphinx*' and 'if the old flagstaffs are unserviceable and you wish to put up new ones, Inshallah, the Captain, will assist you in the matter.'[83]

Failure to be a match for British military power, as demonstrated in the Anglo-Iranian War of 1857, in general, the lack of a naval force worthy of the name, in particular, and the explicit British threat to use force were the main reasons for the inability of the Iranian central government to resist the British move. Although Tehran's efforts to build up a navy, as described earlier, helped assert its authority over Iranian subjects in the Persian Gulf, it was no match for the powerful British flotilla. Thus, Iran's foreign policy in the Persian Gulf could not rely on any means of enforcement, and its weak navy was not in a position to assert ownership over Iranian possessions. Consequently, when in 1904 the British plainly threatened to use military force against the Iranian presence in Abu Musa, the Iranian government saw no option but to submit to the *force majeure*.[84]

Though British motives were partially commercial, as reflected in Kemball's letter, there should be no doubt that British strategic considerations lay at the heart of the calculations that made them so adamant in holding to their positions on Abu Musa and the Tunbs for close to 70 years, despite the tensions that this created in British relations with the Iranians. The addition of Greater Tunb, by the Government of India, to the list of islands that were to be claimed for the chiefs of the Arab coast more utterly relegates the commercial justification to a secondary position.

There are signs indicating that the roots of the British policy on Abu Musa and Greater Tunb, and later on Lesser Tunb, should be sought in the general considerations that brought the British to devise and implement the Curzon strategy, which aimed to uphold British ascendancy in the Persian Gulf and resist 'the establishment of a naval base, or of a fortified port, by any Power' therein. Thus, the more the British controlled territories, the better they were able to ensure the success of the strategy. As confirmed in British correspondence, the Government of India, led by Viceroy Curzon, was very stringent in implementing the strategy everywhere, and not less in the case of the three islands in question.

In this respect, referring to a few pieces of correspondence may further clarify the issue. The British naval commander-in-chief, forwarding to the Government of India a report by the local commander, dated 9 June 1904, on the presence of Persian soldiers and the Persian flag on the island of Sirri, stated that 'Sirri is an important island to us as are the islands of Tamb and Abu Musa' and suggested that 'similar steps be taken with regard to it as were taken in connection with two islands.'[85]

The prevalence of strategic thinking in the British Government of India is also on display in the words of Major Percy Cox, the British Resident, when he wrote on 19 August 1904 that

> signs are not wanting that if we do not maintain a vigorous policy in connection with these islands it will not be long before we are confronted with difficulties in regard to the adjacent pearl fisheries, the preservation of which under the time-honoured conditions has always been one of the fundamental features of our policy in these waters.[86]

Moreover, British official circles widely attributed the Persian move in April 1904 in removing the Arab flag from Abu Musa and Tunb, and the continued Persian protests, 'to Russian Promptings'. Lorimer believed that there

> was reason to believe that the action taken by the Persian Government had been prompted by the Russian Legation at Tehran, who, in view of a tour

made by Lord Curzon in the Persian Gulf, at the end of 1903, were apprehensive of measures on the Gulf on the part of Britain for the consolidation of their position in the quarter, possibly by the occupation of fixed points.[87]

P. Cox claimed that 'one Russian Consular Agent, Bunder Abbas, had accompanied *Darya Begi* on his first trip' to Tunb. In his letter No. 350, dated 23 July 1904, he referred to the Russian intrigues in regard to these islands. He attaches great importance to the island of Tunb from a strategic point of view and suggests that Britain should adopt 'a firm attitude in view of the Persian movements at Sirri and Henjam'.[88]

In the same vein, A. Hardinge stated in communication No. 10, dated 24 May 1904, to Foreign Secretary Lansdowne that

> I have very little doubt in my own mind that the issue of these instructions [to remove the Arab flag] was connected to the Viceroy of India's cruise in the Persian Gulf, and that the Persian Government has been advised by the Russian Legation to anticipate, while there was yet time, any seizure as a possible result of it, on our part, of islands or other strategic points in those waters.[89]

Lesser Tunb

During the drive to claim Abu Musa and Greater Tunb for one of the chiefs of the Arab Coast in 1903–04 and the renewed attention paid to Sirri mostly as a bargaining chip, the British omitted the island of Lesser Tunb. It was a dependency of Lingah, and, as British documents indicate, the Persian flag was flying on Lesser Tunb 'at the time of Persian aggression on Tamb and Abu Musa' in 1904.[90] Likewise, a letter from the Residency Agent at Lingah to Colonel Kemball, dated 4 April 1904 and forwarded by the Agent as enclosure 3 in No. 100, dated 15 April 1904, to the Government of India, indicates that the Persian Director of Customs, Bushehr, after having visited Abu Musa and hoisting the Persian flag there, 'visited the Island of Tamb and Nabiu (the smaller Tamb), where he also hoisted the Persian flag and placed two "*tufangchis*"' (musketeers).[91] The Political Resident reported as well on 24 November 1908 that 'the Shargah flag had not been flown on Little Tamb by the Sheikh.'[92]

Also in 1908, Lesser Tunb came to the attention of the British as a result of red oxide mine exploration conducted by a British company, Messrs. Frank C. Strick and Co. During the survey they made in the Persian Gulf, they visited Lesser Tunb, and, in a communication to the British Foreign Office reporting their finds, they requested to be instructed as to how to take action with regard to obtaining the required concession. Attached to the communication, No. 16 dated 7 October 1908, the company forwarded the report prepared by the captain of the surveying team, in which it is stated 'that the inhabitants of Sirri consider themselves and the Island of Jazirat Nabiyu Tanb as being under the Governor of Lingah, whereas from your letter ... we gather that the rightful owner of both these islands is the Sheikh of Shargah'. They close by asking the Foreign Office 'how and [from] whom [they] should set about trying to obtain the Concession'.[93]

On 13 October, Foreign Secretary Sir Edward Grey wrote to the India Office, proposing 'to inform Messrs. Strick that HM's Government will support their request for a Concession, and if Lord Morley [Secretary of the India Office] concurs, . . . to add that negotiations should be conducted with the Sheikh of Shargah through the British Resident.'[94] Accordingly, a letter addressed to Messrs. Strick informed them that '[a]s regards Tanb, Nabiyu Farur, &c., about which you ask, the information we have shows, as far as it goes, that Tanb belongs to Shargah.'[95]

Later, the Political Resident in the Persian Gulf commented on the issue, in telegram No. 667 of 3 November 1908, stating that:

> Regarding the Island of Lesser Tanb, the Sheikh of Shargah has never flown his flag there, but in case of necessity there appears no reason why we should not claim that its ownership follows that of the island of Greater Tanb and tell Strick to act as indicated by the Secretary of State.[96]

What is noteworthy about the proceedings with regard to Lesser Tunb is that the chiefs of the Arab Coast were irrelevant in the process. It also transpires from related communications that no attempt was made to ascertain the proprietary rights over Lesser Tunb.

After finding itself obliged to first assert its title to the three islands in 1887, the Persian government persistently reasserted it, in 1904, 1905, 1912, 1913, 1923, 1925 and 1928. In the period 1928–53, British reports indicate numerous formal Iranian objections and demonstrations of opposition to what Iran termed 'the occupation' of the three islands.[97]

Following a complaint by Iran in May 1905 on the erection of new buildings at Tunb by the Sheikh of Sharjah, the British took the opportunity 'to make it clear to Persia that the status of Sirri was still *sub judice*, a view in which she acquiesced,' and the Persian Government was warned that 'the revival of its claim to Tanb meant the revival of ours to Sirri.'[98] Early in 1912, when the British decided to erect and maintain a lighthouse on Tunb, the Political Resident, Sir Percy Cox, wrote to the Sheikh of Sharjah that 'while it was desirable that the Shargah flag should always be *en evidence* on Tanb, now at all events this island will be preserved for you by the mere presence of the lighthouse.'[99]

In February 1913, when the Iranian Foreign Ministry protested the erection of a lighthouse on Tunb, Percy Cox threatened that 'if the question was now reopened, His Majesty's Government would no doubt revive the question of Sirri.'[100]

In May 1923, in response to a reassertion of Persian rights to the Tunbs and Abu Musa, P. Loraine, the British Minister in Tehran, was instructed by the Foreign Office to draw the attention of the Prime Minister to the incident of 1904, when the British Government 'had been prepared to take naval action to remove the Persian flag from Tamb and Abu Musa, and hint that revival of the Persian claim might lead His Majesty's Government to take the measures then contemplated.'[101] Following the dispatch of a launch in the autumn of 1925 to Abu Musa by Iranian customs officials to inspect the red oxide deposits and remove one bag, and the

The Curzon strategy 53

assertion by the Iranian government, in response to the British protest, that Abu Musa belonged to Iran, the British Minister in Tehran warned the Iranian acting foreign minister that persistence in the Persian claim would make it necessary 'to request the Government of India to dispatch a ship of war to Abu Musa to uphold the rights of the Sheikh of Shargah.'[102]

The above documents bring clearly to light the policy of the British Government to rely manifestly on the threat to use force to quash Iranian protests against what Iran saw as the illegal occupation of the three islands.

In the history of Britain's long and arduous efforts to preserve the three islands for the Arab chiefs, the harsh and unforgiving way in which it dealt with Sheikh Sultan, the ruler of Ras al-Khaimah, when he decided not to pursue his claim over the Tunbs in 1935, was of great significance. 'He removed his flag and flag-staff from Tamb Island and was reported to be intriguing with the Persians. He wholly replaced his flag and its staff when threatened [by the British] that the island would be handed over to the Sharjah.'[103]

Sheikh Sultan had succeeded his father, Sheikh Salim, in 1919, and obtained recognition as an independent ruler in 1921. He had a strained relationship with the British, and was described by them as having 'neglected the interests of his State and on several occasions adopted an unsatisfactory attitude towards His Majesty's Government.' In February 1948, Sheikh Sultan was overthrown in a coup while absent, and Sheikh Saqr, the third son of Sultan's brother, seized the fort at Ras al-Khaimah and assumed his position. The British Political Resident recommended that Saqr be recognized as ruler as soon as he had given an undertaking to observe all previous treaties and engagements, and authority was received to act accordingly. He gave the required undertaking and was formally recognized by the British on 16 July 1948. The British attempted to arrest and banish Sheikh Sultan, who refused to acquiesce in his replacement by Saqr and intrigued against him.[104]

As in other cases such as Bahrain and Kishm, the British authorities had earlier recognized Iranian title to the three islands before claiming them for the Arab sheikhs under their protection. As an official British memorandum acknowledged, 'Up to about 1873, owing to the close connection existing between Tamb and Lingah, the Residency authorities at Bushire took the view that Tamb was Persian, and in the period ending 1879 several inquiries regarding it are stated to exist in the Residency records.'[105]

Following disputes in 1873 between the Qasimi groups on Lingah and the Arab coast over grazing domestic animals on the islands in question, and enquiries carried out by British agents at Lingah and Sharjah, Edward Ross, Political Resident in the Persian Gulf, wrote to the Sheikh of Ras al-Khaimah, on 19 April 1873, stating that Tunb Island belonged to Lingah and that the inhabitants of Ras al-Khaimah should refrain from annoying Iranian livestock breeders there.[106]

However, the recognition of Iranian title to those islands was not confined to the period before the 1880s. A map 'recently issued by the Intelligence Department of the War Office' for presentation to the Shah on behalf of Her Majesty's Government and communicated under cover of a British note dated 27 July 1888 – signed by His Majesty's Minister under instructions from the Marquess of Salisbury, then Secretary of State for Foreign Affairs – as well as Lord Curzon's Map of Persia of 1892 and the Survey of India Map of 1897, all depicted the three islands in the colour for Persia. Later, in 1928, the British Foreign Office described, in an internal memorandum, the showing of the islands in Persian colour as 'the error in question' and found it to be 'extremely regrettable from the standpoint of His Majesty's Government.'[107]

Indeed, the issue of Tunb and Abu Musa was first raised when Iran hoisted its flag on Sirri in September 1887. According to a telegram dated 16 December 1887 from the British chargé d'affaires in Tehran to the Political Resident, 'the Persian Government stated that for nine years Sirri and Tamb had paid taxes to the Persian Government'.[108] A Foreign Office memorandum dated 11 December 1905 also stated that 'when, in September 1887, the Persian annexed Sirri, the management, administration, and jurisdiction of the island [of Abu Musa] had been for many years vested, by common consent, in the Chief Jowassimi, Sheikh of the Persian coast, who was at the same time Governor of Lingah and a Persian subject.' And, according to the same memorandum, it had just been reported that Iran had already hoisted its flag on Tunb. It goes on to add that 'nearly all the standard maps mark Tamb as Persian . . . and St. Martin's Geographical Dictionary describes Tamb as "a dependency of the [Iranian] Province of Lar". It may be added that in the Indian Survey Map of the Persian Gulf, printed in Simla in 1897, both islands [Tunb and Abu Musa] are coloured as Persian.'[109] On 28 April 1888, the British Resident informed the British Minister in Tehran of 'a new claim put forward by [the Persian government] to the Island of Abu Musa.'[110]

All in all, the control of the three islands by the British was a significant step towards strengthening their position in the Persian Gulf in general and their control over the entrance to the Gulf in particular. It was all the more important as the British, already encountering Persian resistance, had failed to control any of the Persian islands lining the north shores of the Strait of Hormuz or to secure a strong position there.

Whereas, based on the Curzon strategy, the main, long-term objective the British pursued was the consolidation of their position in the Persian Gulf and the implementation of a 'Monroe Doctrine' that they established over the Gulf in 1903 – that is, resisting 'the establishment of a naval base, or of a fortified port, by any Power' in the area – London sought also to achieve certain secondary, immediate goals as well. Laying out these goals, a memorandum by the Foreign Office, dated 12 October 1928, stated that '[t]he satisfactory disposal of the matter [of the three islands] is important in view of its immediate reactions on the Trucial Coast, and the wider reactions on Mohammedan feeling in India of disturbance in that region. But its importance from its possible reactions on the relations of the Trucial Chiefs with Ibn Saud is hardly less great.'[111]

Later, the negotiations with the Russians that finally led to the Anglo-Russian treaty of 1907 on British and Russian spheres of influence in Iran attenuated the Russian reaction that might have otherwise included demanding acquisitions of Persian territory in the north. Although the Russian Revolution in 1917 removed this counter-weighing power from the Persian scene, rising Iranian nationalism turned out to make it unexpectedly more uneven and difficult to navigate for Britain.

The revival of controversies over Sirri Island

As discussed earlier, the Persian government enforced its actual jurisdiction over the island of Sirri in 1887. Although later Britain tacitly acquiesced, albeit under protest, in Persian sovereignty over Sirri, and no move on the part of any Arab chief came to notice at the time, the British continued to use the status of Sirri, especially in the 1900s and beyond, as a means of bringing pressure to bear on the Persian government and as a bargaining chip in the advance of its plans for other Iranian possessions in the area.

In the aftermath of the dispute over Abu Musa and Greater Tunb in April 1904 and beyond, which followed the removal by the Iranians of the Sharjah flag from those two islands, as discussed below, the Government of India entertained the possibility of reopening the question of Sirri. And, indeed, it was discussed in British communications and raised frequently in their talks with the Persian government as a threat by which to induce Iran to abandon its position on Abu Musa and Tunb.

In a telegraph dated 31 May 1904, Major Cox suggested to the Government of India that 'the present opportunity might be embraced to take some action regarding the Sirri island, in connection with which the position seemed identical with that of Tamb and Abu Musa islands.'[112] And in a letter dated 11 June 1904, he suggested that 'we should press the matter again on the Persian Government on a request to be made by the Chief of Shargah.'[113]

In repeating this view in telegram No. 277, dated 15 July 1904, to the British Minister in Tehran, the Government of India stated:

> Owing to the delay which has occurred in urging Arab claims, our case is not strong, but if the Persians advance further right to Abu Musa and Tamb, claim to Sirri might perhaps be revived and at any rate pledge secured that the island will never in any way be conveyed to any other power.[114]

With reference to the said inquiry by the Government of India, Hardinge stated, in his letter No. 34 dated 22 July 1904 to the Government of India, that it was up to His Majesty's Government or the Government of India if they deemed it desirable 'to reopen the question of Sirri . . . without the necessity of a reference to the Sheikh of Shargah.' He, however, warns that 'I would not wish to revive any hopes which the latter Chief may entertain of recovering Sirri, in the loss of which he has long *de facto* acquiesced, in case we should find it convenient to drop the question.'[115]

In the meantime, Hardinge managed to carry out the instruction he received from the Government of India. He informed the Foreign Office in his telegram No. 292, dated 19 July 1904, that he had explained to M. Naus, the Belgian administrator of the Persian customs offices, that 'we prefer that a regular customs station should not be established there while the question of ownership was still uncertain.' He thought, however, that 'we might recognize Persia's sovereignty over Sirri in return for abandonment by Persia of all claims to Tamb and Abu Musa and a pledge that it should never be ceded to any Foreign Power.' He also raised the same theme in his later talks with the Iranian Prime Minister and foreign minister, and threatened that Britain would reopen the issue of Sirri if Iran did not abandon the issue of Abu Musa and Tunb.[116] He finally secured agreement from M. Naus that Sirri be crossed out of the list of places where customs offices were to be set up.

When, in May 1905, Iran complained about an Anglo-Arab move on Tunb, the Persian government was warned that 'the revival of its claim to Tamb meant the revival of ours to Sirri.'[117] A similar threat was renewed in February 1913 by the British. In May 1908, the British government informed a British firm that, although the status of the island was in dispute, 'they had never acquiesced in the Persian claim to dispose of the concessions [to mine red oxide] on it regardless of Great Britain';[118] and the British Minister at Tehran presented a protest to the Persian government in April 1909 against their action in granting a concession, in which he reminded them of the *Caveat* entered by the British government and asked them to arrange for the discontinuance of operations on the island by their concessionaire.[119]

Meanwhile, it is noteworthy that while Britain actively pursued the case of Sirri in certain periods, the chiefs of the Arab littoral were not reported to show any enthusiasm towards the case, to the point that no reference is made to them in the major British documents on this issue, referred to later.

A review of the British arguments

As stated earlier, it is not intended here to address the legal aspect of the dispute between Iran and Britain on the three islands. However, a very brief review of this aspect may help further clarify the issue.

British arguments in support of their claim that the Tunbs and Abu Musa belonged to the chiefs of the Arab littoral were based on what they referred to as the 'double capacity' of the Joasmis as both Persian officials and members of their tribes. These arguments were set forth in detail in the three official documents written by British officials on the status of the island of Sirri in reaction to the Persian government's response to the note from the British chargé d'affaires dated 11 September 1894, referred to earlier. The documents[120] are:

- the memorandum of May 1894, written by F. A. Wilson, Political Resident in the Persian Gulf (referred to hereafter as 'the Memorandum');
- the semi-official report, dated 13 December 1898, by Lieutenant-Colonel Meade, and brought onto the official record in June 1904 (referred to hereafter as 'the Report');
- Lieutenant-Colonel Kemball's report, dated 15 April 1904, to the Government of India.

The Curzon strategy 57

During the dispute over Abu Musa and the Tunbs in 1904, the British extended these arguments to these three islands as well, opining that they were in terms of history and status analogous to Sirri; the Government of India indicated in its telegram No. 10, dated 23 April 1904, that the '[s]tatus of Abu Musa and Tamb is similar to that of Sirri before its seizure by the Persians in 1887.' It then invoked the documents referred to above as the basis upon which the British case rested,[121] and circulated copies of them to the British missions in the region. Thus, a review of these three letters, taken as containing the essence of the British arguments, may clarify the merit of their case in support of their claim to the Arab ownership of the Tunbs and Abu Musa, at least as far as the argument of double capacity is concerned.

The double capacity argument

The British put forth the double capacity argument in the course of discussions lasting from September 1887 till August 1888. When the British Legation in Tehran asked the Persian foreign minister to state on what grounds the Persian government had annexed Sirri, the answer, reflected in the letter from the Persian Minister of Foreign Affairs to the British Legation dated 10 March 1888, was that the Governors of Lingah had always held possession of the place, exacted taxes from its people and exercised jurisdiction over it.[122]

The British Legation concurred in reply that 'it was quite true that the Deputy Governors of Lingah had exercised jurisdiction over the Island of Sirri.' And that was what the two sides agreed upon from the outset; but they diverged when it came to details. The British Legation argued that although the government of Lingah

> had exercised jurisdiction over Sirri, . . . this was not in their capacity as Governors of Lingah, but as Joasmi Sheikhs, that they had traditional rights over the Island of Sirri apart from the position as Governors of Lingah under Persian Government, . . . and that their Arab kinsmen on the Oman Coast shared in these rights, which the Persian domicile of the Lingah Joassmi Sheikhs could not take away from them.[123]

In another round of dispute over Sirri in 1894–99, C. Greene, the British Minister in Tehran, in a note dated 11 September 1894 addressed to the Amin-us-Sultan, the Iranian foreign minister, repeated the same argument of double capacity, maintaining that 'although the Government of Lingah exercised jurisdiction over Sirri, they had not done so in this capacity as Governors of Lingah, but as Joasmi Sheikhs.'[124] In a response dated 6 November 1894, the Iranian foreign minister maintained that '[e]ven when the Joasimi Sheikhs were not Governors of Lingah, the Persian Government had always exercised jurisdiction over Sirri Island.' The Sad-ul-Mulk governorship of Lingah, which exercised jurisdiction over Sirri, was referred to in the letter as an example.

Colonel Wilson rejected this argument in his memorandum, on the basis of the short duration of the governorship named, stating that the 'Sad-ul-Mulk held this charge from June 1883 to March 1884, or about 9 months, in which short period, proof of an alleged long established jurisdiction can hardly be found.' However, this period, though short, was significant as it did not result in any resistance or protest on the part of those the British recognized as owners of Sirri. In this regard, Colonel Meade in his report admitted the exercise of jurisdiction by the Sad-ul-Mulk on behalf of the Iranian Prime Minister and the investiture of day-to-day administration of Lingah, including its dependencies, to a Qasimi sheikh. He stated that 'the Joasmi Sheikhs have been the *de facto* rulers of Lingah for over 100 years. The Sad-ul-Mulk governed Lingah along with Bunder Abbas and the other Gulf ports on behalf of the sadr Azam from June 1883 to March 1884, but never actually interfered in the affairs of the place . . . by leaving the Government of the port of Lingah to Sheikh Yusuf.'

The second argument set forth by the Persian Prime Minister in his reply to the British note maintained that the 'Arab Sheikhs have always farmed[125] the Government revenues of the island from the governors of Lingah. One of these Sheikhs is Sheikh Yusuf who, a few years ago, farmed the revenues from Sad-ul-Mulk, and with His Excellency's permission constructed certain works, such as a reservoir, etc, on the island.'

While the Prime Minister might have been referring to 'the short period' when Sad-ul-Mulk was in charge, Colonel Wilson simply found this 'difficult to understand,' and confined himself to repeating that 'Sheikh Yusuf . . . according to the views of the British Government [was] concerned with the administration of the island on behalf of the Joasimi.'

Wilson stated in his memorandum that 'there is no proof' that 'the Persian possession has been quite independent of the Joasmis, who held authority on the Persian coast' and, despite British demands, the Persian authorities did not give proofs to justify their allegations. On their side, the Iranians considered the exercise of jurisdiction by the governors of Lingah, as Iranian officials, over the islands, Sad-ul-Mulk's governance of Lingah, and the farming by Qasimi sheikhs of government revenues of the islands from the governors of Lingah as proofs of Iranian sovereignty over Sirri, and by extension over the Tunbs and Abu Musa.

What is also noteworthy is the fact that neither the British formal note, Wilson's memorandum nor Meade's report made any reference to any protest by the sheikhs of the Arab coast following the Persian moves on Sirri and Lingah in September 1887. As mentioned in Colonel Meade's report, deputies of the Governors of Bushehr exercised sovereignty over Sirri since 1887 by sending 'one official each year to levy taxes of one bag of rice from each large boat . . . and no Persian officials live there permanently.' This demonstrates that, despite the British claim of the Joasmis' rights to Sirri, the Persians had exercised sovereignty over the island without any difficulty.

To establish the double capacity argument, while Colonel Meade admitted that '[t]he two leading Chiefs of the Joasmi tribe are the Sheikhs of Ras al-Khymah and Shargah', he, as well as Colonel Wilson and C. Greene, were silent as to why a group that had splintered from the main seat of the tribe on the Arab coast and become Persian subjects should have 'carried with them to their new settlement a possession in the islands which they already possessed', and why 'tribal custom' put this splinter group in possession of common tribal rights over the outlying islands of Sirri, the Tunbs and Abu Musa, instead of 'the two leading Chiefs of Joasmi tribe.'

Moreover, the theory of double capacity cannot explain what happened to the jurisdiction over the three islands when the Persian government replaced the Qasimi ruler of Lingah by a non-Qasimi ruler in 1887. Nor why neither the British nor the sheikhs of the main branch of Qasimis lodged any protest or took any action with regard to the continuation of the Persian rule over the dependencies of Lingah, including the three islands, until 1903 and 1908.

In fact, it is an abstraction to assume that the Governor of Lingah could have ruled dependent islands of the governorate, not as the governor but as holder of another legal title. It is questionable whether there has been any precedent to this.

Evaluating the legal merit of the dual legal status, Sir Edward Beckett, the Foreign Office legal expert, ruled the following in 1932:

> My conclusion, is that, unless further evidence is forthcoming that it can be proved that during the period 1880–1887 the [Qasimi] Sheikh of Lingah ruled the islands under some title different from that under which he ruled the mainland (I doubt that it will be easy to show this), the Persians did possess sovereignty over Tamb and Abu-Musa during those years.[126]

The letters

The other evidence the British furnished to prove the title of the sheikhs of the Arab littoral to the islands consisted of translations of three letters provided, in 1882, to the Residency Agent stationed in Sharjah. Addressed to the Arab sheikhs by the Sheikh of Lingah, the letters apparently acknowledged the sheikhs' ownership of the islands. However, as the Political Resident stated in 1928, 'Endeavours are now being made to see if the originals can be produced.'[127]

The British, and, especially later, the United Arab Emirates (UAE), also based their claims to the islands on a number of letters exchanged over the three islands between the Sheikhs of Sharjah and Ras al-Khaimah, on the one hand, and the Qasimi Sheikhs of Lingah on the other. Wilson's memorandum makes a reference to a letter, dated 29 March 1884, written by Sheikh Yusuf, the Governor of Lingah, to the Chief of Ras al-Khaimah, 'fully admitting the possession of the Island of Tamb by the Joasmis.' This letter is important because, among the various arguments put forth by the British, it is the one most frequently referred to by the UAE. In this letter Sheikh Yusuf refers to the complaint already made by the chief of Ras al-Khaimah about denying his subjects access to the island of Tunb by the tribesmen of the Iranian coast and states that '[t]he Island of Tunb is actually an island for you o' the Jowasim of Oman, and I kept my hand over it, considering that you are agreeable to my doing so'.[128] This letter followed disputes in 1873

60   The Curzon strategy

and beyond that resulted in the tribesmen of the Iranian coast preventing Ras al-Khaimah's subjects from entering Tunb to graze their animals. As referred to earlier, following inquiries carried out by the British agents in Lingah and Sharjah, Edward Ross, Political Resident in the Persian Gulf, wrote to the Sheikh of Ras al-Khaimah on 19 April 1873, stating that Tunb Island belonged to Lingah and the inhabitants of Ras al-Khaimah should refrain from annoying Iranian livestock breeders there.[129]

The complimentary nature of the letter, sent after the dispute and aimed at restoring friendship, was evident, especially when it stated a few lines later: 'And the town of Lengah is your town.' This phrase made clear that the letter was only a piece of oriental flattery, indicating that the phrase on the Tunb should not have been taken literally either.

With regard to the letters, one important question went unaddressed and remained unanswered: while the letters, written in 1884 and earlier, are said to establish the ownership of the sheikhs of the Arab littoral over the islands, the question is why the Qasimis of Lingah continued to administer the Tunbs and Abu Musa until 1887 and the non-Qasimi governors of Lingah until 1903, despite the on-again, off-again disputes that characterized the relationship between the two branches of the Qasimis.

Moreover, a cursory search turns up numerous similar letters in the Middle East exchanged among sheikhs and rulers. For example, in reply to the King of Arabia, who had complained about the treatment of his subjects in Bahrain, the Sheikh of Bahrain wrote to him stating that, 'Bahrain, Qatif, Hasa and Nejd are all one and belong to Your Majesty.' Certainly, the inclusion of Bahrain in the list could not have been anything but compliment.[130] Another example is the one referred to earlier in this book, in which the Imam of Muscat, in reply to the British request for his consent to use Kishm Island as a base, responded in May 1820 that 'God knows . . . that I do not reckon these dominions as appertaining to me, but as appertaining to the Honourable Company.'[131]

The priority-in-occupation argument

In a departure from the previous British line of argument, Arthur Hardinge, the British Minister in Tehran, in a note dated 15 June 1904 to the Iranian Foreign Ministry, put forward a new argument specifically about Tunb, stating that 'What [the Sheikh of Shargah] did was to hoist his own flag upon the islands, which were not yet formally occupied by any other Government, and he has the right to fly it as the first occupant, till his lawful possession of these islands is disproved.'[132]

There are a number of facts that render this argument implausible:

- First, Iran had already asserted its sovereignty over Tunb and Abu Musa in 1888. As referred to earlier, the British records indicate when the the British Legation in Tehran made representations to the Persian government on hearing of the raising of Iran's flag on Tunb, 'the Persian Government advanced a new claim to the Island of Abu Musa' in reply on 28 April 1888.[133]

- Second, Sharjah was a tribal entity with no territorial dimension in the modern sense. There is consensus among post-colonial academics as there was among British colonial officials that the concept of territorial sovereignty was non-existent in eastern Arabia up to the mid-twentieth century. As J. B. Kelly reiterated, 'Before the advent of oil, the desert was in many ways similar to the high seas. Nomads and camels roamed across it at will and, though there were vague tribal limits, there were few signs of the authority of any established government outside the ports and oasis.'[134] It was not until 1955 that sheikhs of the coasts felt the need to have clearly defined borders – and even then, they were pushed into it by the British Agent of the time, Julian Walker, on behalf of the British government. As a result, Walker and his successors had to travel around remote parts trying to decide which sheikhs owned which bit of the barren landscape.[135]
- Third, Iran was already a major government located a very short distance from these islands, the British had already recognized that the Governors of Lingah exercised jurisdiction over them and British official maps had depicted them in Iran's mainland colour.
- Fourth, the act of marking the ownership of territories by hoisting a flag was an alien practice to the tribal entities on the Arab littoral.

The factor of prescription

Given Iran's continuous protest and campaign against the occupation of the three islands during the 68 years that followed the raising of an Arab flag on Tunb and Abu Musa in 1903, there remains no room for the factor of prescription. British reports are indicative of numerous Iranian formal objections and demonstrations of opposition to what they termed 'the occupation' of the three islands.[136]

Seeking to lease or purchase the islands in the Strait of Hormuz

Seeking to obtain leasehold over a number of Iranian islands, especially those lying off the north shores of the Strait of Hormuz, was the last method with which the British tried to expand their control in the Persian Gulf. In 1913, the British focused their attention once again on the Strait of Hormuz and the Iranian islands along its north shores. The proposed Trans-Persian Railway was the new development that prompted them to take up the matter anew. On the assumption that the railway would touch coast at Bandar Abbas, the British Government of India proposed, in a telegram from the Government of India to the Secretary of State dated 8 January 1913, several alternatives that in its view were 'necessary to secure naval control of the Gulf.' The alternatives included such actions as 'holding positions on Hormuz, Larak, and Kishm islands . . . and securing our positions in regard to [these] islands either by agreement with Persia or by *de facto* occupation'.[137]

As telegram No. 107 dated 17 April 1914 from Walter Townley, British Minister in Tehran, suggests, while referring to the financial difficulties in which the

Persian government found themselves at the time, Townley broached for the first time the issue of purchase or acquisition on long lease of the islands of Larak, Henjam and the whole of Kishm in a meeting with Persian foreign minister. As his report to London suggests, the Iranian minister replied that 'sale would be impossible but that lease might be arranged if terms were made attractive.' According to the telegram, the British Minister explained to his interlocutor that 'a lease would of course imply a total surrender, for period of its duration, of the islands upon which British flag would be hoisted as H. M.'s Government might require.'[138]

Lord Commissioners of the Admiralty, whose view had been solicited on the idea, stated in communication No. M-631/14 dated 5 May 1914 that 'the control of the islands would undoubtedly be eminently desirable from the standpoint of naval and national interests.' It continues that '[t]he importance of these islands from a strategic point of view cannot be too strongly insisted upon. They command the only deep water sheltered anchorages in the southern end of the Gulf, and they provide a possible base from which the whole trade of the Gulf can be controlled, if necessary, in time of war. They give absolute command over the terminus of the projected Trans-Persian Railway and the proposed line of route of the extension between Bander Abbas and Karachi.' The increase in 'the British influence in these regions', the strengthening of the Biritish position on the Trucial coast, providing Britain with 'a more direct interest in the conservation of the pearl fisheries,' and facilitating 'the working of the patrols maintained for the conservation of peace in those waters,' were among the benefits of the acquisition of the islands in question that the Commissioners of Admiralty referred to in their telegram.[139]

The Viceroy of India followed suit and, in his telegram dated 22 May 1914, found that 'both from the strategic and political points of view, the acquisition of Kishm, Hengam and Larak on a long lease, e.g., 99 years, is highly desirable and would greatly strengthen our position in the Gulf both now and prospectively.' Moreover, he strongly recommended the inclusion of the islands of Hormuz and Shaikh Shuaib in the bargain.[140]

As both the British and Persian governments were in principle in agreement over the lease, soon the bargaining over the financial offer began. The British Minister in Tehran reported on 21 June 1914 that, upon the inquiry made by the Persian foreign minister, he said to him that 'the most H. M.'s Government could offer would be £25,000 for Kishm, Henjam, Larak, Hormuz and Sheikh Shuaib.' He then explained that 'His Excellency's face fell', and that he let it be understood that he expected a lot more.[141]

With the persistence of Iran's financial difficulties, the British records show that Britain decided to take a shot at the possibility of purchasing the islands in question. A *note verbale* sent by the British Minister to the Persian government on 14 October 1914 contained an offer to purchase the islands. Referring to 'the painful financial difficulties' the Persian government found itself in, the note proposed the sale to Britain of certain islands in the Persian Gulf in proximity of Bandar Abbas, specifically, Hormuz, Kishm, Larak, Henjam and Shaikh Shuaib. The note proposes the payment of £300,000, plus cancellation of the Persian debt to Britain equalling £790,000.[142]

In reply, the Iranian Foreign Ministry sent a note, dated 1 November 1914, to the British Legation in Tehran, in which it was stated:

> His Excellency no doubt concurs with me that the contents of his memorandum must have surprised and grieved the Persia Government. The Minister for Foreign Affairs feels sure that the British Government, who have on more difficult situations given their sincere support to Persia, would not take advantage of the Persian financial difficulties and make such proposals which the Persian Government would be unable to accept, and, if accepted, would bring her face to face with a more serious crisis.[143]

In the covering letter, No. 1, Walter Townley explains that, given the delay in replying to his note, he had requested a meeting with the Iranian prime minister, Mostufi ul-Mamalek, and heard from him that 'the scheme was one that was of such vital importance to Persia, since it concerned the sale of a portion of her territory, that the Government could not deal with it without the presence of the Madjless, which would meet in a very short time.' And as noted in the note, the Prime Minister said in reply to his insistence for an assurance that the measure would be laid before the Madjless as soon as it assembled and would receive the strong support of the Cabinet, 'Mustaufi ul-Mamalek did not commit himself to this, and said that he must consult his colleagues'.[144]

In 1918, when the renewal of this offer was under consideration, the addition of the three Iranian islands of Hinderabi, Kais and Farur to the list to be communicated to Persia was approved.[145]

The general British policy of expanding control

The direct control of territories by the British, and the British claiming of territories for their subordinates at the expense of regional powers in the wider region, were not confined to Iranian possessions. The British tended almost invariably to enter into forays in support of small local entities under British protection as opposed to regional or global powers. It was a general policy pursued by the British throughout their ascendancy in the region, by which they aimed to control territories and deny them to actual or perceived rivals. A few examples are as follows:

Cape Musandim

The British hold over the harbours and islands of Cape Musandim, belonging to Oman, was also being strengthened at the turn of century. Despite the fact that the Sultan of Oman's demeanour 'was that of a loyal feudatory of the British Crown rather than of an independent Sovereign, and it is clear that he trusts implicitly to the British Power for support and protection,' as Viceroy Curzon described him in his account of his tour in the Persian Gulf in November 1903,[146] nonetheless, the British were averse to consigning to his care strategically important pieces of lands within his territory.

Viceroy Curzon, in a minute dated 6 October 1902, opined that '[t]he ascendancy of Maskat over the littoral in question is so indeterminate that our own officer, Major Cox, advises us that we can either recognize or ignore it as we please. There is therefore no question of established or admitted right of sovereignty, to which we could appeal.[147]

As a result, and relative to the question of a naval base in the Persian Gulf, communication No. 245, dated 17 January 1903, from the Foreign Office to the India Office, let it be known that the Commissioners of the British Admiralty had 'no objection to the proposals of the Government of India that steps be taken to reoccupy the old telegraphic buildings at Elphinstone inlet [Khor ash-Shem], and to regard the strip of coast between Khor Kalba and Dibba [all belonging to Oman] as part of the territory of the Chief of Shargah.'[148] In so doing, it was believed that 'we should have no difficulty in arranging with the local tribes – who consist only of a few miserable communities of fishermen . . . and acknowledging no chief or master'.[149]

Kubbat Ghazira (Malcolm Inlet) and 'Sheep island, which constitutes the outer protection of Khor Kawi,' were later added to the list. Finally, as indicated in a letter dated 25 November 1904, from T. W. Kemp, Commander and Senior Naval Officer, Persian Gulf, to his superior, flagstaffs were erected in the above islands.[150]

Zakhnuniyeh

Zakhnuniyeh is an island located 10 miles south of Ujair, in the vicinity of Qatar. In one of the latest rounds of disputes over Zakhnuniyeh, the Turks raised their flag there in March 1909 and arranged to keep a guard there. On the recommendation of the British Government of India, the British ambassador in Constantinople made a protest. Although the Turks and Qatari sheikhs claimed it, the British claimed the island for the Sheikh of Bahrain, who was under *de facto* British protection.[151]

In general, the British and the Ottomans were at loggerheads over Qatar and its possessions. While the Turks claimed Qatar as part of the Nejd, and took action in the 1870s to assimilate it into other provinces of their empire, the British vilified the Arab sheikhs for collaborating with the Turks. The British never admitted the validity of the Turkish claim and, as they put it, '[they] treated misbehaviour on the part of the local Chiefs without much regard to Turkish pretensions, though the Turks have, at the invitation or with the connivance of those Chiefs, established small military posts at Ojeir, Zobara and El Bidaa.'[152]

The islands of Verba and Bubiyan

In the case of Verba and Bubiyan, too, the British followed the rule of supporting small local entities under its protection as opposed to regional or global powers. British support of the Sheikh of Kuwait, who had signed an exclusive treaty with the Britain in 1899, was instrumental in strengthening his hand against the Ottomans, who endeavoured to control these two islands. In June 1905, Major Cox made clear that Britain recognized the Sheikh of Kuwait's claim over Bubiyan and Verba, and that the British were advising him to institute or supporting him in instituting a post or posts there.[153]

Kolba

The Kolba case is another instance of British territorial engineering in the area in furtherance of Britain's interests. In 1936, the British provided for the secession of Kolba, an island on the Gulf of Oman, from Sharjah. The Air Ministry and the India Office in London were very anxious to establish an emergency landing ground in Kolba for the route to India of Imperial Airways. The headman of Kolba, himself a Qasimi, refused to guarantee the safety of the landing ground unless granted independence from Sharjah. Since the ruler of Sharjah was clearly unable to impose his authority over his distant cousin, and since the safety of the landing ground was essential to the air route, the India Office sanctioned the independence of Kolba. Thus, the day he signed an agreement with Imperial Airways in August 1936, Sheikh Said bin Hamad al-Qasimi became the ruler of a new Trucial state.

Deeply embittered by the loss of Kolba to his cousin, the ruler of Sharjah felt betrayed by Britain, which had only recently guaranteed his independence and sovereignty, also in return for another air agreement. This agreement was made in 1932 when he had given Imperial Airways permission to construct what was in effect the first airport in the Persian Gulf. The British Political Agent had promised him in writing that the British government would guarantee Sharjah's complete independence and would do nothing to take away his lands from him.[154] Previously, in 1921, the breakaway territory of Ras al-Khaimah had obtained British recognition as an independent state.

Buraimi

The dispute over control of the Buraimi Oasis dated back to the 1800s. It was a continuing source of contention and minor military skirmishes between Britain, acting on behalf of Abu Dhabi, and Saudi Arabia. Tensions came to a head in 1933, when Ibn Saud granted a concession to Standard Oil of California for the 'Eastern part of our Saudi Arab Kingdom within its frontiers', without defining those frontiers, largely because no one knew where they were. The British chose the so-called 'Blue Line' agreed upon between Britain and Turkey in 1913. Saudi Arabia refused to accept it.[155]

In 1949, the British Political Agent, driving hastily across the desert, tried to intercept a party of oil company surveyors escorted by Saudi guards. The Saudis detained the Agent, who claimed to represent Abu Dhabi in the case, for few days. Upon protest by the British government, the Saudis, far from backing down, claimed even more territory, including the Buraimi Oasis. After a few skirmishes and a failed arbitration attempt, the Trucial Oman Levies, led by the British

Colonel Eric Johnson, intervened, and the Saudi contingent on the ground was forced to give up. However, diplomatic activities dragged on.[156]

The affair reached a climax in 1952 when the Saudis, with the tacit support of the United States, occupied the oasis and claimed it as part of their kingdom. The issue was referred to international arbitration in 1954. The negotiations quickly broke down and the Saudis were expelled by force by Omani troops, led by British officers. In the mid-1960s, as the time for British withdrawal drew closer, the Saudis pressed their claim further, leading to more incidents, more drilling controversies and a sequence of claims and counter-claims. British departure from the Persian Gulf left Saudi Arabia with the upper hand, and the Saudis obtained major concessions from Abu Dhabi between 1972 and 1977. In the process, Abu Dhabi gave up part of its western territory and its right to the Zarara oilfield in the south for Saudi recognition of the UAE and the Buraimi Oasis.[157]

Kuwait

In the case of defending Kuwait against Iraq, the British invoked an exchange of letters in June 1961 abrogating the 1899 agreement between themselves and Kuwait, on the grounds that it was inconsistent with the independence of Kuwait, and concluding a treaty of friendship between the two countries. Under this treaty the two countries committed themselves to 'consultation' on matters affecting them both. There was also a clause providing for Britain to give assistance to Kuwait should it be requested. This exchange of letters, by its reference to a 'sovereign and independent State', in fact dismissed the Iraqi claim to Kuwait. A contingent of 3,500 British troops was dispatched to Kuwait in July 1961 to defend Kuwait against Iraq.[158]

The First World War and its aftermath

In the wake of the First World War, two different trends in the Persian Gulf were noticeable – trends that affected the issue of the three islands and made the British more adamant in claiming the islands for their protégés on the Arab coast. The first trend was the strengthening of British control over the Persian Gulf and its Arab littoral states, and the second was growing animosity between Iran and Britain.

Growing British domination over the Persian Gulf Arabs

By and large, in the aftermath of the developments of 1903 and 1904, Britain's grip over the Persian Gulf reached its climax. The regional supremacy it declared unilaterally was recognized by all its imperial rivals during the course of diplomatic negotiations conducted in 1904–14. The supremacy of Britain was also ratified by the results of the First World War.

The only weak links, from a British perspective, in the whole system of the Persian Gulf at this stage were Mesopotamia, which remained under the Ottomans till the First World War, the Persian coast and Saudi authority, which was rather limited to inner Arabia. The First World War enabled the British to finally take control of Mesopotamia. They had been interested in doing so for a long time in order to, among other things, protect the northern approaches of the Persian Gulf from European ambitions and Ottoman expansionism. Newly established Iraq formally became a British Mandate, sanctioned by the League of Nations.

Although they were pacified and disciplined in the nineteenth century, the Trucial states were not incorporated into the British Empire. The need for mobilizing considerable financial and military resources to do so was the main impediment. Although it was thoroughly discussed in British circles, in the end Britain refrained from establishing a formal protectorate regime on the Arab littoral. Britain relied mainly on its maritime supremacy to establish its hegemony over Arab Persian Gulf entities; to do so, the suppression of piracy and the slave trade conveniently served the purpose.

In the 1920s, the British referred to Arab tribes of the lower Persian Gulf as 'constituting a sort of veiled Protectorate', to Bahrein as 'under British protection' and to the Arab state of Muscat as 'being predominantly controlled by British influence' for years; 'its trade is similarly in Anglo-Indian hands; and its Ruler has not merely for years been subsidized by the Government of India, but in 1891 entered into an Agreement with the British Government to alienate any portion of his dominions to any other Power.'[159]

With British supremacy in the Persian Gulf finally and unquestionably assured, the thrust of British policy increasingly turned toward involvement in local politics of the Arab littoral to protect its growing list of accrued interests. As a result, the British policy of refraining from interference in the affairs of the Arab littoral states changed in the 1920s. After the war, Britons were even employed in the governments of local Arab rulers as advisers and administrators.[160] Cost-effective policing made possible through increased speed of communication and advances in technology – especially the airplane – played an important role in adopting the new intrusive policy.

The granting of oil concessions in the 1930s drew Britain into a closer and more involved relationship with the Trucial states, thus hardening further the British attitude toward strengthening the Trucial states' status. Previously British concerns had centred on the security of imperial lines of communications, which were essentially maritime. In the major case in which they were not – the Indo-European telegraph – the telegraph line had been deliberately laid along the Persian coast in order to avoid the lack of security on the Arab littoral.

The new policy led to the establishment of a chain of aerodromes and emergency landing grounds on Arab territory. A civil air agreement signed with Sharjah in 1932 opened this new age, and Dubai followed suit in 1937. These agreements enabled the British to intervene in order to settle dynastic and inter-state quarrels,[161] which finally led to the introduction of a fresh condition for the recognition of new rulers by Britain, namely, that they must accept any advice of the Political Agent.[162]

As part of the new policy, the British Foreign Office agreed with the suggestion of the Political Resident in April 1951 on the establishment of the Council of Rulers, which would meet roughly every three months for the discussion of matters of common interest under the chairmanship of the Political Resident. Meanwhile, the Foreign Office 'instructed the Political Resident to keep the possibility of the formal federation of the States in mind and to report in due course...'[163] The Council established committees in 1958 for public health, agriculture and education. It sat in the courtroom at the Political Agency.[164]

Seeking to have an effective military instrument, a decision was taken to establish a force called the Trucial Oman Levies, to be led by a British officer. It was regularly expanded and was renamed the Trucial Oman Scouts in 1956. All these led to a change in the role of the Political Agent in the Persian Gulf, who could now settle inter-state disputes. With the new force they had a ready means of preventing the parties from fighting.[165]

Iran's continued defiance

With Iraq and the lower Persian Gulf submitting to British dominance, the British navy unrivalled on Gulf waters and Saudi authority confined largely to its Najdi base, the Iranian coastline was the only one not controlled by the British.

Moreover, in full contrast to developments in the lower Persian Gulf, signs of Iranian hostility against the British influence on the upper coast multiplied after the victory of the Constitutional Revolution in 1905–06 and the establishment of the Majlis (parliament). The employment of advisers, including the American financier Morgan Shuster, from major countries other than Britain and Russia to overhaul Iran's administration continued despite British opposition.

At the same time, the significant surge in British attempts to establish control over Iranian politics in the aftermath of the Russian Revolution and the Russian withdrawal from Iran was warded off by a more assertive Iranian nationalism. Chief among the British plans was the one personally masterminded by Lord Curzon in 1919. Once installed in the Foreign Office in January, he tasked Sir Percy Cox, already installed by Curzon as British Minister in Tehran, to secure 'the permanent maintenance of British influence in a country bordering on the Indian Empire', and he himself directed the negotiations from London. Signed in August 1919 after the Iranian Prime Minister and two ministers received 400,000 tomans (£131,147 in the money of the day) as a bribe, the agreement would have given Britain a free hand, to the virtual exclusion of others, in an Iran under British tutelage.[166] It was left to Herman Norman, who replaced Cox in Tehran in June 1920, to brief Curzon on 'the immense unpopularity' of the agreement and its authors.[167]

A popular uprising against the agreement led to the fall of Prime Minister Vusuq al-Dawlah, who had signed it, and the two following Prime Ministers refused to submit it to the Majlis. It was formally denounced a few weeks after Reza Khan's coup in February 1921. Initiated in 1918 by the Eastern Committee of the British Cabinet, then chaired by Lord Curzon, the agreement had been opposed by the British Government of India as 'an ambitious and hazardous experiment, likely to be opposed by Persian national sentiment as making for a protectorate.'[168] It was, as described by Harold Nicolson, who worked under Curzon in the Foreign Office, 'the most galling, because the most personal, of his many diplomatic defeats.'[169]

At the same time, this episode bore testimony to the fact that, while Russia's role as a counterweight had contributed to Iran's endeavours to foil British efforts to dominate the country, it was not, however, the determining factor.

The invitation to American oil companies to seek concessions in Iran (1920–21), the cancellation of the Anglo-Iranian oil concession in 1933 – which resulted in the British militarily threatening Iran in the Persian Gulf – and the rescission of the concession of the (British) Imperial Bank in 1928, among other events, finally culminating in Iran leaning toward Germany in the 1930s, demonstrated the deep resentment on the part of the Iranians towards Britain. With Bahrain, Tunbs and Abu Musa dominating the endless Anglo-Persian negotiations of the late 1920s and early 1930s and no resolution to these issues on the horizon, Britain's decision to abandon Basidu and Henjam in 1935 ushered in less tense phase in Anglo-Persian relations.

As referred to briefly earlier, the question of maintaining facilities at Basidu and Henjam had returned to plague Anglo-Persian relations in the late 1920s and early 1930s as the two states sought at great length to settle their outstanding differences on Gulf questions. Following the failure of the British to substantiate any right in Basidu, as discussed earlier, the Iranian side embarked on certain actions that could be said to amount to harassment tactics, aimed at evicting them from the island. The tension culminated in the arrest by the British of the Iranian head of customs, while he was engaged in inspection in Basidu. Discussing this issue with an Iranian official at the Foreign Ministry in October 1933, the British chargé d'affaires stated, 'the detention of the head of Customs relates to a series of incidents that began a while ago in the Persian Gulf and can't be considered in isolation. The way the navy of the Imperial Government deals with the Gulf's Arabs and the issue of the hauling down of the British flag at Basidu[170] and the insistence of the Iranian officials to enter into the British area in Basidu have all led to this incident.'[171]

The British military claimed the rights to provide 'security for British subjects and their belongings' on Henjam, to deny the Iranian military access to 'the British concessionary land' on the island and to 'interfere with the British navy and telegraph office or possessions of British subjects' there, as expressed in a letter signed 'Commander of the British forces on Henjam' to his Iranian counterpart and reported to the Iranian Foreign Ministry by the Ministry of War on 4 Tir 1307 (25 June 1929). Rejecting these claims as running counter to Iranian sovereignty on Henjam, the Iranian Foreign Ministry reiterated in a *note verbale*, dated 31 Tir 1307 (22 July 1929), to the British Legation in Tehran that: first, Iran had not accorded any concession in those areas; second, Iranian forces were responsible for providing security for foreigners lawfully present on Iranian soil; and third, offices and possessions legally acquired by foreigners on Iranian territory were subject to the law of the land and the Iranian government did not allow foreign forces to interfere.[172]

70 *The Curzon strategy*

Finally, in a note dated 28 Shahrivar 1311 (19 September 1933), the Iranian Foreign Ministry informed the British Legation in Tehran that the Iranian government had decided to turn Henjam into a naval base for its newly bought warships and demanded that the British government stop stationing its own warships on that island.[173] This demand set off a series of bitter communications between the two governments, but finally led to the British evacuation of Henjam in 1935.

In continuation of the policy followed successfully on the Persian mainland in the mid-1920s aimed at extending its authority across the country, Tehran also embarked on new efforts to reassert its sovereign rights over Iranian waters, islands and ports in the Persian Gulf. In this period, Iran adopted an active policy in the Persian Gulf, which brought it into conflict with British interests. At the insistence of the Iranian government in 1923, the British government agreed to provide a list of their vessels in the Persian Gulf at the beginning of each month, to notify the Iranian authorities in advance if British naval vessels intended to visit Iranian ports and, finally, to report the names of British navy crews to the Iranian authorities a few days prior to their visits.[174]

Reluctant acquiescence to the British policing of the Persian Gulf had been one of the major outcomes of Iranian naval weakness. Effective measures could not be initiated to rectify this weakness until after the emergence of Reza Shah, although the resulting naval force of Iran was still far from a match for the British navy. Nonetheless, this did not stop Reza Shah's government from demanding that the policing of the Persian Gulf be entrusted to Iran.[175]

The expulsion by Persia of the Sheikh of Henjam, a Qasimi Arab and the father-in-law of the Sheikh of Dubai, in May 1928, the arrest of a Trucial dhow plying between Dubai and Khassab, which raised the question of the status of Tunbs, the continued questioning by Persia of the independence of the Trucial states, and claims of ownership of the Tunbs and Abu Musa were among developments that affected the political trend.

In relation to a representation made by the British in 1928 on behalf of the Trucial sheikh of Ras al-Khaimah, the acting Iranian foreign minister formally stated that 'my Government cannot in any way approve the attitude that the British Government have adopted on the pretext of having treaties with the above-mentioned Sheikh, and cannot accept resulting declaration which you make of protecting him.'[176] The Foreign Office instructed its chargé d'affaires in Tehran in reply to communicate officially the text of the Exclusive Agreement of 1892 with all the Trucial chiefs and to state that the British government could not permit direct dealings between the chiefs and the Persian government.[177] A Persian reply held to the views expressed in their note and added that 'all agreements made with Trucial Chiefs which harm or limit the rights and interests of Persia cannot be recognized as valid or legally be cited as reason for measure against Persian Government.'[178]

The rejection by the Persian government of the independence of political entities on the Arab littoral, and of the special relationship between them and Britain, was not confined to the Trucial states; Iran also refused to recognize Kuwait, Qatar, Bahrain and even Oman as independent states.

In addition, the Iranian government's 'third-power policy', to which it had nearly always resorted as a way to ward off its aggressive and intervening neighbours, Russia and Britain, assumed a new vigour in the late 1920s and further strained Anglo-Persian relations.[179] Unlike the previous immediate governments that had favoured the United States, Reza Shah's government chose Germany as the favourite third power. A Treaty of friendship signed between Iran and Germany on 17 February 1929 was followed by several trade agreements between the two countries. As a result, Iran's imports from Germany rose from 7.7 per cent in 1929–30 to 47.87 per cent of total imports in 1940–41, and its exports to Germany rose to 42.09 per cent of Iran's total exports from just 4 per cent in the same period. Iran's *rapprochement* with Germany also took the form of employing German advisers and firms. The British and Russian demand that the Iranian government expel several hundreds of German nationals created a crisis on the eve of the Second World War.[180]

Following up on its practice in the nineteenth century, notably in 1838 and 1857, Britain frequently resorted, or threatened to resort, to using its warships against Iranian targets in the Persian Gulf, including on occasions in 1904, 1913, 1923, 1925, 1933 and 1953, to counter Iran's defiance. Relations between Iran and Britain plunged to a new low after the Iranian Minister of Finance sent a note to the Director of the Anglo-Iranian Oil Company on 27 November 1932 announcing the cancellation of the D'Arcy oil concession. On 2 December the British government demanded that Iran immediately withdraw the cancellation.[181] Subsequently, the British Undersecretary for Foreign Affairs announced in the House of Commons that Great Britain 'would not tolerate interference by the Persian Government with the Anglo-Persian Oil Company.'

The British Minister in Tehran also threatened the Iranian government with the landing of troops and reminded the Iranians of the fate of Amanullah Khan, King of Afghanistan. In a *note verbale* dated 8 December 1932 to the Iranian Foreign Ministry, it was threatened that 'His Majesty's Government will regard themselves as entitled to take all such measures as the situation may demand for that company's protection.'[182] On 9 December reports received in Tehran showed that the British had strengthened their naval forces in the Persian Gulf. Two destroyers were anchored 3 miles from Abadan and a gunboat had been dispatched to Bushehr. And on 13 December news of uprisings among Baluchi tribes and the Arabs of Khuzistan reached Tehran.[183] Nineteen years later, Iranian Prime Minister Mossadegh, arguing before the UN Security Council against the validity of the new concession granted in 1933, said that 'the Shah was under pressure and his resistance might have cost him his throne.'[184]

Following the nationalization of the Iranian oil industry in March 1951, the British placed a full-fledged blockade against Iran in the northern Persian Gulf, which was joined by the other major oil companies. In this connection, further threatening measures were taken, including the dispatch of a British paratroop brigade to Cyprus in mid-May and of the cruiser *Mauritius* to the Iranian oil terminal at Abadan.

The British concluded that the maintenance of their influence in the Persian

Gulf was a matter of paramount importance, from both the imperial and the Indian standpoint; and if they were no longer to enjoy on the south Persian coast the privileged position that they had had in the past, then the consolidation of their influence on the Arabian shores was a matter of much greater and more definite importance than at any earlier period.[185]

Thus, Britain became more adamant in its determination to rule out any flexibility when it came to accommodating Iran's stance in the disputes over Bahrain, the Tunbs and Abu Musa. Consequently, these standoffs lingered on until such time as the Britain saw no other way but to leave the Persian Gulf altogether in 1971.

3 The restoration of Persian Gulf autonomy and the issue of the three islands

The announcement of the British withdrawal from 'east of Suez' on 16 January 1968 set in motion a series of activities that prepared the Persian Gulf for a historic change. The new, viable regional structure that the British government wished to see established before the end of 1971 required the removal of a series of impediments, mostly relics of the colonial era. It was a critical period during which there could be no further escape from addressing and settling a number of grave outstanding issues.

Britain's wish to see the small sheikhdoms of the Persian Gulf pull together and organize themselves in a more defensible federation was at the centre of British efforts to establish a security structure that would survive the pullout of their troops. The Iranian government, in turn, had made clear that the creation of such a federation could only follow, and not precede, the settlement of some relevant outstanding territorial and border disputes in the area. Among these disputes, the restoration of Iranian sovereignty over the three islands was high on Tehran's agenda. In the process, Iran also expected that its historic position in the Persian Gulf, denied only during the British supremacy in the area, be reinstated.

In the meantime, how to fill the power vacuum that the British pullout at the end of 1971 would leave was the overarching question that preoccupied regional and global actors. As the Persian Gulf took on greater importance, due to the increasing economic and strategic value of oil, the looming power void appeared more menacing and the need to address it more pressing.

This chapter aims to discuss the end of the *Pax Britannica* in the Persian Gulf, which enabled Iran to actively pursue and resolve the dispute over the three islands and to reinstate its own supremacy in the region. British weakness, the inability and unwillingness of the United States to replace Britain, and Iran's growing power and rising stature were the most important factors in several historic developments in the area at this juncture. While briefly reviewing these factors, the main focus of this chapter will be on Britain's policy reversal and its main consequences, or specifically, the expedient abandonment of Britain's claim of the three islands for its Arab protégés, and the emergence of Arab radicals as the new main pretenders to the islands, rejecting their appurtenance to Iran.

The end of the Pax Britannica

The announcement made in the House of Commons on 16 January 1968 by Labour Prime Minister Harold Wilson of Britain that there would be a total withdrawal of British forces stationed east of Suez by the end of 1971 was a turning point in the history of the region.[1] As discussed in Chapter 1, Britain had begun the process of establishing the *Pax Britannica* in the region in the 1810s for reasons of imperial strategic interest. Facing a multifaceted crisis in mid-1960s, the Labour government found it imperative to commit to leaving for domestic political and financial reasons.

Upon assuming office in 1964, the Labour government inherited an unprecedented balance of payments deficit of £800 million. This massive and mounting deficit, the biggest since the war, was the Wilson government's first major problem. Wilson himself called it 'the central problem' of his administrations from 1964 to 1970.[2]

As a result, the government soon found it essential to take drastic measures, including making large cuts in the defence budget. Reductions in Britain's overseas commitments figured prominently among the measures put on the agenda to stabilize the financial situation. The government could more easily agree on defence cuts in British commitments east of Suez – including Aden, the Persian Gulf, Singapore, Malaysia and Hong Kong – where the largest number of troops outside of Europe were stationed at an annual cost of around £400 million.

In fact, the mid-1960s financial crisis was the *coup de grâce* that left no other choice for the British but to radically reconsider their international commitments. The decline of British standing in the Middle East had begun at end of the Second World War. The independence of India and Pakistan in 1947, the rise of Iranian and Arab nationalism in the Middle East, the nationalization of the Iranian oil industry in 1951, the coup in Egypt and the loss of British military bases there in 1954 and in Kenya and Aden in 1960 and 1967, respectively, the Suez War débacle in 1956, the Iraqi leftist coup in 1958, American competition and the exigencies of the Cold War had already sapped the Empire to a point past repair. Moreover, the experience of decolonization movements in the 1950s and 1960s, most of which mired the colonialists in self-defeating, bloody conflicts, could only have presented a bleak prospect to British politicians weighing whether to stay in the Persian Gulf.

The British Conservative Party, while in opposition, sharply criticized the decision made by the Labour government. In their view withdrawal amounted to dishonouring obligations to friends and allies in the Persian Gulf and would endanger stability in the area. However, as described later, after they won the elections in June 1970 and assumed power, in the end they abstained, despite a great deal of hesitation and manoeuvring, from reversing the Labour government's decision, and carried it out exactly according to the schedule previously established.

In the Persian Gulf, the sheikhdoms whose external security had been guaranteed by Britain for over 150 years received the British withdrawal announcement with dismay. However, at a time when the British were busy with more pressing domestic and foreign concerns, the repercussions of ending Britain's commitments in the Persian Gulf were of little interest to London. Most Arab sheikhs in the Persian Gulf described the British announcement as shocking. The ruler of Abu Dhabi was reported to have proposed that the Arab littorals should offer to pay the entire cost of maintaining the British forces in the area in an attempt to reverse Britain's decision. This offer was rejected by the British government on 22 January 1968.[3]

Thus, the protectorate regime established in the nineteenth century aimed at guaranteeing regional security in Britain's own interests and in those of its Western allies in the Persian Gulf was set for abolition.

Iran reclaims its 'natural' position

The announcement of the British withdrawal from the Persian Gulf provided the Iranian leadership with a historic opportunity to reclaim the age-old position it had lost in early nineteenth century to British ascendancy in the region. In fact, as soon as signs had appeared in the mid-1950s indicating that British colonial power in the Persian Gulf was faltering, Iran, as the main regional power, began preparing itself for the big event. As Iran's interests were always in conflict with those of Britain in the Persian Gulf and the British had sought for more than one and a half centuries to restrain and contain Iranian influence there, Tehran stood to gain the most as a result of the British military presence coming to an end. In other words, unlike many regional players, Iran had no reason to fear the consequences of Britain's retreat.

Despite the close strategic relationship that developed between Iran under Shah Mohammad Reza Pahlavi and the West, competition between Iran and Britain in the Persian Gulf continued unabated in the pattern set in the early nineteenth century. Acrimony and bitterness had intensified during the reign of Reza Shah and led to his dethronement and exile by the British in 1941, following the Allied invasion of Iran, which deepened the distrust and suspicion of the last Shah of Iran towards them. As a result, the Iranian government received the news of Britain's departure with all the more delight. After the announcement, Tehran intermittently launched diplomatic and media campaigns to discourage the British from reversing their decision or delaying its implementation. These campaigns intensified in the wake of the Conservative Party victory in the British elections in June 1970.

The factors that significantly contributed to and facilitated Iran's ascendancy in the Persian Gulf in the aftermath of the British withdrawal can be grouped in the following three categories: Iran's inherent and historic position, Iran's growing interests and power, and the international environment.

Iran's inherent and historic position

Iran, regardless of the political players at its helm, has always been the major power of the Persian Gulf area, by virtue of geopolitical dictates, and with an historic claim to supremacy in the region. It maintained this claim throughout history, including during the period in which the British dominated the Gulf. As discussed previously, the first formal Persian reaction against British military presence in the Persian Gulf dated back to a note of 9 December 1820 to the British Legation in Tehran. In this note the Persian government strongly remonstrated against the British presence on Kishm Island and demanded their 'return to India and . . . in future to avoid such acts'.[4]

When Britain left the region, Iran believed itself to be fully qualified to reclaim the role it had played throughout most of its history. Iran was by far the most powerful nation on the Persian Gulf in terms of historical, geopolitical and military power. It had played an historic role from the Achaemenian and Sassanian eras up to the Safavid and Nadder Shah periods on both sides of the Persian Gulf. It had enjoyed a position of strength unrivalled among political entities in the area, and which had been superseded only by the British superior naval force of the early nineteenth century.

As described in Chapters 1 and 2, Iran refrained by and large from acquiescing to British dominance, and the relationship between Britain, as the major world power, and Iran, as the major regional power, was, throughout this period, a strained one most often fraught with suspicion and animosity. As the largest and most populous littoral state, with 31 million in population in 1971, with the longest coasts, stretching the full length of the northern Persian Gulf and the Sea of Oman, and as heir to a great ancient civilization with unprecedented state continuity in the region, Iran considered itself fit to reclaim and resume a leading regional role in the wake of Britain.[5]

In sharp contrast, the size and structure of the newly established riparian states and sheikhdoms indicated that they were in no position to help fill the vacuum left by Britain. Kuwait had a population of 750,000; Bahrain 200,000; Qatar 90,000; and the UAE 185,000. Saudi Arabia, with a population of 5 to 6 million inhabitants, was not yet really living in the twentieth century, and was just beginning to take an interest in the Persian Gulf. Radical Iraq, with a population of 10 million, beset with internal problems, and unwelcome in the otherwise conservative environment of the Gulf, was not in a position to challenge Iran as the major power in the area.

Iran's growing interests and power

Iran's interest in the Persian Gulf grew considerably during the decade preceding the British withdrawal announcement, and accordingly the Iranian government became more closely involved in the area. The developments that prompted the Iranian leadership to focus on the Persian Gulf and adopt an assertive approach toward it can be summarized as follows:

Deterioration in Iranian–Arab relations

The 1958 coup in Iraq altered the perception of threat in Tehran and prompted the Iranian government to give serious consideration to defence of its southern boundaries, especially by rebuilding the navy destroyed during the Second World War. The growing Soviet–Iraqi relationship, especially from the late 1960s, also may have implied that the Soviet threat had jumped over the Zagros Mountains and into the Persian Gulf.

The first challenge in this respect was the belligerency emanating from Arab radicalism and the deterioration in relations between Iran and radical Arab states in the 1960s, led by Iraq and Egypt. The Iraqi coup of 1958 had already eliminated a conservative monarchical regime and replaced it with a revolutionary, pan-Arab regime on Iran's border, and at the same time had led to the collapse of a pillar of the 'containment policy' against the Soviet Union, namely, the Baghdad Pact, later replaced by the Central Treaty Organization (CENTO).

Iran's *de facto* recognition of Israel on 24 July 1960 drew vehement condemnation by several Arab states. Egypt launched a verbal attack on Iran's territorial integrity by claiming the province of Khuzistan, or 'Arabistan' as they called it, as part of the Arab world. On 26 July the United Arab Republic broke off diplomatic relations with Iran, and President Nasser denounced the Shah in a speech on 28 July. The Arab League declared a boycott against Iran on 8 August.[6]

This represented a potentially powerful challenge. The Shah saw in Nasser and the radical doctrines of Arab nationalism an anti-monarchical threat. The scale of Egyptian military activity in Yemen and the possibility of a British withdrawal from Aden raised the spectre of subversion against conservative Arab governments of the Persian Gulf and threats to Iran's economic lifeline – its oil exports. Even though Arab radicalism reached its apex on the eve of the Arab–Israeli War in June 1967 and began to decline thereafter, it remained potent enough to be a constant source of apprehension for the Iranian royal government up to the Islamic Revolution – a challenge that imperial Iran mobilized to defend against, and the Persian Gulf was to be the main battleground.

Growth of importance of the oil and gas sector

The strategic importance of the Strait of Hormuz grew along with the importance of oil to the world economy. The waterway became the international oil highway and a global checkpoint connecting the world's largest single site of oil reserves and production with world markets.

Further development of oil exploitation capacity, including activities in offshore oilfields and the construction of the immense oil export terminal on Kharg Island, also made the Persian Gulf take on more significance in Iranian eyes. The security of the Gulf was becoming vital on the grounds that it was the only export outlet for Iranian oil. Given the growing importance of oil in the international economy, and the fact that the Persian Gulf was already an international oil highway, the filling of the vacuum created by the British withdrawal was of great importance for both Iran and the international community.

From the Iranian point of view, threats to this oil highway could come from a number of directions, especially given the weakness of the Lilliputian states in the Persian Gulf region after British withdrawal. The uncertainties that followed the

British withdrawal from Aden and the rebellion in Dhofar from 1965 were held up as examples.

At the same time, Iran's success in leading oil-producing countries in a campaign aimed at overhauling the nature of the relationship between the oil-producing countries and Western oil companies and at increasing oil prices in early 1970 was an achievement that helped enhance Iran's regional posture and, as the Shah's Court Minister Asadollah Alam believed, 'was a triumph [that] confirmed us in unrivalled leadership of the entire Gulf'.[7] During this episode the British were accused by Iranian officials of supporting oil companies and running the negotiations from behind the scenes.[8]

The Iranian military build-up

Tehran's focus on the Persian Gulf led it to accord higher priority to strengthening Iranian naval and air forces. The Shah declared in March 1965 that Iran's military preparation would henceforth be focused on the Persia Gulf. In the autumn of the same year the Iranian legislature passed a bill to strengthen Iran's armed forces at a cost of some $400 million. A large part of this sum – and of later allocations – was devoted to the creation of a modernized Iranian navy and air force.[9] There can be no doubt that the decision to accelerate arms purchases to the levels seen in the 1960s was prodded significantly by Iran's apprehensions about the power vacuum that was expected to emerge in the Gulf region.

The military build-up enhanced Iran's status as the most powerful littoral state on the eve of and in the wake of the British withdrawal, and as the only regional country having a naval force that deserved the name. The rise in oil revenues in the early 1970s allowed a more rapid increase in military spending and the expansion of armed forces. As a result, in the ten years following Wilson's announcement, Iranian arms purchases rose sixteenfold,[10] resulting in an unprecedented arms race in the region. During the same period, Iraq's arms purchase rose sixfold and Saudi Arabia's twenty-three-fold.[11]

Moreover, Iran and its main rivals in the Persian Gulf were wide apart in terms of military power. Iran's total military manpower in 1969 was about 221,000, with a growing navy and air force, whereas Saudi Arabian manpower did not exceed 34,000 that year. The Iraqi and Kuwaiti figures stood at 78,000 and 10,000, respectively.[12] The Saudi navy at the time was a 1,000-man force with only several small craft at its disposal.[13] Assessing military capabilities of the major regional powers in the Persian Gulf in 1971, the International Institute for Strategic Studies (IISS) concluded that Iran's air force and navy were a match for the forces of all of the Arab littoral states combined.[14]

Iran's emphasis on regional autonomy

Relying on its historical and geopolitical position and its military strengths, and resolving to tend to its growing interests, the Iranian authorities did not hesitate to broadcast their views maintaining that Iran should be the dominant power around her own shores.[15] They also insisted that responsibility for the security of the Persian Gulf should rest only with the countries that surrounded it. These views found expression in increasing media and diplomatic campaigns against the continuance of the British military presence and outright rejection of any foreign military forces stationed in the Persian Gulf.

As the British withdrew, the initial US attempt to secure a small military presence in Bahrain faced strong opposition on the part of Tehran. In a controversial move on 6 January 1972, Bahrain granted the United States the use of its naval base. It was announced in Washington that Bahrain had agreed to lease part of its naval base, formerly used by Britain, to the United States as a station for the latter's small Middle East fleet of one flagship and two destroyers manned by 260 men. The agreement had been signed on 23 December 1971 but at Bahrain's request not immediately publicized.[16]

The Shah had already made clear 'his determination to prevent [the] American Navy ... from replacing Britain as Bahrain's protector.' This was recorded in an interview of the Shah in the *New York Times* in March 1969 and the complaint that Court Minister A. Alam received from the US ambassador about it is referred to in an entry dated 26 March 1969 in Alam's memoirs.[17] Such opposition to intervention by external powers in Gulf affairs was rising at a time when some members of the British Conservative Party were arguing for a reconsideration of Labour's decision to withdraw from the Gulf. This led the Shah to tell Alam, on 27 March 1971, that, 'the British have no desire to see the entire Gulf dominated by Iran'.[18]

Iran did not consider itself underqualified to take up the role the British had once assumed in the Persian Gulf, and, with early signs indicating the British retreat well before the official announcement in 1968, the Iranian government had begun in the mid-1960s to make clear its views on a Persian Gulf without British dominance. Court Minister A. Alam told Ambassador Denis Wright on 17 February 1969 that 'we are prepared to draw up a fifty year's defense agreement with [the Arabs of the lower Gulf] ... all in all it will be much the same as the agreement they once had with the British.'[19] Whereas psychologically and in view of Nasserite propaganda against Iran, such a remark could seem far-fetched, in view of the wide gap between the actual power and capabilities of Iran and the Arab littoral states, it was not baseless.

The international environment

The international environment played a favourable role in furthering the policy that the Iranian government was embarked upon. With Britain weakening and withdrawing and the United States unable and unwilling to replace it, it was inevitable that the Persian Gulf region could regain, to a large extent, its autonomy from global powers, and a laissez-faire attitude prevailed. This meant that both world powers had a limited influence on the outcome of events from 1968 onward; the region would be left to its own devices to manage its own affairs. Even though drastic events in 1979, such as the Islamic Revolution in Iran, the Soviet invasion of Afghanistan, and the series of events in the Horn of Africa and in Yemen, shook the basis of regional autonomy, it remained intact in its main features up to the massive American force deployment to the region in the wake of Iraq's invasion of Kuwait.

During the Cold War it was imperative for Western policy-makers in general to try to contain the Soviet Union by controlling the regions surrounding it, but the Gulf proved to be one of the weak links requiring a great deal of effort on the part of Western strategists. At one point, Western-oriented countries in the oil-producing region were encouraged to join together by concluding the Baghdad Pact, but this proved short-lived due to the leftist coup in Iraq in 1958.

Prompted by the importance of Saudi Arabia's oil resources and the Persian Gulf's significant strategic position between Europe and the Pacific, the American government had made efforts to gain a minimum diplomatic presence in the Gulf but had been thwarted by Britain in the past, and even prevented for several decades from establishing any sort of diplomatic representation in the British dominion in the Persian Gulf except for a consulate in Kuwait.[20]

However, the Anglo-American competition was generally confined to economic interests. Britain was expected to play a primary role in defending the region against perceived threats from the East and from local unrest and to ensure the general interests of the West in the region. Under such circumstances, Harold Wilson's January 1968 announcement was made against the advice of Washington, which urged Britain to delay withdrawal until the mid- or late 1970s. Clearly uneasy over the prospect of Britain's withdrawal, US officials did their best to head off a precipitous decision to accelerate the removal of the British military presence from the Persian Gulf. Following a personal message sent by US Secretary of State Dean Rusk to his British counterpart, President Johnson sent a message, dated 11 January 1968, to Prime Minister Wilson stating 'I have just heard from Dean Rusk of your plans for total British withdrawal from the Far East and the Persian Gulf by 1971 . . . I cannot conceal from you my deep dismay upon learning this profoundly discouraging news. If these steps are taken . . . the structure of peace-keeping will be shaken to its foundations.' He asked Wilson to 'to review the alternatives before you take these irrevocable steps.'[21]

Johnson sent another letter four days later in which he reminded Wilson that 'the announcement of accelerated British withdrawal both from its Far Eastern bases and from the Persian Gulf would create most serious problems for the United States and for the security of the entire world.'[22]

At the time, the United States was deeply involved in Vietnam and was in no position to make a direct military commitment to the Persian Gulf to replace the departing British forces. The new situation confronted the United States with the dilemma of how to ensure the security of this area of vital strategic and economic interest.

With the United States preoccupied by the Vietnam War, there was no Western global power interested in replacing Britain. Massive US force deployment in the Far East and domestic constraints, notably the widespread protests against the Vietnam entanglement, meant that there were neither resources nor support in

American society or government for new commitments. Moreover, the Americans had other pressing foreign policy priorities, such as the consequences of the 1967 Arab–Israeli war and European defence against the Warsaw Pact.

Moreover, a strong US presence in the Persian Gulf could have been a prelude to more serious efforts on the part of the Soviet Union to achieve the same. The Soviets were already, more or less and in different forms, present in Iraq and South Yemen; Moscow pursued its goals by conventional diplomacy too, such as by improving relations with Iran, North Yemen and Kuwait.

American authorities were aware that Iran and a few other actors in the Gulf were more or less opposed to US military presence there, as it would run the risk of making the area another theatre of the Cold War. Iran, on numerous occasions, as discussed later, had made it clear that regional security should be left to the littoral states to provide and no outside power should interfere therein.

Consequently, the United States was careful to clarify that it had no interest in getting directly involved in helping fill the power vacuum. A circular telegram, No. 118823, dated 21 February 1968 and signed by US Secretary of State Dean Rusk, to certain posts summarized the hands-off policy adopted by the Johnson administration in the wake of the British withdrawal announcement. It read in part: 'We have, however, no plan regarding developments in this [Persian Gulf] region and do not expect to be consulted by states concerned as to any political arrangements which they may find useful or desirable for themselves.'[23] Along the same lines, telegram No. 116285 of 16 February 1968 to Dhahran noted that the State Department 'believed it important to continue to avoid any possible erroneous impression that the United States was planning to "replace" the British in the Gulf or that it favoured certain specific solutions to Gulf problems.'[24]

Likewise, in a message to the Shah, Lyndon Johnson wrote: 'the United States interest in the security of the area does not, however, envisage that we would wish either to replace the British military presence or participate in any new regional security arrangement. The US looks to the countries in the area to ensure the area's security.'[25] The State Department spokesman stated publicly on 16 January that 'the US regrets the British Government's announcement regarding its forces in South Asia and the Persian Gulf', but that the United States had 'no plans to move in where the British forces pull out.'[26]

Under such circumstances, and given the importance of the region for the outside world, soon the question as to who should take over from Britain and provide the area with a security umbrella came to the fore. The large Persian Gulf Arab states, Iraq and Saudi Arabia, were no substitute. Iraq's pan-Arabist ruling regime was perceived as a source of threat rather than of regional stability, particularly following the threat by Qassim's regime to invade Kuwait in 1961. Saudi Arabia lacked the military might, as discussed earlier, to play the role of protector of the Persian Gulf. Moreover, the involvement of these two states in the Arab–Israeli crisis prevented them from being seen favourably enough by the West to assume a major role in the area.

This ultimately led to both the United States and Britain finding no choice but to favour Iran as the guardian of security and safety in the Persian Gulf in the wake of the British forces' withdrawal, and as a bulwark against revolutionary change in the region. This further enhanced the status of Iran in the area and, in the process, helped Iran secure its right to the ownership of the three islands with actual British assistance and tacit American backing.

The US government tried to adapt itself to the new environment in the Persian Gulf by devising a set of policies compatible with the new developments. Finalization of a new policy towards Iran, under consideration since the mid-1960s, topped the American agenda in the Gulf. The recognition of Iran's growing power was the main characteristic of the new American policy in the area.

The 'twin pillars' strategy took shape in US policy discussions immediately after the British withdrawal announcement in January 1968. Walter Rostow, President Johnson's Special Assistant, in a memorandum to the President dated 31 January 1968 encouraging him to send a message to the Shah (referred to above) to try to dissuade him from cancelling his visit to Saudi Arabia, argued that 'our main concern anyway is not the immediate issue of the visit but the future of the Persian Gulf. Good relations between Iran and Saudi Arabia will be necessary to keep things under control when the British leave. The alternatives are instability with strong chance of an increased Soviet presence. We don't want to have to replace the British, and we don't want the Russians there. So we must count on the Shah and Faisal.' A note indicated that Johnson approved the message.[27]

Richard Nixon placed US Gulf policy in a more global context, compatible with Washington's wider policy for dealing with all challenges at the international level. The Nixon doctrine, essentially devised to allow an exit from Vietnam, was soon found to be applicable to the Persian Gulf too. This doctrine advocated the need for the US allies to be able to defend themselves against regional threats without direct American military assistance. Nixon emphasized in Guam on 25 July 1969 that the United States was going to encourage, and had a right to expect, that problems of internal security and of military defence be increasingly handled by, and the responsibility for it taken by, the Asian nations themselves.[28] The Guam doctrine, as such, reaffirmed regional autonomy and helped Washington maintains its policy of no direct involvement in the Gulf affairs.

Within the confines of this doctrine, and despite the gravity of the Persian Gulf situation for the West, the United States chose mainly not to interfere in interactions among the regional states. American officials basically concluded that the best option for the United States was to rely on Iran and Saudi Arabia to work together as guardians of the Gulf, an approach that came to be known as the 'twin pillars' policy. This policy was implemented after 1971 when Britain's forces left the region for good. It was maintained throughout the 1970s and, as a result, Iran obtained overwhelming US support, which in turn caused Iraq, Iran's main regional rival, to seek arms from the Soviet Union.

Nonetheless, the wide military power gap between Iran and Saudi Arabia meant that the burden was unequal. Some argue that the policy was misrepresented and was 'more of a one pillar and a half.'[29]

In fact, Iran was to play a larger military role as a naval power successor to Britain and as a force against hostile regional powers, such as Iraq, while the Saudis were expected to try to ensure stability in the lower Gulf, not through military means but rather through political mediation and conciliation and by guarding against Nasserite penetration of the Gulf.

Settling outstanding issues

Once Britain's decision to withdraw from the Persian Gulf had been taken, the creation of a viable state and a stable, self-sustaining regional structure that could survive the pullout soon moved to the top of the British regional agenda. The achievement of this objective required, first and foremost, attending to the territorial issues and disputes among the regional political units, which came immediately to the fore. Created mostly as a result of Britain's territorial engineering, and having been swept under the carpet by the British for so many decades, these issues were the most important obstacles blocking the establishment of a new security order in the Persian Gulf.

At the UN Security Council meeting on Abu Musa and the Tunbs on 9 December 1971, the British representative summarized the priorities of his government with regard to the Persian Gulf as follows:

> The primary concern of the British Government has been to ensure that the stability which our presence in the area had helped to preserve for nearly 150 years would continue after our departure. As we saw it, there were two important prerequisites if this aim was to be achieved: first, that the nine States concerned, especially the States of the Trucial Coast, most of which were too small to be politically and economically viable on their own, should succeed in their efforts to come together in some form of federation or union, preferably between all nine of the protected States or, failing that, at least between the seven Trucial States; and, secondly, that we should help to the best of our ability to promote the settlement of outstanding territorial differences in the area. The majority of those differences concerned conflicting claims by the Arab States and Iran to certain islands in the Gulf.[30]

Iran's determination to recover the three islands

Iran was directly involved in the most important disputes and had leverage that the British had no choice but to take into consideration in their preparation for establishing a new regional security order, in which they themselves could no longer play a pivotal role.

Concerned about the security of the Persian Gulf after its departure in general, Britain focused on the political and structural inter-relationships among the nine tiny states from Bahrain to Fujaira, in particular. As the termination of the British treaty relationship with the sheikhdoms meant that they would not be guaranteed British protection any longer, Britain regarded as essential some kind of union that could be able to stand on its own feet. The concern was strategic: nine separate tiny states in a very important region could have been more vulnerable to radicalism emanating from inside and outside than would a union that encompassed them.

Therefore, British efforts aimed at inducing small emirates to close ranks, which had already started in the 1950s, found a new impetus during the days after the announcement of the British intention to pull out.

In parallel, the Iranian government was preoccupied with several issues of great importance for its future role and influence in the Persian Gulf, including the disputes with Britain over Bahrain and the three islands as well as a maritime dispute with the Saudis over the division of oil from the mid-Gulf. This last dispute, which culminated in an Iranian gunboat driving an ARAMCO drilling rig out of Gulf waters claimed by Iran in February 1968, was resolved amicably in October that year.[31]

The Iranian government took a series of measures designed to communicate to Britain and other parties its seriousness and resolve with regard to the three islands. These measures can be summarized as follows:

The Bahrain–three islands linkage

Mindful of the need to reach an accommodation with the neighbouring states, especially Saudi Arabia, Iran considered practical and realistic steps to back up its long-standing claim to Bahrain. In a landmark statement at a press conference held in New Delhi on 4 January 1969, the Shah announced that Iran would not use force to regain what belonged to it by right; rather, as he put it, Iran 'prefers to see the Bahraini people make their own free choice.'[32] This statement implied the acceptance by Iran of the UN option that had already been presented to him by the British ambassador on Christmas Eve 1968. It was later revealed that he made the statement without the prior knowledge of any of his ministers – an example of the Shah's one-man rule.[33]

The status of Bahrain was finally settled through action by a representative of the UN Secretary-General, who was mandated to 'ascertain the wishes of Bahrain's people'. They were found to be enthusiastic to remain Bahrainis, and thus were put on the path towards independence.[34] The successful conclusion of the Bahrain dispute improved the regional climate. At the same time, giving up on Bahrain put the Iranian government in a difficult domestic position, making more difficult the acceptance of any outcome less than the restoration of full Iranian control over the three islands. Therefore, Iran pursued its position on them resolutely, making it clear that under no circumstances could there be any compromise on the issue of the islands.

While efforts aimed at resolving the Bahrain dispute were under way, the Iranian government had made clear to its interlocutors that it viewed the disputes over Bahrain and the three islands as part of the same package. Iran now indicated that since it had given up on Bahrain, it expected that Britain and the sheikhdoms of the Persian Gulf would compromise over the three islands.

Thus, having secured the independence of Bahrain, the British could not overlook Iran's view on the islands. They adopted a soft and cautious approach towards the Iranian claim, quietly carried out by Sir William Luce, the British especial envoy, who started his mission in August 1970 and frequently visited the region.

The Arab Federation–three islands linkage

Iran made a similar linkage between the return of the three islands to Iran and Iranian recognition and support of the federation of Arab emirates that the British were eager to establish and make sustainable.

According to Adnan Pachachi, the United Arab Emirates' representative to the United Nations, in his statement in the Security Council meeting on the islands on 9 December 1971, '[t]he Iranian Government reiterated its view that it would not negotiate this dispute with the Government of the UAE, but that it would try to prevent the proclamation of the independence of the federation and that it would settle the island problem before the emergence of independence of the UAE.'[35]

The lower Persian Gulf states, excluding Saudi Arabia and Kuwait, had been spurred by London since the 1950s to rally their forces to form a 'federation of Arab emirates' and to achieve this before the British withdrawal. An agreement was quickly drafted and agreed upon by rulers at a summit conference held in Dubai on 27 February 1968. Supported by the British and signed by the rulers of Bahrain, Qatar and the seven Trucial sheikhdoms, the agreement sought to set up a Supreme Council that would be responsible for all international matters of politics, defence, economics and culture, leaving the domestic issues to the respective rulers.

The agreement was more a declaration of intent than a plan for a fully formed federal state. However, the British project to create an Arab federation soon hit two main impediments: first, the age-old rivalries among the Arab sheikhs were not easy to surmount; second, the Iranian government strongly opposed the plan on the grounds that the biggest of the sheikhdoms, Bahrain, was an Iranian province, and two other sheikhdoms, Sharjah and Ras al-Khaimah, were purported to include the three islands of Abu Musa and Tunbs, which Iran considered parts of its own territory.[36] Since Britain was still the protecting power, the removal of these obstacles was its responsibility.

The attempt to include Bahrain, Sharjah and Ras al-Khaimah in the federation was enough to provoke Iran's anger. Iran soon made clear that the return of Bahrain and the three islands to Iranian sovereignty would be required before it could remove its objection to the union and allow its creation. As Sir Denis Wright put it, 'the Shah saw this as a dirty British trick to confront him with a *fait accompli* whereby he would either have to recognize a union that included Bahrain and the other disputed islands or else run foul of the Arab world by refusing recognition.'[37]

The Shah clarified his position, which in its essentials had never changed. In an interview in May 1968 with the Kuwaiti journal *Al-Ra'y al-Amm*, he said that Iran did not oppose Arab federalism, 'as long as its historical and territorial rights are observed in its foundation. There is a possibility that the federation could inherit the old British colonial policy, which opposes the interests of Iran.'[38]

In a statement on 1 April 1968 the Iranian foreign minister elucidated the Iranian government's perspective, declaring that Britain could not give away to others what it had obtained by force. Iran reserved its rights in the Persian Gulf and would not accept this 'historical injustice.'[39] On 24 May 1968, the Shah explained in an interview that Iran's opposition to the proposed federation stemmed from its 'imperialist' origins, and accused Britain of 'manipulation.'[40] The Iranian position caused complications of grotesquely disproportionate size.

The Iranian media spoke of the federation as a British plot to maintain an imperialist policy that Iran could not tolerate. In the words of Denis Wright, 'the tightly-controlled Tehran press, instructed from on high, was equally hostile and offensive.'[41]

A sign that attempts to establish the federation were facing difficulties was the inaction regarding the Dubai agreement, which was supposed to come into force on 30 March 1968. The message sent by the British Political Agent to the fifth meeting of the Supreme Council, held in October 1969, which was failing to deliver any result, conveyed the degree of Britain's enthusiasm to see the project through: 'I know that some difficulties have arisen at the conference. My Government will be extremely disappointed if these difficulties cannot be overcome. I believe that the failure of the meeting would be most unwelcome to other Arab countries whose future support for the Gulf is important.'[42]

Later, in the meeting of the Security Council held to consider Iran's takeover of the islands, the representatives of the United Arab Emirates described the whole process this way:

> [The] Arab emirates agreed on 18 July 1971 on the constitution of an independent State, which they called the United Arab Emirates (UAE). But Iran made clear that not only would [it] not recognize the Union if the dispute on the islands were not settled, but that it would do everything in its power to disrupt that Union and prevent its creation. We were therefore advised that we should delay the proclamation of our independence and postpone our application to the UN in the hope that a satisfactory settlement could be reached with Iran.[43]

Iran's show of determination

In the run-up to the British withdrawal from the Persian Gulf, Iranian officials used every opportunity to communicate to the British their resolve to recover the islands. The memoirs of the then-Minister of Court, Assadollah Alam, record some of the most categorical positions in this respect.

Alam's entry on 27 May 1969 reads: 'the British continue to drag their feet in respect of restoring our islands of Tunbs and Abu Musa. As I told [British Foreign Secretary Michael Steward], he must be well aware that Britain had gained unlawful possession of these islands and handed them as a blighted inheritance to the Shaikhs of Sharja and Ras al-Khaimah whom his Government now supports against Iran. We can see no sense in this policy, since Iran is set to become the Emirates' sole protector once the British withdraw.'[44]

In a meeting with Denis Wright, the British ambassador, on 13 July 1970, Alam threatened that Iran would resort to force, saying that '[t]here can be no way forward until the issue of the islands has been resolved. If the British refuse to act, then it is we that shall be forced to make the running by resorting to military occupation.' Wright replied that 'while he appreciates the depth of Iranian feeling over the matter, he regards a military solution as being unlikely to cause anything but harm to our standing in the Persian Gulf'[45] – a position that could have been taken only as recommendatory, and thus indicative of an important change in the British approach. Sir Denis Wright later wrote that 'I had also to warn the Iranians that any attempt to seize the islands before the abrogation of our protective treaties with the Sheikhs [on 1 December 1971], whose sovereignty over them we recognized, would bring us into armed conflict with Iran.'[46] Given Iran's takeover of the three islands on 30 November 1971 and the British inaction in its wake, as well as some other British actions and positions, referred to later, it seems that Alam's account of the exchange between himself and Wright is more accurate than Wright's account in 1991. It shows how the British position had changed from fervently claiming the islands for the Arab sheikhs to neutrality.

Iran also launched a public campaign aimed at indicating the impossibility of any retreat on the Iranian part. In February 1971 the Shah publicly declared that, if necessary, Iran would resort to force to regain the islands. Simultaneously, the government moved to stir up and mobilize public emotions on the issue by means of a press campaign.[47] The public campaign was important in the sense that through it the Iranian authorities bound themselves into a situation in which their prestige at home and abroad was staked on the outcome of the dispute.

Throughout 1971 the Iranian authorities invariably stressed Iran's right to the islands and its willingness to use any means to regain them. Prime Minister A. A. Hoveida, in a speech on 27 June 1971 to the people of Bandar Abbas, reiterated Iran's historical and legitimate rights in the Gulf and asserted that Iran would use 'whatever means necessary' to recover them.[48] Foreign Minister A. Zahedi said in an interview during his trip to Bahrain that 'it is a fact that these islands in the Persian Gulf have been and are part of Iran, and will continue to be so. These islands were occupied by British troops nearly 75 years ago but now that the British are leaving the area they should be returned to Iran; that is, to their original owner. Of course, Iran will do its best to solve this problem by peaceful means, but if it is not successful in this attempt then it will use any step necessary to regain these islands.'[49]

The Shah, answering a question about a comment made by Sir William Luce to the effect that Iran would use force to regain the islands, said 'what Luce has said is true. The islands belong to us. I hope the issue will be resolved peacefully. But I must again stress that we are determined to regain what is ours. I cannot sit here watching my country being auctioned off and handed over to the ruler of another country.'[50]

Another move that evinced the lengths to which the Iranian government was prepared to go was an incident in May 1971 in which Iranian armed forces fired upon British aircraft that were harassing Iranian naval forces in the Gulf, particularly near to the disputed islands.[51] The mild reaction on the part of Britain allowed the incident to pass without long-lasting effect.

Yet another event demonstrating not only the Iranian resolve but also London's inclination with regard to the islands was the action the British took in response to the Iranian protest against drilling by the American oil company Oxy under a concession it had been granted by Umm al-Qawain in November 1969. When the company started drilling 9 miles from Abu Musa in early 1970, and Sharjah also laid claim to the same waters, Iran warned the British ambassador on 22 May 1970 that

> Should the Sheikhs of Sharjah and Umm al-Qawain make an attempt to drill for oil in the waters around Abu Musa . . . Iran will not baulk at military intervention. Abu Musa is ours and Britain must bear in mind that it is we who they will be up against in any attempt to support the Sheikhs. Not that any such Anglo-Iranian confrontation would be without its positive side. It would clear the decks in more ways than one. Iranian pride would be satisfied, and having defeated the British we would be in a position to force the Sheikhs to accept a solution over the Islands.[52]

The Shah insisted that 'for us to ignore such a deal would be an implicit admission that they have a valid claim.' In response, Wright asked the Iranian government to show restraint and promised that he would do 'all in his power to prevent drilling around the island.'[53]

The situation threatened to lead to a political crisis between Iran and Britain and to the latter's embarrassment in the case of military action by Iran. In deference to Iran's threat of armed intervention and to prevent an Iranian–Arab confrontation, the British government directed the American company to stop drilling operations off Abu Musa Island. Sir Stewart Crawford, the Political Resident in Bahrain, instructed John Cole, then Assistant Political Agent in Dubai, to go aboard a Royal Navy frigate carrying orders to Oxy to halt drilling and move the company's oil rig out of disputed waters. Oxy complied and an immediate political crisis was averted.[54]

An official British statement at the time confirmed the impression that Iranian pressure was the driving force behind the order: 'this action does not imply acceptance of the Iranian claim, although the reassertion of [the] Iranian threat of force was a major political factor.'[55] There should be little doubt that the British action was another sign indicating a reversal in the British position on the status of the three islands and that it was prompted by the Iranian threat to put an end to the drilling.

Iran also brought pressure to bear on the Arab littorals, especially Sharjah and Ras al-Khaimah, and offered them increasing economic assistance. The Shah made this clear in December 1970, saying that after an agreement was reached on the islands the sheikhdoms could 'count all the more on Iran's economic aid.'[56]

Indications suggest that the cumulative effect of these actions by Iran was the British conclusion that Iranian officials were not bluffing when they spoke of resorting to military action, if necessary, to regain the islands. This led the British to redouble their efforts to work out a compromise.

A half-solution option

Britain's attitude towards Iran's efforts to regain the islands was crucial. The events unfolding during the run-up to the British withdrawal from east of Suez demonstrated that Britain adopted a forward-looking approach, which consisted essentially of refraining from resisting Iran's moves and of seeking a compromise outcome that would allow the furtherance of their objectives.

Britain's strategic self-interest calculations that ran counter to Iran's interests at the turn of the twentieth century had undergone substantial modifications in the late 1960s, and a convergence of interests between the two countries was developing at a time when the British, and indeed the entire West, needed Iran to serve as the main source of security in the region. Thus, in dealing with the issues at hand in the new era, the British abandoned the imperatives of imperial thinking, which had once required deterring foreign rivals and containing major regional powers. Viewing Iran as the only Western-oriented military power on the oil-rich Persian Gulf and the main source of stability, London chose expediently and once more out of self-interest to reverse its stringent approach vis-à-vis Iranian positions, in favour of adopting a moderate, pragmatic policy focused only on achieving its main objective of stability by enlisting Iran's help.

Kuwait's representative to the UN said in his speech at the Security Council meeting on the islands that '[t]he British Government, through Sir William Luce, approached us many times and sought our assistance to encourage the Rulers of the Emirates, especially Sheikh Saqr of Ras al-Khaima, to co-operate with Sir William in finding a formula that would satisfy Iran at the expense of the territorial integrity of the Emirates. The Government of Kuwait rejected that approach'.[57]

Consequently, Britain opted rather to act as a neutral provider of good offices, and assumed a mediating and consensus-building role. In other words, after 75 years of insisting on Arab sovereignty over the three islands, the British role was overnight reduced to one of mediator. The statement made by Colin Crowe, Britain's permanent representative to the UN, in the Security Council meeting on the three islands on 9 December 1971, as discussed later, marked the formal discontinuance of the British policy of adamantly claiming the three islands for their protégés on the Arab littoral. The new British approach helped enormously to ease the disputes and tensions that had pitted Iran and Britain against each other in unending controversies and removed the main impediment to the return of the three islands to Iran's possession.

Thus, the cornerstone of British policy in the Gulf, particularly after Harold Wilson's Labour government was defeated by the Tories in June 1970, became support for Iran to take over as guardian of the region, a role the Iranian government was eager to assume. As a result, once the British had decided that the Shah had acted in a reasonable and responsible way by virtually abandoning claim to Bahrain, they saw no reason why he should not be compensated.

In explaining the British about-face, some scholars have gone so far as to attribute it to Iran having signed an agreement for £100 million worth of British military equipment, such as Chieftain tanks and communications material.

According to this theory, the British feared that any confrontation with Iran would have jeopardized this lucrative contract.[58]

The Guardian newspaper attributed the policy change to the British embarking on a realist path, writing that, 'given the military predominance in the area of the forces of Iran, and the very considerable British financial interest in the Iranian oil industry, the path of realism would appear to be to accept the inevitable and recognize the determination of the Shah's government to occupy Abu Musa as soon as the British forces are gone.'[59]

However, the British were not in a position to reverse officially and publicly the policy they had pursued since the early twentieth century. During this long period of maintaining that the islands belonged to the Arab sheikhs, Britain had committed itself to enforcing this view by securing the islands for sheikhs under their protection. This dilemma led the British to seek a face-saving half-solution, one analogous to those they applied in so many other areas at the end of their colonial presence, solutions that, as referred to earlier, Jack Straw correctly lamented.

Therefore, the British faced a dilemma: they could either allow the Iranian forces to land on the islands without lifting a finger to stop it, or withdraw from the region without seeing the Arab union come about. The British chose the first solution, even though, as explained by Glen Balfour-Paul, it was humiliating for the British Empire, since this option entailed non-compliance on their part with an agreement to which they still were committed.[60]

As to how such a half-solution could be achieved, it seems that the numerous entries in Alam's memoirs in which he gives account of his negotiations with British officials on the islands can shed light on British thinking. The conciliatory approach with regard to the islands can be traced back to 9 November 1969, when Sir Denis Wright told Alam that

> we are bound by our commitments to the Sheiks of Sharjah and Ras al-Khaimah, but nevertheless, we encourage them to reach some sort of accommodation with Iran, provided always that you confine yourselves to an occupation based on mutual agreement or a lease, and do not insist on pressing a claim to occupy the islands by legal right.

As Alam explains, the Shah was outraged: 'he's talking out of his ears . . . The islands belong to us.'[61]

On 17 February 1969, shortly after Iran implied its preparedness to drop its claim to Bahrain, Alam recorded his conversation with the British ambassador, writing that 'in strict confidence he [Wright] told me that the islands of Tunbs are certain to be handed over to Iran. The British have warned the Sheikh of Ras al-Khaimah that the islands lie on our side of the median line, and that unless he comes to some sort of understanding with us we shall simply take them, legally and if needs be by force.' According to Alam, when Wright mentioned that Abu Musa was lying below the median line, Alam replied that 'we are sufficiently powerful to disregard the line. We joked for a while . . .'[62]

The restoration of Persian Gulf autonomy 91

Having summoned the British ambassador on 29 May 1970, and warned him that 'his country would forfeit all credibility if there were no new initiative soon,' the ambassador asked 'why were we so insistent on the question of legal sovereignty over the islands? Far simpler for us just to occupy them. Solve the issue at one fell swoop.'[63] Alam's entry dated 19 March 1969 indicates that Wright told Alam that the Tunbs 'will be easy for [Iran] to recover but not Abu Musa, which lies too close to the Arabian Peninsula.' Alam points out that he responded 'this didn't alter Iran's right nor entitle the Arabs to hold on to Iranian territory; which HIM [the Shah] will never abandon.' The ambassador suggested a linkage with the federation and said Iran could occupy Abu Musa in the interests of joint security in the Gulf.[64]

Wright was later quoted in private interviews as saying that he 'never said such a thing [on legal sovereignty over the islands] to Alam.'[65] Nonetheless, in one interview in 1997 he did say that he had believed that 'Britain should allow Iran to take the islands as he thought the Shah would inevitably secure them anyway.'[66] In the same interview, he recalled that the Conservative Party came to the conclusion that withdrawal was inevitable; they instructed 'Britain's local representatives to put more pressure on the Sheiks to come to an agreement with Iran.'[67]

British records also confirm that Sir Denis believed that an agreement on the islands was possible 'if the question of sovereignty was fudged.'[68]

Moreover, numerous signs indicating that Britain had decided to accommodate Iran and, to this end, reconsider its previous position on the islands cast doubt on the accuracy of Sir Denis Wright's later denial. It was quite conspicuous at the time that the British had stopped claiming the islands for the Arab sheikhs, contrary to the emphatic British approach of the preceding decades, when they never let any Iranian assertion to Iran's ownership of the islands go unanswered.

Britain, instead, focused on deterring the Iranian government from resorting to force in the case of the islands before the expiration of its commitment to the sheikhs on 1 December 1971. The exchange between Alam and Wright on 13 July 1970, referred to earlier, in which the British ambassador only tried to moderate the Iranian approach by cautioning against any action that 'may lead to trouble with the Arabs',[69] was an early indication of the new and rather recommendatory British position. The British could not have missed the fact that their new approach would be interpreted by the Iranian government as one of neutrality and resignation and by some Arab parties as ranging from abandonment to collusion with imperial Iran on the three islands on the eve of their withdrawal from the Persian Gulf.

In carrying out the new British policy, at one point Sir Denis Wright suggested to Alam that Iran 'approach the Sheikh of Sharjah as we did the Sheikh of Ras al-Khaima. A deal might be struck and the British would back us. I said I would pass it on to the HIM but was in no position to comment myself.'[70]

The Conservatives, after returning to power in June 1970, considered reversing the Labour government's decision to withdraw from the Gulf. However, they were faced with declarations from not only the Iranian government but, less predictably, from the governments of Saudi Arabia and Kuwait, all decrying the idea of Britain retaining a military presence in the Persian Gulf area after 1971.[71] The process of forming the federation was already in motion, and a reversal was impractical.

A meeting between the Shah of Iran and Sir Alec Douglas-Home, the new Conservative Foreign Secretary, held on 10 July 1970 in Brussels, was instrumental in terms of charting the way ahead. In this meeting, Douglas-Home heard from the Shah that, now that the dispute over Bahrain had settled, he had no objections to the federation provided there was a satisfactory agreement on the islands dispute. In this meeting the Shah also opposed the continuation of Britain's treaties with the emirates, but did not object to the federation entering a defence agreement with Britain, or to Britain retaining an indirect presence through CENTO.[72] As Sir Denis Wright, who was present in this meeting, later stated, '[Douglas-Home] found the Shah uncompromising both on British withdrawal from the Gulf and Iran's claims to the islands and I have little doubt that this Brussels meeting was a major factor in the Government's ultimate decision to withdraw from the Gulf by the end of 1971 and let the Shah have the disputed islands, though for years we had upheld the Arab Sheikhs' claims to the them.' Interestingly, he called it 'an example of *realpolitik* – and not for us British a particularly happy ending to 150 years of *Pax Britannica.*'[73]

In order to exert pressure on the ruler of Sharjah and Ras al-Khaimah to accommodate Iran's demands, Britain dispatched Sir William Luce as special envoy of the Foreign Secretary to the Persian Gulf region in June 1971. He was instructed to 'tell the rulers of Sharjah and Ras al-Khaimah that they could expect no help from Britain if the Persians saw fit to occupy Abu Musa and the Tunbs by force, and that they would be wise, therefore, to seek an accommodation with the Shah.'[74] Jasim M. Abdulghani says that this was confirmed to him by several UAE officials who participated in the talks with Luce. Luce was reported to have threatened Sheikh Khaled of Sharjah that his political power might be jeopardized if he did not acquiesce to the Shah's demands.[75]

It is well to remember that the parties engaged in efforts to break the impasse were working under the constraint of a deadline. A solution had to be found before 1 December 1971, the date when the British protection agreement with the would-be members of the proposed union was to expire. It was clear that, in the absence of any agreed solution, the only sequence of events that might secure the establishment of the union in time to conclude with the testamentary agreements would presuppose the Shah's seizure of the islands before Britain's relationship with the union's prospective members was terminated. In that case, the value of the British protection would be shown to be illusory. However humiliating it might have been, the scenario indicated must have seemed a lesser evil given the British interest in the Gulf's future stability than withdrawing with the islands problem unresolved and with no union established.[76]

Evidence also suggests that at least the American Embassy in Tehran held a view on the islands that was similar to the one held by the British. In a telegram to Secretary of State Dean Rusk, the US ambassador in Tehran opined that, in return for an agreement on the Bahrain dispute, Iran should be allowed to announce 'exclusive rights to fortify the Tunbs and Abu Musa, rather than the Iranian sovereignty over the islands.'[77] This view was in harmony with the top US priority in the Persian Gulf, which was to secure the stability of the region, and with the US position that Iran should bear the major responsibility in this respect, for which it would purportedly need to turn the islands into military bases.

As to the relevant Arab rulers, the visit to Tehran of the Sheikh of Ras al-Khaimah long before the final stage of negotiations made clear that there could be no hope of reaching an agreement with him on the Tunbs. Earlier in June 1970 the British had provided him with a tentative proposal almost along the same lines as the agreement later incorporated in the Memorandum of Understanding with Sharjah, but which he rejected.[78] Referring to the sheikh's presence in Tehran, which had been invited by the foreign minister, Alam noted on 20 December 1969 that he saw no chance of a settlement.[79] Three days later the Shah too expressed dissatisfaction 'over negotiations with the Sheikh of Ras al-Khaimah.'[80]

But the flexibility demonstrated by the Sheikh of Sharjah allowed for a Memorandum of Understanding to be agreed upon by Sharjah and Iran and formally confirmed by an indirect exchange of letters on 18 and 25 November 1971, respectively, between the two sides through the British Foreign Secretary. On 29 November Sheikh Khaled, the ruler of Sharjah, made public the conclusion of the MoU with Iran over the disputed island of Abu Musa. According to the MoU, 'Neither Iran nor Sharjah will give up its claim to Abu Musa nor recognize the other's claim.' Against this background the parties agreed that

1. Iranian troops will arrive in Abu Musa. They will occupy areas the extent of which have been agreed on the map attached to this memorandum.
2. (a) Within the agreed areas occupied by Iranian troops, Iran will have full jurisdiction and the Iranian flag will fly.
   (b) Sharjah will retain full jurisdiction over the remainder of the island. The Sharjah flag will continue to fly over the Sharjah police post on the same basis as the Iranian flag will fly over the Iranian military quarters.
3. Iran and Sharjah recognize the breadth of the island's territorial sea as twelve nautical miles.

Articles 4, 5 and 6 of the MoU provided for an equal sharing of oil revenues from the exploitation of the petroleum resources of Abu Musa, equal fishing rights for both sides' nationals, and financial assistance to be paid to Sharjah by Iran, amounting to, as agreed upon later, £1.5 million a year until such time as the emirate's annual receipts from oil totalled £3 million.[81] As will be discussed later, Articles 1 to 3 of the MoU had certain implications with respect to the issue of sovereignty over the island. In accordance with the agreement, Iranian troops landed on Abu Musa on 30 November. On the same day, the landing of Iranian troops on the Tunbs was effectuated as well.

When they arrived on Abu Musa, the Iranian troops were greeted by the brother of Sheikh Khaled of Sharjah. The landing on the Tunbs, as discussed later, took place without any agreement with the ruler of Ras al-Khaimah, Sheikh Saqr, and followed a military clash between the parties.

The Arab researcher Hussein al-Baharna described the British policy in this way:

> The case of Abu Musa and the Tunbs islands reveals certain interesting features of British operations *vis-à-vis* the Gulf countries. It may be recalled that Britain had not yet legally ended its special treaties with the Rulers of Sharjah and Ras al-Khaima when Iran landed its troops. Legally they were still under British protection. But Britain took no action to stop the Iranian occupation. On the contrary, it negotiated with the Shah of Iran and the Ruler of Sharja a MOU agreeing to Iran's occupation of part of Abu Musa. As to the Tunb islands, Britain maintained that it was impossible to stop the Iranian action just one day before the termination of the treaty relations. Apart from not being a convincing argument, it demonstrates that Britain probably had its own special interests to protect that could not be sacrificed for the sake of upholding a principle of treaty. Expediency prevailed over the law.[82]

Regarding the date and the way in which the islands were returned to Iranian possession, note should also be taken of the following:

First, the military takeover took place exactly one day before the termination of Britain's treaties with the Trucial states. It was timed to confirm the nature of the dispute as one between Iran and Britain and, further, to signify the rejection on the part of the Iranians of the colonial commandeering of Iranian possessions in the Persian Gulf. Moreover, since the establishment of the UAE was not to be officially announced until 2 December, Iran's move on the islands could not be construed as an act against an Arab state.

The Times of London conceded Britain's responsibility for responding to Iran's action when it wrote that 'from the point of view of stability in the Gulf in the future, there is some advantage in the fact that Iran seized the islands while Britain was technically still responsible. The seizure is technically, therefore, not a seizure of Arab territory from Arabs, since it was under British protection.'[83]

Second, the British plan B – convincing Iran not to take action before the British withdrawal – failed too. It was to be implemented in case plan A, the full agreement between Iran and the Arab sheikhs, proved impossible. As Wright wrote, the British hope was then that Iran 'won't seize the islands while we are still bound by our treaty, if [Iran] does we will be in a state of war with our ally.'[84] The British ambassador to Tehran, Peter Ramsbotham, who replaced Wright, recalled hinting to the Shah that he should be ready to move in to the island the day Britain left the Gulf in order to avert a direct confrontation with Britain.[85]

The only positive outcome from the British perspective was that Iran moved on the islands one day before the termination of the British treaty commitments. It enabled the British to argue, not quite persuasively, that it was not possible to enter a war with Iran on its last day in the Gulf. Undoubtedly, as the Arab reactions later indicated, the timing was in part responsible for much of the resulting Arab odium falling on Britain's head.

Third, indications suggest that the British knew of the date that Iran was going to land troops on the islands. The UK Foreign Secretary told the Cabinet on 18 November 1971 that the failure to reach agreement over the Tunbs 'made it virtually certain that the Shah would take control of the islands in his own time.'[86] The presence of a British carrier in the immediate area during the Iranian takeover, and a number of other British actions, indicated British foreknowledge of Iran's move. Moreover, the presence of the brother and heir apparent of the ruler of Sharjah on Abu Musa to greet the Iranian forces indicates that Sharjah and the British knew of the exact timing of the takeover.

As John Bulloch, a British journalist and the author of *The Persian Gulf Unveiled*, wrote, 'only a couple of weeks before a senior Air Force officer dealing with the evacuation of British personnel and stores from Sharjah had assured me that if Iran tried to seize the islands by force, Britain would act, "right up to the last minute".' He adds, 'Clearly this officer was not in the confidence of those making the decision. As it was, the last Political Resident, Sir Geoffrey Arthur, was awoken by an aide very early in the morning to be told of the Shah's moves; perhaps it was significant that Sir Geoffrey was particularly short with the keen young Foreign Service officer, who had disturbed him, and that he promptly went back to sleep.'[87]

On 2 December, following Iran's regaining of the islands and one day after the treaty between Britain and the Trucial sheikhdoms expired, the rulers of six of the sheikhdoms, Ras al-Khaimah excluded, formally announced the formation of the United Arab Emirates as a free and sovereign state at a meeting in Dubai. They actually made official announcement of the agreement that had already been reached on 18 July 1971 but had been postponed in the face of the continued Iranian position of withholding recognition and support of the federation until the islands dispute was settled. Sheikh Saqr of Ras al-Khaimah submitted a formal application for admission to the UAE on 23 December 1971. However, because of the demands and conditions attached – that the UAE sever diplomatic relations with Iran in protest 'over that country's occupation' of the three islands, and that the sheikhdom be granted powers equal to Abu Dhabi and Dubai in the Supreme Council of Rulers – the application was rejected.[88]

Also on 2 December, a treaty of friendship between the UAE and Britain was signed by Sheikh Zayed and Political Resident Sir Geoffrey Arthur.[89] The UAE was accepted as the eighteenth member of the Arab League at an emergency session convened at the request of Iraq, Syria and Ras al-Khaimah on 6 December to discuss the takeover by Iran of the three Persian Gulf islands. As in the case of the Bahrain and Qatar admissions, the only dissenting voice was that of South Yemen, though Iraq's recognition of the new state was declared to be conditional on the annulment of the Abu Musa agreement.[90] The UAE's application for UN membership was approved by the Security Council on 8 December and agreed by the UN General Assembly on the following day. There too, the only hostile voice was that of South Yemen. On 10 December the UAE took its seat as the 132nd UN member.[91]

Later, Sheikh Saqr dropped his conditions and Ras al-Khaimah was accepted, on 10 February 1972, as the UAE's seventh member.

Controversies over the Tunbs

As British efforts to draw Sheikh Saqr of Ras al-Khaimah into a compromise agreement had failed, the sheikh's forces on Greater Tunb resisted the landing of Iranian troops. Several soldiers on the both sides died in the fighting that ensued. The sheikh promptly complained to the Arab League and the British government about the incident.[92] On 8 December, however, the Arab League Council rejected the request by Iraq and Ras al-Khaimah that all Arab countries sever ties with Britain and Iran.[93]

During meetings with Saqr in May and twice in September 1971, Sir William Luce had advised the sheikh of Iran's firm demand for sovereignty over the islands and presented a compromise solution in which the sheikh would retain some limited right on the Tunbs. Abandoning a position that Britain had sought to defend for close to one hundred years, Luce argued that his government could not enforce a settlement as it was playing the role of 'a mediator' rather than taking sides. He added that time was running out and, at that point, mentioned a detailed proposal drafted by the Shah and his ambassador to London, Amir Khosrow Afshar, as well as a draft series of pledges to be signed by the rulers separately that would commit them to the terms of agreement.[94]

Refusing any compromise, on 2 December 1971 Sheikh Saqr appealed to the Arab states to force Iran off the Greater and Lesser Tunb islands. He also appealed to Libya and Kuwait to repel the Iranian forces that had occupied the islands. Although Sheikh Saqr's messages to Libya and Kuwait were the only ones recorded, it was understood that he had written in similar terms to the leaders of the entire Arab League.

On 10 December 1971 his son, Sheikh Khaled bin Saqr, arrived in Benghazi where he told journalists that he had come to 'explain the situation regarding Iran's occupation of Arab Islands ... and to ask fraternal Libya to back and support us'.[95] His trip to Baghdad in 1970 was referred to in Alam's memoirs, where he quotes the British ambassador as saying that he had been unable to dissuade the Sheikh of Ras al-Khaimah from taking that trip.[96] The conservative Arab countries of the Persian Gulf gave only token support to Ras al-Khaimah in its protest against Iran's regaining of the three islands, with almost no lasting effect, as radical Iraq was their most immediate concern.

There is a spectrum of views as to why the ruler of Ras al-Khaimah, Saqr bin Muhammad al-Qasimi, resisted any understanding with Iran and Britain. Faisal bin Salman al-Saud stated in his book that 'a combination of reasons were referred to as explaining Saqr's behaviour that range from his hope to gain more from oil exploration in and around the Tunbs, his tribal and religious belief and also hope in the Arab world rising against Iran.'[97]

Anthony Cordesman attributed the sheikh's inflexibility to 'his desire to become a major leader of the UAE'. As he put it, the sheikh based his claim on the fact that Ras al-Khaimah then had most of the UAE's water and much of its arable land, and these were the traditional sources of power. This assessment ignored the new reality created by oil wealth and Ras al-Khaimah's dependence on grants by Abu Dhabi and Dubai. But Sheikh Saqr continued to resist British and Iranian pressure to turn islands over to Iran.[98] Cordesman wrote elsewhere, 'Ras al-Khaimah's ambitious Ruling Sheikh – sometimes jokingly referred to as the "Napoleon of the Gulf" – initially tried to stand on his own, in part because of his long standing rivalry with a branch of the royal family in Sharjah and his jealously of the oil wealth of Abu Dhabi and Dubai.'[99]

Glen Balfour-Paul referred to Sheikh Saqr as 'particularistic as ever' and reminded that 'he also continued to hold out against the participation in the proposed union of the seven, though this had not discouraged the remaining six, led by Abu Dhabi and Dubai, from pressing ahead with plan for its formation.'[100] Advised by Sir William Luce that Britain 'had done her best but could not contemplate forcibly opposing the seizure of the Tunbs, which might take place any day now, Sheikh Saqr resigning himself to losing them, he refused, however, any action that would indicate his foreknowledge of Iranian intentions. He would not, for example, give any warning to his posse of police on the larger Tunb, much less withdraw them and avoid the risk of casualties.'[101]

Rosemarie Said Zahlan was of the view that Sheikh Saqr, who had overthrown and replaced his uncle, Sheikh Sultan, in 1948, refused to join the UAE in 1971 in hopes of an oil discovery analogous to that of Abu Dhabi. He resented the fact that his state would be accorded only a minor role in the forthcoming federation because of its low income and small population, and was convinced that this would change once oil and gas in substantial quantities were discovered.[102]

J. B. Kelly described Sheikh Saqr as 'the Bonaparte of the Trucial Coast.'[103] And similarly, in late November 1971, the *Times* of London noted that 'if Iran carries out its threat to seize the Tunbs, Shaikh Sakr has only himself to blame.'[104]

Amir Khosrow Afshar, the Iranian negotiator, commenting on his meeting with Sheikh Saqr, stated, 'I met Sheikh Saqr in the Iranian Embassy in London and told him we were prepared to extend financial assistance to Ras al-Khaima, provided that he officially renounced his opposition to the reassertion of Iranian sovereignty on the two Tunbs. He said he saw no sense in not doing so, but such an official declaration would put his life in jeopardy with the fanatics.'[105]

The reviews of Sheikh Saqr's policy warrant that his other moves are also taken into consideration. He laid informal claims to Sharjah on the grounds that it was legitimately a part of a larger Qawasim state. He did not fully support the UAE before the Shah's fall, and at one point unilaterally invited Soviet military technicians to Ras al-Khaimah.[106]

In the mid-1970s, Sheikh Saqr made recurrent efforts to claim territory and offshore rights from Oman. In November 1977 these efforts finally led to an armed confrontation between Ras al-Khaimah and Oman that ended like 'a comic opera' when the large number of Omanis in Sheikh Saqr's forces refused to fight Oman's forces. Moreover, the president of the UAE, Sheikh Zayed of Abu Dhabi, backed Oman in the dispute, which exposed the UAE's vulnerability to pressure from

Oman and led to continued tension between Sheikh Saqr and other members of the UAE.[107]

The issue of Iranian sovereignty over the islands

Sir Denis Wright, who left Iran in April 1971, felt that he was successful at least in 'getting the [Shah] to agree not to force the sovereignty issue for the time being. Maybe this provided a way out.'[108]

Some British sources claimed that Iran had told Luce that it would not insist on resolving the issue of sovereignty over the islands, provided that Iranian troops could be stationed there. Nonetheless, in a memorandum sent to all Arab leaders by Sheikh Khaled bin Muhammad al-Qasimi of Sharjah on 24 August 1971 and published in full by the Lebanese newspaper *Al-Anwar* on 30 November 1971, he described the Iranian position as seeking recognition of its sovereignty over the island after an initial period of two years. In the memorandum the sheikh refused to accept the Iranian claim of sovereignty but was willing to negotiate and pleaded for the support of Arab leaders in countering the Iranian claim to Abu Musa. According to the same newspaper, only four unnamed Arab leaders responded to the memorandum.[109]

Adnan Pachachi, the UAE representative at the UN, stated during the Security Council meeting on the islands on 9 December 1971 that

> Iran insisted on taking over those islands and insisted on the view that those islands were Iranian historically and that, therefore, Iranian sovereignty had to be restored to them. Their insistence was centered on the question of sovereignty. All proposals which were made to the Iranian Government regarding the possibilities of cooperation between the Arab sheikdoms concerned and Iran in respect of these islands were rejected, and only the surrender of sovereignty of these islands to Iran was acceptable to the Iranian Government.[110]

Although the articles of the MoU are not explicit on the question of sovereignty over the island, the document implicitly recognizes Iranian sovereignty over Abu Musa: Article 2 allows Iran to deploy military forces on the northern part of the island; Article 3 recognizes the Iranian law of territorial waters for Abu Musa, whereas the breadth of Sharjah's sea territory was, at the time, 3 nautical miles, in accordance with the British law.[111]

Moreover, the Iranian foreign minister, A. A. Khalatbari, in letter No. M/21284 dated 25 November 1971, informed the British Foreign Secretary that 'Iran's acceptance of the arrangements relating to Abu Musa set out in the enclosure to your aforesaid letter is given on the understanding that nothing in the said arrangements shall be taken as restricting the freedom of Iran to take any measures in the island of Abu Musa which in its opinion would be necessary to safeguard the security of the island or of the Iranian forces.' He closed the letter by asking 'for confirmation that this understanding has been conveyed to the Ruler of Sharjah.' Foreign Secretary Alec Douglas-Home's letter dated 26 November 1971 in reply to Khalatbari's indicates that 'I have taken note of the understanding on which your government's acceptance of the arrangements relating to Abu Musa is given and have conveyed that understanding to the Ruler of Sharjah.'[112]

Although the word 'sovereignty' is not used in Khalatbari's letter, what is referred to therein could mean nothing else. The content of Alec Douglas-Home's reply and Sharjah's silence should be interpreted as acceptance on their part.

Statements by the Iranian officials at the time also assert their understanding of the terms of the MoU – statements that were disputed neither by the British nor by Sharjah. The Iranian prime minister told the Majlis immediately after the Iranian forces landed on the three islands:

> The Government of His Imperial Majesty has in no conceivable way relinquished or will relinquish its incontestable sovereignty rights and jurisdiction over the whole island of Abu Musa. Thus, the presence of local agents in part of Abu Musa should in no way be interpreted as contradictory to this declared policy.[113]

In an interview on 29 January 1972, the Shah confirmed this, when he categorically stated that 'we maintain our position that the whole of the island [of Abu Musa] belongs to us.'[114]

In this regard, it is also important to note that Iran had already rejected other proposals that might have adversely effected the question of its ultimate sovereignty over the islands. These included permanent demilitarization of the islands to assuage Iran's fear of their use against tanker traffic, the equal partition of the islands, a lease of the islands to Iran for 99 years and the stationing of a joint Iranian–Arab garrison on the islands.[115]

Yet the fact remains that all of the endeavours during the years leading up to Iran's repossession of the islands did not lead to the explicit recognition of Iranian sovereignty over them. This created an opportunity for Arab radicals, on the one hand, and the conservative-moderate Arab camp, on the other, who were at loggerheads with Tehran before and after the Islamic Revolution, respectively, and who tried to keep the issue alive and turn it into a rallying point in the Arab world against Iran. Thus, the half-solution the British helped bring about, and the inability of the Iranian imperial government to strike a more clear-cut deal, created a situation that is not much different from that in some other regions where the British once ruled.

Arab radicals pick up the banner

Since the announcement in January 1968 of the British withdrawal from the Persian Gulf and Iran's reassertion of its ownership of the three islands in November 1971, Arab radicalism, led by Iraq, has played the leading role in opposing Iran's move, reviving the issue intermittently and sparing no possible effort in galvanizing Arab quarters in regard to the three islands.

Thus, as the British were preparing to withdraw their forces, Ba'athist Iraq had its own agenda in the Gulf, one that ran drastically counter to that of Iran. This conflict soon focused, *inter alia*, on the issue of the three islands and, ironically, the banner of opposition to Iran's title to these islands, which the British struck on the eve of their departure, was hoisted by Arab radicals, in both governments and other groupings, led by Iraq.[116]

Baghdad, notably, led the anti-Iranian pack from this period, and the active hostility shown by the Iraqi government endured for many years, in fact, up to the conclusion of the Algiers Agreement between Iran and Iraq in 1975; it then resurfaced in the wake of the 1979 Islamic Revolution. In the process, it widely affected, as described later, several aspects of Iraq's foreign policy, including its relations with Kuwait and the Persian Gulf sheikhdoms.

Arab sources subscribing to Arab radicals' views on the issue of the three islands admit that '[a]s a matter of fact, only Iraq challenged the Iranian occupation of these islands. Even the United Arab Emirates itself – except for complaining for a short time – kept silent about the matter, at the request of the British.'[117]

Burdened with an inherited legacy of intermittent and inconclusive wars between the Ottoman and Persian empires, and following its own geopolitical interests in the Persian Gulf and its own ideological persuasion, Iraq soon placed itself at the forefront of the Arabs opposing Iran on the issue of the three islands.

There were continuous sources of disputes and rivalry between Iran and Iraq, regardless of the nature of the political establishment in either country. Even when both countries were ruled by conservative, monarchical regimes from the 1920s to the 1950s, the similarity of their political orientation did not preclude the eruption of multiple crises over a disputed boundary. They did, however, cooperate to counter shared threats against their conservative regimes. After the 1958 coup in Iraq, however, common interests evaporated and rivalries between the two countries took on a strong ideological aspect as well.

As to the Persian Gulf issues, Iraq, by virtue of its size and pan-Arab orientation, saw itself as the guardian of Arabism in the Gulf, and believed that it 'carries the main burden in safeguarding the area.'[118] Later, the Ba'ath Party, convinced of its messianic pan-Arab role and bent on establishing a new socialist revolutionary order in a unified Arab state under its leadership, saw Iraq as the launching pad from which to overthrow the political status quo in the Persian Gulf.

Moreover, the increase in oil production led Iraq's leaders to pay more attention to the main route of its exports to the outside world, that is, the Persian Gulf. Iran's swift action to fill the vacuum left by the British in the 1970s heightened further the sensitivity of the Iraqis with regard to developments in the Gulf. From this juncture on, Iranian moves became, in fact, an important factor in shaping Iraqi attitudes in foreign policy and even affected certain important aspects of Iraqi domestic policy.

In general, the foreign policy of Iraqi regimes, especially since 1968, was influenced by, among other things, the desire to achieve predominance in the Persian Gulf region as a prelude to realizing the Ba'athists' ultimate dream, the leadership of the Arab world, by taking up the position Abdul al-Nasser of Egypt had left behind. Gaining a preponderant position in the Persian Gulf was to pave the way for the Ba'athists to claim Nasser's legacy, that is, leadership of the Arab world.

Thus, the islands issue was just another element now added to the historic rivalry between Iran and Iraq, which had deep roots in their clashing perceptions of national interests. Out of two major contentious issues – rivalry over the Persian Gulf and the Shatt al-Arab boundary dispute – the Iranian move on the islands could have possibly affected the first one. Hence, Iraq was reacting in part to the greater control that had been given over its lifeline through the Persian Gulf to Iran by the British. Moreover, the British effort to link the UAE's security to Iran threatened this lifeline from both sides of the Gulf and was a major challenge to the Ba'athist cause of an Arab national consciousness.[119]

The repudiation by Iran on 19 April 1969 of the 1937 treaty covering the Shatt al-Arab border with Iraq had already exacerbated Iran–Iraq relations. Iraqi reactions to that move had included the expulsion of Iraqis of Iranian origin; the provision of assistance to Iranian dissidents, including by making radio transmitters available to them with which to voice hostility against the Shah; and revival of the issue of 'Arabistan', by using that name for the Iranian province of Khuzistan, and by forming the 'Popular Front for Liberation of Arabistan'.

At the same time, the Iraqi claim to ascendancy in the Persian Gulf had little substance. Strategically and militarily, Iraq was no match for Iran. While the Iranian coastline stretches the full length of the northern Persian Gulf and the Sea of Oman, the Iraqi coastline of mere 40 kilometres is short and shallow, and the Iraqi seaports unreliable. Moreover, Iraq lacks a reliable strategic depth vis-à-vis Iran. All important Iraqi centres of population, business and industry lie within 150 kilometres of the Iranian border, whereas the extensive Iranian strategic depth provides it with a much larger margin for manoeuvre.

All in all, Iran, assisted by the entire West, regarded itself as the guardian of the status quo in the region and as the gendarmerie providing security to the conservative establishment in the region, including the sheikhdoms. Conversely, the Iraqis, supported by the Soviets, perceived themselves as the standard-bearers of revolutionary change, militancy and Arab nationalism in the Persian Gulf, whose calling was to plant the seeds of Arab nationalism in the area. As such, there could be no let-up in its enmity-ridden rivalry with an Iran that befriended the West and was determined to safeguard the Persian Gulf region against the powerful waves of radical Arab nationalism.

Under such general circumstances, reactions by the radical Arab states, led by Iraq, to Iran's move on the three islands can be summarized as follows:

Arab radicals' moves against Iran and Britain

Iraq was already in a state of political confrontation with Iran and Britain, and Iran's move and the indications of British support triggered an explosive Iraqi response against those countries, including the breaking of diplomatic relations with Britain and Iran, the nationalization of the remaining British holdings of the Iraq Petroleum Company, sporadic skirmishes on Iran–Iraq borders and the expulsion of Iranians from Iraq.

On the day that Iran's troops landed on the islands, Baghdad radio announced that Iraq had decided to break off diplomatic relations with Britain and Iran,

102　*The restoration of Persian Gulf autonomy*

because of Iran's 'flagrant aggression in collusion with Britain' against the Greater and Lesser Tunb islands. Following up on that, Baghdad radio reported on 5 December that the Iraqi Foreign Ministry had ordered the British ambassador and the chargé d'affaires at the Iranian Embassy to leave Baghdad by 12 December, and their respective staffs to leave by 16 December.[120]

Libya, in its turn, seized on the incidents to nationalize assets of the British Petroleum Company as punishment for Britain's alleged complicity in Iran's seizure of the islands.[121] On 8 December Libyan radio quoted the Libyan premier, Major Abd al-Salam Jaloud, as saying in a newspaper interview that 'the Arab Republic asked permission from the Iraqi authorities to land airborne forces at Basra airport, preparatory to moving them to the islands. The Iraqi authorities approved Libya's application, some in the Gulf refused'. He continued, 'Iran's ambition will not end with the occupation of the three islands. It plans to take control of the entire Gulf.'[122]

At home, the Iraqi Ba'athists expelled thousands of theology students, pilgrims and businessmen 'accused of being of Iranian origin', despite their having been in Iraq for generations. On 30 December 1971, 60,000 'Iranians' were deported from Iraq. It was reported that Iraq expelled a further 60,000 Iranians from its territory over the following few days and that these included women and children. Convoys of buses took them in freezing conditions to the border and left them there. In a speech on 31 December, Saddam Hussein, Deputy Chairman of the Revolutionary Commanding Council, said that Iraq was deporting all aliens who had entered Iraq illegally.[123]

On 3 January, the Iranian authorities spoke of a daily influx of 1,000 refugees from Iraq. It was reported that, on 19 January, Iran sent a memorandum to the UN Commission on Human Rights asking that effective measures be taken to protect the remaining Iranian community in Iraq after the recent expulsions.[124]

The Iraqi government in its hostility against Iran went so far as equating 'Persian nationalism' with Zionism. It considered its primary role to be the preservation of the Arab nature of the Gulf and the integrity of the Arab homeland by combating what it described as systematic Persian infiltration of the Arab side of the Gulf. The Political Report of the Eighth Congress of the Arab Ba'ath Socialist Party, held in Iraq in January 1974, drew a parallel between Palestine and the Gulf: it saw the centre of the conflict as a struggle between Arab nationalism on the one hand, and Zionism and Persian nationalism on the other. Immigration and settlement of the Persians in the Gulf sheikhdoms was described by Iraq 'as a colonialist phenomenon, posing a threat to the Arabism of the Persian Gulf analogous to the Zionist colonization of Palestine.'[125] This immigration and 'Iran's occupation of the three Arab islands' were seen as an 'imperialist plot whose objective was to circumscribe centers of revolution, primarily Iraq, and work for their enfeeblement and fall.'[126]

The Iraqi government also decided to promote itself as the protector of Arab lands in the area. A passage from the Political Report read:

> Political, economic, cultural and other activities needed to face up to [the

The restoration of Persian Gulf autonomy 103

imperialists'] aggressive ambitions could not flourish for reasons peculiar to the [Gulf] area, particularly the weakness of the popular movements vis-à-vis the regimes. These regimes did not oppose the threats to the Arab character of the Gulf with an effective policy, in spite of the pressure of public opinion within the area and elsewhere in the Arab homeland. Iraq's initiatives in this domain met with anti-nationalist mistrust, on the false pretext of fear for our country, a pretext inspired by the imperialists and others, whose design was to keep the area apart from its biggest and most powerful Arab neighbour.

The threat to the countries of the Arabian Gulf grew greater at a time when the Revolution was deeply involved on both the military and political fronts with the Palestinian question and with resistance to Zionism and imperialism, so that Iraq's activities in the area were reduced in both scope and kind.

But the growing threat met only silence or indifference in the Arab world, due either to deliberate collusion or to ignorance and preoccupation with Zionist enemy in the Palestinian arena. Some regimes used these pretexts to close their ears to Iraq's urgent warnings of danger in the Gulf area. They withdraw from moral or even symbolic obligations, to the point of improving relations with Iran before and even after its occupation of the three Arab islands of Abu Musa and Greater and Lesser Tunb.

These regimes' alliance – especially at this point – with the Saudi Arabia, which has an essential role in the imperialist plan for the Arabian Gulf, gave Saudi reaction a free hand and an effective political cover for it to exert great influence on the area, in collaboration with the Iranian regime and the reactionary regimes of the Gulf.

Other Arab regimes paid no attention to events in the Gulf, either willfully or from heedlessness, and were not prepared to participate in resistance to the danger. On the contrary, most tried directly or indirectly to suggest that Iraq's concern for this subject and its appeals for action were but a pretext for avoiding its obligations in the Palestinian arena.[127]

In 1980, Ba'ath Party and government official Tariq Aziz said:

Some might say that Iraq brought up the question of the three islands, of Arabistan and of the Shatt al-Arab agreements, prompting Iran to respond in this fashion. Yes, Iraq did indeed bring up these three issues, but is it so strange for Iraq to want the return of the three islands occupied by the Shah of Iran with his military forces . . . ?[128]

Iraq's moves at the United Nations

On the multilateral scene, Iraq and Libya, joined by Algeria and South Yemen, took the case of the three islands to the UN Security Council. In a letter dated 3 December 1971 and addressed to the President of the Security Council, the permanent representatives of these four member states requested 'an urgent meeting of the Security Council to consider the dangerous situation in the Arabian Gulf

104 *The restoration of Persian Gulf autonomy*

area arising from the occupation by the armed forces of Iran of the Islands of Abu Musa, the Greater Tunb and the Lesser Tunb on November 30, 1971.'[129] It should be noted that the complainants included the island of Abu Musa in their letter, thus disregarding the understanding reached by Iran with the Sheikh of Sharjah.

This letter effectively put the issue on the agenda of the Security Council and enabled different groupings of Arab countries with varying political inclinations to activate it in accordance with prevailing situations in every period since.

Furthermore, Talib El-Shibib, Iraq's permanent representative to the UN, in another letter, dated 7 December 1971 and addressed to the UN Secretary-General, transmitted 'the text of a cable received by [his] Government from the Ruler of Ras al-Khaima.' In the cable, after a description of the events of 30 November, it is stated that

> The two islands of Tunb are and have always been, since ancient times, an indivisible part of the territory of Ras al-Khaima, and their occupation by Iran is a blatant aggression not only against Ras al-Khaima alone, but against all the Arab people.[130]

Acting on the letter dated 3 December, the President of the Security Council held a meeting on 9 December 1971 to consider the issue. As it is the only Security Council meeting ever held on this subject, it warrants a thorough consideration. The following points are noteworthy:

- It is significant that in the meeting the representative of Iraq sat at the Council table as the counterpart to the Iranian representative, and the remaining representatives on the list of speakers, including that of UAE, sat on the side of the Council Chamber. In other words, Iraq stood as the main complainant challenging Iran on the issue at hand. Note also should be taken of the fact that, as indicated by the President of the Council, the UAE's request to participate in the debate was received by the president while the meeting was already in process. (At the time, Ras al-Khaimah was yet to be part of the UAE.)
- The Iraqi representative was the first speaker on the issue. He said he came to the Council 'to submit not the complaint of [his] own Government only, but also that of a small and helpless Arab State, which has no means to defend itself against the aggression.' He rejected the Memorandum of Understanding between Iran and Sharjah, arguing that on the basis of the exclusive agreement between Britain and the Trucial states, 'the alleged agreement between the Government of Iran and the Ruler of Al-Sharja was concluded at a time when the latter had not yet fully regained the right to enter into any international commitment'.[131] He went on to consider '[t]he invasion of the Tunb islands and the partial occupation of the island of Abu Musa' to be 'the latest step in a policy of expansion by the Government of Iran, a blatant demonstration of the collusion between Iran and the United Kingdom Government'.[132]
- The Iraqi representative dealt extensively with the Persian Gulf's general issues. He said, 'the Straits of Hormuz and the strategic three islands now

The restoration of Persian Gulf autonomy 105

illegally occupied by Iran do control the lifeline of the littoral states, which have no outlet to the high seas other than through the Strait. Iraq is among those States, whereas Iran . . . has direct outlets on the Arabian Sea.' He further stated that 'we reject the appointment of Iran, or any other single state, as guardian or guarantor of the continuation of the flow of oil to the outside world. Iraq also rejects the control by Iran of the only outlet of Iraq's commerce to the high seas.'

- Referring to age-old commonalities between the Arabs and the Persians, the representative of Kuwait extensively informed the Council of 'Kuwaiti efforts with a view to amicably resolving the dispute, but to no avail.' He repeated his government's view that 'these islands are always Arab islands and [Kuwait] disapproves of the Iranian occupation, and deplores the use of force.' He was less clement towards Britain, 'whose history' in his words 'is characterized by a chronic disease of pulling out and leaving behind explosive situation'. He went on to consider it 'the country which deserves severe condemnation.'[133]
- Colin Crowe, the British permanent representative, in his statement in the Council, referring to the Tunbs, said: 'Both islands lie near the Iranian shore and have long been claimed by Iran. For many years the British Government has been trying to bring about an agreed solution between Iran and the Ruler.' He went on to say, 'The ending of Britain's special position and responsibilities with the Gulf has inevitably meant the striking of a balance between the conflicting claims of neighbouring States, and the taking into account of realities.' He portrayed the outcome of the efforts as 'a reasonable and acceptable basis for the future security of the area', and added, 'I cannot see how the representative of Iraq can describe the present situation as dangerous or as threat to peace.'[134] This statement marked the formal discontinuance of the British policy of adamantly claiming the three islands for their protégés on the Arab littoral. Just as that policy had been born of mainly strategic considerations, it was laid to rest owing to much the same type of consideration, albeit these were of a different nature in the new era.
- The Iraqi representative, in making a second statement in exercise of the right to reply, said: 'I asked [the UK representative] two questions and he answered neither of them. The first was: were these islands Arab, and did they belong to Sharjah and Ras al-Khaima? I do not think we have received an answer to that question. The second question was: was not Britain duty bound to defend the territorial integrity of these islands until the final second of the expiration of British responsibility for their protection and defence, or do British obligations have a duration of a period minus one or two days? Is this a new precedent in respect of treaties and the carrying out of obligations of States?'[135]
- Adnan Pachachi, who had been an Iraqi foreign minister in the 1960s but who now represented the UAE at the United Nations, made a statement in the Council after the Iraqi representative spoke for the second time. He recalled his intervention at the General Assembly on the same day, adding that 'I

expressed the deep regret felt by the people of the country which I have the honor to represent and its Government at the action taken by Iran in forcibly occupying the Arab islands in the Gulf.' In closing his statement, Pachachi said, 'it is our sincere hope that the Iranian Government will consider its position on these islands and will find it possible to settle this problem in a way that befits relations between neighbours and the deep spiritual and cultural ties that have bound the Arab and Iranian peoples over the centuries.'[136]

- The Iranian representative, Amir Khosrow Afshar, told the meeting in his brief statement that 'We strongly believe that it is for the Persian Gulf States alone to deal with this vital international waterway . . . any interference by outside Powers in the affairs of the Persian Gulf would undoubtedly endanger peace and stability in the area.' He also stated that the Libyan Minister of Industry had declared to the press in Kuwait that the Libyan planned to dispatch troops to occupy the islands.
- The representative of Somalia, a member of the Arab League, helped find a way out: 'In the view of my delegation it would be precipitate at this stage to recommend any recourse under Article 36. I say this because my delegation understands that some States friendly to both the complainants and Iran have initiated contact, at government level, in an attempt to bring both sides together so that the matter might be resolved without acrimony and with justice.' He further stated that 'My delegation would therefore suggest that the Council defer consideration of this matter to a later date, so that sufficient time is allowed for these efforts of quiet diplomacy to work and to materialize.'
- The President of the Security Council, repeating the suggestion made by the Somali representative and hearing no objection, proceeded accordingly. The meeting came thus to an end, and the three islands issue, despite remaining on the agenda of Council, has never again been discussed in a Council meeting.
- It should also be noted that only six out of 22 Arab countries spoke in this open debate, which had been requested by four Arab countries.

In the debate at the UN General Assembly on the admission of the United Arab Emirates to membership in the United Nations, the radical Arab states brought strong pressure to bear on the UAE in respect of the three islands issue. South Yemen's representative stated in the meeting that in the view of his government 'the declaration of the so-called independence of the UAE is a great farce.' He accused 'the rulers of the so-called UAE and their patrons' of reacting 'passively in complete apathy and utter connivance' against the Iranian action on the three islands, and described it as the 'selling out of part of the territory of the Arabian Gulf.'[137] In the recorded vote that followed, South Yemen voted against admission of the UAE to the United Nations and Iraq was absent.[138]

In the closing part of his statement in the General Assembly, Adnan Pachachi, the UAE's representative, touched briefly upon the issue of the three islands, 'expressing the deep regret felt by the people and the Government of the UAE at the action taken by Iran in forcibly occupying some Arab islands in the Gulf.'

The restoration of Persian Gulf autonomy 107

He described the Iranian action in using force to settle a territorial dispute 'not only contrary to the Charter of the UN, but also incompatible with the traditional friendship that has bound together the Arab and Iranian peoples.'[139]

The only other action taken collectively by a group of Arab countries at the United Nations before the Islamic Revolution was the issuance of a letter, dated 18 July 1972, addressed to the Secretary-General and signed by the representatives of Algeria, Bahrain, Egypt, Iraq, Kuwait, Lebanon, Libya, Morocco, Oman, South Yemen, Sudan, Syria, Tunisia and the UAE; Jordan, North Yemen, Somali, Qatar and Saudi Arabia did not join in. In this letter, the signatories stated the following:

> We reiterate . . . our position regarding the three Arab islands, namely Abu Musa, the Greater Tunb and the Lesser Tunb, which have been militarily occupied by Iran and the question of which is before the Security Council. Our position has been very clear on this question. We affirm that the islands are Arab, and history attests to the continued Arab identity and character of these islands.[140]

In reply to this letter in August, Iran's permanent representative to the UN stated that 'the renewal of Iranian administration in the islands . . . is not "military occupation" . . . Iran has only re-established its rightful authority over the islands after its long interruption by colonial domination of the Persian Gulf'.[141]

The July 1972 letter was the last letter to the United Nations on the islands before the one sent to the UN Secretary-General by Sadoon Hammadi, the Minister for Foreign Affairs of Iraq, eight years later in April 1980, referred to in Chapter 4. In the UN General Assembly, too, the UAE did not raise the issue of the three islands on its own initiative or in its main statements up until 1992. Nonetheless, in this span of time, UAE officials were twice dragged by Iraq and in the exercise of the right of reply into responding to Iran's reactions against Iraqi statements.[142]

Iraq was, thus, the only country that continued bringing up the issue of the three islands for two more years (1972 and 1973[143]), using it as a tool in its disputes with Iran over a range of issues, before declining to raise it in 1974 and shelving it after 1975 when an agreement was reached with Iran ending the dispute over the Shatt al-Arab waterway that had pitted the two countries against each other. As we will see later, in the aftermath of the Islamic Revolution in Iran, Iraq started another short round of controversies within and outside of the United Nations.

Iraq's moves against conservative sheikhs

Following Iran's move on the three islands, Iraq refused to recognize the newly established federation of the United Arab Emirates in protest against Sharjah's agreement with Iran on Abu Musa. The Iraqi government made its recognition of the UAE conditional upon the latter's cancellation of the agreement and upon its commitment not to establish diplomatic relations with Iran before Iran returned the three islands[144] – a demand that went unheeded.

More importantly, evidence suggests that Iraq matched its public criticism of Iran's move of taking over the islands with active attempts to subvert the process:

- An aborted coup on 24 January 1972 by a rebel force of eighteen, led by Sheikh Saqr ibn Sultan, the ruler's cousin, who had been deposed as ruler in 1965 and since lived in Cairo, disrupted Sharjah. It resulted in the killing of the ruler, Sheikh Khaled bin Muhammad al-Qasimi, who had signed the Memorandum of Understanding with Iran, and nine members of his family.[145] Despite the death of Sheikh Khaled, the coup failed and Sheikh Khaled's brother replaced him.
- Sharjah's authorities alleged, on 7 February 1972, that arms used in the attempted coup had been shipped from Basra with Iraqi connivance. In December, 71 shots were fired at Sheikh Saqr ibn Muhammad, Sharjah's deputy ruler, but only grazed his shoulder. Sheikh Saqr had represented his brother, Sheikh Khaled, in receiving the Iranian landing party on Abu Musa Island on 30 November 1971.[146]
- Sharjah's new ruler, Sheikh Sultan ibn Muhammad, said in an interview on 2 February 1972 that he would keep to his brother's agreement with Iran on the partial occupation of Abu Musa, but would try to achieve a new understanding with the Shah on the issue.[147]
- Lebanese newspapers reported on 17 February 1972 that ten suitcases seized at Manama airport contain machine guns and other weapons. Classified as diplomatic mail, the suitcases were carried by an Iraqi diplomatic official, Abd al-Hamid Kharbit, and contained machine guns, hand grenades, bazookas, small arms and ammunitions. Kharbit was quoted as telling the Bahraini authorities that the arms were gifts from the Iraqi Government to the leaders of Bahrain in view of 'their well-known love of hunting.'[148]

International and regional repercussions

The intensifying conflict with Iran prompted Iraq to seek the support of transregional powers. Baghdad's relations with Cairo were marred by previous tensions, its ties with the radical Arab states were not close, and with Syria they were tense. Iraq was also isolated in the conservative Arab world, including in the Persian Gulf. Its activism against what it termed as 'Arab reaction' had put Iraq at odds with the sheikhs and kings and other moderates in the area, in such a way that they were much hated and, at the same time, feared by the Persian Gulf Arab monarchs. Consequently, Iraq's reactions to the restoration of Iranian sovereignty over the islands included the strengthening of its relationship with the socialist camp as well.

On the same day that Iran's troops landed on the islands, Abd-al-Baqi, the Iraqi foreign minister, met with the ambassadors of the Soviet Union, China and France in Baghdad to inform them of the Iranian 'aggression' and to urge these states to request that Iran withdraw from the islands.[149] Earlier in the same month, Al-Bakr, the Iraqi president, declared that 'the confrontation against Israel and the protection of Arabism of the Gulf required augmenting ties with the international forces supporting Arab rights, especially the Soviet Union and the People's Republic of China.'[150]

Further Iraqi efforts resulted in Soviet Defence Minister Andrei Grechko's visit to Baghdad on 14–22 December 1971. An article published in *Al-Thawrah* on 17 December maintained that the conquest of the three islands by Iran required raising the Iraqi–Soviet relationship to the level of a 'strategic alliance.'[151] This and what followed it, that is, the conclusion of the Friendship Treaty between the two countries, demonstrated how far Baghdad was ready to go in its enmity against Iran.

Notwithstanding Iraq's efforts, the way the events relating to the islands were reported in the Soviet media, including *Pravda*, demonstrated a pro-Iranian or neutral inclination on the part of the Soviets, as mostly Tehran's version of the events was reflected. This indicated that the Soviets preferred Iranian to British influence in the Persian Gulf as the lesser evil. In the joint statement issued at the conclusion of Grechko's visit, there was no reference to the issue of the islands, reflecting the gap between the two sides' stances. However, the phrase 'to promote ... military cooperation' in the statement indicated an upgrading of the military relationship between the two sides, attributable to Iraq's need for Soviet weapons after the escalation of tensions with Iran.[152]

During the exchange of visits by Saddam Hussein and Soviet Premier Alexei Kosygin in February and April 1972, respectively, the Iraqis tried unsuccessfully to insert language into their joint statements deploring the Iranian move on the three islands. 'In his speech in Moscow, Saddam alleged that "plots" were being hatched against Iraq by US and British "imperialist circles" and that the Iranian reaction has committed some provocations on our border, and also [has occupied] "three Arab islands in the Gulf".' He spoke of the need for 'a firm strategic alliance' between the two countries.[153]

The signing of the Friendship and Cooperation Treaty between Iraq and the Soviet Union took place in April 1972. The signatories pledged to contact each other in case of 'danger to the peace of either party' and to refrain from joining an alliance with a country or a group of countries against the other. They also resolved to 'develop cooperation in strengthening their defense capacity.'[154]

Iraq's treaty with Moscow led the United States to further develop its own relationship with Iran and to support it even more. In May 1972, President Richard Nixon announced that Iran could buy any non-nuclear American weapons it chose to. The United States also deepened its involvement in the Kurdish crisis, providing more assistance to the Kurds fighting Iraqi central government forces.

At the regional level, Arab radicals and anti-Western states such as Algeria, Libya and South Yemen joined Iraq in resolutely condemning the Iranian move. The Arab conservatives and moderates did not follow Iraq's lead in reacting to the landing of Iran's troops on the islands, and, as an important sign, they did not take part in the Iraqi action at the UN Security Council against Iran. Egypt, apprehensive over the growing tension in the Persian Gulf and afraid it might overshadow the Arab–Israeli dispute, appealed for moderation. It called upon Iran to withdraw from the islands and to enter into negotiations to attain a just and peaceful settlement. Saudi Arabia, as a conservative and pro-Western state, indicated only its dissatisfaction with the Iranian move and did not even directly urge an Iranian pullout. Nor did it take part in the meeting of the Security Council held on 9 December 1971.

The islands incident also helped lead to more Iraqi pressure on Kuwait with regard to the islands of Verba and Bubiyan. In the early 1960s, Iraq's claim to all of Kuwait had contributed substantially to Iraq's isolation and inhibited the development of strong links with its Arab neighbours in the Persian Gulf. In the later 1960s, concerned about its conflict with Iran since 1969 over the Shatt al-Arab and wishing to secure strategic depth in the Persian Gulf, Iraq had already began to press Kuwait to cede to it those two Kuwaiti islands. The Iranian move on the three islands in 1971 exacerbated the situation for Iraq and made it press more severely upon Kuwait. Iraq's foreign minister stated in April 1973 that without these islands, Iraq could not become a Gulf power, and hence Iraqi control of the islands constituted a prerequisite for the delineation of the Kuwait–Iraq borders.[155] Only a combination of Saudi and Iranian pressure and a Kuwaiti payment of several hundred million dollars led to a less aggressive Iraqi policy.[156]

Nonetheless, the Iraqi theory that the Shah of Iran was a more dangerous threat to the Arabs than Israel suffered during and in the aftermath of the 1973 Arab–Israeli war. The Iraqi government, under pressure from the Arab streets, dispatched military forces to the Syria–Israel border and re-established diplomatic relations with Tehran, an action that, however, failed to bring about any improvement of the relationship between the two countries.

In the aftermath of its signing with Iran of the 1975 agreement, Iraq moved gradually away from its ultra-radical, anti-Zionist stance as its attention became focused on its role in the Persian Gulf.

Iran's ascendancy in the Persian Gulf

With *Pax Britannica* winding down and the islands issue settled on Iranian terms, the era of Iranian ascendancy in the Persian Gulf was ushered in, and Iran as a conservative state tried to maintain the status quo as befitted its perceived national interests.

Regardless of the rhetoric on the part of Arab radicals, led by Iraq, and despite the evidence of Iranian aggrandizement, the Arab Persian Gulf sheikhs and monarchs continued to feel more comfortable with Iran throughout the 1970s. They regarded Iran as a conservative, status quo-oriented power, and preferred it over Iraq's revolutionary and ideological regime. At the same time, Iran's perceived role as the guardian of Gulf security was more or less in conflict with Iraq's perception of its own role as the guardian and bulwark of Arabism in the Persian Gulf.

Iran shared certain characteristics with the Arab states of the Persian Gulf: suspicion of Arab radicalism and of Iraq in particular; apprehension over internal

The restoration of Persian Gulf autonomy 111

upheaval encouraged by Arab radicals; a close relationship with the West, and the United States in particular; a desire to minimize Soviet influence; an interest in higher oil prices and the security of oil supplies; and a tendency to keep aloof from the impacts of the Arab–Israeli dispute.

These commonalities led many to expect that a system of Arab–Iranian Gulf security could emerge in the 1970s, under US direction and as a concrete implementation of the Twin Pillar policy proclaimed by Washington. No such security system came about; rather, there was a *de facto* unilateral Gulf security system, one of Iranian hegemony.[157] In this period, Iranian actions such as moving on the three islands, containing Iraq from 1969 to 1975 (directly or by proxy), and deploying troops in Dhofar from 1973 benefited the conservative Persian Gulf rulers.

A degree of pragmatism demonstrated by Iran, which helped to restore relations with Egypt after the death of Nasser and to cultivate good relationships with some other Arab states, contributed to thwarting the possibility of a unified Arab position against Iran.

As it became clear that Iran's interest was best served by the maintenance of peace and stability in, and the autonomy of, the Persian Gulf, as well as the independence of the conservative sheikhdoms, Iran enjoyed a brief period of close relationships with the sheikhdoms and provided them with protection against radicalism through 1978. This period began with the Iranian government moderating its policy and seeking *rapprochement* with other Gulf states from early 1972. Strengthening this approach between 1974 and 1979, Iran succeeded in systematically mending fences with conservative Gulf States. It supported Kuwait during its periods of tension with Iraq, enhanced cooperation with Bahrain, provided aid to the United Arab Emirates, and Dubai in particular, gave military support to Oman in suppressing the Dhofar rebellion, helped North Yemen replace its Soviet arms and furnished arms to Somalia. Iran also signed an agreement with Oman in December 1977 providing for joint patrol of the Strait of Hormuz (the key channels of which are in Omani waters).

Iran followed up its *rapprochement* with the Arab Persian Gulf states with a thaw in its relations with Egypt. In January 1975 the Shah visited Egypt and Jordan, a step indicative of Iran's desire to improve relations with the Arab world. President Sadat of Egypt greeted him as a 'dear brother' and called his visit a 'turning point in the history of the region'.[158]

Despite Arab concerns over Iran's long-term goals in the region, Iraq was not able to project her influence and win the trust of the Persian Gulf Arab states. Iraq became soon isolated in the region and portrayed as a threat to the conservative Arab regimes in the area. This was a function of its radical revolutionary orientation, its anti-monarchical, anti-Western slogans, its support for revolutionary movements in the area, its expansionist drive with regard to Kuwait and its attempts to propagate, aid and abet Ba'athist revolutionary cells throughout the region.

Oman did face in reality a serious threat from Arab radicalism. The revolutionary movement in Dhofar remained active until the end of 1975, and a state of cold confrontation with South Yemen persisted until 1982. Dhofar guerrillas presented themselves from 1968 until 1974 as the Popular Front for the Liberation of the Occupied Arab Gulf (PFLOAG), which meant to cover the United Arab Emirates, Qatar, Bahrain and, sometimes, Kuwait; their threat was taken seriously enough by the Gulf rulers to cause them to back Oman quietly. Iran intervened massively to crush the movement, and to this end, according to the Iranian Foreign Ministry, deployed some 3,000 troops in Oman.[159]

The British commander of Oman's defence forces announced on 2 February 1975 that Iran had guaranteed air support against foreign intrusion into Oman's airspace as requested. Press reports on 2 January had reported that Iran had extended its naval presence in Oman under an agreement for joint naval operations in the crucial Strait of Hormuz. The Omani Minister of State for Foreign Affairs, Qais Abd al-Moneim al-Zawawi, said that Iran would have the major responsibility for implementing the agreement, which was aimed at keeping the waters on both sides of the Strait 'secure and free.' He denied that the operations were a threat to Iraq, saying that 'we are committed to a policy of free passage ... about 20 million of barrels of oil a day were carried by tankers through the Strait.'[160]

At the same time, Iran's military superiority continued uncontested and its military build-up went on unabated. Iran's expenditure on US armaments was to reach $10.4 billion between 1972 and 1976. In 1973 alone Iran bought $2.2 billion worth of US weaponry, in 1974 $4.4 billion and in 1975 $3 billion. Its defence budget had soared from $800 million in 1970 to $6.325 billion in 1975. During their meeting with the Shah in 1972 in Tehran, President Nixon and Secretary of State Kissinger had promised the Shah that Iran might purchase any US non-nuclear weapons systems in quantities, which the Shah could specify. By 1973 Iran had become the largest single purchaser of US arms in the world.[161]

Iran's military build-up presented little tangible threat to most other Persian Gulf states. As Anthony Cordesman put it, Iran's 'military build-up relieved the Arab littoral states of immediate concern for their external security and of the need to develop close ties or seek collective security.' Basically, Iran had a long-term interest in preserving the stability of the other Gulf states and in keeping them immune from radicalism. Iran also had an equal interest in avoiding any instability that might exacerbate the competition among big powers in the Persian Gulf and end up undermining the autonomy of the area, which would in turn be detrimental to its supremacy.[162]

Conversely, the Iraqi government, as a close friend of the Soviet Union and a state with a radical posture on all Arab issues that aimed to take over the Arab leadership from Egypt, alienated the moderates and conservatives in the area. The memory of Iraq's aggressiveness towards Kuwait in 1961 and its belligerent attitudes against sheikhs and monarchs in the area since 1971 exacerbated the situation. The Iraqi claim to Kuwait was never formally dropped, and some political support was initially given to the PFLOAG.[163] Its belligerency culminated in aggression against Kuwait in 1973, which pushed Iraq's regional standing to a new low and effectively ruled it out as a serious challenger to Iran's status in the region.

The restoration of Persian Gulf autonomy 113

South Yemen, ruled by a radical regime and supported by the Soviets, was perceived as another threat to the status quo in the Persian Gulf. South Yemen fought two border wars with North Yemen in 1972 and 1979, and until 1982 provided support to the underground guerrillas active in the North. South Yemen backed the guerrillas in Dhofar not only up to the end of the fighting there, but, in political form, for seven years afterwards. South Yemen also appeared to present a threat because of the facilities it had given to Soviet naval and air forces in Aden and the close military and political ties between Aden and the Soviet Union.[164]

Though arrived at relatively late, the Algiers Agreement of 6 March 1975, which paved the way for the Treaty concerning the State Frontier and Neighbourly Relations, between Iran and Iraq, was a landmark development in the area with far-reaching effects. Feeling increasingly isolated in the Persian Gulf and beset with unending Kurdish insurgency and other troubles inside the country, the Iraqi government finally agreed to recognize the deepest navigable channel (the thalweg line) in the Shatt al-Arab as the fluvial border between the two countries.

In addition to easing tension between Tehran and Baghdad, the agreement had a positive impact on the relations between Iraq and other Gulf states as well. It reinforced the ongoing process of strengthening relationships between Iran and the Arab states on the lower Persian Gulf and enabled Iraq to get on board. As a result, it ushered in a process of reconciliation and *rapprochement* between Iraq and its Arab neighbours in the Persian Gulf, which was welcomed by them. Foreign Minister Ahmad al-Suwaidi of the UAE described it as a 'positive step' towards achieving security and stability in the region.[165]

The agreement meant, among other things, that the Iraqi regime, too, implicitly accepted the status quo in the region, which resulted in a relative relaxation of tensions in the Persian Gulf. In practice, Iraq played down the importance of its political differences with conservative Arab littoral states and worked towards closer relations with them. Consequently, it cut off its aid to the Dhofari rebels and established diplomatic relations with Oman. Symptoms of tension and disenchantment in its relations with the Soviet Union began to appear in 1976.

Nonetheless, Iraq made an exception when it came to Kuwait and continued to pursue its claim to the islands of Verba and Bubiyan, as it felt even more in need of a deep port facility after agreeing to divide the Shatt al-Arab along the thalweg line. Moreover, although the Iraqis moderated their approach after making their peace with Iran in 1975, their appetite for greater influence in the Persian Gulf did not diminish. They merely chose thereafter diplomatic rather than clandestine or revolutionary means to achieve it.

The autonomy of the Persian Gulf and the re-establishment of Iran's supremacy there were the major outcomes of the developments that followed the announcement of the British withdrawal from east of Suez in January 1968. Iran's inherent position as well as its close relationship with the West and tension-free relations with the East helped it overcome Arab radicals' vociferous protests and foil their efforts to achieve different outcomes. As a result, while relinquishing its claim to Bahrain, Iran proved unyielding about recovering the three islands. The exit of the dominant foreign power from the Persian Gulf and the following period, characterized by the absence of a global power in the area unprecedented for centuries, enabled Iran to restore its control over these islands and strengthen its position in the Gulf. Initial opposition, which lasted only for few months, soon faded away and the regional actors acquiesced in Iran's role and position in the area, which continued unchallenged until after the Islamic Revolution.

4 Transitional period

The 1979 Islamic Revolution in Iran and other momentous events around the same time in the region introduced a new chapter in the history of the Persian Gulf, thus affecting to some extent the evolution of the issue of the three islands. The new era began with the relationship between Iran and the conservative sheikhs deteriorating and the US government embarking definitively on a new policy of enhanced military presence in the region.

The cumulative result of these two mutually reinforcing trends was a transitional period in the 1980s during which the regional autonomy of the Persian Gulf became increasingly constrained and the historic Iranian ascendancy therein more challenged. This decade was also transitional in that a global power had yet to return to supremacy in the area. Although the United States made some advances in the 1980s with the aim of establishing its dominance in the Persian Gulf, the indecision and wavering reaction to this by most littoral Arab states and the bipolar environment did not yet allow American dominance. Equally important was Iranian resilience and its upper hand in the war with Iraq for most of the decade. As a result, uncertainty and indecision reigned for the most part and any clear-cut policy on the part of most actors proved elusive. Consequently, the intense rivalry in the area, involving both local and global powers, remained largely inconclusive up to the beginning of the 1990s.

In parallel, the events of 1979, coupled with the ostracism of Egypt in the wake of its separate peace with Israel, opened a new window of opportunity for Baghdad to try to champion the Arab cause. While, due to the lack of a global power's supremacy in the area, a favourable environment for the Arab sheikhs to actively pursue the issue of the three islands was still absent, the Iraqi government's domestic and regional priorities dictated anew the raising of most issues that it had had to shelve under Iran's *ancien régime*, including the issue of the three islands. Consequently, Baghdad resumed the function of being the most interested in and vocal on the islands, and spared no effort to revive the issue and use it as a tool to rally the Arabs, both governments and public opinion, around its anti-Iranian stance.

A subdued approach by the Arab sheikhs, due to uncertainty in the area and the absence of a global dominating power that could provide the least necessary protection, among other things, defeated Iraq's wide-ranging, though isolated, efforts at the beginning of the 1980s to place the issue of the three islands on the regional political agenda. Thus, except for few brief moments, the issue lay dormant throughout this period too.

The main purpose of this chapter is twofold: to review the overall situation in the Persian Gulf after the Islamic Revolution in Iran in 1979, in general, and the issue of the three islands, in particular, and to describe Iraq's attempts to revive the three islands issue and the reasons that these attempts ended in total failure.

Regional realignment

As the 1970s drew to a close, the Iranian Revolution, as well as other important events in the wider Middle East region, from the Horn of Africa to Afghanistan, ushered in a new era in the Persian Gulf. The success of the Islamic Revolution in bringing about the collapse of the millennia-old monarchy in Iran had a tremendous impact on the area. It dramatically upset the balance of power in the region by sweeping away, in one stroke, a pro-Western government in Iran, thereby costing the United States the main pillar it relied on to safeguard its interests in the Persian Gulf and the wider region. The hostage crisis in Tehran, unrest among Shi'ite minorities across the region, the seizure of the Grand Mosque in Mecca, which brought to light major challenges to another important US ally in the area, and the Soviet invasion of Afghanistan in the same year, which brought the Russians closer than ever to the Persian Gulf, all played their synergic roles in reshaping the region.

The Revolution replaced a pro-Western Iranian government with a new political establishment that displayed a clearly antagonistic approach towards the Israeli and Western interests in the region. It changed the situation in the Persian Gulf entirely by putting an end to Iran's cooperation with the United States and Israel and by disassociating Iran from ongoing actions against non-conformist elements in the region, including the radicals in Oman.

The collapse of the Shah's regime meant, therefore, the simultaneous collapse of the most important pillar of US foreign policy in the region. The Islamic Revolution in Iran resulted in the breakdown of the 'twin pillars' policy pursued by Washington, and the regional power structure underwent a major shift. The Revolution not only cost the United States the pillar it had relied upon since 1971 to safeguard its interests in the Persian Gulf, it also set Tehran and Washington on a collision course in the area for many ensuing years. Therefore, in sharp contrast to the policy pursued in 1971–79, when the Americans did whatever was in their power to enhance Iran's power and help upgrade its status in the region, soon after the Revolution the erosion of the foundations of the Iranian position in the Persian Gulf became a high priority on the American regional agenda.

At the same time, radical developments in Iran initiated a tumultuous period in the region characterized by the fear of regional states of the 'export' of the Iranian Revolution, through direct actions or indirectly by influencing the peoples of the region. Relevant developments such as the Iran–Iraq War, tensions and confrontations at the annual Hajj pilgrimage, and so forth, coupled with growing US presence in the region, which climaxed in 1991, profoundly affected the relationships among regional actors.

The collapse of the imperial regime in Iran gave rise to mixed feelings in Persian Gulf conservative circles. The rulers of the Arab littoral states had disliked the Shah and his dominance over the Persian Gulf, his arrogance and the way he looked down upon them; therefore they were pleased that the 'gendarme of the Gulf' was gone and that Iran's dominant position might be undermined down the road. At the same time, the overthrow of the Shah's pro-Western, monarchical regime seemed ominous in so far as its impact on certain segments of the population, Soviet policy in the area and the opening for a more assertive role by Iraq in the region were concerned. There are signs indicating that the common interests linking the Iranian and Arab monarchical regimes clearly outweighed their differences, to the extent that Saudi Crown Prince Fahd issued a statement, on 6 January 1979, expressing the Kingdom's support for the Shah's regime, which he described as based on 'legitimacy'.[1]

The new government in Tehran adopted policies that were a marked departure from those pursued by the defunct imperial regime. It soon decided, among other things, to pull out the 200 remaining Iranian troops from Oman, to withdraw from CENTO and to join the Non-Aligned Movement. It adopted a vocal pro-Arab and pro-Palestinian orientation, which, although formally welcomed by the conservative Persian Gulf regimes, at times embarrassed them.

The appointment of personal religious envoys to the Persian Gulf states by Imam Khomeini, the idea that the Revolution could be exported and media campaigns directed against some of the conservative Gulf regimes alarmed the Arab sheikhs. Informal Iranian support for dissident Islamic movements in the region, such as those in Bahrain and Saudi Arabia, irredentist comments by an Iranian religious dignitary on Bahrain and an allegedly Iranian-backed coup in the same country sent shock waves throughout the area.[2]

This seminal event in Iran and what followed it awoke the Arab rulers to their precarious situation and the peril presented by the Islamic and revolutionary message that seemed to be getting across in their societies. Unrest in the oil-rich, predominantly Shi'ite Hasa Eastern Province of Saudi Arabia, including the commemoration of Ashura in 1980 by reportedly 90,000, who defied the government ban, was a case in point. It led to the first Shi'ite uprising there, in which several Shi'ites and security personnel were killed and wounded and many others arrested.[3] Iran's combined attacks on monarchy as an un-Islamic institution and denunciation of the Gulf rulers as corrupt resonated widely on the lower coast of the Persian Gulf.

The Islamic Revolution in Iran, as an encouragement for religiously motivated and social-revolutionary forces throughout the Middle East, undermined the conservatives particularly in the Persian Gulf states. Its anti-American and anti-Western ideas and messages could, it was feared, easily find favour with the peoples on the opposite side of the Persian Gulf. Open ties with the West, previously perceived as a security guarantee, now became a handicap, as they could provoke internal opposition in an environment in which the new government in Tehran had immediately declared its solidarity not only with the Palestinians but also with 'liberation movements' in the area.

The Gulf states and the United States shared the fears of both Soviet intervention and the spread of what they termed Islamic fundamentalism. Based on their experience, another concern of the littoral states was military domination by Iran and the continuation of its supremacy, this time with an Islamic colour, bent on exporting its revolution – a concern that, under the new circumstances, the United States shared. The panic of the littoral Arab states over the Islamic Revolution and their search for both a global and a regional power to support them created opportunities for both the United States and Iraq.

Consequently, the conservative Arab states moved in two directions: on the one hand, they embraced the increasing US military presence in the area, and on the other, they rediscovered Iraq and tried to bolster it on the eve of its invasion of Iran and thereafter. In the meantime, what was of great importance was the fact that their position and their increasing support of Iraq stood in sharp contrast to that of the members of the Steadfastness Front (a conglomeration of Arab states opposed to the Israeli–Egyptian peace agreement) who shunned Iraq and its war effort against Iran. At the same time, given the paradoxical situation and deep mixed feelings, while trying to undermine Iran's standing in the area, they did their best not to antagonize it.

The cumulative effect of these developments made the Arab littorals fall back on Arabism and Arab collective security in order to check Iran's ideological onslaught. Availing itself of the new opportunity, Iraq very soon moved closer to the conservative sheikhs and monarchs and became the pace-setter of events. Thus, the Islamic Revolution served as catalyst for closer Iraqi–Saudi relations in particular and for closer Iraqi relations with the Persian Gulf states in general. Saddam Hussein spared no efforts to spread fear among the sheikhs, and indeed all Arab governments, of the 'export of revolution', and to muster support for his regional designs against Iran.

The growing relationship between Iraq and the Saudis manifested itself in Iraq's helping to defuse the Saudi–South Yemeni confrontation, curtailing of its relations with the Marxist government of South Yemen in 1979, cooperating with the Saudis in weaning the North Yemeni away from Soviet influence and establishing a united front of groups opposed to the Soviet-backed Marxist government of South Yemen.[4] Iraq also strongly criticized the Soviet invasion of Afghanistan, describing it as extremely worrisome to friends of the Soviet Union.

The *rapprochement* between Iraq and the conservative rulers was meant, among other things, to erode Iranian status in the Persian Gulf. This policy emerged from both a shared uneasiness with Iran's supremacy in the area and fears of the ideology associated with the Islamic Revolution.

The Iran–Iraq War further polarized matters. The Arab conservatives more or less helped Iraq in its war efforts. However, they were split into two groups. In general, Saudi Arabia, Kuwait and, to some extent, Bahrain actively supported

Iraq, as they feared the export of revolution and the spread of the war to their territories. Oman, UAE and Qatar were geographically farther distanced from the war fronts, and the UAE in particular had good trade relations with Iran, so these nations tried to appear to be neutral. As discussed later, Iranian relations with the latter group were more conciliatory.

There were persistent reports of Riyadh allowing Iraqi warplanes to use Saudi airspace and even its airbases. The Saudis also let their ports in the Red Sea and the Persian Gulf be used for military and civilian imports for Iraq, and they financed Iraq as well: by the end of 1981, Saudi lendings to Iraq amounted to $10 billion.[5] Kuwait too increasingly provided Iraq with financial and logistical aid, with 500 to 1,000 heavy trucks a day carting goods to Iraq. To its interest-free loan of $2 billion to Iraq in the autumn of 1980, it added two further sums of $2 billion each in April and December of 1981.[6]

Altogether, by 1983, the six Arab states had loaned Iraq around $24 billion. As the war progressed, these sums given grew accordingly. As a result, financial aid to the rest of the Arab world had to be reduced radically. Kuwait, for example, cut 39 per cent of its aid to Jordan, Syria and the PLO because of its budget deficit. The war in the Persian Gulf took precedence over the war with Israel, and by 1987 Kuwait had ceased to provide Syria – Iran's ally – with aid.[7]

Since the days of the conflict between Oman and Ras al-Khaimah in 1977 and the adventures of Sheikh Saqr, the most important differences between the Gulf Emirates have been in their policies towards Iran and Iraq. Abu Dhabi backed Iraq during the Iran–Iraq War, and strongly supported efforts to build-up the Gulf Cooperation Council. Dubai and Sharjah tried more to appear neutral during the best part of the Iran–Iraq War, and Dubai opposed efforts to create and strengthen a common military force, because this might have increased the influence of Abu Dhabi.

Qatar and the UAE maintained official silence on the Iran–Iraq hostilities. In the UAE's case, this was the result of differences among the seven constituent principalities: three were pro-Iranian, two pro-Iraqi and two non-partisan. The pro-Iraqi emirates of Abu Dhabi and Ras al-Khaimah had loaned Baghdad $1.3 billion by the end of 1981, with Qatar providing another $1 billion.[8]

Sharjah remained dependent on Iranian cooperation for its oil wealth. Dubai also has long had close ties to Iran and has a significant Shi'ite minority of Iranian origin. Dubai and, to a lesser extent, Sharjah, enjoyed a brisk and lively trade with Iran during most of the Iran–Iraq War. They were therefore loath to relinquish their neutrality in the war. Moreover, Sharjah had an agreement with Iran at the time regarding the oil resources of Abu Musa Island, providing another incentive to maintain good relations with Iran.[9]

Abu Dhabi did not necessarily share the same attitude. Sheikh Zayed, its ruler and the president of the UAE, was outspoken in his support of a pan-Arab stance towards the war, and thus favoured Iraq. Abu Dhabi was imprudent in publicizing its initial support of Iraq in the war. In November 1986, two missiles hit an offshore oilfield in Abu Dhabi; both Iraq and Iran denied having fired them.[10] Iran also needed to put political pressure on those states that acted against it by supporting Iraq in its war effort. Meanwhile, Oman had a particular interest in keeping the Persian Gulf open to international shipping through the Hormuz Strait.

Faced with the new situation in the region and deprived of the stability that had prevailed in the 1970s, Arab conservatives felt it imperative to formulate a new security concept for the Persian Gulf. The most tangible outcome of this reorientation was the effort undertaken to institutionalize regional cooperation by the constitution of the Gulf Cooperation Council (GCC). Trying to turn the instability into advantage and use it to expand their strategic perspective, the Saudis endeavoured to emerge as a major military actor in the region. The only way to achieve this objective was to spearhead the development of a regional security arrangement, whose military capabilities could be developed with the support of the United States. The Saudis hoped that eventually such an organization might serve as a deterrent against the manoeuvres of Iran. The GCC was established for that purpose.[11]

The GCC was said to seek to secure the Persian Gulf Arab countries' objectives of maintaining domestic stability and external security. In fact, the GCC was in many ways a direct response to the challenges of the day in the wider region as well, chief among them the creation of the radical Steadfastness Front, which consisted of Arab states opposing the Israeli–Egyptian peace; the weakening of the moderate camp due to Cairo's peace treaty with Israel; the disappearance of a moderate pro-Western regime in Iran; the Soviet invasion of Afghanistan; the Iran–Iraq War and, finally, threats from a powerful Israeli war machine that could, theoretically, attack any of these states at will without risking retribution or military response from a united Arab body.[12]

As a subregional organization, the GCC could call upon the West for military assistance in the event its members perceived internal or external threat to one or more of themselves. It was created at a time when the United States was in the process of rethinking its policies and bringing about radical changes in its involvement in the Persian Gulf. It was also a time when the Iranian Revolution had escalated the security-related fears of the Gulf states whose political orientations were analogous to those existing in Iran prior to the Revolution.

In the 1970s, despite several efforts, it had not been possible for a security framework to evolve among the Arab states around the Persian Gulf. Previous attempts to form a regional organization had failed owing to the rivalries among Iran, Iraq and Saudi Arabia. With Iran and Iraq engaged in a conflict and weakened, Saudi Arabia got its chance to lead the formation of the GCC. The exclusion of Iran from a regional security gathering in the Persian Gulf was a meaningful development and indicated an intention on the part of the founders of the new organization to embark upon a new, separate path. This stood in contrast to the efforts of the 1970s, when Iran together with the other six Gulf countries had endeavoured to reach an understanding on security arrangements in the Persian Gulf and Iraq had been the only odd party out. Despite the growing relationship between Iraq and the Six, the Iraqi Ba'athists were not invited to join this time either, a decision that signalled the degree of caution the lower Persian Gulf conservatives wanted to demonstrate.

Although the GCC pronounced itself against foreign presence in the Persian Gulf, the congruity between the real policies of the GCC states and the strategic objectives of the United States was manifest in a number of ways:

- First, the Arab littoral states and the United States both strongly favoured the current political status quo in the lower Persian Gulf.
- Second, both envisioned the GCC as a vehicle for promoting political stability and order in the region.
- Finally, GCC member states continued their heavy reliance on Western military equipment and on the use of Western military advisers to build their armed forces and military infrastructures.

With the liberation of Khorramshahr in May 1982 by Iran, the Arab littoral states adopted a more cautious stand. Following a GCC meeting in emergency session in Kuwait on 15 May, the UAE took the initiative to bring about peace between Iran and Iraq. Two weeks later, when the ministers met again in Saudi Arabia, they decided to renew their effort to bring an end to the war. Iraq, losing ground, expressed its readiness to halt the fighting.[13]

Renewed Iraqi interest in the three islands

With the Shah out of the scene, Baghdad soon returned to the hostile approach that had characterized the Iran–Iraq relationship during the years leading to the Algiers Agreement in 1975.

Iraq's national and regional ambitions

Several nearly simultaneous developments – the Islamic Revolution in Iran, the signing of the Camp David agreement between Egypt and Israel, and Saddam Hussein's assumption of the presidency in Iraq – set Baghdad on a new, adventurous track that affected the entire region in a dramatic way. The Iraqi government, a loner in inter-Arab affairs for the best part of the 1970s, now sought to be seen as a leader of 'the Arab nation'.

The Iraqi bid for Arab leadership was actually launched when Baghdad hosted the anti-Sadat Arab summit in November 1978. The Ba'ath Party now hoped to take advantage of the upheavals in Iran and on the Arab–Israeli scene that had wracked the Middle East from 1978 onward. Capitalizing on the impact of the Islamic Revolution on the Persian Gulf Arab states and the strained relations between Iran and those countries, Iraq renewed more vigorously its policy of projecting itself as the defender and guardian of Arabism in the Persian Gulf. Accordingly, and given the importance of territorial issues in the Middle East in bestowing legitimacy upon political leaders, Saddam found himself obliged to give territorial expression to his otherwise highly personalized claim to authority.

On behalf of Iraq, but perhaps especially on behalf of the restoration of his own prestige, Saddam –who himself had signed the Algiers Agreement, which regulated the Iran–Iraq border on land and through the Shatt al-Arab waterway – increasingly put forward claims focusing on the Shatt al-Arab, demanding that Iran recognize Iraq's full sovereignty over the entire river. Increasingly, therefore, there was a tangible, territorial concession to be wrung from Iran, if Saddam Hussein's credibility was to be maintained. Thus, he wanted public acknowledgement by Iran of Iraqi sovereignty over the entire Shatt al-Arab, with all the historical, political and regional resonance that such a concession would have with the region. This suggested a more offensive or active strategy than had hitherto been adopted by the Iraqi regime.

Based on such an observation, S. Chubin and C. Tripp refer to the Iran–Iraq War as a 'war for political gain through territorial concession.' As they maintain, 'war was the only feasible course for wringing the kinds of concessions from Iran that Saddam seemed to believe were not simply desirable but necessary.'[14]

Iraq initiated border provocations in March 1979 by violating Iranian airspace and conducting artillery attacks on the border town of Qasr-e Shirin, and such acts continued. In October that year, Iraq threatened to abrogate the 1975 Algiers accord. Constant border clashes occurred during the first half of 1980.[15]

At the same time, Saddam Hussein increasingly adopted the persona of champion of Iraq's rights and sovereignty, as well as the rights and sovereignty of the 'Arab nation'. This translated concretely into his demand, on behalf of the Arab nation, that Iran relinquish its title to Abu Musa and the Tunbs. It was also reflected in his championing of the 'cause' of the Arab inhabitants of the Iranian province of Khuzistan.

Moreover, Saddam Hussein did not confine himself to territorial claims. Declaring himself the champion of the Arab cause, he presented himself as the only Arab leader who could save the Arabs from Islamic Iran. In February and October 1979, Iraq offered to send troops to Bahrain and Kuwait to defend them in case of an Iranian attack. Vowing to defend the sovereignty of Bahrain and Kuwait, he stated that 'we will not allow anyone to harm the Arabism of the Gulf or its land and people.'[16] He added that 'the Iranians know perfectly well that they cannot reach Abu Dhabi before they have broken down the great barrier of Iraq. Abu Dhabi seems to know this too, and is reassured by this fact.'[17]

Saddam clearly aimed to emerge from such a triumph as the new guardian of the 'Arabian Gulf' and the leader of the pan-Arab movement. That ambition was not unwelcome to rulers of Persian Gulf sheikhdoms, who felt that their political survival was threatened by Iran's Islamic Revolution.

The revival of Iraq's interest in the three islands

The sudden upsurge in Iraq's interest in the three islands was also well timed to exploit the constant fears of the Arab Persian Gulf states that the religion-inspired turmoil on the opposite shores might spill across the waters to theirs. As later events demonstrated, the Iraqi leadership believed that if it could take advantage of these fears to slip down and seize the three islands, it would emerge considerably stronger in the area, not only militarily but also politically. Accordingly, the

Iraqi government invariably singled out the issue of the three islands as a litmus test of Iran's new pro-Arab credentials and consistently argued that the return of the islands should be a prerequisite for harmonious Arab–Iranian relations.[18]

While Iran was undergoing a tumultuous period after the victory of the Islamic Revolution and the details of its foreign policy were yet to be worked out, the Iraqi government, as early as June 1979 – around four months after the Revolution – began claiming the three islands for 'the Arabs.' The two Iraqi government newspapers, *Al-Thawrah* – the government-run paper – and *Al-Jumhuriyah* – the Ba'ath Party-run paper – raised this issue while attacking what they termed as 'Iran's hostile policies in the Arab Gulf.' Under the headline 'the Tehran authorities follow the steps of the deposed Shah,' *Ath-Thawrah* wrote, 'The provocative statements made by a number of Iranian officials against several Arab countries and the Gulf area call to mind the picture which prevailed during the Shah's rule.' The paper added that the threats during the Shah's rule took the form of direct intervention against the revolution in Oman, 'the occupation of the Arab islands – Greater Tunb, Lesser Tunb and Abu Musa' – and then the organized immigration of Iranians to all parts of the Gulf, the aim of which was to implement a scheme to make the Gulf area Persian. *Al-Jumhuriyah* stated that the Tehran authorities were behaving towards 'the Arab Gulf area in a haughtier and more cunning, conspiratorial and dangerous manner than in the past.'[19]

Tariq Aziz, a member of Iraq's Revolution Command Council and the deputy prime minister, was the first Iraqi official that broached the issue of the three islands. He stated in August 1979 that Iraq would like to stress one central issue, namely 'the Arabism of the Gulf and the need to keep the Gulf area from any kind of foreign influence.' He added that Iraq wanted the area to be completely independent of imperialist and colonial influence. Aziz also said that Iraq considered the three islands 'to be Arab' and believed that 'a friend should deal with the Arab nation from the position of friendship in every way and on all levels.'[20]

On 3 November 1979, Iraq first formally demanded the revision of the Algiers Agreement of 1975. Iraq also said that 'Iran must give up three Gulf islands and provide self-rule for Iran's Arab, Kurdish and Baluch minorities.' Iraq's ambassador to Lebanon, Abdul-Hussein Moslem Hassan, in his interview with *An-Nahar* on 3 November 1979, said the improvement of relations between Iran and Iraq depended on the realization of the following conditions:

- Revision of the 1975 Algiers Agreement with regard to Shatt al-Arab;
- Granting of autonomy to Kurd, Baluchi and Arab minorities in Iran;
- Withdrawal of the Iranian armed forces from the Tunb and Abu Musa islands.[21]

The spokesman for the Iranian Foreign Ministry reacted to the Iraqi ambassador's statement by condemning it and rejecting the three conditions.[22]

Ratcheting up the controversy, the next Iraqi move was to raise the issue at the United Nations. Iraq's foreign minister, in a letter to the UN Secretary-General, demanded an immediate Iranian withdrawal from the three islands, the official

Iraqi news agency reported on 6 April 1980.[23] This letter could have been intended to precede an attempt by Iraq to attack and occupy the three islands, as described later.

In a speech on 15 April 1980, Saddam Hussein recounted his talks with Iran's foreign minister, Ibrahim Yazdi, held on the margins of the meeting of the Non-Aligned Movement in Havana in 1979, saying:

> I said to him: first you have behaved badly towards us and you should stop this immediately. He replied: What more? I said: The three Arab islands of Greater Tunb, Lesser Tunb and Abu Musa are Arab and should be returned to their owners [prolonged cheers]. He said: What more? I replied: An agreement between us was concluded under special circumstances in 1975 in which you unjustly took a part of Shatt al-Arab. That must be returned to Iraq [cheers]. I said: Another point is that you must behave properly towards the Iranian peoples. This is our advice to you. You must behave properly towards your peoples. In order to deal correctly with your peoples you must respect their national rights. You must know that those who are in Arabistan [Khuzistan] are Arabs, and the blood in their veins is Arab [prolonged cheers].[24]

According to the Iranian sources, the Iranian foreign minister meeting Saddam in Havana proposed to the Iraqi side 'to cooperate to implement the protocol concerning frontier security, good neighbourly relations, commercial, technical, and economic dealings, pilgrimage tours, and the security of the Persian Gulf.'[25]

Pointing out that 'there was no difference between the Shah's regime and the present Persian regime', Iraq's ambassador to the Soviet Union, Abd ar-Rahman Ahmad ad-Duri, said that Iran 'should have ended the past commitments and returned the three Arab islands to the Arab nation.'[26]

In June 1980, Saddam said in a speech: 'we now have the military strength to take back the three islands in the Persian Gulf occupied by the Shah. We have never remained silent since the occupation of these three islands and have constantly prepared ourselves militarily and economically to recapture them.'[27]

At the same time, various visits between Saddam and Kuwaiti and Saudi officials took place in May and August 1980 and further contacts were pursued with Oman and Ras al-Khaimah in order to build an anti-Iranian axis.[28]

A plan to attack and seize the three islands

Evidence and recurring reports suggest that Iraq in its obsession with the issue of the three islands went so far as planning to invade and occupy them. According to a Middle East News Agency dispatch dated 5 December 1979, the weekly magazine *Akhir Sa'ah* reported from Cairo, quoting Palestinian sources, that the recent sudden visit of Yasir Arafat, PLO Executive Committee Chairman, to Baghdad stopped an 'Iraqi military operation aimed at invading and forcibly occupying three islands in the Gulf which Iran is now occupying.' The magazine said that the PLO representative in Tehran had told Arafat that Iraq was likely to invade the three islands – the Lesser and Greater Tunbs and Abu Musa. Arafat quickly contacted Iraq and then left for Baghdad 'to convince Saddam Hussein not to invade the three islands and, thus, avoid an armed confrontation with Khomeini.'[29]

Other sources credited Western intelligence services with uncovering and foiling the plot with a view to avoiding the spread of the conflict and deflecting the threat against the flow of oil through the Strait of Hormuz. Based on these sources, it was reported from Washington on 3 October 1980 that diplomatic pressure by the United States, Britain and some Persian Gulf countries had prevented the use of Omani territory by Iraqi planes and troops for attacks against the islands of Abu Musa and the Greater and Lesser Tunbs. Intelligence reports were said to have been received on 28 September indicating that Iraq had sent troop-carrying helicopters and planes to Oman and had been asking the Omanis for permission to use their territory to carry out the assault.

It was feared that an Iraqi attack would widen the war by provoking retaliatory Iranian action against Oman as well as against Saudi Arabia and Kuwait and might result in the closing of the Strait of Hormuz to oil shipments.[30]

According to Dilip Hiro, 'When British intelligence in Oman discovered that Iraq had assembled helicopters and troops in Oman to carry out the plan, the British and American governments pressured the Omani Ruler, Sultan Qaboos bin Said, to scuttle the Iraqi plan. Later, Saudi Arabia persuaded Iraq to abandon the idea of retaking the islands in the Gulf.'[31] This action, reportedly taken by the Western governments and supported by the Saudis, if accurate, aimed at keeping the war localized, maintaining the flow of oil through the strait and preventing the conflict from affecting the whole Persian Gulf, including by putting navigation through the Strait of Hormuz in jeopardy.

John Duke Anthony, too, refers to 'Western diplomatic intervention during the early stage of the war' resulting in 'Iraq's curtailing its earlier intentions to wrest control from Iran of the three disputed islands'.[32]

According to Anthony H. Cordesman, the start of the Iran–Iraq War 'was accompanied by the covert efforts of several of the southern Gulf states to use the Iraqi attack to reclaim the Tunbs and Abu Musa'.[33] Elsewhere in the same book he says that the new situation 'led Bahrain, the UAE, and Oman to initially support Iraq's plan to attack the Iranian-held Tunbs and Abu Musa islands'.[34]

In reality, Iran was so busy with its domestic post-revolutionary situation that did not have much time to pay attention to what was going on in the region. Even the Iraqi invasion on 22 September 1980, launched after one and a half years of border skirmishes and troop movements along their common borders, had taken Iranian officials by surprise.

Raising the issue at the United Nations

Sadoon Hammadi, the Minister for Foreign Affairs of Iraq, in a letter dated 29 April 1980 to the UN Secretary-General, stated that '[t]he Government of the Republic of Iraq would like to emphasize its non-recognition of Iran's illegal occupation of the three Arab islands (Greater Tunb, Lesser Tunb and Abu Musa) and the consequences that may ensue from such occupation, and demands the immediate withdrawal of Iran from those islands'. In the first paragraph of the letter, the Iraqi official refers to a statement made in an interview by the Iranian president, A. H. Bani Sadr, in which he said that 'Iran would not forgo or restore the three Arab islands and that Arab states (Abu Dhabi, Qatar, Oman, Dubai, Kuwait, and Saudi Arabia) are not independent States'.[35]

It is important to note that, after the letter of 17 July 1972 (S/10740) by the representatives of several Arab governments about the three islands, this was the first statement about the islands circulated as a document of the Security Council. It is important as well to note that in this letter the islands are twice referred to as 'the three Arab islands' and no mention of any particular title-holder is made.

Reacting to the Iranian foreign minister's response[36] to the letter from Iraq's foreign minister, the permanent representative of Iraq wrote another letter, dated 19 August 1980 and addressed to the UN Secretary-General, in which he indulged in legal argument in a bid to prove the 'Arab' title to the three islands. He states in the letter that

> at no time in history has any of the three islands been subjected to Iranian rule. The true fact is that the British did not occupy the said islands separately, they occupied Ras al-Khaimah in 1819 when they defeated the Kawassims. The three islands comprised part of the territory of Ras al-Khaimah since 1750 and they remained so without any interruption.

Rejecting the Iranian arguments, he then argued about the inadmissibility of maps as evidence of the title in territorial and boundary disputes and 'the inability of the Iranian representative to prove that the islands were in fact historically part of Iran in the meeting of the Security Council held in December 1971 upon the request of Iraq.' He also likened the Iranian statement to that of the representative of Iran 'when it was under the rule of the Shah'.[37]

Iraq also raised the issue of the three islands during the general debate in the UN General Assembly on 3 October 1980. Referring to the two letters discussed above, Foreign Minister Saadon Hemadi of Iraq said in his statement:

> If the ruling authorities in Iran do not really intend to expand at the expense of Arab national interests and if they honestly stand for the defense of those interests against the Zionist enemy, then we are entitled to wonder about the reasons for their retention of the three Arab islands, Abu Moussa, the Greater Tunb and the Lesser Tunb, which Iran occupied in the time of the Shah.[38]

Iraq's statement in terms of its reference to the issue of the three islands contrasted with the statement of the UAE in the same general debate during the same session of the UN General Assembly, which made no reference to this issue.[39]

It is interesting that, at a time when Iraq's war efforts were floundering, the same Iraqi foreign minister in the general debate of the UN General Assembly in 1981 did not mention the three islands. He did come close to the issue and accused 'the successive regimes of the Persian state' of having 'pursued a policy of expansion ... particularly in the Arab Gulf region,' but he did not refer specifically to the three islands.[40]

In general, during the first phase of the war, when the Iraqi army was on the offensive, Iraq held to its conditions for ending the fighting, which, as a spokesman for the Iraqi government said on 23 September 1981, included the return to Iraq of the three islands. He pointed out that the three islands 'which were occupied by Iranian troops nine years ago – must be turned over to Iraq.'[41]

Shelving the issue

When the first phase of the war, in which the Iraqi army was on the offensive, came to an end and Iraq began retreating on all fronts, Iraqi officials chose to abandon every reference to the three islands altogether. In fact, they gave up on all preconditions for ending the fighting, including that relating to the Shatt al-Arab waterway, which they had set out in the period 1980–81. Actually, this was the last period when Iraq formally raised the issue of the three islands. Not even in his extensive letter addressed to the Iranian president on 14 August 1990, in which he signalled Iraq's readiness to negotiate a border and territorial settlement with Iran on the basis of the Algiers Accord of 1975, did Saddam raise the issue.

During the years 1979 and 1980 when Baghdad aggressively pursued the issue, Iraqi officials were clear on one point: the three islands did not belong to Iran. However, they left ambiguous the question as to whom they did belong. At a news conference in September 1980, the Iraqi defence minister said that what he referred to as 'the Arab islands' near the entrance to the Persian Gulf were seized by the Shah in 1971. 'Before that time and throughout history, the inhabitants were Arab and they fell within the Arab region,' he said. 'Iraq is quite clear who they belong to.'[42] As the preceding references demonstrate, Iraq never claimed the three islands for the UAE. The Iraqi media, as referred to earlier and later, were also ambiguous as to whom the three islands belonged. They usually demanded the return of the islands to 'their legitimate owners.' The scheme, referred to earlier, to attack and seize the islands is also important in this context. It would be difficult to assume that Saddam Hussein intended to seize the islands and hand them over to the UAE.

This ambiguity gave rise to speculation as to what Baghdad was up to. Some observers did not rule out the possibility that Baghdad was contemplating bringing the three islands under its direct control in a quest to imposing its leadership over the Persian Gulf as a prelude to fulfilling its dream of assuming the leadership of the Arab world. With this in mind, John Kifner of the *New York Times* wrote:

> It would be shortsighted to treat the war as a limited crisis. Iraq's proclaimed intention to liberate the strategically situated islands of Abu Musa and the two Tunbs is dangerously ambiguous. Iraq has no legitimate or historical claim to them... Iraq either intends to take the islands as spoils of war or restore them to their former owners ... Either step would dramatically demonstrate

Iraq's domination of the Gulf and provide a pretext for Iraq to establish itself as guardian of the strait. More dangerous are Iraq's past claims to the whole of Kuwait. They were asserted in 1961, dropped in 1963, reasserted in 1973 in more-limited form as claims to Kuwaiti territory close to Iraq's Gulf port of Umm Qasr and to the Kuwaiti offshore islands of Bubiyan and Warbah. Any Iraqi seizure of Kuwaiti territory could threaten the integrity of other Gulf States.[43]

Why did Iraq's attempts fail?

As described above, Iraq spent a great deal of political capital in 1979 and 1980 reactivating the issue of the three islands. However, its attempts to seize them or even put the issue on the agenda of regional actors failed badly. The schism in the ranks of the Arab governments, in which the Arab radicals, still powerful, supported Iran, on the one hand, and the UAE was reluctant to pursue the issue, on the other, were two immediate reasons for Iraq's failure. Nonetheless, the underlying cause lay elsewhere. Regional autonomy proved its resilience in the 1980s, and, given the upper hand that Iran enjoyed in the war with Iraq and the lingering impact of the Arab–Israeli conflict on the Persian Gulf region, the United States, as a global power, could not prevail in the area. Thus, without a global power hostile to Iran dominating the Persian Gulf, the requirements for the revival of the three islands issue were yet to be developed.

The Persian Gulf autonomy strained but enduring

In the transitional period, the United States tried but failed to impose its hegemony over the Persian Gulf. Thus, in this period the area continued to be mainly autonomous and free from the decisive influence of a global power. This autonomy was an important characteristic that helped result in the dormancy of the issue of the three islands and the inaction of the sheikhdoms thereon, as in the 1970s.

Nonetheless, the way that local and global actors reacted to the ground-breaking events of 1979 and ensuing years set a trend in motion that gradually chipped away at the regional autonomy of the Persian Gulf achieved in the early 1970s. Although these events initiated developments that led to the US claim of ascendancy in the area in the wake of dislodging Iraq from Kuwait in 1991, in the 1980s, for reasons referred to later, Gulf autonomy endured.

The same trend affected in a negative way Iranian predominance in the Persian Gulf, which had been gradually secured in the aftermath of the British withdrawal from east of Suez in 1971. However, it failed to affect the Iranian status in a decisive way in the 1980s. Thus, Iraq remained the only party to challenge the Iranian title to the three islands in the opening phase of this transitional period. Only new power realignments in the region in the early 1990s enabled the UAE and some others to enter into the fray.

The establishment of the Islamic Republic in Iran, the hostage crisis, the seizure of the Grand Mosque in Mecca and, more importantly, the Soviet invasion of

Afghanistan later in the same year, which brought the Russians closer than ever to the Persian Gulf, caused the United States to search seriously for an alternative to the 'Twin Pillar' policy. The events in the 1970s in the Persian Gulf and the wider area had already reminded policy-makers in Washington of the centrality of the wider region to the interests of the United States. The Arab–Israeli War of 1973, the subsequent Arab oil embargo against the West and these events of the late 1970s demonstrated the importance of the Persian Gulf for American interests.

Therefore, after the severe blow dealt to its strategic position stemming from the ouster of the Shah, the American leadership decided that it needed to show determination in salvaging the remainder of the status quo in the Persian Gulf and preventing the total collapse of its credibility in the eyes of the Arab littoral states through committing itself to the use of its military might, if necessary.

With the Nixon doctrine, which relied on indigenous forces to respond to regional threats, becoming obsolete, and finding itself unable to respond to the double threats emanating from the ouster of the Shah and the Soviet invasion of Afghanistan, Washington turned to the establishment of the Rapid Deployment Force in 1979 and the announcement of the Carter doctrine in January 1980. These were two major steps towards an emerging new policy that was meant to be based essentially on direct US intervention in the region – a policy that ran counter to the autonomy of the region from global powers and inherently endangered Iranian regional ascendancy.

The formation of a quick-response combat force to be airlifted into the region as well as the *maintaining* of a continuously upgraded naval presence in the Arabian Sea and northwest Indian Ocean 'to satisfy Saudi desires for a US presence "over the horizon," out of Arab sight except in an emergency' were publicly discussed at least since June 1979.[44] On 5 December that year, before the Soviet invasion of Afghanistan, US Marine commanders disclosed that they had been ordered to organize a 50,000-man spearhead for President Carter's Rapid Deployment Force.[45]

Four weeks after the Soviet invasion of Afghanistan, President Carter announced, in his State of the Union address on 23 January 1980, a doctrine that amounted to a unilateral extension of NATO alliance to cover the Persian Gulf. The Carter doctrine proclaimed: 'An attempt by any outside force to gain control of the Persian Gulf region will be regarded as an assault on the vital interests of the United States of America. And such an assault will be repelled by any means necessary, including military force.' He explained that the 'grave threat' to the Persian Gulf security had to be met by 'collective efforts' and 'consultation and close co-operation with countries in the region'.[46] The striking similarity between the Carter doctrine and the policy set out by the British foreign minister in 1903 for the same area, as discussed in Chapter 2, should not escape notice.

At the same time, though absent from Carter's statement, the control and curtailment of oil supplies, not only by an outsider but also by a belligerent insider such as revolutionary Iran, were being actively discussed as foreign policy measures within and outside the administration.[47] The new US policy also declared the Persian Gulf vital to America's national security and committed itself to keep it open. Its other objective, though unstated, was to shield Saudi Arabia and other conservative Arab states in the region against the possible effects of the Islamic Revolution on the opposite shores of the Persian Gulf.

Although the Carter doctrine was announced in the wake of the Soviet invasion of Afghanistan, it was clear that the US administration meant to send a warning to Iran, cautioning it against attempts that might be interpreted as exporting its revolution to the other part of the Persian Gulf and threatening retaliatory American action to back up its message.

To secure these goals, President Carter set up a special joint task force, namely the Rapid Deployment Joint Task Force, which was put into operation on 1 March 1980 and tasked with, as its commanding general put it, being prepared to 'send troops to the oil-rich Persian Gulf within hours' in order to 'help deter Soviet aggression and protect petroleum supplies for the West'.[48] The Rapid Deployment Force evolved later into a separate command analogous to those in Europe, Asia and Latin America, and after 1 January 1982 was renamed the US Central Command, or CENTCOM. The RDJTF and CENTCOM aimed to militarily bind various Gulf countries in a US-centred order.

However, these efforts lacked credibility as they were not accompanied by the presence of reliable allies in the area or permanent American bases in the Persian Gulf. Pentagon officials conceded that it would take two weeks to move 25,000 troops with light tanks into the area and that six months would be required to put into action a force of 100,000 men supported by heavy tanks and other major weapons. Therefore, once CENTCOM was in place, the United States embarked on a long path to secure permanent bases in the lower Persian Gulf – an effort that proved complicated and unfruitful, due to the unwavering support of the United States for the Israeli policies in the region, up till Iraq's invasion of Kuwait.

Nonetheless, the Carter doctrine and CENTCOM, as such, represented a major policy shift and were the first actions to set in motion a series of activities by a global power since the British withdrawal from the area. This policy direction culminated later in the establishment of a strong American presence in the Persian Gulf and in the United States seeking a position of dominance in the 1990s and beyond. Later confirmed by the Reagan administration, the Carter doctrine and CENTCOM formed the basis of US policy in the area up to Iraq's invasion of Kuwait.

The outbreak of the Iran–Iraq War on 22 September 1980 enabled the American government to enter into the second phase of enhancing its military presence on the ground. A US military build-up in the Persian Gulf region had been under way already before the war. US aircraft carriers and Marine detachments were dispatched to the Arabian Sea from their traditional patrolling areas in Europe and Asia. Seven ships loaded with tanks and ammunition had been positioned in the Indian Ocean as floating warehouses should more troops be dispatched in an emergency. Defense Secretary Harold Brown had announced that the United States would have to spend $20 billion to $25 billion over the following five years to build a much more credible rapid deployment force for such troublespots as the Indian Ocean and the Persian Gulf region.[49]

Washington, in effect, announced that it had assumed responsibility for ensuring the continued flow of vital Persian Gulf oil and deterring attacks on other Persian Gulf states. Within a fortnight of the outbreak of Iraq's invasion of Iran, the Carter administration had dispatched four Airborne and Warning Control System (AWACS) to Saudi Arabia, with a supporting contingent of several hundred servicemen, and had strengthened Saudi Arabia's air defences with a mobile, ground-radar station, communications equipment and roughly 100 airmen.[50] It further pledged to honour 'requests for assistance from non-belligerent friends in the area who feel threatened by the conflict.' Deputy Secretary of State Warren Christopher stated in a major policy speech on 7 October 1980, three weeks into the Iran–Iraq War, that 'the United States has vital interests at stake in the Persian Gulf region, [and] we will defend them.' He said those nations 'deserve our help, when they ask for it, in deterring the possibility of unprovoked attack.'[51]

US envoys in such Gulf states as Kuwait, Oman and the United Arab Emirates had informed the leaders there of the US readiness to provide them with protection, using the four radar planes in Saudi Arabia and other defensive equipment, against any Iranian air attack, State Department officials said.[52] These moves unfolded against the background of an unprecedented deployment of American naval and air power in the region. Then operating in the northern Arabian Sea were two carrier battle groups comprising 37 warships. These forces were built around two carriers that could launch approximately 160 combat aircraft. US Defense Secretary Harold Brown described the armada as 'the most powerful concentration of naval forces, including naval air forces, that have ever been in that area.' And, he added, 'We have more capability than all the other countries in the region combined.'[53]

In February 1982, the US Defense Secretary obtained Riyadh's agreement to form a joint Saudi–US military committee, something the Saudis had refused to do in the past. The reaction by anti-American elements in the Arab world to this move demonstrated the obstacles in the way of US military cooperation with moderate Arab states and how far the United States still was from its objective of acquiring permanent military base rights in the region in the 1980s. A top-ranking PLO leader, Salah Khalaf (Abu Iyad), denounced the Saudi–US accord as a cover for establishing a foreign base in an Arab country and expressed concern that other Gulf states would soon follow suit, asserting that '[t]his move may benefit the Americans but it most certainly will not serve Saudi interests.'[54]

Against this background, the Pentagon issued a secret directive in March 1982 that widened the scope of American military involvement in the Persian Gulf. It stated: 'What ever the circumstances, we should be prepared to introduce American forces into the region should it appear [that our] security of access to the Persian Gulf oil is threatened.'[55]

However, without fixed military base rights in the Persian Gulf, the US presence on the ground was considered to be neither reliable nor sustainable. Overextension and awkwardness of supply lines and the difficulty of securing base rights in a region simultaneously both dependent on and antagonistic towards the United States, among other factors, hindered CENTCOM and its predecessor, the Rapid

Defense Force. At a time when Soviet aircraft were a mere two to three hours' flying time away from Aden, Socotra, Baku or Afghanistan, and the Iranian navy was present in the Gulf, the United States, by contrast, needed between fourteen and seventeen hours to arrive from the US mainland. The US geopolitical predicament was exacerbated at a time when no Arab state, Egypt included, appeared inclined to accede to a US request for bases.

At the same time, US fervour was quite real. At the Senate Foreign Relations Committee hearing on 6 and 7 February 1980 concerning the issue of US bases in the region, an expert from the Center for Strategic Studies declared, 'The process of disintegration of the Arab tribal states in the Persian Gulf is well advanced: the Saudi Arabian government may have only a few months of life left unless we make serious moves to shore it up'.[56]

Nonetheless, the results of the US efforts to secure military base rights in the Persian Gulf remained minimal mainly until after the invasion of Kuwait by Iraq. The uneasy relationship between the Arab littoral states and the United States was one of the reasons making the Arab rulers hesitant on the issue of the base rights. Confidence in Washington's reliability was low because of its growing strategic cooperation with Israel. This was further aggravated by simultaneous events in the Arab world in connection with the Arab–Israeli conflict – the Camp David agreements – which led to further splits among the Arab states. The consistent American position vis-à-vis the Arab–Israeli conflict put serious strains on the relations between the United States and the so-called moderate Arab Persian Gulf states, which – with the notable exception of Oman – condemned the Camp David peace process.

In the 1980s, Oman, the one Persian Gulf state to have participated in joint manoeuvres with the United States, agreed to permit that country limited use of an airfield and conditional access to three other airbases. Bases with the most necessary requirements, such as exclusivity of access and jurisdiction, however, have remained elusive.

Although the Americans made huge progress in enhancing their military presence in the Persian Gulf, the littoral Arab countries remained reluctant in the 1980s to enter into a close military relationship with the Americans and to provide them with the possibility of using their territories for military purposes. Three main reasons can be given to explain such reluctance:

- First, the considerable friction between the United States and Arab countries, in general, on the issues pertaining to the Palestinian question, including the status of Jerusalem. Too close a US embrace of any Persian Gulf state could become especially problematic in terms of the domestic legitimacy and regional political acceptability of the country concerned. Earlier, in this respect, reference was made, as an example, to the strong reaction by the PLO against a joint Saudi–US military committee. Moreover, the Palestinian communities living in the Arab littoral states and their grievances stemming from the strategic alliance between Washington and Tel Aviv had a strength that could not be overlooked. Four US experts back from a trip to the Persian

Gulf in January 1980 concluded that 'there was general agreement among Gulf leaders that the US strategic alliance with Israel is a much greater danger to the area than possible Soviet aggression.'[57] Consequently, the attitude of the Arab Persian Gulf rulers toward US military aid was summed up this way: 'They want you as a friend in the closet or behind the curtain.'[58]

- Second, the dynamism created by the Islamic Revolution in the region and its inspirational impact on existing and emerging social and political forces. Moreover, given the degree of animosity between Iran and the United States in the 1980s and the balance of power at the local and global levels, the regional countries needed to think twice before making any decision on granting military base rights to the United States.
- Third, superpower rivalry. There was an understanding among Persian Gulf countries that they needed to refrain from any act that might provoke the spread of superpower competition to the Gulf.

Under such circumstances, the serious efforts aimed at fully re-establishing the dominance of a global power in the Persian Gulf and bringing the regional autonomy, achieved after the withdrawal of the British, to an end led nowhere in the 1980s. As we will see in Chapter 5, only Iraq's invasion of Kuwait in 1990 provided the Arab littoral states with convenient justification to embrace the dramatic US military build-up in the Persian Gulf by, *inter alia*, granting full military base rights to the Americans. Consequently, the full resumption of the Arab claim to the three islands needed to wait until after the perceived establishment of American hegemony in the area after 1991, as had been the case during colonial rule.

Disarray in the Arab camp

The realignment of forces at the regional level, brought about in part by the collapse of the Iranian imperial government, and the desertion of Iraq by Arab radicals, who for the first time began ignoring its call on many issues, including the three islands, were the most important reasons leading to Iraq's failure to bring the UAE on board and place the islands issue on the Arab agenda.

As discussed in Chapter 3, before the Islamic Revolution Arab nationalists and radicals tended to regard Iran as a thorn in their side and, conversely, Arab moderates and conservatives looked to it as a force for stability. While the opposition of the Arab radicals to the Pahlavi regime was categorical, the Arab moderates and conservatives identified themselves with imperial Iran's general game plan, executive strategies and strategic outlook, although they were never fully convinced of the innocence of the Shah's regional aims. As A. Ehteshami has observed, 'the legacies of that era have continued to haunt Arab policies as well as the Arab–Iranian relationships that have taken shape since the overthrow of the institution of monarchy in Iran in 1979.'[59]

Despite the unity of the Arab states in the face of Egypt's separate peace agreement with Israel, the strong and modern military forces of Iran under the Shah and of Egypt and Israel far outweighed those of any combination of Arab armies.

The Iranian Revolution and other events helped upset the balance between the conservative-moderate camp, on the one hand, and the Arab radicals, on the other, and inevitably led to a realignment of forces in the already fragmented Arab world. Had it not been for the Islamic Revolution, Iran's close relations with Egypt and Israel in the preceding years could have dramatically changed the situation in the Middle East in favour of Israel and the West and undermined the Palestinian cause and its radical Arab allies. Arafat clearly had this in mind when he said that 'the Iranian revolution has turned the power balance in the Mideast upside down.'[60] It opened up prospects for militancy for several decades that positively affected the Palestinian as well as the Arab radicals' cause.

The rejectionist Arab camp – Algeria, Iraq, Libya, South Yemen, Syria and the PLO – formed the United Steadfastness Front, which opposed Egypt's separate peace with Israel. The moderate-conservative Arab states that either would not or could not take a more active role in undermining the Camp David Accords stood outside of this group. Iran's entry into the fray on the side of the rejectionists served to weaken the conservative-moderate camp. This served as an additional element of tension in the relations between Iran, under its new government, and the Arab moderate-conservative camp, which already felt unease over the side effects of the Revolution and its militant Islamic ideology on their political systems. Therefore, a combination of these elements set the two sides on different, contradictory tracks right from the beginning.

The political muscle Iraq was building up in the Persian Gulf – through its security agreement with the Saudis as well as through other means – was balanced by setbacks in its relationship with the radical Arab states. Its relations with neighbouring Syria remained strained, and Syria's allies in Steadfastness Front, Algeria and Libya, openly snubbed Iraq by refusing to participate in a much-vaunted 'Arab popular conference' in Baghdad in early April 1980. Algeria's president Chadli Benjedid even turned down an invitation from Iraq's president Saddam Hussein to co-chair the conference.[61]

With Iraq's invasion of Iran, the split among Arab nations followed bizarre lines. Jordan's moderate and pro-American King Hussein was the first to declare unequivocal support for the radical, hard-line Iraqi regime. He was motivated by his hatred for the Islamic Revolution and its anti-monarchical message as well as by his desire to repay Baghdad for its financial aid. On the other hand, as the war progressed, a number of radical Arab and Soviet-supported states, already at the forefront of struggling against the imperial Iranian government and backing heretofore-considered radical Iraq, extended various forms of support to Iran. The government-run Syrian newspaper *Al Ba'ath* described Saddam Hussein as a 'pervert' and 'an agent of imperialism and reaction who wants to play the role of the shah' as the predominant power in the Persian Gulf. It continued, 'The purpose of the war is very clear. It is to divert attention from the main struggle with Israel and give the United States and Zionist forces the alibi to interfere in the Gulf region with the blessing of Arab reactionary regimes.'[62]

The Syrians airlifted Soviet-made arms and ammunition to Iran and provided Tehran with intelligence on Iraq; Syrian airplanes also repeatedly violated Iraqi airspace in order to divert Iraqi air forces. Syria–Iran bilateral ties developed to include an arms deal, a ten-year trade pact and the bartering of oil for cash and goods, which led to the closure of the Iraqi pipelines passing through Syria on 10 April 1982.

Libya was another Arab country that airlifted Soviet-made weapons to Iran in October 1980 and declared its support for Iran in the war with Iraq. The Libyan leader said that he saw the hand of the United States in the Iraqi invasion.[63] In messages sent to King Khalid of Saudi Arabia and other rulers of Persian Gulf Arab riparian countries, Colonel Muammar el-Qaddafi, the Libyan leader, said it was their 'Islamic duty' to align themselves with the Muslims of Iran. The Libyan announcement came amid increasing reports that both Libya and Syria had been airlifting military supplies to Tehran. Colonel Qaddafi also demanded that King Khalid evict from Saudi Arabia the four AWACS the United States has stationed there.

At the same time, Iraq decided to break relations with Syria, Libya and North Korea.[64] The position of the other members of the Steadfastness Front ranged from mildly supportive of Iran to more neutral and meditative. Their support of Iran, which contrasted with the support of Iraq by the Arab moderate-conservative alliance, had the side effect of weakening Iraq's portrayal of the war as an ethnic and nationalist conflict pitting Persians against Arabs.

Saddam classified Arab states as pro-Iraqi, neutral or traitor. In the first category came first Jordan and, to a lesser extent, North Yemen and Morocco. He was so incensed with the 'traitors' and 'opportunists' of the states of Syria and Libya that he severed diplomatic ties with them in October 1980. To a lesser extent, he was unhappy with Algeria and South Yemen for maintaining cordial relations with Tehran. He did not name the neutral countries. Despite the generous material and logistical aid he received form Saudi Arabia and Kuwait, he described their contributions as 'much less than what duty dictates.'[65]

Iraq's need for various kinds of assistance from the West and for the financial and logistical support of Arab oil-producing countries was, among other things, responsible for eroding Baghdad's alignment with the rejectionist Arab camp. The Friendship Treaty with the Soviets already became dormant, since they had both disregarded one of its most important clauses – the obligation of one signatory to inform and consult with the other in advance of any military action – when the Soviets invaded Afghanistan and Iraq invaded Iran.[66]

Despite the widespread public image in the United States of the Baghdad regime as one that continued to harbour and sponsor terrorists, Iraq was removed from the State Department's list of countries supporting terrorism in February 1982[67] and diplomatic relation between the two states resumed in 1984. This was so despite Iraq's long and multifaceted relationship with the Soviet Union, with which one might have expected the Reagan administration to be considerably preoccupied. Iraq turned mostly to the West for weapons and equipment, with several Persian Gulf Arab countries paying the bill.

For the West as well as for the Arab Gulf states, Iran was more worrisome than Iraq. In fact, Iran was perceived to be moving away from and Iraq moving towards them. Iraq had virtually ended its support for the Popular Front for the Liberation of Oman, steadily improved relations with Saudi Arabia, reduced tensions with Kuwait and forged a broad range of cooperative ties with other Gulf states aimed at enhancing their respective capabilities against Iranian-sponsored activities.

The Western and Gulf states maintained that the setback for their interests should Iran defeat Iraq was beyond question. They had an interest in seeing that Iran did not emerge from the conflict with the capacity to export its own radical ideology to lands beyond its shores.

On the other hand, Iran's open support for the PLO, in spite of the fears of the Persian Gulf states regarding their own Palestinian 'guests', and the pursuit of close ties with the radical Syrian government, worried the conservative Gulf states sufficiently for them to contemplate assisting Iraq in its war efforts against Iran. As J. D. Anthony put it, 'Iran advanced its own cause and embarrassed the Arab regimes by being the first – and only – regional state to provide actual military assistance to the Syrians, Lebanese and Palestinians during the Israeli invasion of Lebanon in the summer of 1982.'[68]

After the Iranian rejection of the Soviet offer to sell it weapons directly, the Soviets allowed Syria and Libya to airlift arms and ammunition to Iran. On the other hand, the Soviets stopped supplying arms to Baghdad, and Iraq publicly complained that the Soviet Union had not implemented 'its pre-war contracts with Iraq' since the outbreak of the war. Iraq succeeded in purchasing Soviet-made weapons and ammunition from Somalia, North Yemen and Egypt, which had in the past received them, and having them shipped through Saudi Arabia.[69]

Ignoring the Arab League's boycott resolution against Egypt, Saddam Hussein also approached Cairo for Soviet-made arms and ammunition, and received them, which was the first sign of a diminution of hostility towards Egypt in the Arab world.[70]

In sum, the effect of Saddam's attack on Iran was to throw the Arab world into disarray, split the Arab front against Israel and undermine the position of the PLO. Politically, President Saddam Hussein's bid for leadership of a pan-Arab movement appeared thoroughly discredited. As prominent Arab League members sided with Iran, the Saddam plan to portray his war against Iran as the one carried out on behalf of the Arab nation failed. So did his effort to rally the Arabs behind his bid to move the issue of the three islands to the top of the Arab agenda. When the Iraqi foreign minister raised the issue in the UN General Assembly in October 1980, no other Arab representative followed suit. The Iraqi media campaign on the three islands did not resonate well anywhere outside Iraq.

Nonetheless, in parallel with the support provided to Iraq's efforts against Iran by the Arab moderate-to-conservative camp in the 1980s, a few signs emerged that presaged this camp's activities on the issue of the three islands in the 1990s. While the Arab radicals, who were at the forefront of challenging Iran's title to the three islands in the 1970s, sided with Iran after the Islamic Revolution, Arab moderates and conservatives, moving away from Iran, also began showing interest in the three islands. However, they refrained from raising the issue formally, and stayed subdued at the informal level too. Among the rare references to the three islands, this comment by Cairo Voice of the Arabs from 16 September 1979 is worth mentioning:

> The ruling Iranian authorities did not, however, express any readiness to return the three Arab islands in the Arab Gulf to the UAE – the islands of Abu Musa, Greater and Lesser Tunb – despite Khomeini's personal declaration prior to the success of the revolution that the three islands were Arab and would be restored to their legitimate Arab owners. The leaders of the Iranian Revolution soon retracted their pledges. They went even further in hostility to their neighbours, the brothers, by uttering scores of statements claiming Bahrain was Iranian and that the majority of the inhabitants of Kuwait were Iranians or of Iranian descent, and that the whole of the Gulf complemented Iran and was also Persian.[71]

UAE and the issue of the three islands in the 1980s

During a brief period from August 1980 to March 1981, UAE officials undertook a series of activities related to the issue of the three islands, the most important of which were the submission of two letters to the UN Secretary-General. This episode, uncharacteristic of the 21-year period from 1971 to 1992, should be understood in the light of these seven factors:

- Iran was swept by a popular revolution and deeply preoccupied with the typical problems and predicaments of a post-revolutionary situation; doing away with the remnants of resistance loyal to the *ancien régime* and survival topped their list of priorities. The new government was thus inward-looking and less interested in foreign policy issues. The new authorities had yet to set foreign policy, let alone become acquainted with the islands issue.
- Iraq's star was ascending. It was trying to take full advantage of the collapse of the Shah's regime and the perceived power vacuum that had unexpectedly emerged in the Persian Gulf.
- If the Iranian government, busy with the domestic issues, failed to notice signs of a gathering threat coming from Iraq, the Persian Gulf Arab states did not. Terrified by the impact of the revolutionary message on their societies and regimes, they, in fact, followed eagerly Iraq's preparations for the invasion of Iran and hoped impatiently to reap some benefits from the results.
- Some circles in the UAE were chief among those who harboured hope in Iraq's efforts. They calculated that, with the Iranian armed forces seemingly in a state of disintegration, they would be able to take over the three islands, thanks to a lightning victory by Iraq.
- Enormous Iraqi pressure on the small Persian Gulf states, too, should be taken into account. As described earlier, Iraq's provocations related to, and its fixation with, the three islands, which began almost a month after the victory of the Islamic Revolution, would not have gone unnoticed in the UAE.
- In fact, the UAE did not start this episode on its own initiative but was coerced

138 *Transitional period*

- into it by pressure tactics employed by a rising Iraq. As will be discussed, the two formal letters from the UAE to the UN Secretary-General regarding the islands were a reaction to the exchange of letters between Iran and Iraq through the UN Secretary-General.
- Finally, it is noteworthy that this seven-month episode corresponded to the period in which Iraq looked to be either on the rise or politically and militarily victorious. The first UAE claim, dated 8 August 1980, came when Iraq was deeply involved in its military preparations for invading Iran, which included making necessary arrangements with the Persian Gulf Arab conservatives. The episode ended when Iraq unexpectedly stalled on all war fronts and lost momentum, and the recoiling period began. The brief period of UAE activity related to the three islands began with the perception that Iraq was at its peak and ended with actually seeing it falter.

Thus, the circumstances in 1980 appeared to certain circles in the UAE and the region to provide a suitable political setting in which to reactivate the issue of the three islands. Nonetheless, although such a setting was an essential prerequisite, it was not alone sufficient to justify putting these UAE officials on a path towards serious conflict with Iran. It took them more than a year and half to formally raise the issue, and their toying with it lasted only for several months.

To the author's knowledge, the first talk of the three islands held inside the United Arab Emirates came from Sheikh Saqr Bin Muhammad al-Qasimi, the ruler of Ras al-Khaimah, on 3 April 1980. The Kuwaiti News Agency quoted him as saying in an interview with the Kuwaiti newspaper *Al-Hadaf* that he believed that 'Iran will return three islands it occupied during the era of the deposed Shah near the Strait of Hormuz nine years ago.' He welcomed the statement attributed to President Bani-Sadr of Iran, in which he was quoted as saying that Iran would not return the three islands . . . as long as the American military presence continued in the Persian Gulf region.[72] This cautious statement on the three islands by one of the Emirate sheikhs, the most vociferous one among them, was made in the context of almost daily mention of the issue, as referred to earlier, by Iraqi officials and media, since about a month after the Iranian Revolution.

The first UAE formal statement on the issue of the three islands came in a reaction to an exchange between Iran and Iraq. Rashid Abdullah, the UAE Minister of State for Foreign Affairs, reacted to an Iranian letter of 26 May 1980 to the UN Secretary-General[73] by sending his own letter to the Secretary-General, dated 8 August 1980, raising the UAE claim to the three islands. As discussed earlier, the Iranian foreign minister, Sadegh Ghotbzadeh, in his response to the letter of his Iraqi counterpart had rejected Iraq's claims related to the three islands and stressed that they 'have always been throughout history an integral part of Iran.' He also had recalled that '[i]t took Iraq almost eight years to break the silence and to raise this question anew.'[74]

In his reaction to this Iranian letter, the UAE foreign minister stated, in part, that 'the Government of the United Arab Emirates finds itself obliged to re-emphasize its firm attachment to those islands, which form an integral part of the territory of our State whose sovereign rights thereover are indisputable and unimpeachable, and reaffirm its readiness to furnish substantive proof to that effect.'[75]

The acting foreign minister of Iran, M. K. Khoda Panahi, in a letter dated 12 November 1980 to the UN Secretary-General, responded to the Minister of State for Foreign Affairs of the UAE on the issue of the three islands. In his letter, he restated the Iranian position on the issue, stating, *inter alia*, that 'the fact that [these islands] belong to Iran cannot be subject to consideration and discussion under any circumstances'.[76]

Iraq welcomed the letter by the UAE foreign minister. In a commentary on the official statement in which the UAE had called for the restoration of the three islands – Lesser Tunb, Greater Tunb and Abu Musa – to 'their legitimate owners', the newspaper *Al-Thawrah* wrote: 'The UAA's [sic] total rejection of any non-Arab sovereignty over the three islands constitutes a public rebuttal of the racist Persian regime's allegations and fabrications that the Arab islands belong to Iran.' The paper added: 'The statement came as a categorical reply to the lies circulated by the President of the Iranian regime in which he claimed that the Arab islands were not occupied by force but by agreement between the Shah's government and the owners of these islands.' *Al-Thawrah* further asserted that 'Iraq, which is waging its national and pan-Arab war against the Persian aggressors, has been seriously and sincerely determined to sort out all the national and pan-Arab rights between the Arabs and Iran out of its commitment to safeguarding the security, liberty and independence of the Arab Gulf and the stability of world security.'[77]

Other than the existence of the exceptional situation in the area, referred to earlier, and the pressure brought to bear on the UAE by Iraq and Iraqi actions, a third element that provided an opportunity to those in favour of reviving the issue and that finally caused the UAE to take a position in that particular point in time should not be omitted: the Iranian letter in response to Iraq's letter, which some in the UAE found provocative and insisted on the need to react to.

Nonetheless, the official letter to the UN Secretary-General was the first formal, individual position the UAE took about the issue of the three islands during its brief history. Its previous stance had been set out in a collective letter to the President of the Security Council signed by seventeen Arab countries on 17 July 1972. Earlier than that, the UAE representative had joined a meeting of the Council that had been convened upon request by the Iraqi representative.

In the meantime, Sheikh Saqr Bin Muhammad al-Qasimi, the ruler of Ras al-Khaimah, was quoted by the UAE newspaper *Al-Fajr* as saying during his visit to Iraq on 16 September 1980 that 'the UAE recently informed Iraq about its view on the issue of the three islands'. The paper went on to state that he had discussed with President Saddam Hussein of Iraq the issue of the three islands, 'which historically belong to the UAA [sic], border problems between Iraq and Iran and the situation in the Arabian Gulf.' Saqr also revealed to the paper that Saddam had informed him of the contents of the speech he would he later deliver at the Iraqi National Assembly in which he declared the abrogation of the 1975 Algiers Agreement between Iraq and Iran.[78]

Meanwhile, the only other UAE move on the issue in this period came in the form of another letter, which was a reaction to an interview attributed to President A. Bani Sadr of Iran that was published by the French magazine *Nouvel Observateur* on 13 October 1980. He was quoted as saying that 'the former Shah of Iran had paid sums of money to certain sheikhs in return for their silence regarding Iran's occupation of the islands.' While rejecting such allegations, the UAE's permanent representative to the UN, in his letter to the UN Secretary-General dated 1 December 1980, stated that 'we believe that such statements are detrimental to the reputation of the Government of the United Arab Emirates and to harmonious brotherly relations between the Arab and Iranian Muslim peoples.' In this letter, claims to the three islands analogous to those already raised by Rashid Abdullah in his letter were repeated.[79]

As referred to earlier, despite the raising of the issue of the three islands by Iraq in the general debate of the UN General Assembly in October 1980, in his statement in the same debate the UAE foreign minister refrained from making any reference to this issue, which is the most important annual occasion for the member states to declare their positions.[80]

Apart from those two formal letters to the UN Secretary-General, a few statements to the press by UAE officials were reported between August 1980 and March 1981. In January 1981 the UAE Minister of State for Foreign Affairs stated that the Emirates 'still have rights to these islands and we are still calling for the return of the Islands'.[81] On 28 March 1981, the ruler of Ras al-Khaimah was reported to say in an interview that 'the three islands are an Arab right about which there could be no discussion. Iran's rulers know this better than others; however, no contact on this issue has been made between us with them.'[82]

The regional arrangement meticulously engineered by Baghdad for close to two years began collapsing soon after Iraq's invasion of Iran foundered during its first several weeks. A rearrangement of priorities rapidly became imperative as survival of the Iraqi regime moved to the top of the agenda, and that required an end to the war. A new division of labour was devised among Iraq's allies, including those on the lower shores of the Persian Gulf, that took into consideration the particularities of each state, including its perceived level of risk, vulnerabilities, proximity to the battlefields, domestic politics, demographic composition, and so forth.

A change of heart was one consequence of the new situation. The UAE not only chose to fall back into another long period of dormancy on the issue of the three islands, but also took upon itself to mend relations with Iran and for the most part to try to adopt a neutral stance in the war between Iran and Iraq. From this point on, the UAE chose to maintain a relatively controversy-free, if not friendly, relationship with Iran. Iraq's occasionally coercive attempts thereafter failed to persuade the UAE to reopen the issue of the three islands and initiate a dispute thereon. A new round of activity by the UAE was initiated only in 1992, as discussed in Chapter 5, under totally different circumstances, in the wake of the Americans driving Iraq out of Kuwait.

As Iraq's ascending star began unexpectedly to descend several weeks after the outbreak of the war, it became again important for the smaller Arab states to consider maintaining the balance of power between Iran and Iraq in order to help neutralize the perceived threats emanating from the Islamic Revolution. The UAE and Oman, in particular, had only to gain by remaining neutral. They were the two main GCC mediators working with Iran. As Rosemarie Said Zahlan has indicated, Oman and the UAE enjoyed good relations with Iran throughout the war; the argument was that to continue a dialogue with Iran would make a negotiated peace settlement more likely.[83] And as Marschall notes, in 1983 the UAE continued to play the main role as a mediator to bring about an end to the war.[84]

A combination of endemic difficulties involving demographic make-up, domestic politics and economic interest led the UAE to favour a *rapprochement* with Iran. The country had profited economically from trade with Iran. Bilateral trade had steadily increased since the outbreak of war, and it was not in either country's interest to alienate the other. However, since the Iraqi occupation of Khorramshahr, Iran's main commercial port and the only one that handled large container ships, Iran had conducted most of its trade with or through Dubai.[85]

The emirates of Dubai and Sharjah stayed on particularly good terms with Iran throughout the war and the ensuing years. They were major entrepôts of trade and providers of services. Dubai also became the main Persian Gulf port for servicing and repairing international shipping. For Sharjah, good relations with Iran were important to secure the continuation of the agreement on the shared oil resources of Abu Musa Island.[86]

Almost throughout the 1980s, the UAE played the most prominent role within the GCC by talking directly to Tehran. Various Iranian delegations visited the UAE during this period, discussing the situation in the war as well as the expansion of economic ties and their common opposition to any foreign interference in the region.[87]

During a regional tour in May 1987 that was described as a 'diplomatic offensive',[88] the Iranian deputy foreign minister, Ali Muhammad Besharati, praised 'the UAE's policy towards Iran and thought it could serve as an example for the other GCC countries.' He said that 'the Persian Gulf was of strategic importance and, therefore, all countries of the region had to maintain its security.' Sheikh Zayed bin Sultan al-Nahyan, the UAE president, confirmed everything Besharati said and replied that any disadvantage to Iran was also a disadvantage to the UAE. Both the UAE and Qatar subsequently issued statements opposing foreign intervention, and Oman advocated a regional solution to the problem of shipping safety.[89]

Afterwards, A. A. Velayati, the Iranian foreign minister, discussed in Abu Dhabi how Security Council Resolution 598 could be implemented, and in Muscat he reviewed the same subject. Perhaps as a result of these talks, at its summit at the end of December 1987 the GCC decided to negotiate with Iran and delegated the UAE as mediator because of its good ties with that country. Prime Minister Musavi declared that Iran was ready to receive the GCC envoy.[90] Consequently, the UAE representative, Saif Said, went to Tehran, declaring that the cooperation between the GCC and Iran would curb the influence of foreign powers.[91] All in all, the GCC put much emphasis on the UAE to break the stalemate.

142 *Transitional period*

According to Rosemarie Said Zahlan, the Sharjah newspaper *Al-Khalij* was the only one to publish the entire report of UN Secretary-General de Cuellar's September 1987 Persian Gulf visit. It showed Iran's willingness to negotiate a just and lasting peace settlement through the United Nations.[92] Whereas the Arab League's meeting in early November 1987 in Amman had condemned Iran for its continued intransigence regarding the cease-fire and for its occupation of Iraqi territory, Iran was neither condemned nor even criticized at the GCC summit held in Riyadh one month later.[93]

The relatively good relationship between Iran and the UAE survived a few incidents in the 1980s:

- In November 1986 the main pumping and loading facilities in the Al Bakush offshore oilfield, off Abu Dhabi, was attacked from the air. Iraqi air strikes had already damaged Iranian facilities that drew oil from the same reservoir. Abu Dhabi continued producing oil from this common reservoir in spite of Iranian protest. Iran and Iraq both denied that they had undertaken the attack.[94]
- Iran was accused of launching attacks on oil tankers crossing the Persian Gulf, operating, among other places, from Abu Musa.[95]
- International media, quoting well-informed Persian Gulf diplomats and shipping sources, reported in 1987 that Iranian Revolutionary Guards had fortified the three islands. According to these reports, 1,000 Revolutionary Guards, plus attack helicopters and speedboats, were stationed on the islands of Abu Musa and the Greater and Lesser Tunbs. One report quoted a Gulf shipping source as saying, 'we know for a fact that the Iranians have fortified their bases on the islands,' and added that 'during his frequent runs through the strait he had seen heightened Iranian military activity on and around the three small islands since the middle of June. The source also stated that 'we've seen helicopters taking off and landing from Abu Musa and lots of Iranian gunboats moving between the islands.' According to this report Western diplomats in the Persian Gulf, who kept close watch on the so-called 'tanker war' in the conflict between Iraq and Iran, corroborated the accounts of the shipping sources. They said the Iranians had built a helicopter pad and a small airport on Abu Musa.[96] A State Department official in Washington also said the shipping sources' account was consistent with what the United States knew, which included the fact that 'Iran [had] maintained a paramilitary presence on Abu Musa and the Tunbs since 1971. He claimed that since the summer of 1986 when Iran switched its tactics from air attacks on Iraqi-related shipping to hit-and-run raids, the islands [had] served as occasional forward bases for missile-firing Iranian helicopters and speedboats.'[97]

Reports claimed that the reinforced presence of Revolutionary Guards on the islands appeared to have resulted not from the heightened tensions after the US decision to reflag Kuwaiti tankers but from Iran's response to the short-lived palace coup in Sharjah on 17 June 1987. The emirate's ruler since 1972, Sheikh Sultan bin Muhammed al-Qassimi, was replaced by his brother, Sheikh Abdel-

Aziz, plunging the sheikhdom into a political crisis. Iran, which supported Sheikh Sultan, immediately moved about 1,000 Revolutionary Guards to the three islands – the equivalent of Sharjah's entire armed forces – plus reinforcements of helicopters and high-speed gunboats to pressure the emirate to return Sheikh Sultan to power. The Iranian move sent shock waves through the Persian Gulf, where regional leaders, including Saudi Arabian King Fahd, voiced concern over the situation at a time when tension was already high because of the Iran–Iraq War. Fahd warned against aggravating the situation lest there be 'foreign intervention.' Diplomats in Dubai said he was clearly referring to the possibility of an Iranian attack against Sharjah to reinstate Sheikh Sultan.[98] On 20 June Sultan was reinstated under a compromise that named the rebellious Sheikh Abdel-Aziz as crown prince and chairman of the country's Executive Council.

Though it got what it apparently sought, Iran reportedly did not reduce its reinforced presence on the three islands. The forces there were now in an excellent position to step up raids against Gulf shipping, particularly American-flagged cargo ships and warships, both diplomats and shipping sources said. 'Nothing has been withdrawn,' a knowledgeable diplomat claimed, and '[t]here is now a serious danger that Iran will use the islands to stage attacks against US ships.' Shipping sources said the three fortified islands, besides being used for possible Iranian helicopter and gunboat attacks, could also serve as operational bases for mining the shipping channels leading into and out of the Strait of Hormuz.[99]

Sailing towards the lighthouse on the island of Abu Nuayr off the coast of Abu Dhabi, a convoy of eleven US-escorted reflagged ships also passed near the islands of Abu Musa and the Greater and Lesser Tunbs, 'where Revolutionary Guards recently have reinforced their positions with additional troops, helicopters and attack boats,' as reported by a section of media.[100]

In September 1987, when the 'tanker war', which had begun in July, was at its peak and the United States accused Iran of seeding explosives in the waterway entering and exiting the Persian Gulf in retaliation for an American attack on an Iranian vessel earlier in the same month, there was also speculation about mines being dropped from small boats operating from Abu Musa. The mines did not damage any vessels, but shipping executives said 'the channel was one of the busiest and is parallel to an 'exclusion zone' that Iran has declared around Abu Musa.'[101]

It is important to note that, although the reports referred to above went unheeded by UAE officials, the UAE did adopt the policy, from 1992, of protesting against any even minor civilian activities by Iran on the three islands.

5 Confrontational phase

The period covering 1992 to the present time has been characterized by efforts undertaken by the UAE to reactivate and internationalize the issue of the three islands by raising it in multilateral forums, with the aim of buttressing its position by drawing support primarily from GCC member states and the Arab League and ultimately from larger global organizations. Ending a long period of dormancy for the issue since 1972, the current period of activity came about in the wake of dramatic, mutually reinforcing developments at the local, regional and global levels.

The end of the Cold War and the liberation of Kuwait by the United States in the early 1990s brought about the dawn of what was later called 'the American era' in the region.[1] They enabled the United States to enjoy unprecedented influence and freedom of action in the Persian Gulf, and, thus, to present a serious challenge to Iranian primacy in the area, as the Britain had in its time. Accordingly, the more the United States gained prominence in the Persian Gulf, the more the local autonomy of the area was undermined. These seminal developments also allowed the conservative-moderate Arab camp to strengthen its position throughout the region. Assisted by the United States, this camp was able to pursue more forcefully the policies that it desired but that had remained largely inconclusive during the transitional period in the 1980s.

Consequently, attempts were made to reinstate some of the broad policies that had prevailed up to the British withdrawal from the Persian Gulf, including the policy of containing the major regional power. The containment of Iran has figured prominently on the agenda of the United States in the Persian Gulf ever since, as was once the case under the British. This, coupled with a major realignment of power across the Arab world in favour of the conservative-moderate camp, set the stage for the local Arab sheikhs to revive the issue of the three islands. Regardless of whether or not the United States has played a direct role in the issue of the islands, this issue has in practice benefited the US containment policy against Iran, just as the British drew benefit from the same controversy in their time.

In this chapter, the revival of the issue of the three islands is explored as a side effect of several new trends in the Persian Gulf, as US status has grown and the autonomy of the Gulf has faltered. The humiliating defeat of Iraq in 1991 and its exclusion from the power balance in the Persian Gulf was worrisome to certain littoral states, which had pinned their hopes on Baghdad as a counterweight to Iran in the area. Iran's frustration with the unfavourable GCC reaction to the diplomatic overtures it made at the end of the Iran–Iraq War also affected future courses of action.

This chapter begins by reviewing unsuccessful efforts on the part of Iran to remove tension in its relations with GCC countries. It then examines the events leading to the close involvement of the United States and its allies in the security arrangement devised for the Persian Gulf. An assessment follows of the newfound strength of the conservative-moderate Arab camp, which contrasts with its weaker status in the 1980s. The chapter closes with a review of the new cycle of activity embarked upon by the UAE and its allies, taking into account all of these trends.

Iran's diplomatic overtures and their outcome

Iran's efforts to normalize its ties with the Arab littoral states intensified soon after the cease-fire in the Iran–Iraq War and in parallel with its efforts aimed at reconstructing the country. The littoral states failed to react favourably to Iran's overtures, however, and looked to more distant foreign powers to provide for regional security to the exclusion of Iran from the relevant arrangements.

Iran's efforts to normalize ties with the GCC

Focused on post-war reconstruction, the new Iranian president, Akbar Hashemi Rafsanjani, elected in July 1989, put policy emphasis on economic development and rebuilding. His first five-year plan (1989–94) depended on attracting foreign capital, increasing oil revenue and importing modern technology. Thus, he had to improve Iran's relations with the outside world, especially the countries neighbouring Iran. Consequently, Iran made significant conciliatory gestures towards the six monarchical conservative Persian Gulf Arab states, and proposed a complete break from the strained to hostile relationship of the 1979–88 period.

Framing Iran's policy with regard to GCC countries, Speaker Rafsanjani in early 1989 had already declared that 'the Islamic Republic of Iran was ready to improve relations with the Gulf littoral states in various fields in order to repair the economic damage of the war.' Addressing the Iranian diplomatic corps to the Persian Gulf in Tehran, he added that '[t]he wartime conditions inflicted substantial economic losses on all of us and now since the war has apparently ended, efforts should be made to make good on the losses.'[2]

While running for president, he also said that 'as regards the Arabic countries, especially the Persian Gulf littoral states, our policy is based on the expansion of relations and good neighbourliness. There are no obstacles on our part. Recently, we have received positive signs from the Persian Gulf littoral states.'[3] He urged Iran's southern neighbours 'to cooperate with us in order to resolve existing issues concerning the oil market, maritime laws and Security Council Resolution 598.'[4]

Iran was also concerned about Iraq's policy in the Persian Gulf region, and containing Iraq became its other major objective in the wake of the war. This goal also required the improvement of relations with GCC countries, which could then put pressure on Saddam to implement UN Security Council Resolution 598. Thus, the objectives of advancing post-war reconstruction and thwarting an Iraq that sought to become the gendarme of the Persian Gulf framed Iran's policy towards GCC countries, prompting some experts to note what they termed as 'the clear shift in Iranian foreign policy towards national interest and away from revolutionary ideology.'[5]

In the weeks that followed the Iraqi invasion of Kuwait Iran's foreign minister, Ali Akbar Velayati, visited the UAE, Oman, Bahrain, Qatar and Syria, where his meetings included sessions with Kuwait's foreign minister. During these visits, Velayati portrayed Iran as 'the only regional power that can resist Iraq', and offered military assistance to GCC member states.[6]

The expansion of the presence of US-dominated military forces, in response to the Iraqi invasion of Kuwait, however, provided ammunition to the hard-liners in Iran, who opposed the moderate foreign policy pursued by President Rafsanjani that was based on, among other things, *rapprochement* with GCC countries. Rafsanjani was running a political risk, then, as Iran's hard-liners opposed any *rapprochement* with Saudi Arabia. The president largely outflanked them in a policy struggle that broke out after the war, even though the challenges presented to him continued unabated. Tehran's radical daily *Kayhan* dismissed a regional security arrangement that the government pursued as 'a mirage' and warned that Iran would be 'the only loser.'[7]

Nonetheless, by the middle of September 1989, Iran had upgraded its diplomatic relations with both Kuwait and Bahrain and staged negotiations with the Saudis on improving bilateral relations. Between September and October 1989 high-level Foreign Ministry officials paid at least three visits to smaller GCC member states.[8]

A regional security arrangement

Opposing the stationing of foreign forces in the region, Iran called upon GCC countries to minimize their dependence on the United States and rely on themselves to maintain regional security. In the first instance, the Iranian reaction to the deployment of US forces in the Persian Gulf region in 1990 came in a keynote speech by the Iranian supreme leader, Ayatollah Khamenei. He said, 'Anyone who fights America's aggression, its greediness and its plans to encroach on the Persian Gulf region has engaged in *jihad* in the cause of Allah and anyone who is killed on that path is a martyr ... We will not allow the Americans to gain a foothold in an area where we are present and turn it into their sphere of influence.'[9] His speech came amid signs that the United States and its allies were preparing to increase the momentum of the military build-up to confront Saddam Hussein following the Iraqi invasion of Kuwait in August 1990.

As an alternative, a new regional security arrangement for the Persian Gulf that would include all littoral states and exclude foreign powers reappeared at the top of the Iranian priority list for the region. Iran based its position on paragraph 8 of UN Security Council Resolution 598, in which the UN Secretary-General was asked to 'examine in consultation with Iran and Iraq and with other States of the region measures to enhance the security and stability of the region.'[10] This was a proposition that Iran strongly favoured and upon which it predicated its policy in the Persian Gulf in the ensuing phase, when it undertook enduring efforts to realize it.

Initial signals from GCC countries were promising, and well received in Tehran. Talk about including Iran in a future regional security agreement during the GCC summit in Doha, held on 22–25 December 1990, less than a month before the US attack on Iraqi forces in Kuwait, raised Iran's hopes of becoming an active player in Persian Gulf security. On the eve of, during and in the wake of the Doha Summit, which was aimed mainly at developing a security strategy for the Persian Gulf, GCC officials signalled clearly that Iran should be included in any new regional security arrangement after the liberation of Kuwait.

Sultan Qabus of Oman called for regional cooperation, which would include Iran, to establish security in the region.[11] Kuwait's Minister of State for Foreign Affairs, Sheikh Nasser Mohammed al-Sabah, stressed during a visit to Tehran before the summit that '[w]ithout the powerful presence of Iran, no regional security is possible or practical.'[12] The Qatari foreign minister and the spokesman for the summit, Mubarak al-Khater, stressed that Iran would be included in any regional arrangement and contacts were already under way.[13]

Moreover, in an unprecedented gesture, all foreign affairs ministers of GCC member countries and Abdullah Bishara, the GCC Secretary-General, met with the Iranian foreign minister, Ali Akbar Velayati, over a dinner in the Mission of Iran in New York, and discussed developments in the region.[14] The mere mention of a security role for Tehran represented a reversal of the situation of a decade before, when the GCC was formed in the face of what was seen then as the main threat: revolutionary Iran.

Attesting to this promising environment for regional cooperation, the closing statement issued by the Doha Summit signalled openness on the part of the GCC to embrace Iran's diplomatic overtures. The paragraph on Iran in the statement reads:

> The GCC Higher Council welcomes the desire of the Islamic Republic of Iran to improve and promote its relations with all GCC countries. The GCC Higher Council underlines the importance of serious and realistic action to settle the outstanding differences between Iran and the GCC Member States so that the countries of the region can proceed to achieve their cherished goals and exploit their resources for comprehensive economic development. The GCC Higher Council stresses its desire to establish distinguished relations with Iran on the basis of good-neighborliness, non-interference in domestic affairs and respect for sovereignty, independence and peaceful coexistence deriving from the bonds of religion and heritage that link the countries of the region.[15]

Nonetheless, in the aftermath of Kuwait's liberation, these hopes were soon dampened. The extraordinary ministerial meeting of the GCC held in the wake of the liberation of Kuwait, in Kuwait City on 5 May 1991, omitted any reference to Iran in its final communiqué.[16] And most of the GCC states, in fact, began looking elsewhere for security assistance, clearly preferring the permanent presence of foreign forces and fully reversing their favourable inclination to consider a regional security arrangement that could involve Iran.

Iran, however, continued to stick to its position under the new circumstances, and kept demanding the withdrawal of foreign forces from the area. Kamal Kharrazi, a former permanent representative to the UN and foreign minister of Iran, reiterated Iran's belief that security and stability of the Persian Gulf region should be maintained solely through the cooperation of the Persian Gulf states. He said that paragraph 8 of Security Council Resolution 598 had created the necessary grounds for the establishment of peace and security in the region through the cooperation of the Persian Gulf States, far from any foreign interference.[17]

In early March 1991, Kharrazi transmitted to UN Secretary-General Javier Perez de Cuellar a message from Foreign Minister Velayati urging that paragraph 8 of UN Security Council Resolution 598 be implemented. Earlier, President Rafsanjani of Iran told Iran's Supreme National Security Council that the continuing allied presence in Iraq had 'no justification whatsoever.'[18]

Nonetheless, as soon as Iraq was driven out of Kuwait, the conservative Arab regimes stopped showing any interest in building regional security on the basis of cooperation among all the riparian states to the exclusion of foreigners. The Director of the Department of GCC and Gulf State Affairs in the UAE Foreign Ministry, Khalifa Shaheen al-Merree, candidly summarized in an interview the gist of the Arab sheikhs' views:

> We cannot have a regional security arrangement because of Iran. To have [a] reliable security arrangement, the first thing you need is trust. That's why we see the solving of the islands dispute with Iran, as well as boundary problems within the GCC, as a pre-requisite. Since 1991, we [have] detected some intention by Iran to establish itself as the regional power after Iraq's defeat. They wanted to exercise their influence. Iran opposed the Damascus Declaration. When we held the six-plus-one talks with Iran in 1991, Iran very much opposed the participation of foreign forces in Gulf security. This is where the gap between Iran and the UAE lies.[19]

Thus, the littoral Arab states clearly demonstrated that still they viewed a role for Iran in the Persian Gulf as worrisome. In this connection, they also were said to be troubled about Iran's efforts to revive its armed forces, which had gone through an eight-year devastating war with Iraq.

The Director-General of the Persian Gulf Department of the Iranian Foreign Ministry, Hossein Sadeghi, described the mood in Tehran in a bitter way:

> In the meetings at the UN in September 1990, we offered them our help in solving the Crisis and in securing the region, but after Kuwait was freed we

saw that they did not want our support. Kuwait, Saudi Arabia and the others in the meeting said they would help us reconstruct our economy, but after Kuwait was liberated they forgot.[20]

Six plus Two failure

After the lightning defeat of Iraq, and while the United States was considering the ways and means to make its military presence in the Persian Gulf permanent, the Gulf Arab states initially preferred that the permanent US military presence did not include American ground troops. The humiliating Iraqi defeat, however, and the continuation of comprehensive UN sanctions against it virtually excluded Iraq from the balance of power in the Gulf. Nor did the conservative sheikhs trust Iran, and Iraq could not be perceived as in a position to balance it out. Thus, the option of depending on outside protectors was raised higher on the list for consideration.

Under such circumstances, the Persian Gulf Arabs, still preferring to avoid associating themselves closely with the West, explored for a while the possibility of relying on militarily powerful Arab states and creating what was dubbed 'pan-Arab security arrangements' in the Persian Gulf. Thus, they briefly considered an Arab defence alliance including Egypt and Syria.

In mid-February 1991, representatives of the GCC member states plus Syria and Egypt met in Cairo and considered, among other things, 'the region's security and stability as an integral part of the Arab world's security and stability.'[21] A month later, the 'Six plus Two' signed the Damascus Declaration, which, *inter alia*, stated that:

> The eight States consider that the presence of Egyptian and Syrian forces on the territories of the Kingdom of Saudi Arabia and other States in the Gulf region represents a nucleus for an Arab peace force to guarantee the security and safety of Arab States in the Gulf region, and a blueprint that would guarantee the effectiveness of the joint Arab defensive security system.[22]

It was widely understood at the time – particularly by Egyptian officials – that most, if not all, of the 38,000 Egyptian and 20,000 Syrian troops who took part in the war against Iraq would remain in the Persian Gulf as the foundation of the new regional security set-up. In return for providing the troops and weaponry to protect Saudi Arabia and other Persian Gulf states, these two countries would be assured of significant financial flows to sustain their economic development. Egypt and Syria were talking of an annual $15 billion provided by GCC countries.[23]

Having laid the framework for a regional security agreement in their meeting in Damascus, the foreign ministers of the Six plus Two states later met James Baker, the US Secretary of State. The Arab ministers, in a statement issued after their meeting with Baker, 'expressed their appreciation for the statement delivered by President George Bush before the United States Congress, which dealt positively with the security of this region and the Palestinian question.' The statement added, in a clear allusion to the future American presence in the Persian Gulf, that the

Arab ministers agreed that the task of establishing peace and security in the Middle East was 'for all the peoples of the region and outside parties prepared to play a constructive role.'[24]

The endorsement of Mr Bush's plan meant that the Arab countries agreed that the American military presence in the Persian Gulf region would continue to be larger than it was before the Iraqi invasion of Kuwait, which, together with agreement to the US plan on the Palestinian question, constituted a breakthrough in Arab–American relations. The substance of the meeting suggested that they were then prepared to consider all sorts of unprecedented approaches, including continuing and open military cooperation with the United States.

Reflecting on the security structure that would replace the 500,000 American troops still in Kuwait and Iraq, James Baker said, after his meeting the Six plus Two group, that he and the eight ministers had agreed it would consist of an Arab peace-keeping force made up of the six Arab Persian Gulf states, plus troops from Egypt and Syria, and an enhanced American naval presence in the Persian Gulf, along with regular joint training exercises between American air and ground forces that would be assigned to the region on a non-permanent, rotating basis. It would also include the pre-positioning of large amounts of American equipment in Saudi Arabia and elsewhere so that if American troops had to be quickly reintroduced into the region, part of their weapons and supplies would already be in place.[25]

In an effort to avoid antagonizing Iran, the Arab ministers emphasized in their statement that this security structure was not aimed at Iran, which had expressed displeasure with the concept and, it was feared, could end up actively opposing it. To this end, the statement read:

> They are also eager to develop friendly relations with Iran, and are looking forward to cooperating with it on the basis of mutual respect and the principles of international law, which govern friendly relations among states.[26]

The Saudi foreign minister also stated that the eight Arab states 'are keen to develop cordial relations with Iran.' He added, 'They reiterate that whatever arrangements they may agree upon shall not be directed against any other party. In fact, the reference in the Damascus Declaration to a dialogue with Islamic and international parties clearly indicates a willingness on their part to have a dialogue with Islamic countries, including Iran.'[27]

Iran reacted angrily to the prospect of being excluded from a security arrangement in the Persian Gulf. Foreign Minister Velayati delivered a message from President Rafsanjani to Sultan Qabus stressing Iran's desire to take part in the security plan.[28] Sultan Qabus, who headed the GCC committee for regional security arrangements, explained to Velayati that he hoped to create a collective security system in the first phase among the GCC members, and later in principle among all the Gulf countries. He stated that Egypt and Syria could not act as guardians of the GCC.

Sultan was only partly right. The Damascus Declaration was soon dead, and, in May 1992, Egypt began to withdraw its troops from Saudi Arabia and Kuwait. Unable to rely on its own forces and wary of Iranian motives, the GCC preferred Western protection.

Egyptian president Hosni Mubarak's decision to pull nearly 40,000 Egyptian troops out of Saudi Arabia and Kuwait signalled the unravelling of a highly publicized plan, only two months old, to establish a pan-Arab security force in the Persian Gulf. The pullout also highlighted the preference of the Persian Gulf Arab states to have the militarily dominant United States, rather than weaker and less reliable Arab nations, guarantee their national security. Egyptian military and political officials in Cairo said in interviews that the decision reflected Egypt's impatience with Saudi and Kuwaiti foot-dragging in implementing a proposed pan-Arab Persian Gulf security arrangement first announced on 6 March 1991.

The Kuwaitis and the Saudis, who long had sought to keep their countries free from any foreign military presence and then appeared averse to having a large number of Arab troops on their soil, ended up opting to consolidate defence ties with the United States, which had proved its readiness to guarantee their security during the seven-month-long crisis brought about by Iraq's invasion of Kuwait. A question asked by a Persian Gulf Arab diplomat well describes the mentality of the Arab littoral states: 'When you have a visible security link to the United States, who's going to attack you if they know the United States will come and protect you?' He added: 'With Washington's now-clear commitment to maintain the Gulf States' independence, there is less need for Arab ground forces in the region . . . The Gulf states didn't really want massive Syrian or Egyptian ground troops in the Gulf.' As stated by an Arab journalist of the Persian Gulf, 'They want blue-eyed soldiers to protect them'.[29]

According to an Egyptian military source, Mubarak's decision was a result of 'the hesitation of the Gulf countries about what they want to do. They did not make decisions.' Other Arab analysts suggested that Mubarak also was annoyed at being pushed to the periphery in what had become primarily a discussion between the United States and the Gulf nations on future security arrangements in the region.[30] Deep down, the Persian Gulf Arabs knew that Arab solidarity was a sham. They were only paying lip service to it for home consumption.

When the United States emerged as the sole protector of the Arab monarchies, as discussed later, Iran's relationship with the Gulf Arabs deteriorated. In addition to Iran feeling betrayed by its Persian Gulf neighbours and dismayed by their drawing closer to the United States, its position on another important development, namely, the Arab–Israeli peace conference of October 1991, further affected the divided environment in the Persian Gulf. Economic *rapprochement* between Israel and the GCC countries also contributed to a change in their perception of the major threat, and Arab Gulf enmity was shifted away from Israel to Iran, which opposed the peace process. In turn, this shift brought the Arab littoral states more firmly into the Western economic and security system, as Iran continued to move in the opposite direction.

Local autonomy of the Persian Gulf in danger

Just as the British presence in the Persian Gulf was once maintained at Iran's cost, the US military presence, begun in the 1980s and dramatically increased in the early 1990s, was to proceed at Iran's expense. The strengthened presence of the United States in the Persian Gulf was also to cost its autonomy from global powers.

As described in Chapter 4, the efforts on the part of the local Arab states and global powers aimed at containing Iran's Islamic Revolution resulted, advertently or otherwise, in the undermining of the autonomy of the Persian Gulf region from outside powers, achieved in the aftermath of the British withdrawal from the area in 1971. As Iran had dominated an autonomous Persian Gulf region since 1971, the re-emergence of an outside power was seen as providing a counterweight to Iran's primacy. However, despite moves by the United States in this direction in the 1980s, welcomed and facilitated by the conservative Arab sheikhs, the global power could only begin to challenge the Iranian position in the 1990s, as before that time the United States did not really have the teeth to back up its policies, including the Carter doctrine. It lacked the necessary conventional forces on the ground to enforce its policies if they were challenged. This situation began to change in the later years of the 1980s.

Increasing US military presence

The year 1987 was a decisive period for the UAE *rapprochement* with the West, which, coupled with the developments of 1990–91, served as a prelude to the new UAE policy on the three islands that became effective in 1992. The relationship between the UAE and the United States began to blossom in 1987 when Abu Dhabi supported the United States in the 'tanker war', and continued to improve in 1990–91 when it provided important financial and logistical assistance to Operation Desert Storm.

A new, more aggressive US policy against Iran, the 'tanker war', wider international pressure on Iran, the reflagging of Kuwaiti vessels, the clash in Mecca between Iranian pilgrims and Saudi forces during the Hajj ceremony, which led to the death of around 400 Iranian pilgrims, and the risk of the Iran–Iraq War escalating into a regional confrontation all laid the groundwork for developments in the 1990s.

At the same time, the side effects of the Iran–Iraq War facilitated the *rapprochement* between the GCC and the United States. As the war, showing no sign of let-up, increasingly impinged on GCC countries, they drew closer to the West and the United States, in particular.

In October and November 1986 oil platforms belonging to the UAE came under attack. In the first attack, the raiding Iraqi aircraft, intending to attack the nearby Iranian Sassan oilfield, misfired. In the November attack, a 'lone foreign aircraft' fired two missiles that hit two linked UAE oil platforms.[31] Abu Dhabi responded by turning to the United States for aid to improve its air defences.[32] Later, reports about mines planted in the southern shipping lanes, and more attacks on UAE offshore oil facilities in 1988, further strengthened the trend.

With the inception of this new tense phase, the US presence in the Persian Gulf acquired dimensions beyond the merely symbolic. These incidents led to increasing cooperation between Abu Dhabi and the United States, including Operation Earnest Will, begun on 22 July 1987, in which the Western power escorted reflagged Kuwaiti oil tankers through the Strait of Hormuz and into and out of the war-torn Persian Gulf.[33] This operation continued into 1988.

Beyond escorting the reflagged ships, US military detachments became engaged in mine-sweeping operations, issued periodic warning to the Iranian navy, and attacked Iranian helicopter and vessels in October 1987 and April 1988, in addition to attacking two Iranian oil platforms and finally an Iranian airliner in July 1988. Through these naval actions the United States sought to demonstrate its seriousness and commitment to maintaining the security of the conservative sheikhs and bringing about a new order in the Persian Gulf with itself at its helm.

Following the clashes in Mecca, the embassies of Saudi and Kuwait in Tehran were stormed by demonstrators protesting the killing of the Iranian pilgrims. Around the same time, an explosion hit an ARAMCO gas plant, and several offices of Saudi airlines across the globe were bombed, as were a few installations inside the country.[34] Following these incidents, relations between Iran and the Arab Persian Gulf states deteriorated considerably.

These events came on the heels of a new policy, adopted by the Reagan administration following the Iran-Contra fiasco. The American government meant by the new policy, among other things, to re-establish its credibility with the Persian Gulf Arab states that had been taken aback by the news of the United States providing Iran with arms. The new policy aimed to close off all international sources of arms sales to Iran and to encourage the provision of arms and intelligence to Iraq and the Arab littoral states. This new policy significantly helped these states.

The new, aggressive US policy with regard to Iran marked the beginning of of a brief tense phase in the region, which started when Kuwait asked the United States to protect its ships and lasted until July 1988 when Iran accepted UN Security Council Resolution 598. This phase is viewed by some as marking the end of 'the appeasement phase', which had started when Iraq faltered in its war efforts in 1981 and which was viewed as a remnant of the peninsular states' tacit acceptance of the regional dominance of Iran under the Shah.[35]

The return of a global power to the Persian Gulf

In the 1990s, the United States adopted the policy that the British had applied in the region for one and a half centuries: guaranteeing the external security of the Arab Persian Gulf states by its direct presence and through, *inter alia*, the containment of Iran, as the most powerful regional state.

The early years of the 1990s saw the development of a new Persian Gulf, characterized mainly by the assumption by the United States of a new role in the region. Building on what preceded in the previous years and capitalizing on the end of the Cold War as well as Iraq's absurd invasion of Kuwait, the US government found a welcoming environment to rapidly enhance its military presence in the Persian Gulf. The conservative sheikhs, too, took advantage of the opportunity to allow US military forces on their soil for the first time – an opportunity that could not have been otherwise available to them. These developments and the way they were exploited left their deep imprint on the region for many years to come. They provided the United States with wide latitude to pursue its policies against its local nemesis, including through devising the 'dual containment policy' – a policy that both helped create an appropriate context for the revival of the issue of the three islands and needed it to develop.[36]

The easing of Cold War tensions affected the situation in the Persian Gulf much earlier than other parts of the world. The United States and the Soviet Union began cooperating at least as early as 1986 to pressure Iran to end the war, with methods including the consideration of a comprehensive arms embargo on Iran in late 1987, should Tehran have failed to accept Security Council Resolution 598.[37] Although the Persian Gulf was never a theatre in the US–Soviet Union Cold War, and the Russians never really penetrated the region, the end of the Cold War and the collapse of the Soviet Union allowed the United States more latitude to pursue its policies in the Gulf region. The disintegration of the Soviet Union had an adverse impact on radical forces throughout the Middle East, thus easing much of the tension in the area and boosting the conservative-moderate camp's self-esteem. Accordingly, it also further enabled the conservative monarchies in the area to feel freer to expand relations with the United States and the West in general, with less concern over a backlash from the regional Soviet allies and the Palestinians. Had it not been for the a thaw in the Cold War standoff in the first place, the task of the United States to flush the Iraqis out of Kuwait would have been much more complicated, if not outright impossible.

Facing a worsening economic situation, but still harbouring his ambitions to lead the Arab world through controlling the Persian Gulf, Iraqi president Saddam Hussein saw the takeover of Kuwait in August 1990 as a step toward seizing or controlling the assets of the Arab monarchies and placing himself firmly at the head of the Arab world. This Iraqi action radically altered the shape of strategic affairs in the Persian Gulf.

Feeling threatened, the Persian Gulf Arab monarchies reacted by inviting in Western help, which led to the unprecedented step of the Arab monarchies' allowing foreign troops onto their soil to protect them from Iraqi aggression. The United States, in an attempt to forestall any Iraqi designs on Saudi Arabia and to flush the Iraqis out of Kuwait, launched the largest American force mobilization since its involvement in Vietnam.

The Iraqi invasion of Kuwait created a situation in the Persian Gulf that enabled the Americans to enter a new phase in their direct presence. Upon the invasion, the US government led the international response and tried, in the meantime, to overcome the long-standing obstacles to its primacy in the region. After the invasion, the United States took three weeks to move a small rapid deployment force into the area and several months to move in enough equipment to enter the battle.

After the war, American military planners set out to tie the region into the US security web as never before, to cultivate indigenous armies and air forces that would be technologically compatible with their US counterparts and to negotiate access to airstrips, ports, roads, buildings and intelligence links should the United States choose to move into action itself.

Iraq's invasion galvanized considerable more unity among GCC member states. They all denounced the invasion and provided support to the Coalition during Operation Desert Storm. The UAE, which had supported the United States and the United Kingdom during the 'tanker war' of 1987–88, strongly supported the Coalition forces during the war over Kuwait, providing troops, extensive financial aid, basing rights and aid in kind. It spent a total of roughly $10 billion on the war. This reflected the fact that all the Arab sheikhs saw Iraq's move on Kuwait as a common threat.[38] The UAE steadily strengthened its strategic cooperation with the West after the Gulf War as well, and offered to host a pre-positioned US Army brigade on its soil.

After the Kuwait crisis, the United States was portrayed as the only country that possessed the capabilities needed to defend the Persian Gulf monarchies. It was claimed that 'none of the countries outside the greater Middle East, with the exception of the United States, seems capable, much less inclined, to project power into the region for the foreseeable future.'[39]

President Bush, in an address to a joint session of Congress celebrating the US victory over Iraq, announced his government's new policy with regard to the Persian Gulf and signalled a turning point in the American presence there. In his speech, he emphasized that 'commitment to peace in the Middle East does not end with the liberation of Kuwait.' He said that there would be an enhanced American military role, including 'a capable naval presence' in the Persian Gulf and regular exercises by US air and ground forces. 'Let it be clear,' he said, 'our vital national interests depend on a stable and secure Gulf.' He said the countries of the region would bear the principal burden of securing the peace in the wake of the victory over Iraq, but added 'America stands ready' to back up any security arrangement of the Persian Gulf nations.[40] His description of the US military role in the Persian Gulf was his most explicit at the time and reflected planning under way inside the administration and in the region for many weeks.

On the other side, as the brief moment of entertaining the use of Arab ground troops on their soil came to an end, the Persian Gulf Arab states soon turned almost exclusively to the United States and the West for protection. In this new situation, the United States was perceived as the Arab sheikhs' single protector.

The announcement in May 1992 of Egypt's decision to pull its troops out of Saudi Arabia came as the US Defense Secretary, Dick Cheney, was touring the region and discussing the details of future US military arrangements for the Persian Gulf Arab states. He reported 'significant progress' in his talks with them on regional security arrangements. At that stage, the United States was seeking to store large amounts of equipment in Saudi Arabia and other Arab states for use by US troops in a future crisis, and to conduct military manoeuvres with the Arab littoral states on a regular basis.[41]

Returning to Washington, Cheney revealed that he had reached general understandings with Saudi Arabia and other Arab governments on storing American military equipment in those countries, along with agreements to hold joint exercises. This paved the way for detailed negotiations and produced some progress with the smaller Arab countries, including the signing of a formal defence co-operation accord with Kuwait. The United States was seeking a strong security pact to prevent a return to the loose arrangements that had existed before Iraq's invasion of Kuwait.

In September 1991, Kuwait and the United States signed a ten-year renewable defence pact, which, as explained by the Pentagon, gave the United States the authority to pre-position stocks of weaponry and support materiel inside Kuwait, allowed US military personnel to conduct joint exercises with the Kuwaiti defence forces and permitted the Americans to obtain certain types of logistical support from Kuwait, such as the use of its ports by US Navy ships.[42] It was the first in a network of pacts signed by the United States and GCC member states.

At the conclusion of a six-day visit to Saudi Arabia, Kuwait, Bahrain, the United Arab Emirates and Qatar in March 1995, US Defense Secretary William Perry announced that 'the countries I visited are willing to work with the United States as we follow a policy ... to prevent aggression by Iraq and Iran.' Pentagon officials disclosed later that Perry's meetings with Qatar's emir resulted in an agreement 'to speed up plans to store enough supplies to support about 5,000 troops in battle. One brigade's supplies were already stationed in Kuwait, and the United States wanted to put [supplies for] a total of three brigades in the Gulf region in order to field an entire armoured division of about 15,000 to 17,000 soldiers should a new land war erupt.'[43]

Eventually, five of the six GCC member states – Bahrain, Kuwait, Oman, Qatar and the UAE – signed elaborate defence cooperation agreements with the United States. Saudi Arabia revived a 1977 training agreement and developed the most extensive relationship with the United States. The agreement with Qatar gave the United States 'unimpeded access' to its international airport, seaports, army bases and other military facilities. It also stipulated that the United States might, if necessary, pre-position in Qatar non-lethal equipment and supplies, oil, fuel, bombs and ammunition. It gave US military personnel access without passports.[44] Bahrain became the first Persian Gulf country to allow a permanent US naval presence on its territory.

Together with the deal with Saudi Arabia, this network of defence agreements allowed the United States flexibility in peacetime military exercises and in dealing with threats against the Arab oil powers in the area. More than ever, the United States could place itself in the position of unchallenged protector of the Arab conservative states in the area. While the rulers of Persian Gulf nations remained leery of a large foreign presence on their soil, they abandoned many of their traditional reservations after the United States led the coalition that drove Iraq from Kuwait.

As a result of these agreements, then, in a massive but still discreet strategic shift of US military assets, the United States positioned hundreds of warplanes, dozens of warships and tens of thousands of troops on the land of and offshore from its six Arab allies. This stood in sharp contrast to the situation before the military build-up leading to the 1991 Persian Gulf War, when the United States had watched the region from spy planes and stationed troops and equipment for emergencies well out of sight, 'over the horizon.'

While in the aftermath of the Cold War US forces were downsizing in every other part of the globe, they were on the increase in the Persian Gulf, to back up what was known as the 'dual containment policy' and to monitor and intimidate Iran and Iraq. As Iraq was already devastated and firmly subject to crippling comprehensive sanctions, the US government relied on its military might in the Persian Gulf to challenge Iran's supremacy in the area and to bolster the Arab states.

Consequently, in the mid-1990s about 9,000 US troops were stationed on GCC countries' territory, most of them in Saudi Arabia. Another 15,000 sailors and Marines were on the fifteen to twenty Navy warships in or near the Persian Gulf at any given time. Headquartered in Bahrain since 1994, the ships of the US 5th Fleet carried up to 100 warplanes and more than 100 Tomahawk missiles. Nearby was positioned one, sometimes two, nuclear submarines. Normally there were also thirteen Army and Marine ships, virtual floating equipment bases with enough tanks, artillery and supplies for 5,000 Marines and 5,000 soldiers. Besides the Navy planes, the US Air Force had stationed an estimated 170 warplanes, including fighters, bombers, tank-killers and intelligence and electronic warfare planes. Most were on the Arabian Peninsula in support of Operation Southern Watch, which enforced the UN-imposed 'no-fly zone' in southern Iraq. Some were stationed in Kuwait and Bahrain.[45] According to US spokespersons, at the same time, around 6,000 Air Force and other military personnel were based in Saudi Arabia.[46]

Troop strength was, and continues to be, significantly enhanced by year-round bilateral or multilateral exercises. Before the war, Oman was the only country to practise with US troops. In 1995 there were about 60 exercises in the region involving 50,000 US troops and virtually all indigenous Arab armed forces.[47]

In addition to the troop build-up, a brigade of American civilian contractors soon became involved in coordinating an unprecedented flood of US weapons sold to the region and in training the militaries of these countries in how to use their new arms. US military planners brought in American arms manufacturers and contractors to build sites and teach the Persian Gulf countries about the equipment they were buying. About 5,000 US government personnel and contractors operated in the region to implement these deals. Between 1990 and 1995, the countries agreed to purchase about $72.5 billion in weapons, equipment and military construction, according to the Pentagon.[48]

In the new security environment the UAE received special attention. Its strategic importance lay in both its location and the fact that it possessed around 5 per cent of the world's oil reserves. It was assumed that if Iran ever planned to disrupt the flow of oil through the Persian Gulf, the West would depend heavily on the UAE to challenge it. The UAE's strategic location has made it critical to collective military efforts in the southern Persian Gulf and has ensured that it will play an important future role in posturing against Iran in any perceived encounter in the area in the future.

The relationship between the United States and the UAE, which had blossomed in the late 1980s when Abu Dhabi supported the 'tanker war' and in the early 1990s when it provided important financial and logistical assistance to Operation Desert Storm, gained new momentum under the new security arrangement with the United States. They cooperated closely during the 'tanker war' and the Gulf War, and the UAE provided port call facilities and support during Operation Earnest Will. The US Navy and the US Marine Corps have conducted joint exercises with the UAE since July 1990, when Saddam Hussein first began to threaten the UAE. The UAE provided the United States with $6.572 billion in direct aid during the Persian Gulf War of 1991, and $218 million in goods and services.[49]

The UAE negotiated a security arrangement with the United States in 1992 that offered the United States access to UAE air and naval facilities. They signed a more comprehensive defence agreement on 23 July 1994. As a result, the US Navy is on the record as having made nearly 300 ship visits a year to the UAE during most of the 1990s. The UAE signed a similar agreement with the United Kingdom and France.[50] It has also emerged as one of the world's largest markets for US arms manufacturers; Abu Dhabi purchased $360 million in US arms in 1992–94 alone.[51]

Since the Persian Gulf War, Jabel Ali port in Dubai has become crucial to the US naval operations in the area, because it is the safest liberty port in the region and the only harbour deep enough to berth an aircraft carrier. Fujayrah, which faces the Indian Ocean and is connected to the Persian Gulf coast by a modern road, would be critical to American operations should the Strait of Hormuz be closed off. US warplanes have also flown out of UAE airbases on support missions for Operation Southern Watch over Iraq, and the United States has pre-positioned materiel on UAE soil.[52]

The US Navy maintains a small pre-positioning facility at Jabel Ali, uses Dubai as its main R&R port in the Persian Gulf and has a small naval support facility at Fujayrah. From the 1990s to 2003, the UAE permitted US tanker aircraft to operate out of the country in support of the 'no-fly zone' in southern Iraq, and cooperated with the United States in contingency planning. The UAE agreed in 1995 to pre-position one US Army armoured brigade in the country. The force included 120 tanks and 70 AIFVs. The UAE negotiated a status of forces agreement with the United States and the details of a pre-positioning agreement and suitable cost-sharing.[53]

Dual containment

Extensive efforts were also made by the United States to complement its newly enhanced military presence in the Persian Gulf by bringing more pressure to bear on Iran at the political level. The Clinton Administration embarked on a new path of trying to weaken and isolate Iran with a view to preventing it from re-emerging as an effective power in the area. The new US government also meant to rearrange the Middle East to suit 'the Middle East peace process.'

Confrontational phase 159

For much of the 1980s, the United States had sought to play Iran and Iraq against one another. But with UN sanctions imposed on Iraq after its invasion of Kuwait, the Clinton administration adopted a new course of action, dubbed 'a strategy of dual containment', which emerged from a comprehensive policy review ordered by President Clinton. Secretary of State Warren Christopher hinted at the emerging shift in February 1993 by branding Iran an 'international outlaw' and a 'dangerous country' for 'the support of terrorism' and 'the pursuit of nuclear weapons.'[54]

The broad outlines of the new approach were described in a speech in May 1993 by Martin S. Indyk, the Senior Director for Middle East policy at the National Security Council, to the Washington Institute for Near East Policy, a research group. He stated that the new policy stemmed from 'a clear-headed assessment of the antagonism that both regimes harbor toward the US and its allies in the region'.[55]

He added, 'We do not seek a confrontation but we will not normalize relations . . . until and unless Iran's policies change across the board.' He said the administration was concerned that if Iran was left unchecked, its military power and influence within five years could be comparable to Iraq's before the 1990 invasion of Kuwait. 'Iran does not yet face the kind of international regime that has been imposed on Iraq,' Indyk said. But he added that Washington would 'work energetically to persuade our European and Japanese allies, as well as Russia and China,' not to allow Iran to build up its military. He said bluntly, 'If we fail in our efforts to modify Iranian behavior, five years from now Iran will be much more capable of posing a real threat to Israel and to Western interests in the Middle East.'[56]

This policy departed from the past US practice of helping to build up one of the countries in hopes of balancing the other's military and political influence. The new US objective was to ensure that both Iran and Iraq remained equally weak for an indefinite period.

As the clock had been set back in Iraq for so many years as a result of the ferocious American military campaign and crippling global sanctions imposed by the United Nations against that country, the new policy mainly targeted Iran and meant to ensnare it in a tight web of international trade restrictions aimed at depriving it of the income and technology it needed to develop its economy after the eight-year war with Iraq. More concretely, the Americans sought to exclude the largest Persian Gulf littoral state – Iran – from regional affairs. The Clinton administration worked under the assumption that it would be easy to sell the new policy to its Arab partners, who had just been threatened by Iraq and remained suspicious of Iran's revolutionary foreign policy.

Contrary to the twin pillars policy, the dual containment policy aimed at depriving Iran of its advantages in the region and pushing it into isolation. The dual containment policy went into effect on 6 May 1995, when President Clinton issued an Executive Order banning US trade with and investment in Iran. The unilateral sanctions were toughened on 5 March 1996, when Clinton signed legislation that would impose a 'secondary boycott', that is, a series of sanctions on foreign companies or individuals who did business with Iran.[57]

A side effect of this new policy was its divisiveness, in the sense that it had the potential of pitting Iran and the lower Persian Gulf Arab sheikhs against each other. There were growing signs that the new US policy included the portrayal of Iran as a threat to its neighbours in the Persian Gulf. CIA Director Robert M. Gates said on 27 March 1992 that 'the Iranian government is buying $2 billion worth of weapons from foreign suppliers each year in a drive to again become the preeminent power in the Persian Gulf region.[58]

Rosemarie Said Zahlan has drawn a parallel between the new American policy and the order that the British maintained for a long period in the Persian Gulf, viewing the introduction of the dual containment policy as a form of return to the old policy pursued by the British prior to their withdrawal.[59] Such a policy formed the basis and set the context for the issue of the three islands to re-emerge once again.

Contributing factors: shift and realignment in the Arab world

At the same time, parallel and matching developments in the Arab world facilitated the increasing US presence in the Persian Gulf region and led to the lessening of its cost for the local Arab monarchies. These developments included the weakening of Arab radicals in the Arab world and the strengthening of the conservative-moderate Arab camp at the expense of the Palestinian movement and the Arab radicals who supported it. This trend, described as 'a mood of pragmatism', which had already begun some time in the late 1980s, culminated with the collapse of the Soviet Union and the humiliating Iraqi defeat in 1991.

The weakening of Arab radicals

The Arab League summit of November 1987 was a victory for the conservative-moderate Arab camp. The summiteers not only invited Egypt back into the Arab fold and called for an increase in Cairo's politico-military role in the Persian Gulf, but also compelled Syria to join in the official condemnation of Iran for occupying 'part of Iraqi territory and its procrastination in accepting UN SCR 598' and to endorse the Arab League's support of 'Kuwait in confronting the threats and aggressions of the Iranian regime.' They also condemned Iran for what they termed as 'bloody criminal acts perpetrated by the Iranians in the vicinity of the Holy Mosque in Mecca.'[60]

The visit to Kuwait of the Egyptian defence minister only a month after the Amman Summit and the Egyptian security guarantees offered to GCC states reinforced the marginalization of Syria in the Persian Gulf and the failure of Iran to cow the conservative Persian Gulf states into abandoning Iraq.

The cease-fire between Iran and Iraq also further reduced the tension in the Arab world and stimulated diplomatic interaction among Arab states. In the months of November and December 1988 Algeria and Egypt restored full diplomatic relations. Saddam's official visit to Libya and Egypt led to the improvement of Iraq's bilateral relations. The creation of the Maghreb Union in mid-1988 was different from previous Arab association in that it brought together governments proclaiming all three prevalent Arab political lines (radical Libya, non-aligned Algeria and the pro-Western states of Tunisia and Morocco) under one roof.

The return of Egypt to the fold of the Arab League in May 1989, following the withdrawal of Syria's objections as the last obstacle, and without Syria receiving any concession on its standoff with Israel, was the ultimate sign of a major shift and realignment within the Arab world.[61] The new trend put Iran and Syria under pressure and on a different track from the mainstream in the region. This transformation in the world of Arab states came at the cost of Iran's foreign policy objectives and resulted in a weakening of Iran's regional posture.

The defeat of pan-Arabism

Iraq's invasion of Kuwait struck a near-fatal blow to the pan-Arabist project held dear by, among others, the Iraqi Ba'athists, and to its drive to inflame what it described as historic rivalries between the Persians and the Arabs. With the invasion and ransacking of one Arab state by another, pan-Arabism lost most of its appeal in the Persian Gulf and, to a large extent, ceased to be the impediment to a strategic *rapprochement* between the Arab conservatives and the West in the post-Kuwait war era that it had been since the British withdrawal.

This development helped substantially to decrease Iraq's activism with regard to the three islands and removed a dual constraint on the GCC countries, including the UAE: on the one hand, they were relieved, to a great extent, of the potential for pan-Arabic agitation within their societies and from the larger Arab world; on the other, they were allowed a wider margin of manoeuvre free from Iraqi heavy-handedness.

As a result, pragmatism could now become the watchword in the area. This approach helped remove the obstacles to the UAE embarking on the path of *rapprochement* with the West – without the fear of a backlash from within the UAE or the Arab world.

The Palestinian effects

The situation of the Persian Gulf was affected in varying degrees by the evolution of the Palestinian question for the best part of the twentieth century. The importance that the Arabs 'on the street' attach to Palestine subjected also the Persian Gulf Arab rulers to considerable strain. Especially in the wake of their independence, the Palestinian question further preoccupied the Persian Gulf rulers, as they daily found themselves confronted with different issues stemming from or affected by the Palestinian question.

One of the goals the British pursued during their presence in the Persian Gulf area was to keep the Arab sheikhs aloof from trends in other parts of the Arab Middle East. In so doing, they succeeded more or less in charting a different socio-political course for the Persian Gulf Arabs and in barring them from actively interacting with the larger Arab world. This policy served the interests of the United Kingdom by minimizing the impact of Arab nationalism and the Arab–Israeli conflict on the Arabs in the Persian Gulf area.

The departure of the British rendered it difficult to keep the Persian Gulf separated from the trends and divisions in the wider Arab world. The conservative sheikhs lost the ability to shield themselves from the main currents in the region, such as the Palestinian movement and the Islamic Revolution in Iran. The impact of developments in adjacent areas was also compounded by the presence of large Palestinian and Shi'ite communities in the Persian Gulf.

Palestinian expatriates were important in spreading the creed of Arab nationalism in the Persian Gulf. After the 1948 exodus, many Palestinians settled in Kuwait, Saudi Arabia, Qatar, Abu Dhabi and Dubai, and managed to establish large communities there. They became teachers, managers and civil servants, and gradually helped make the Palestinian problem the key element of Arab nationalist thinking, and kept it alive in the forefront of people's minds. The liberation of Palestine became the ultimate goal of all Arabs, and Arab unity was seen as the only way to achieve it.[62]

After the Arab–Israeli War of 1967, the Kuwaiti and Saudi governments provided funds to the front-line Arab states, which helped these Gulf governments to buy the stability of their own regimes in the midst of the upheavals of nationalist feeling that followed the Arab defeat. The Arab–Israeli War of 1973 further promoted the Palestinian cause throughout the Persian Gulf and forced the local Arab rulers to distance themselves from the United States.

After the disappearance of the Shah from the scene and the Soviet invasion of Afghanistan, as the United States worked to improve its Persian Gulf relationships, the unresolved Palestinian issue remained one of the most important impediments. This issue acquired a new acuity in the field of US–Persian Gulf relations and remained the most immediate source of misunderstanding and distrust between the United States and conservative Arabs. All of the Persian Gulf States refused to back the March 1979 Egypt–Israel treaty because it fell short of providing for Palestinian self-determination.

In the 1980s, the Islamic Revolution further complicated the situation. Saudi Arabia drew closer to Syria, declared its total opposition to the Camp David accords and distanced itself from Anwar al-Sadat and his public embrace of America and the American presence. The Saudis refused to take part in Alexander Haig's 'strategic consensus' scheme, whereby the Reagan administration proposed a sad replica of the defence pacts of the 1950s.[63] In other words, not every Arab country could side with the Americans within the framework of anti-Soviet 'strategic cooperation' as long as Israel opposed the minimal aspirations of the Palestinians. The Palestinian question was one of the obstacles that precluded the establishment of US supremacy in the Persian Gulf in the 1980s.

As Anthony Cordesman wrote in 1984, 'The Palestinian issue is a popular cause whose importance is steadily increasing', adding that, 'virtually every citizen in the Gulf under the age of 25 has grown up in a political atmosphere that has made the Palestinian issue a sine qua non of Arab consciousness.'[64] Thus, no Gulf state could afford to ignore the Palestinians in shaping its relations with the West. This meant that the Gulf rulers 'must balance their need for partnership with the West against the need to respond to each crisis in the Arab–Israeli conflict'.[65]

While the US options on the security of the Persian Gulf and the Palestinian question were quite limited – either accommodate the Arabs or incur their resentment – the crisis over Kuwait provided a strategic way out. The PLO's support of Saddam's invasion of Kuwait and the enthusiasm with which some Palestinians in Kuwait greeted the invaders provided the Arab conservatives in the area with an excellent opportunity to detach themselves from the Palestinians. It was important in the sense that it helped the littoral Arab states to unlink the Palestinian question from the issue of security in the Persian Gulf, and to enter into strategic relationships with the Americans.

Consequent upon this development, all of the Persian Gulf Arab monarchies agreed to attend the 1991 Madrid Conference, which involved them for the first time in face-to-face negotiations with Israel. While Saudi Arabia and Kuwait were less enthusiastic, the other sheikhdoms went even the extra mile towards normalization with Israel.

Furthermore, the support of the Gulf states for the Palestinian–Israeli peace process and their economic *rapprochement* with Israel, before the Netanyahu government, led to a shift in their major threat perception and enmity away from Israel to concentrate on Iran, which opposed the peace process. In turn, this shift also brought the Arab littoral states more clearly into the Western economic and security system and left Iran isolated.[66] To some extent, the Arab Gulf conservatives came to view Israel as an additional balancing factor that would deter the Arab radicals from threatening them.

Therefore, as was the case with Britain, the new intervening global power succeeded in charting a distinct course for the Persian Gulf sheikhs independent of that of the rest of the Arab world, disengaging them from such broader Arab issues as the Palestinian question and reducing Persian Gulf financial aid to other Arab countries to a trickle. At the same time, while Israel had always viewed any special relationship between Arab Middle Eastern countries, especially Egypt and Saudi Arabia, and the United States as a dangerous threat to its national security, this was not the case as far as the small Persian Gulf Arab states were concerned.

A new cycle of activity on the islands

In early 1992 several striking trends were already in progress in the Persian Gulf area:

- With the policies of excluding Iran and containing it definitely on the agenda of the West and the conservative sheikhs on the one hand, and Arab radicals undermined on the other, it became soon clear that the policy of *rapprochement* with the GCC countries that Tehran had adopted and pursued after the cease-fire in the Iran–Iraq War was leading nowhere.
- Excluding Iran and reneging on their agreement with Egypt and Syria, the

Arab littoral states were firmly embarked on the path of relying on the West, and the United States in particular, in establishing a new security arrangement in the region.
- With Iraq effectively neutralized, the sheikhs and the West found themselves in agreement on a shared strategy to counter-balance Iran, contain it in the region, and deny it the role it considered itself fit to play by virtue of its natural position in the area.
- With Iraq's humiliating defeat, the entire radical tendency in the Arab world found itself on the defensive and in decline.

In view of these trends, the UAE and its allies in the GCC perceived the Persian Gulf emerging from the Kuwait crisis in quite a new light. These trends brought them to reconsider the tacit recognition of Iranian supremacy in the Gulf in which they had acquiesced during the 1970s and, to a lesser extent, in the 1980s. Especially with Iraq being excluded from the power balance in the area, the UAE, along with the conservative-moderate Arab camp, perceived it all the more necessary to contribute effectively to the US policy of containing Iran that was already in place.

Concurrently, they found more general developments in the wider region to be promising, providing them with wider latitude to disregard the declining Arab radicals and to build a more sustainable relationship with the West. Other than these new trends, the perception of the UAE and its partners in the GCC that the Iranian economy was ravaged and its military prowess undermined as a result of the Iran–Iraq War, which had, in their view, ended on terms different from those that Iran had sought, played an important role in their decision to chart a new course in the area.

The new cycle of activity over Abu Musa, in early 1992 and onwards, was a byproduct of these new trends and the deterioration of the relationship between Iran and certain GCC countries that they had brought about.[67] The Abu Musa controversy was, therefore, both an effect and a means of furthering the strategy of outweighing, containing and isolating Iran, and it did not cause the relationship between the two parties to worsen. Bilateral ties had already suffered as a result of the Arab littoral states' failing to acknowledge Iran's diplomatic overture, the continued overwhelming on- and offshore military presence of the United States and its allies in the area and the increasing strength of the conservative-moderate Arab camp in the region.

April and August 1992 incidents

The UAE's perception of the new situation prevailing in the Persian Gulf and the wider region paved the ground for the policy it adopted in the spring of 1992. While allowing Iran to register its discontent over the new trend in the region, incidents in April and August 1992 also provided the UAE and the conservative-moderate Arab camp with an opportunity to embark upon a new active policy against Iran. They first focused on the island of Abu Musa and then escalated the controversy by extending it to the islands of Greater and Lesser Tunbs.

The Kuwait crisis and the security developments that ensued, especially the growing American presence in the area, had made Iranian authorities uneasy and further focused their attention on Iran's lifeline and strategically important territories in the Persian Gulf – reminiscent of the early 1960s when Iran's imperial government accorded new priority to the Persian Gulf in its foreign policy. A tour of the three islands by President Rafsanjani in February 1992 highlighted the importance Iran attached to the stability of the Gulf as its strategic lifeline and as an important part of its foreign policy. During the trip, he ordered the opening of a slaughterhouse and the creation of an industrial fishing fleet.[68]

Accordingly, the security agreements that the Persian Gulf states were signing with outside powers, the growing and hostile US military presence, the role Egypt had tried to play in the Persian Gulf, coupled with the hostility it expressed against Iran, were all alarming to the Iranian authorities. Tehran reacted with anxiety and suspicion to certain activities in and around the three islands and soon became apprehensive about the possibility that the UAE, assisted by local and global powers, was trying to undermine its position with regard to the islands by various means, such as sending increasing number of foreign nationals to Abu Musa.

Iran had always been suspicious of such activities. According to Richard Schofield, Iran had complained in 1983 that there were too many foreigners on the jointly administered island. Since then, in response to the growing visits by non-Sharjah nationals to the island, Iranian patrols in the southern part of the island under Sharjah administration became increasingly regular. In 1989, Iran agreed that the patrols would not enter into Arab villages.[69]

Moreover, the brief cycle of activity on the islands in 1980 by Iraq and, to a much lesser extent, by the UAE was still fresh in the Iranians' memory. The Iranians always noted such activities with distrust, which had begun in the aftermath of the Islamic Revolution at a time when the new political establishment was yet to settle down. Saddam's plan to raid the islands and take them over in 1980, referred to earlier, and the preparations made to turn the lower Persian Gulf into a foothold from which to carry this out had already alarmed Iranian authorities.

Some analysts also attributed Iran's new measure related to Abu Musa to larger strategic goals, including Iran's wish to send a message to Washington that Tehran was displeased with the large US post-war military presence in the Persian Gulf and with the United States's attempts to isolate Iran in the area. The Abu Musa move 'is a security, strategic-driven decision, and so it would be very difficult to believe that it's not related to the increased US presence' in the Persian Gulf, said Rouhollah Ramazani, an analyst at the University of Virginia. Tehran was saying that it 'is a player and has got to be taken into account, whereas everything the United States has done so far has been exclusionary' of Iran, Ramazani said.[70]

Iranian diplomatic sources also were quoted as saying that Iran wanted to counter the growing US influence in the region after military agreements had been signed with Kuwait, Bahrain and Qatar. According to these sources the Iranian move was aimed, therefore, at preventing the UAE from providing any facilities to the United States on the islands.[71]

Note should also be taken of the fact that the largest single group of foreigners on Abu Musa Island was Egyptian and, given the long-standing enmity between

166 *Confrontational phase*

the governments of Iran and Egypt at the time, the presence of a large number of Egyptians on the island would simply have added to the sense of alarm on the Iranians' part.

The UAE reactions to Iran's placement of certain restrictions on the entry of non-UAE citizens working on the jointly administered island of Abu Musa in April and August 1992 served as the starting point for a new round of activity over the three islands. Reports of what actually happened in these two incidents are highly contradictory and it is out of the scope of this research to discuss them in details. What is extremely important is the escalation of the controversy out of proportion to the initial incidents and, despite Iran's later remedies, its extension to the Greater and Lesser Tunbs.

Beginning on 14 April 1992, a section of the international media, quoting 'diplomats and travelers', reported that in early April Iran had taken control of the entire island of Abu Musa. According to these reports, 'Iran threw out an unknown number of the 700 Arabs living on Abu Musa.' They were also quoted as saying that 'Iranians also closed the only school, the desalination plant and the police station on the UAE side of the island.' The sources all spoke on condition of anonymity.[72] Persian Gulf-based diplomats were also quoted as saying, 'It is a very serious situation . . . this raises a lot of questions about Iran's intentions in the region, particularly at a time when they are re-arming as quickly as they can.'[73]

It is noteworthy that all media reports on the evictions and closures on Abu Musa originated only from anonymous sources, and none was attributed to UAE officials.[74]

Iran's foreign minister Ali Akbar Velayati almost immediately denied that any Arabs had been expelled from Abu Musa.[75] He renewed Iran's denial of its reported takeover of Abu Musa Island a week later as well, reaffirming that 'the Arab citizens on the island have rights [equal] to those of the Iranian citizens on it'.[76] He also explained on Iranian television that

> during the past few years great many measures have been adopted to develop Abu Musa Island. Included among these measures is the upgrading of the island, in the administrative organization of the country, from a district to a governorate. It has been said that the Islamic Republic of Iran intends to expel the Arab residents of the said island. We categorically deny that [claim]. That is not the case whatsoever. The Arab residents of the island, like other residents, are respected and held in esteem; their rights are preserved.[77]

Deputy Foreign Minister Besharati of Iran also noted that '[th]ese days the issue of the Abu Musa Island is in the air and several details have appeared in the media which have no truth at all. We abide by what Iran agreed with the United Arab Emirates shortly after its creation in 1971.'[78]

Several months later, President Rafsanjani, recalling the incident in April during a Friday Prayers Sermon, tried to throw some light on what led to the controversy in April:

Lately, some seven or eight months ago, we arrested a few individuals in the territorial waters of the island. They were armed and had come there on armed boats. They could provide no explanation of why they had come over there. They could be neither fishermen nor anything else. They were neither Iranians nor Arabs. At present one of them is still in prison; he is from the Netherlands. Now what an armed Dutchman has got to do around Abu Musa Island, on an armed boat, is something which must be explained. This is, seriously, a curious issue.[79]

In late September 1992, Fumani-Ha'eri, the Director-General for the Persian Gulf in the Iranian Foreign Ministry, provided a similar explanation in an interview:

Some eight months ago, a boat carrying weapons and ammunition and including a Dutch passenger was stopped by Iranian authorities near Abu Musa Island. The Islamic Republic of Iran, in view of the sensitivity of the region and the need to maintain its security, adopted certain security measures for foreigners. However, nothing has happened with regards to the people of Sharjah who live in the island. We told our UAE brothers that the policy of the Islamic Republic of Iran towards the Abu Musa Island has not changed and that all agreements already reached between Iran and Sharjah remain valid.[80]

What may be concluded from available sources can be summarized as follows: Iran's security concerns related to Abu Musa Island led the Iranian authorities to suggest that it should issue passes to non-UAE nationals. In other words, from the Iranian perspective, this was a dispute over the right of access to Abu Musa, which essentially raised the issue of sovereignty. By virtue of the letter Iran's foreign minister had sent to the British Foreign Secretary dated 25 November 1971, referred to in Chapter 3, Iran considered itself entitled to 'take any measures in the island of Abu Musa which in its opinion would be necessary to safeguard the security of the island or of the Iranian forces.' The British response to this letter indicated that it had been conveyed to the ruler of Sharjah, who had made no comment on it.

Nonetheless, the UAE refused to agree to this measure. These circumstances led to the incident in April. Later, after a four-month interval, which might have allowed UAE officials to make their minds up after consulting with regional and global friends, they came back by dispatching a passenger ferry, the *Khatir*, with mostly foreigners aboard, to Abu Musa and, as a result, the issue got blown out of all proportion. The issue came to a head on 22 August 1992 when Iranian officials turned back the *Khatir*. What was noteworthy about this incident was the fact that it received full media coverage in the Arab world and in the West.

The *Khatir*, while carrying around 100 teachers to work on the island of Abu Musa, was refused permission by Iranian authorities to dock, the official Emirates news agency WAM reported. 'Iranian officials on the island intercepted the ves-

168 *Confrontational phase*

sel and prevented it from docking at the port after detaching its anchors,' WAM said. Teachers on the ship told the Associated Press that most of the passengers were Palestinians, Jordanians and Egyptians. There were ten UAE nationals, they said.[81] According to a police spokesman in Sharjah, the passengers had waited aboard the ship for three days to land, but had been refused the right to do so until such time as they had obtained either visitors' or residential visas from the Iranian authorities. These demands were contrary to 'political agreements with the Iranian authorities', the spokesman added.[82]

The Islamic Republic News Agency (IRNA), for its part, reported that a passenger ship of Sharjah with 104 passengers aboard, which had been seized at Iran's Persian Gulf island of Abu Musa for unauthorized entry at its port, returned to Sharjah on 24 August. According to IRNA, while the ship was in custody, her passengers, who were nationals of countries other than those of the Persian Gulf, as well as her crew members, were offered food and conventional services. Iranian Foreign Ministry spokesman Morteza Sarmadi said entry of foreign nationals to the Iranian island of Abu Musa must be consistent with normal procedures agreed upon between Iran and Sharjah. On the basis of the agreement, arriving vessels had to obtain authorization to enter in the territorial waters of the island, and in order to step onto the island any foreign nationals aboard the arriving ships had to obtain entry permits from the Iranian port authorities.[83]

Finally, in light of further developments, it became clear that the claim that UAE resident nationals had been evicted and that the island had been taken over completely and annexed to Iran was inaccurate.

The UAE's reactions

After these incidents, the UAE adopted an increasingly hard-line position, thus rendering a compromise very difficult, if not impossible, on the issue of access to the island. At the same time, it also displayed a more assertive posture by publicizing its demands against Iran in talks. This attitude was a striking departure from that of the successive UAE governments of the preceding 20 years. Noteworthy among the unprecedented positions the UAE adopted was the raising of the stakes too high by seeking to widen the controversy to include two other islands, the Greater and Lesser Tunbs. The actions taken by the UAE with regard to the April and August incidents can be summarized as follows:

Raising the issue at regional and international forums

The communiqué issued by the 44th session of the Ministerial Council of the GCC, held in Jeddah on 8 and 9 September 1992, referred to the issue of the three islands as the second-most important issue on its agenda, after the situation between Iraq and Kuwait and preceding the Palestinian question. The communiqué stated, in part, the following:

> The Council is attending with great concern to the measures taken by Iran on the island of Abu Musa and to events unfolding there. It expresses its strong

condemnation of the measures taken by Iran on the island, representing as they do a violation of the sovereignty and territorial integrity of a GCC State and a breach of security and stability in the region. The Council calls upon the Islamic Republic of Iran to honor the Memorandum of Understanding concluded by the Emirate of Sharjah and Iran at the relevant time, while stressing the fact that the island of Abu Musa has been the responsibility of the Government of the United Arab Emirates since the establishment of the federation, and it expresses its outright rejection of the continued occupation by the Islamic Republic of Iran of the Greater Tunb and Lesser Tunb islands belonging to the United Arab Emirates.

The communiqué contains two more paragraphs on the islands, dealing with the impact of the issue on bilateral relations and the need to abide by international law. In a letter to the UN Secretary-General dated 15 September 1992, the representative of Kuwait, as the chair of the GCC Council, requested the circulation of the communiqué as a document of the General Assembly and of the Security Council.[84]

The statement issued by the ministers for foreign affairs of the Damascus Declaration countries in their sixth meeting, held in Doha, Qatar, on 9–10 September, in the same way expressed 'strong condemnation of the unwarranted measures [Iran] had taken on the island in violation of the sovereignty and the territorial integrity of the UAE.' It also expressed 'their outright rejection of the continued occupation by the Islamic Republic of Iran of the Greater Tunb and Lesser Tunb islands belonging to the United Arab Emirates.' This statement was also later transmitted to the UN Secretary-General for circulation as document of the General Assembly and of the Security Council.[85]

In its regular session on 13 September 1992, the Arab League adopted a resolution concerning 'the occupation by the Islamic Republic of Iran of the Arab islands belonging to the United Arab Emirates in the Arabian Gulf.' In this resolution the Council decided:

i   To stand by the United Arab Emirates in its adherence to full sovereignty over the islands of Abu Musa, Greater Tunb and Lesser Tunb, and to denounce Iran's illegal occupation of these islands;
ii To state the Council's unqualified support for all measures taken by the United Arab Emirates to assert its sovereignty over the islands and to place the issue of the Iranian violations – which most seriously endanger the security and stability of the region – before the United Nations;
iii To call upon the Islamic Republic of Iran to respect the pacts and covenants it has concluded with the United Arab Emirates, as well as that country's sovereignty over Abu Musa, Greater Tunb and Lesser Tunb islands.

This resolution was also later transmitted to the UN Secretary-General for circulation as a document of the Security Council[86] and of the UN General Assembly.[87]

The UAE's permanent UN envoy also met with UN Secretary-General Dr Boutros Boutros-Ghali on 8 October. According to the UAE news agency, the envoy informed Boutros-Ghali about the latest developments in the region, especially the crisis between the UAE and Iran over the three islands of Abu Musa and the Greater and Lesser Tunbs. He also met the envoys of Britain, Russia, India, Venezuela, Belgium and Austria and explained to them the UAE stance on the three islands and the latest developments in the region.[88]

In late November, UAE Minister of State for Foreign Affairs Sheikh Hamdan ibn Zayed al-Nahayan said that his government had 'taken its dispute with Iran over the three strategic islands to the United Nations.' Quoted by *Al-Hayat* newspaper, he invited Secretary-General Boutros-Ghali to send an envoy to the region. Foreign Minister Rashed Abdallah had also delivered a memorandum on the islands to the UN chief a week earlier, and Boutros-Ghali had then received the Iranian representative to the world body.[89]

Subjecting negotiations to preconditions

In a move that demonstrated the UAE's assertiveness and self-assurance in holding to its hard-line position, Minister of State for Foreign Affairs Sheikh Hamdan ibn Zayed al-Nahayan cancelled, on 10 September, a scheduled visit to Iran to resume talks on the disagreement. He had been invited by the Iranian foreign minister during his trip to the UAE in June as part of a regional tour. As a Western diplomat was quoted by Agence France Presse as saying, it was an 'extremely serious development' that could trigger fresh tension. The same newswire service quoted an unidentified UAE Foreign Ministry official as saying, 'it has been decided to cancel the visit because the UAE is convinced that there is no desire by the Iranian side to ensure the success of the visit.' This source gave two reasons for the cancellation:

> The first is that Iran refuses to issue a statement saying the visit is meant to discuss the island dispute. The second is the statement by the Iranian Foreign Ministry spokesman asserting claim over the three islands. . . Despite the UAE's keenness on conducting a direct dialogue with the Islamic Republic of Iran, the visit became useless. It will not serve the aspired objectives, and its results have become known in advance because those two indications clearly prove that the Iranian side has no desire to respond to this keenness and to the statement issued by the GCC foreign ministers.[90]

The fact that UAE officials expected Iran to accede, even before negotiations, to their demands demonstrated how decisive they perceived the force realignment in the area to be and how they believed their position to be strengthened. This behaviour stood in stark contrast to their approach in the preceding 20 years, and the fact that they had never initiated any move in the past in this respect indicates that they were only dragged into it by others who pursued their own agendas. The

Confrontational phase 171

breaking off of negotiations with Iran, discussed in the following section, further demonstrated the above.

Breaking off negotiations

The UAE's efforts to include the two islands of Greater Tunb and Lesser Tunb in the agenda of bilateral talks and their decision to break off negotiations upon Iranian opposition to their inclusion constituted another crucial development indicating the new and different UAE attitude. Not only had this issue not been raised by UAE officials publicly since April, but also, according to Iranian sources, neither had it been mentioned at the meeting between President Rafsanjani and the highest ranking UAE official (the foreign minister) present at the Jakarta Summit of Non-aligned Nations in September 1992, and the UAE Foreign minister had only registered objections regarding Abu Musa Island.[91] The reference to the Tunbs appeared for the first time in the GCC statement issued on 9 September 1992.

The insistence on the part of the UAE delegation that the Tunbs be included on the agenda of negotiations between Iran and the UAE led to their breaking off. In a statement, Iran's chief delegate to the talks at a lower level said the discussions, held on 28 September in Abu Dhabi, broke down because the UAE 'insisted that the problem of the two Tunbs should be on the agenda. We told them nobody is allowed to talk about the sovereignty of any land of Iran. The case of Abu Musa is different. There exists an agreement between Iran and Sharjah on the island.'[92] He further said that, during the negotiations, 'we announced our readiness to settle the Abu Musa issue, underlined Iran's adherence to the 1971 agreement and invited the UAE delegation to visit Tehran to follow up the talks.'[93]

On the other hand, the hard-line UAE position was reflected in the statement the UAE government issued after the talks broke off. This statement, which sounds like an ultimatum, reads in its main part as follows:

> During these meetings, the UAE delegation presented the delegation of the Islamic Republic of Iran with the following demands:
>
> 1 Ending the military occupation of the islands of Greater Tunb and Lesser Tunb.
> 2 Emphasizing Iran's commitment to the 1971 memorandum of understanding on the island of Abu Musa.
> 3 Refraining from interfering in any way and under any circumstances or pretexts in the UAE's exercise of its full sovereignty over its portion of the island of Abu Musa, in accordance with the memorandum of understanding.
> 4 Canceling all arrangements and measures imposed by Iran on the State organs on the island of Abu Musa, the State citizens and the non-UAE residents.
> 5 Finding an appropriate framework to resolve the issue of sovereignty over the island of Abu Musa within a definite period of time.

172 *Confrontational phase*

> In view of the Iranian side's insistence on refusing to discuss the issue of ending the Iranian occupation of the islands of Greater Tunb and Lesser Tunb or to agree on referring the issue to the International Court of Justice, it has become impossible to continue to discuss the issue and other subjects in this meeting.
>
> The UAE would like to point out in this regard that it has maintained sovereignty over Greater Tunb and Lesser Tunb since early history, and the Iranian military occupation of the two islands in November 1971 will not change their legal status. International law confirms that forcible occupation does not grant the occupying state sovereignty over an occupied region no matter how long this occupation lasts.
>
> The UAE believes the Iranian side is responsible for not achieving any progress in the talks. As a result of this, the UAE has no choice but to resort to all available peaceful means to assert its sovereignty over the three islands.[94]

Iran's assistance in facilitating the reopening of schools in the Arab quarter of Abu Musa and the return of the teachers and their families on 11 November 1992, which was announced on 14 November, did not lead to moderation on the part of the UAE. On his part, the Iranian Foreign Ministry Director-General for the Persian Gulf, who announced the news upon his return from a tour of the island, restated that the policy of Iran towards Abu Musa Island 'has not changed'.[95]

Iran's reaction

The Iranian government responded to the UAE position by reiterating 'its historic and legal title to the three islands'. Reacting to the statement by the GCC foreign ministers dated 9 September 1992, Iranian Foreign Ministry spokesman Morteza Sarmadi pointed out that the 1971 agreement stipulated that Iran should handle security on Abu Musa, thus giving it the right to refuse entry to citizens of third countries. He said that 'on the basis of irrefutable historical and legal documents, the islands of Abu Musa – and the Tunbs – belong to Iran.'

Sarmadi said Arab residents on Abu Musa could live in harmony with their 'Iranian brothers and sisters on the island.' He said that the GCC communiqué was 'a blatant violation of the good neighborly relations.' He added that Iran 'would not allow any country to interfere in its internal affairs or violate its national sovereignty.'[96]

Likewise, Iran's Supreme National Security Council (SNSC), in a statement dated 12 September 1992, termed 'unjustified' the recent stances and propaganda campaign of some regional states on Abu Musa Island in the Persian Gulf, IRNA reported. The statement, issued at the end of a session chaired by President Rafsanjani, held that such acts were the result of the 'hands of discord whose interests lie in seeing the region tense and divided'. The SNSC declared Iran's 'fraternity and good-neighborliness' with the Muslim states of the region, and said that with due respect to their sovereignty and territorial integrity, as well as regional security, 'we will not allow any country to interfere in our internal affairs'. It added,

Confrontational phase 173

'Security at Abu Musa is part of the undeniable responsibility of Iran, and we hope that regional states through cooperation and mutual understanding will maintain the security of the important and strategic Persian Gulf.' The session was attended by all SNSC members, political advisers and top military commanders.[97]

In his Friday Prayers Sermons of 20 September, Rafsanjani, after having explained the incident in April, stated that

> At that time we decided to bring the Island under control; so we said that foreigners who came over there must let us know of their arrival in advance. Their identity must be known before they arrived. And we acted upon that decision. Since then we have had no incidents. Meanwhile, because in some cases some individuals wanted to arrive there without our knowledge, naturally there were disputes between the officials at the island and those individuals. Sometimes the officials send back an individual and this is something which can easily happen. And we have informed Member States of the Cooperation Council of that policy. We have told them that was our policy and we have changed nothing else. Even in Jakarta, which we visited, foreign ministers of some of these countries who were there came to see us. We asked them what all that hue and cry was about. We told them nothing has changed so why do you make an issue of it? Eventually, it was agreed that nothing had changed. They said that what they wanted was for their people to live in comfort and we told them all right, we let them live in comfort. There and then I told them that I would send somebody to the island to investigate. If there were undue restrictions then we would remove them. And we did send somebody. And they know about it.[98]

As tension grew over the islands, the Air Force commander General Mansur Satari announced that Iran was prepared to shoot down any aircraft violating its airspace. He said on Tehran radio on 21 September that his aircraft were stepping up their watch over the three islands and his pilots were ready to repulse any intrusion by 'mischievous foreigners'.[99]

Iran's spiritual leader Ali Khamenei, too, accused the United States, Britain and other 'imperialist powers of attempting to sow discord' between Iran and its neighbours in order to 'justify their illegitimate presence' in the Persian Gulf.[100]

Three months later, President Rafsanjani warned that the Arab countries in the GCC would have to 'cross a sea of blood' to reach the three islands in the Persian Gulf. Raising the level of the Iranian challenge to the GCC countries, the Iranian president said at the Friday prayers of 25 December 1992 that they 'should not repeat the same mistakes as Saddam', who tried to 'transform Iran's Arvand-Roud river into the Shatt al-Arab and Kuwait into an Iraqi province'. He said 'Iran is stronger than you', referring to the Persian Gulf states, and accused the GCC countries of having chosen 'Satan's path'. Rafsanjani was reacting to the affirmation two days earlier by GCC leaders meeting in Abu Dhabi of United Arab Emirates sovereignty over the islands of Abu Musa, Greater Tunb and Lesser Tunb.[101]

174 *Confrontational phase*

International reactions

The GCC, the United States and the United Kingdom, as well as their close friends in the larger Arab world, lent different degrees of explicit and implicit support to the UAE's drive on the issue of the three islands, mainly as a means to bring pressure to bear on Iran. A comparison between their positions in 1992 and those of the same countries in the 1970s on the same issue and a study of their evolution in the 1980s are indicative of the importance of the role of regional and global politics and the irrelevance of legal and historical arguments when it comes to this case. As noted earlier, the West that tacitly or explicitly supported Iran on the issue of the three islands in the 1970s stopped doing so in the aftermath of the Islamic Revolution and turned entirely against Iran in the early 1990s.

In the Arab world, the Arab radicals, who led the campaign against the Shah's act of restoring Iran's ownership to the three islands, mostly sided later in the 1980s with revolutionary Iran. With the Arab radicals losing ground as a result of the realignment of broader forces in the wider region in the 1990s, the conservative-moderate Arab camp, closely assisted by the West, found the opportunity to set the agenda at the regional level. That is why the issue of the three islands could make a comeback.

As it was coming to assume a role in the Persian Gulf analogous to the one that Britain had played in the nineteenth and most of the twentieth centuries, the US government played an important, though partly tacit, role in the evolution of the issue of the three islands in the 1990s. On the basis of its long-standing position of refraining from taking sides or commenting on territorial and border issues in the Middle East, the United States made some effort not to interfere substantially in the three islands issue. However, in contrast to their sympathy for Iran's position during diplomatic activities in 1971 on the same issue,[102] American officials, in a position reversal, explicitly provided similar sympathy to the Arab side in 1992 – a change of heart that could only be explained in terms of the strategic realignment that had taken place in the region in the wake of the Islamic Revolution and especially in the early 1990s.

In the heat of controversy between Iran and the GCC, US Acting Secretary of State Lawrence S. Eagleburger said on 12 September 1992 that 'I don't think there is any question that the issue could become very serious if the Iranians were to decide to resort to force.' The United States believed the dispute 'should be settled peacefully. We're totally opposed to the use of force,' Eagleburger said.[103] Meanwhile, he did not explain why Iran might need to resort to force, as the islands were already under Iranian control.

In separate talks in New York with foreign ministers of the Persian Gulf sheikhdoms, it was reported that Eagleburger conveyed US support in their dispute with Iran over a Persian Gulf island known as Abu Musa.[104]

The remarks made by Edward Djerejian, Assistant Secretary of State for Near Eastern and South Asian Affairs, to the National Association of Arab Americans' 20th Anniversary Conference, held in Washington on 11 September 1992, indicated where the United States was tilting on the issue of the three islands. His statement contained the following passage:

Across the Gulf from our friends and allies lies the Islamic Republic of Iran, an important country that can contribute to regional security, if, if it chooses a constructive path... Iran's policies toward the Gulf Arab states, as exemplified by its heavy handed assertion of authority on Abu Musa Island, have shown it to be an increasingly truculent neighbor. We welcome the firm stand that the Gulf Cooperation Council has taken on this issue.[105]

At the same time, US military and diplomatic officials were often quoted in the US media, on a non-attribution basis, as expressing concern over Iran's intentions. For example, the *New York Times* quoted US military officials as saying that 'Iran might be trying to take control of the islands, strategically located at the entrance to the gulf, to counter military cooperation between the United States and gulf nations. They also speculated that the annexation might be part of plans for expanding Iran's navy.'[106]

In the meantime, British officials were blunter in expressing their support for the UAE. Malcolm Rifkind, the UK defence secretary, from on board HMS *Chatham* in the Persian Gulf on 23 September 1992, promised Western backing for Persian Gulf Arabs against aggression by Iran, at the same time attacking Tehran's arms build-up, including the purchase of three Russian submarines. Speaking on the deck of Britain's most sophisticated anti-submarine frigate, Rifkind disclosed that the leaders of both Saudi Arabia and Kuwait had expressed their deep anxiety to him about Iranian moves.

On the same occasion, Tony Hogg, the *Chatham*'s captain, said that 'advice had already been given in recent weeks to Gulf Arabs about how to conduct submarine warfare. But the question was difficult and expensive because the hot, shallow waters of the Persian Gulf were very bad for sonar detection'. Asked whether Iran had yet responded to demands that the disagreement over the islands be resolved peacefully, Rifkind said, 'It is early days, but it should be quite clear to anyone contemplating aggression that the UN and those nations which are giving the most active support to the UN are prepared to do what is necessary to try to ensure peace in the region.' On the subject of the Tehran naval build-up, he added, 'It is obviously a matter of legitimate concern for other countries in the region. 'It is for each individual country to decide what its proper response to that should be. But we obviously discuss with all our friends and allies what can be done to help if there is any new threat which develops.'[107]

The Egyptian government, as the major pro-Western Arab government, aspired to play a role in the Persian Gulf, which was mostly characterized by its show of enmity against Iran. Its failure to assume a role as protector of the oil-producing sheikhs angered Egypt but did not deter it from pursuing its agenda in the Persian Gulf. It continued an active diplomacy in the area, was especially keen on gaining an economic foothold in the region and kept reminding the local rulers of the potential Iranian threat. Putting the Egyptian role in perspective, it is worth remembering that the interests Egypt sought in the Persian Gulf had collided with Iran's since the nineteenth century and earlier. This conflict culminated in the 1960s when the Persian Gulf became a front line in the struggle between Egypt's pan-Arabism and Iran. The dispute over the very name of 'the Persian Gulf' is a legacy of that time.

President Hosni Mubarak wrote in an Egyptian newspaper article that Iran's behaviour 'raises fears about increasing Iranian ambitions of hegemony over the Emirates and other sister States in the Arabian Gulf. The same source quoted another Egyptian official as saying that 'the Abu Musa dispute indicates that Iranians still have their ambitions in the Gulf. They start with Abu Musa and they might end up with Bahrain... They are back to the policies of the shah.'[108] Amr Musa, the Egyptian foreign minister, announced even ahead of UAE officials that the case would be brought to the UN Security Council, as all communications with Iran on it had failed.[109] The role of Egypt was also instrumental in securing toughly worded statements on the three islands issue by the Arab League.

Though discredited and preoccupied with myriad problems, Iraq, too, mostly at the level of official media, was vocal on the issue of the three islands. On 16 April the newspaper *Al-Thawrah* criticized Arab and world silence on 'the aggressive and expansionist policy of the Iranian regime, a policy that conflicts with all international norms.'[110]

The newspaper *Al-Qadisiyah*, the organ of the Iraqi Defence Ministry, warned on 1 September that 'the Iranian regime may use the Abu Musa Island, which belongs to the United Arab Emirates,[111] as a major military base for aggression against the States in the region.' The paper pointed out that the Iranian authorities' refusal to allow a ship carrying 104 island residents to dock on the island clearly indicated that Iran planned to annex the Arab island. It asserted that 'the Iranian regime has begun to intensify its suspect military presence on this island, particularly after it set up missile battery systems.'[112]

Although it was pleasing to the UAE and other conservative sheikhs that Iraq had sanctioned itself out of all leverage in the Persian Gulf, they occasionally missed it as a counterweight to Iran. Such a mixed feeling lay at the origin of the somewhat ambiguous attitude of the UAE towards Iraq. Whereas the UAE firmly backed Kuwait in October 1994, when Iraqi troops moved to the border area, Abu Dhabi also made public statements indicating that sanctions should be lifted to ease constraints on Iraq. Senior UAE officials, such as Vice President Maktum, argued that a 'militarily strong and united Iraq' was needed to balance Iranian power.[113] President Zayed himself said that Baghdad did not threaten its neighbours, and referred to the Iraqi sanctions regime as unjust.[114] However, American hostility towards Saddam's regime all but ensured that Iraq under his rule would not be integrated into the Persian Gulf's military balance of power.

An unending nuisance?

Since 1992, the UAE has tried to keep alive the three islands as an issue of contention between Iran and the Arab world. Although the controversy over the islands has worked to strain and restrict Iran's relation with the Arab countries, its impact should not be considered bigger than that of the overall opposing directions of their foreign policies. At the same time, both sides, including the UAE itself, have tried to isolate this issue from their economic relationship.

While taking a unified formal stand in opposing Iran on the islands, the individual emirates that constitute the UAE have kept up their economic relations with Iran. The same holds true when it comes to Arab League member states. And for some Arab countries, such as Syria, the issue of the islands has been quite irrelevant with no impact at all on bilateral diplomatic relations with Iran.

So while Abu Dhabi and the Arab League have repeatedly registered their views on the three islands at the United Nations, there has been no appetite on their part to escalate the difference. The reasons for such an approach can be summarized as follows:

- Any major escalation between Iran and the UAE might lead to a confrontation with unforeseeable consequences.
- Militarily, the UAE is too far from being a match for Iran.
- None of the UAE's allies in the Arab world, except for Iraq under Saddam, have seen the issue as a case of naked aggression or as worthy of actual conflict.
- Iran has remained one of Dubai's major business partners, accounting for around 20 to 30 per cent of Dubai's business.
- There is disagreement on the issue among the seven sheikhdoms.

As a result, the issue of the three islands has turned into a means, used by the Arab conservative-moderate camp and supported by the United States, to try to balance its ties with Iran and to curb Iran's influence in the Persian Gulf and wider area, in order to undermine Iran when necessary. Portraying Iran as expansionist can also benefit the conservative sheikhs in their quest to justify their very close security relationship with the West, particularly the United States. The islands issue has also been used to further the objectives of the dual containment policy by restraining Iran's relationship with regional states.

Under President Khatami, Iran's policy of removing tension in its relationships with the outside world created a regional environment more conducive to development of ties among local players. The Khatami government stressed that improving Iran's relations with the GCC and fostering regional stability and security figured among its top foreign policy goals. A fifteen-day visit by ex-President Rafsanjani and visits by Foreign Minister Kharrazi to Saudi Arabia in 1998 opened the way to cooperation and more serious attempts at overcoming distrust. These and many other visits, aimed at building confidence, led to some warming of relations. The signing of a security agreement between Iran and Saudi Arabia in April 1998 aimed at fighting terrorism, smuggling, and border violations signalled greater Arab trust of Iran and could prove to be a harbinger of improved regional relations.

Nonetheless, for its part, the UAE remained sceptical. The Emirates' official news agency noted in March 1998 that '[d]espite Iran's openness since the election of President Khatami, there have not been any worthwhile developments regarding issues of dispute in Iranian foreign policies.' UAE officials were further dismayed by Karrazi's hints 'that it is the US pressure in the Persian Gulf, rather than Iran's takeover of the islands, which hinders better relations.'[115]

178 *Confrontational phase*

The UAE continued to remain anxious about the level of the relationship between Iran and its allies in the GCC under President Khatami and was deeply disturbed at the warming of relations between Iran and Saudi Arabia in 1998–99. The UAE made this position public after a visit by President Khatami to Saudi Arabia in May 1999, and accused Saudi Arabia of bidding for closer ties with Iran at the expense of the UAE. Emirates foreign minister Rashid Abdullah said closer ties between GCC members and Iran ignored his country's dispute with Iran over the three islands in the Strait of Hormuz. 'We think this closeness is at the expense of the UAE,' Abdullah was quoted as saying. 'In fact, it has encouraged Iran to . . . change a lot of the island structure,' he added. Abdullah said the Emirates would rethink its obligations to the GCC if other members continued to ignore the dispute over the islands.[116]

In the long run, however, Abu Dhabi fears the most that Tehran will improve its relations with Washington and avoid the islands issue. This would be a defeat in Abu Dhabi's eyes because it would remove most of the international pressure on Iran.[117]

Conclusion
From containment to containment

The main concern of this book has been to identify a range of factors that lie at the origin of the issue of the three islands of Abu Musa and the Tunbs and that influence its development to date. The islands issue is an important one that once strained the relationship between Iran and Great Britain and that, since the early 1970s, has had a bearing on the relationship between Iran and the radical and conservative groups of Arab countries, each in their turn. By placing the current controversies surrounding the three islands in historic perspective, the preceding chapters aimed to make a contribution towards the understanding of certain old disputes on a wide range of issues that marked the relationship between Iran and Great Britain during the nineteenth century and the best part of the twentieth century. Although these conflicts are part of history, the review and understanding of them are still pertinent as the historic disputes lie at the origin of certain current disputes, and examining them can help shed light on the nature of the new controversies between Iran and certain parties on the lower Persian Gulf.

The origin and development of the issue of Abu Musa and the Tunbs, as discussed in the preceding chapters, make clear that this is not a normal border or territorial controversy analogous to those that pit so many countries against each other. It has been the outgrowth of a host of local, regional and global intricacies, and has echoed and reflected a variety of political and diplomatic agitations and perturbed relationships throughout the region since the late nineteenth century. In the first instance, it grew out of the antagonism that marked the relationship between the prevailing global power, Great Britain, and the major regional power, Iran. Later, it turned into a point of contention between the pro-Soviet Arab radicals and Iran's pro-Western imperial government in the early 1970s. Finally, it was used by the conservative-moderate Arab camp and the United States to further the policy of containment against the Islamic government in Tehran in the 1990s and beyond.

This review of general developments in the Persian Gulf demonstrates that the controversy over the three islands has always been inextricably linked to the geopolitics of the region and the role, or the lack thereof, of global powers therein. In the light of the foregoing chapters, three distinct periods are identifiable in terms of the presence or lack of regional autonomy. The situation in each of these periods has had a direct bearing on the development of the controversies over the three islands:

The *first period* began in the 1820s, when Britain began to achieve dominance in the Persian Gulf, and ended in 1971, when it withdrew from east of Suez. British dominance challenged Iran's historic ascendancy in the Gulf and brought regional autonomy to an end. Having determined that control over the Persian Gulf and the Strait of Hormuz was essential for the security of their possessions in the Indian subcontinent, the British tried to establish *Pax Britannica* in the Gulf, but they faced resistance on the part of Iran, as the main regional power, and almost immediately found themselves needing to contain and constrain that country. Thus the interest of these two powers came into conflict for two reasons. First, the global dominant power, in its quest for a secure environment and base facilities, needed to control Iranian possessions in the area to use for its own flotilla and so that it could deny their use to its rivals. This policy was reflected most visibly in the case of Iranian islands in the Persian Gulf, starting with Bahrain and culminating in the case of the three islands of Abu Musa and the Tunbs after the late nineteenth century. Second, in order to fortify its position and thwart any threats that might come from the Iranians themselves or from European rivals through Iranian territory, Britain sought to curtail Iranian influence in the area in general.

Iran, with an eye on India's experience, looked with suspicion to the steps Britain took in the aftermath of its 1819–20 military operations against the Piratical Coast. These steps, including the signing of a wide variety of formal treaties and agreements with Arab rulers that restricted their international capacity, allowed Britain wide latitude to make the arrangements necessary for its lasting presence in the area. Iran never recognized the special relationship between Britain and the Trucial sheikhdoms and became more suspicious as well as resistant in the face of continuous British attempts to gain control over its possessions in the Persian Gulf through concession, claiming them for the Arab rulers, military occupation and finally lease or purchase.

Thus, this period was characterized by numerous disputes, tensions and even wars between Britain and Iran over territories, not only in the Persian Gulf but also along the eastern Iranian borders adjoining the British dominion and Afghanistan as a buffer zone. The colonial British decision-makers were also haunted by two spectres: on the one hand, the social and political movements in nineteenth-century Iran, inspired by a vibrant Persian nationalism and preoccupied with reclaiming its glorious heritage, that fought both the despotic monarchy and foreign interference, and, on the other hand, the danger of the Iranian court joining with European powers hostile to Britain.

Consequently, the British concluded early in the nineteenth century that they would not be able to subjugate the Iranian body politic in a sustainable way, as they did other political entities throughout the wider region. This conclusion was reinforced by the influential role the Russians played in the Qajar court, and it finally led to Britain's adoption of a containment strategy against Iran that can be described as their overarching policy, in that it guided British activities in the areas surrounding Iran through the nineteenth and the best part of the twentieth century. This policy, coupled with the established colonial tactic of cultivating notables and promoting tribal sheikhs in charge of small political entities as opposed to engaging major regional powers, was the defining factor in the relationship between Iran and Britain in the period under study.

The slow but steady policy of separating the island of Bahrain from Iran, the dispute over the islands lining the north shores of the Strait of Hormuz and the periodic occupation of Kharg Island were the three major and inter-related developments throughout the nineteenth century and the early years of the twentieth century, all of which were guided by the over-all British strategy east of Suez. The controversy over the islands lying at the centre of the Persian Gulf arose during the last quarter of the nineteenth century and culminated in the early twentieth century.

A new British strategy, devised and implemented by Viceroy Curzon in the early years of the 1900s, which aimed to strengthen British control over the Persian Gulf and to thwart its European rivals, led the British to focus more seriously on two groups of Iranian islands – first, the islands of Kishm, Henjam, Hormuz and Larak and, second, the three islands of Abu Musa, Greater Tunb and Lesser Tunb – along with on-and-off attempts to revive the controversy over the island of Sirri as a bargaining chip. These two groups of islands were perceived as more or less dominating the sealanes of communication entering and exiting the Persian Gulf at the Strait of Hormuz. The British efforts led to growing tension between Iran and Britain – a tension that was exacerbated following the hoisting of Arab flags, at the behest of the British, on Abu Musa and the Tunbs. British attempts to control more territory in the Persian Gulf continued, *inter alia*, through seeking to obtain leasehold over a number of Iranian islands in the 1910s, especially those lining the north shores of the Strait of Hormuz.

Thus, a vicious circle at work throughout this long period led to the increasing deterioration of the Iranian-British relationship, culminating in 1857 in the all-out war between the two countries and continuing more or less the same way through the occupation of Iran by the Allied forces during the Second World War and beyond. Territorial disputes reached their apex in 1903–04 when Britain formally claimed the three islands for the Arab sheikhs under its protection. All Iranian protests in this period were rejected and Iranian actions were dealt with heavy-handedly.

The *second period* began in the wake of the British withdrawal from the Persian Gulf, which brought the *Pax Britannica* in the area to an end and opened the way for the revival of its autonomous status. This period lasted for around 20 years and was characterized by the absence of a dominant global power in the region. The departure of Britain, as the global power, from the area led to the removal of tension arising from the competition between the global and the regional powers. One of the immediate results of this historic development was the collapse of the containment policy maintained by the British against Iran during the period of its supremacy in the region.

Enjoying an inherent and historic position in the Persian Gulf, developing growing interests therein and generally acquiring more power as well as benefiting from the international environment as influenced by the Cold War, Iran stood to gain the most from the end of the British military presence, as it could now reinstate its ascendancy in the region. Unlike many other regional players, it had nothing to lose and no reason to fear the consequences of Britain's withdrawal.

Britain's increasing financial hardship, which induced it to leave the Gulf, and the inability and unwillingness of the United States to replace Britain, mostly due to the Vietnam débacle, coupled with Iran's increasing power and rising stature, allowed the advent of a totally different period, distinct from the one that preceded it as well as the one that followed it. It should be noted that it was the only period, though brief, in the past two centuries when the Persian Gulf was left on its own and, in the absence of a prevailing global power, could enjoy regional autonomy.

The new situation called for establishing a viable new regional structure and filling the power vacuum left behind. While the British wished to see the small Arab sheikhdoms pull together and organize themselves in a more defensible federation, the Iranian government attached priority to the restoration of its sovereignty over the three islands.

Under such circumstances, British policy towards the three islands of Abu Musa and the Tunbs underwent a drastic change, amounting to the reversal of the decades-old tactic of claiming the islands for the Arab sheikhs of the lower Gulf. Two reasons for this drastic change can be outlined. On the one hand, the British need to contain Iran, which had diminished since the Second World War, came to an end. On the other, the imperative to prepare for the security of the Persian Gulf and the nine Arab emirates became pressing and moved to the top of the British list of priorities.

The British policy reversal that accompanied its withdrawal from the region – namely, the expedient discontinuance of Britain's claims to the three islands for its Arab protégés – was an important hallmark of the this period. It was a significant and historic development when Britain opted to act as a neutral provider of good offices and assumed a mediating and consensus-building role between Iran and the Arab sheikhs. After close to 80 years of insisting on Arab sovereignty over the three islands, the British role was overnight reduced to that of a mediator. The statement made by Colin Crowe, British permanent representative to the UN, in the Security Council meeting on the three islands on 9 December 1971, marked the public and formal discontinuance of the old British policy. The new British approach helped enormously to ease the tensions that had pitted Iran and Britain against each other for over a hundred years.

The British about-face was indicative of the emergence of a totally new era – an era in which not only did Britain not need to contain and constrain the main regional power, it also needed the same power to fill the vacuum it was going to leave behind.

Although the British ceased to claim the three islands for the Arab sheikhs, they were not in a position to fully, formally and publicly reverse the policy that they had adamantly pursued since the early twentieth century to the point of recognizing Iranian sovereignty over the islands. What the British sought the most was a face-saving solution that allowed for the formation of an 'Arab Union', which they considered critical for the security of the sheikhdoms and the stability of the Gulf. Thus, while withholding their formal recognition of Iranian sovereignty over the islands, they chose not to deny Iran's claim to them outright and they allowed Iranian forces to land on the islands, although this meant non-compliance on their part with the agreements with the Arabs to which they were still committed.

Nonetheless, the face-saving half-solution the British sought and almost achieved proved to be an open sore in the relationship of the regional states, and thus detrimental to the interests of cooperation and harmony in the region. On the basis of this half-solution, the issue of sovereignty over Abu Musa was tacitly addressed and resolved in the Memorandum of Understanding between Iran and Sharjah; but the lack of explicit reference to it left the door open for controversy.

This period was also characterized by silence on and lack of interest in the issue of the three islands, except for two brief moments. The first came immediately after the British withdrawal and the second followed the Islamic Revolution in Iran, and both lasted only for several months. The most important characteristic of this period was the fact that the Arab radicals, led by Iraq, were the only active force on the issue of the three islands, and it was they who initiated these two brief episodes of protest against Iran's action on the three islands. The prospect of Iranian supremacy in the Persian Gulf, coupled with Iran's close relationship with the West and its ties to Israel, had antagonized the Arab radicals. Under the influence of regional politics, heavily tainted by Cold War competition, the Arab–Israeli conflict and the geopolitics of the region, the Arab radicals and pan-Arabists took the lead in trying to agitate Arab public opinion against the way that Iran's pro-Western monarchy and Britain handled the issue of the three islands. That led, *inter alia*, to the raising of the issue at the UN Security Council by Iraq, Libya, Algeria and South Yemen.

When the UAE and the conservative-moderate Arab camp proved indifferent and quite reluctant to follow suit, the islands soon became one of the two main points of contention between Iran and Iraq, the former led by a Western-oriented, conservative monarchy and the latter a revolutionary Ba'athist regime tied to the socialist camp through a friendship treaty. Ironically, Arab radicals, led by Iraq, raised a flag that the British colonialists had barely lowered on the eve of their departure from the Persian Gulf. Significantly, while Iraq was very active on the issue and took it to the UN Security Council, the UAE remained passive and very reluctant to pursue the issue until 1992.

Nonetheless, the subdued approach by the Arab sheikhs, due to reasons including uncertainty in the area and the absence of a global dominating power that could provide the least necessary protection, defeated Iraq's wide-ranging efforts during both moments of activity on the three islands in this period. Although the regional autonomy of the Persian Gulf became increasingly constrained and Iranian ascendancy therein more challenged in the latter part of this period, the supremacy of a global power in the area had yet to return.

In the brief moment after the Islamic Revolution in Iran when Iraq resumed its rhetoric on the issue of the three islands, it found other such Arab radicals as Libya, Syria and the PLO on the side of the new Islamic establishment in

Tehran. Thus, despite a great deal of political capital spent in 1979 by Baghdad to reactivate the issue of the three islands, the result was nothing but failure. The refusal of the UAE and other Arab countries to follow the Iraqi lead, the resilience of regional autonomy and the absence of a global power prevailing in the area were the most important reasons underlying this failure. It was an important hallmark of the period that helped result, among other things, in the issue returning to dormancy for some time to come. The full reappearance of the issue of the three islands on the conservative Arabs' agenda had to wait until after the perceived establishment of American hegemony in the area after 1991, mirroring the case during colonial rule.

The *third period* set in following the Iraqi invasion of Kuwait in 1990, which paved the way for the creation of a completely new situation in the Persian Gulf. In this period the United States was able to build upon the slow but steady military build-up it had carried out in the wider region in the aftermath of the events in the late 1970s and during the 1980s, and was able to begin enhancing massively its military capability in the Gulf. The new situation also opened the way for the United States and the Arab littoral states to reach an unprecedented understanding on such issues as military base rights and the pre-positioning of arms and military hardware on territory of the Arab states. The United States and the Arab conservative camp also capitalized on the end of the Cold War, the weakening of the Arab radicals and the blow dealt to the PLO and the Palestinian communities in the Gulf as a result of their support for Iraq's invasion of Kuwait. The latter event helped the Arab conservatives to unlink the Palestinian question from the security of the Persian Gulf, freeing them to enter into their first strategic relationship with the Americans. As a result, the US government found an unparallel welcoming environment in the region.

Hence, the developments in the early 1990s brought about what was later called the dawn of 'the American era' in the region. The United States was able to enjoy unprecedented influence and freedom to act in the Persian Gulf, and, thus, to present a serious challenge to Iranian primacy there, as Britain had during its era. As Iran had dominated the autonomous Persian Gulf region since 1971, the reappearance in the Gulf of an outside power, seen by some Arab states as a counterweight to Iran's primacy, was thus encouraged. Accordingly, the more the United States gained influence in the Persian Gulf, the more the local autonomy of the area was undermined. These seminal developments also allowed the conservative-moderate Arab camp to strengthen its position throughout the region. This camp, assisted by the United States, could pursue now more forcefully the policies it desired but that had remained largely inconclusive during the transitional period in the 1980s.

Thus, in early 1992 several striking trends were already in progress in the Persian Gulf area. With Iraq's humiliating defeat, the radical tendencies in the Arab world found themselves on the defensive and in decline. The Arab littoral states of the Persian Gulf were firmly embarked on the path of relying on the West, and the United States in particular, in establishing a new security arrangement in the region. With Iraq, once perceived as a counterweight to Iran, effectively neutralized, the conservative sheikhs and the West were in agreement on, and adamant about, the need for a shared strategy for counterbalancing and containing Iran in the region, and denying it the role it considered itself fit to play by virtue of its natural position in the area. Thus, the policies of excluding and containing Iran were put definitively on the agenda of the West and the conservative sheikhs.

As such, this period bears many similarities to the first period, referred to above, in terms of the full-fledged return of a global power to the Persian Gulf, the undermining of the autonomous status of the Gulf region and the recurrence of tension and conflict between this global power and Iran as the main regional power. The containment policy adopted by the new global power against Iran, even in its first guise of 'dual containment', is another striking similarity between the first and the third periods.

In the 1990s, the United States adopted a regional policy much like the one employed by Britain for one and a half centuries, guaranteeing the external security of the Arab Persian Gulf states by its direct presence and by the containment of Iran as the most powerful regional state. The dual containment policy pursued by the United States to date under different forms has aimed at depriving Iran of its advantages in the region and driving it into isolation. The conservative sheikhs, too, took advantage of the opportunity to allow US military forces on their soil for the first time – a possibility that would not have been otherwise available to the Americans. These developments and the way they were exploited left their deep imprint on the region for many years. They provided, among other things, the United States with wide latitude to pursue its policies against its local nemesis and helped create an appropriate context for the revival of the issue of the three islands, which in turn helped the containment policy to continue and develop.

These developments, coupled with the major power realignment across the Arab world in favour of the conservative-moderate camp, set the stage for the UAE to revive the issue of the three islands. Regardless of whether or not the United States played a direct role in the issue of the islands, the issue did in practice benefit the US policy of containing Iran, just as Britain drew the same benefit from the same controversy at its time in the region.

Under the newly prevailing circumstances in the region, the UAE began its own moves on the issue of the three islands in 1992 for the first time, independently of Iraq and the Arab radicals. Thus, the period covering 1992 to the present time is characterized by efforts undertaken by the UAE to reactivate and internationalize the issue of the three islands by raising it in multilateral forums with the aim of buttressing its position by drawing support primarily from GCC member states and the Arab League and ultimately from larger global organizations. Ending a long period of dormancy on the issue since 1972, the current period of activity came about in the wake of dramatic mutually reinforcing developments at the local, regional and global levels.

Notes

1 *Pax Britannica* in the Persian Gulf

1. John Kampfner, 'NS Interview - Jack Straw', *New Statesman*, 18 November 2002.
2. George N. Curzon, *Persia and the Persian Question*, Vol. II, Frank Cass, London, 1966, p. 4.
3. Iran was known as Persia in most parts of the world up until 1935, when the Iranian government requested that foreign governments use the name Iran. Thus, in this book both names are used.
4. Sir Percy Sykes, *A History of Persia*, Vol. II, 3rd edition, Macmillan, London, 1958, p. 431.
5. E. Peterson, 'The Historical Pattern of Gulf Security', in Lawrence G. Potter and Gary Sick (eds), *Security in the Persian Gulf: Origin, Obstacle, and the Search for Consensus*, Palgrave, New York, 2002, p. 8.
6. Donald Hawley, *The Trucial States*, George Allen & Unwin, London, 1970, p. 17.
7. J. G. Lorimer, *Gazetteer of the Persian Gulf, Oman, and Central Arabia*, Vol. I, Part I, Superintendent Government Printing, Calcutta, 1915, pp. 174–7.
8. Tehran was also hopeful of being able to rely on French help to recover Georgia, occupied by Russia, and to guarantee the territorial integrity of Iran.
9. G. R. Tadjbakhche, 'La Question des Iles de Bahrein', Editions A. Pedone, Paris, 1960, pp. 54–5. This treaty would have obliged Napoleon to restrain Russian expansionism in the direction of Persia in return for the Qajar Shah's declaration of war upon Britain and his participation with Afghans in an attack on India. This treaty led nowhere, as France soon reconciled with Russia and Britain.
10. Both 'Qawassim' and 'Joasmis' are used in reference to a tribe on the Arab coast, found mainly in Ras al-Khaimah and Sharjah.
11. Hawley, *Trucial States*, pp. 113–14.
12. Ibid. p. 114.
13. Arab scholars believe that the history of piracy in the Persian Gulf needs to be reinvestigated. They assert that the Arab rulers simply demanded a tariff from merchant vessels traversing the Persian Gulf, and captured those that failed to respond positively – an act that did not amount to piracy. See: Husain M. al-Baharna, 'The Consequences of Britain's Exclusive Treaties: A Gulf View', in B. R. Pridham (ed.), *The Arab Gulf and the West*, St. Martin's Press, New York, 1985, p. 23. Nonetheless, European sources, even the French who then rivalled the British, consider that the Qawassim practised piracy and caused anarchy in the area. See: Tadjbakhche, 'Question des Iles de Bahrein', p. 53.

Notes 187

14 al-Baharna, 'The Consequences of Britain's Exclusive Treaties', p. 24.
15 Curzon, *Persia and the Persian Question*, Vol. II, p. 450.
16 The Political Resident, appointed by the British Indian Government from the Indian Political Service, had functions and status more similar to those of a colonial governor than an ambassador. Bushehr was the seat of the Political Resident for the Persian Gulf until 1947, when, as the colonial era came to an end, the post was transferred to Bahrain and the Foreign Office assumed responsibility for the appointment.
17 For a summary description of the agreements referred to in this section, see: David Roberts, 'The Exclusive Treaties – A British View,' in Pridham (ed.), *The Arab Gulf and the West,* p. 2. For their full texts, see: Hawley, *Trucial States*, pp. 314–22.
18 Curzon, *Persia and the Persian Question*, Vol. II, p. 451.
19 Peterson, 'Historical Pattern of Gulf Security', p. 14.
20 For the transcript of the agreements, see: Hawley, *Trucial States*, pp. 314–22.
21 al-Baharna, 'Consequences of Britain's Exclusive Treaties', p. 18.
22 Ibid.
23 Peterson, 'Historical Pattern of Gulf Security', p. 14.
24 Roberts, 'Exclusive Treaties', p. 11.
25 Sir Denis Wright, 'The Changed Balance of Power in the Persian Gulf,' *Asian Affairs*, Vol. IV, October 1973, p. 256.
26 This was to some extent an outgrowth of the same policy of de-Persianization adopted by the British in the Indian subcontinent in the mid-eighteenth century when they began strengthening their dominance there. The British sought to drive out the Persian language that was widely spoken in the Indian Mughal court before their arrival. For the extent of interaction between Iran and India and the role of the Persian culture in Indian society before the British era, see: John F. Standish. *Persia and the Gulf: Retrospect and Prospect*, Curzon Press, Richmond, 1998, pp. 33–49.
27 *Islands and Maritime Boundaries of the Gulf, 1798–1835*, edited by Richard Schofield, Vol. IV, Archive Editions, Slough, 1990, p. 341.
28 Undoubtedly, the inefficient and deficient way in which the Qajars ran the affairs of state was a main source of popular discontent. However, the inherent strength of the state accorded it a distinguished status in the region.
29 For a thorough discussion of Iranian nationalism rooted in land, see: Firouzeh Kashani-sabet, *Frontier Fictions: Shaping the Iranian Nation, 1904–1946*, Princeton University Press, Princeton, NJ, 1999.
30 *The Persian Gulf Historical Summaries, 1907–1953; Volume I: Historical Summary of Events in Territories of the Ottoman Empire, Persia, and Arabia affecting the British Position in the Persian Gulf; 1907–1928*, (PG 13), Archive Editions, Gerrards Cross, 1987, p. 6.
31 Ibid. pp. 9–10.
32 Curzon, *Persia and the Persian Question*, Vol. II, p. 481.
33 J. B. Kelly, *Britain and the Persian Gulf, 1795–1880*, Clarendon Press, Oxford, 1968, p. 262.
34 Ibid. p. 293.
35 *The Persian Gulf Historical Summaries; 1907–1953, Vol. IV: Memorandum respecting British Interests in the Persian Gulf, 1908*, Archive Editions, 1987, p. 107.
36 The relevant clause in the 'exclusive treaty' prohibited the sheikhs from 'giving,

188 Notes

       ceding, selling, leasing or mortgaging' any part of their territories to any state or person other than Britain or British subjects.

37   The strategic role of the Persian Gulf islands remains as important today as it ever was. The Kuwait crisis of 1990–91, which followed Iraq's failure to secure a lease of the islands of Verba and Bubiyan, is a case in point.

38   Robert Geran Landen, *Oman since 1856: Disruptive Modernization in a Traditional Arab Society*, Princeton University Press, Princeton, NJ, 1967, p. 250.

39   *Islands and Maritime Boundaries*, Vol. I, p. xxxi.

40   Peterson, 'The Historical Pattern of Gulf Security', p. 14.

41   Kelly, *Britain and the Persian Gulf*, p. 167.

42   Ibid. p. 167.

43   Curzon, *Persia and the Persian Question*, Vol. II, p. 413.

44   Kelly, *Britain and the Persian Gulf*, p. 167.

45   Tadjbakhche, 'Question des Iles de Bahrein', p. 56.

46   As explained later, Kharg Island was occupied by the British in 1838 to force Iranian troops to abandon their conquest of Herat. Despite the Iranian retreat from Herat, the British kept the island under occupation for four years.

47   Curzon, *Persia and the Persian Question*, Vol. II, p. 404.

48   The island of Henjam was referred to as Angar by the British at an earlier time.

49   For the full document see: *Islands and Maritime Boundaries*, Vol. I, pp. 523–4.

50   Ibid. p. 526.

51   Sayyid Sa'id, who had come to power in Oman in 1807, committed himself to a close alliance with the British after a period of flirting with the French, and intermittently with the Persians. He joined the British in their expeditions against the Qawasim in 1809 and 1819. See: Hawley, *Trucial States*, pp. 102–5. He later signed the Anglo-Omani treaties of friendship. See: Kelly, *Britain and the Persian Gulf*, pp. 222–3.

52   *Islands and Maritime Boundaries*, Vol. I, p. 527.

53   Ibid. p. 528.

54   Lorimer, *Gazetteer*, Vol. I , Part IA, p. 200.

55   This refers to the on-again, off-again leasehold the Imam of Muscat obtained from the Persian government over Bandar Abbas and its dependencies.

56   *Islands and Maritime Boundaries*, Vol. I, p. 530.

57   Ibid.

58   From the letter dated 16 May 1821, in Volume 20 of 1820–21, from the Bombay Government to Dr Jukes, British envoy to the Persian Gulf, deputed to allay the alarm felt in Persia about the British proceedings in the Persian Gulf, page 592. Cited in: *Islands and Maritime Boundaries*, Vol. I, p. 667.

59   Bombay Government to the Government of India, dated 9 March 1822, No. 469, Vol. 91 of 1822. Cited in: *Islands and Maritime Boundaries*, Vol. I, p. 673.

60   *Islands and Maritime Boundaries*, Vol. I, p. 680.

61   Hawley, *Trucial States*, p. 164.

62   Lorimer, *Gazetteer*, Vol. I, Part IA, p. 200.

63   *Islands and Maritime Boundaries*, Vol. I, p. 693.

64   Curzon, *Persia and the Persian Question*, Vol. II, p. 412.

65   Farhang Mehr, *A Colonial Legacy: The Dispute over the Islands of Abu Musa and the Greater and Lesser Tunbs*, University Press of America, New York, 1997, p. 109.

66   Memorandum by the First Political Department, Ministry of Foreign Affairs, dated

Notes 189

16 Ordibehesht 1307 (6 May 1929). In: *Gozideh-e Asnad-e Khaleej Fars* (*Selected Persian Gulf Documents*), Institute for International and Political Studies (IIPS), Tehran, 1989, p. 399.
67 Ibid. p. 426.
68 Ibid. p. 488.
69 *Persian Gulf Historical Summaries*, Vol. IV, p. 2.
70 Ibid. p. 72.
71 Kelly, *Britain and the Persian Gulf*, p. 30.
72 E. Hertslet's report, in: *Islands and Maritime Boundaries*, Vol. I, p. 343.
73 Ibid.
74 Kelly, *Britain and the Persian Gulf*, p. 163.
75 F. O. 60/17, M. Elphinstone to H. Willock, 15 Dec. 1819. Cited in: Tadjbakhche, 'La Question des Iles de Bahrein', pp. 58–9. (Translated from French.)
76 Ibid.
77 E. Hertslet's report, in: *Islands and Maritime Boundaries of the Gulf*, Vol. I, p. 344.
78 For the full text of the Treaty of Shiraz, see: *Islands and Maritime Boundaries*, Vol. I, p. 681.
79 F. O. 248/48, cited in: Tadjbakhche, 'La Question des Iles de Bahrein', p. 74. With regard to the reaction of Bombay also see: Kelly, *Britain and the Persian Gulf*, p. 190.
80 Kelly, *Britain and the Persian Gulf*, pp. 145–6.
81 Ibid. pp. 222–3.
82 Ibid. p. 165.
83 Ibid. pp. 165–6.
84 E. Hertslet's report, in: *Islands and Maritime Boundaries*, Vol. I, p. 346.
85 Ibid. p. 348.
86 Ibid. p. 350.
87 F. O. 60/113 and 248/121, Aghassi to Colonel Sheil. Cited in: Tadjbakhche, 'La Question des Iles de Bahrein', p. 92.
88 E. Hertslet's report, in: *Islands and Maritime Boundaries*, Vol. III, p. 352.
89 Ibid. p. 353.
90 Ibid. p. 375.
91 Ibid. Vol. V, pp. 223–5.
92 *Persian Gulf Historical Summaries*, Vol. IV, p. 37. For a history of Iranian protest against British handling of Bahrain's affairs from 1928 to 1953, see: *Persian Gulf Historical Summaries*, Vol. II, pp. 38–9.
93 F. O. Correspondence relating to Persia and Afghanistan, J. Harrison and Son, London, 1839, p. 4. Cited in: Kashani-sabet, *Frontier Fictions*, p. 31.
94 Kelly, *Britain and the Persian Gulf*, p. 6.
95 Ibid. pp. 296–9.
96 Ibid. pp. 347–8.
97 Lorimer, *Gazetteer*, Vol. I, Part II, p. 1993.
98 Ibid. p. 349.
99 Curzon, *Persia and the Persian Question*, Vol. II, p. 606.
100 Kashani-sabet, *Frontier Fictions*, p. 32.
101 Kelly, *Britain and the Persian Gulf*, p. 481.
102 For a description of the Anglo-Persian War of 1857, see: Kelly, *Britain and the Persian Gulf*, pp. 452–9, and Curzon, *Persia and the Persian Question*, Vol. II, p. 405.

190 Notes

103 Curzon, *Persia and the Persian Question*, Vol. II, pp. 232–3.
104 Kelly, *Britain and the Persian Gulf*, p. 562.
105 For details see: Kelly, *Britain and the Persian Gulf*, pp. 555–63.
106 Roberts, 'The Exclusive Treaties', p. 11.
107 Sir Percy Cox to Duke of Devonshire, 9 April 1923: Enclosure: Pledges Given to the Sheikh of Mohammerah, p. 1, L/P&S/10/933. Cited in: Kashani-sabet, *Frontier Fictions*, p. 164.
108 Memorandum on British Commitments (During the War) to the Gulf Chiefs, p. 2, L/P&S/10/933. Cited in: Kashani-sabet, *Frontier Fictions*, p. 164.
109 Lansdowne to Hardinge (2 December 1902, Home 2899/02), and Hardinge to Lansdowne (5 December 1902, Home 2069/03), respectively. Cited in: Briton Cooper Busch, *Britain and the Persian Gulf, 1894–1914*, University of California Press, Berkeley, 1967, p. 243.
110 *Persian Gulf Historical Summaries*, Vol. I, p. 34.

2 The Curzon strategy

1 This new strategy was characterized more by its aggressiveness than by the novelty of its substance.
2 *Islands and Maritime Boundaries of the Gulf, 1798–1835*, Vol. IV, edited by Richard Schofield, Archive Editions, Slough, 1990, pp. xvii and xviii.
3 Foreign Secretary Lansdowne in a statement in the House of Commons on 3 May 1903 said the following about the British trade in the Persian Gulf: 'I see that in 1897 the trade was only £260,000, whereas in 1900 it had risen to over £1,000,000. At this moment out of a total trade in the Gulf ports of £3,600,000 in 1901, £2,300,000 represents the commerce of this country.' Ibid. p. 345.
4 Ibid. pp. 353–7.
5 Robert Geran Landen, *Oman since 1856: Disruptive Modernization in a Traditional Arab Society*, Princeton University Press, Princeton, NJ, 1967, p. 261.
6 For French activities in this period, see: J. B. Kelly, *Britain and the Persian Gulf, 1795–1880*, Clarendon Press, Oxford, 1968, p. 835, and David Roberts, 'The Exclusive Treaties – a British View,' in B. R. Pridham (ed.), *The Arab Gulf and the West*, Saint Martin's Press, New York, 1985, p. 10.
7 For details see: Sir Percy Sykes, *A History of Persia*, Vol. II, third edition, Macmillan, London, 1958, pp. 431–3.
8 E. Peterson, 'The Historical Pattern of Gulf Security', in Lawrence G. Potter and Gary Sick (eds), *Security in the Persian Gulf: Origin, Obstacle, and the Search for Consensus*, Palgrave, New York, 2002, p. 17.
9 *Islands and Maritime Boundaries*, Vol. III, p. 657.
10 Ibid. p. 659.
11 The new Iranian territorial policy also had the effect of alerting the British and the sheikhs of the Arab littoral that they should try to salvage as much territory formerly administered by the Qasimi Sheikh of Langah as possible. This, as seen later, affected their policy on Abu Musa and the Tunbs.
12 *Islands and Maritime Boundaries*, Vol. III, p. 658.
13 K. Vadiei, *Joghrafiya-ie Ensani-e Iran (Human Geography of Iran)*, Tehran University Press, Tehran, 1974, pp. 192–3.
14 See the letter from the Persian foreign minister to the British Legation, dated March 1888, reproduced in: *Islands and Maritime Boundaries*, Vol. III, p. 659.

15 *Islands and Maritime Boundaries*, Vol. III, pp. 646–7.
16 Ibid. p. 659.
17 Peterson, 'Historical Pattern of Gulf Security', p. 97.
18 *Islands and Maritime Boundaries*, Vol. III, p. 659.
19 Ibid. pp. 659–61.
20 Briton Cooper Busch, *Britain and the Persian Gulf, 1894–1914*, University of California Press, Berkeley, 1967, p. 242.
21 Farhang Mehr, *A Colonial Legacy: The Dispute over the Islands of Abu Musa and the Greater and Lesser Tunbs*, University Press of America, New York, 1997, p. 45.
22 Sykes, *History of Persia*, p. 378.
23 George N. Curzon, *Persia and the Persian Question*, Vol. II, Frank Cass, London, 1966, p. 394.
24 For these communications, see: *Islands and Maritime Boundaries*, Vol. III, p. 657.
25 Ibid. p. 658.
26 Donald Hawley, *The Trucial States*, George Allen & Unwin, London, 1970, p. 161.
27 See the full letter in: *Lower Gulf Islands: Abu Musa and the Tunbs Dispute*, edited by P. L. Toyes, Arabian Geopolitics series, ed. Richard Schofield, Archive Editions, Slough, 1993, p. 292.
28 Ibid. p. 296.
29 Hawley, *Trucial States*, p. 161.
30 Peterson, 'Historical Pattern of Gulf Security', p. 15.
31 Landen, *Oman since 1856*, p. 250.
32 Ibid. pp. 261–5.
33 John F. Standish, *Persia and the Gulf: Retrospect and Prospect*, Curzon Press, Richmond, 1998, p. 142.
34 For the transcript of the statement, see: *Persian Gulf Historical Summaries,* Vol. IV, p. 107.
35 Ibid. p. 109.
36 Sir Denis Wright, 'George Nathaniel Curzon 1859–1925', *Encyclopedia Iranica*, Vol. VI, ed. Ehsan Yarshater, Center for Iranian Studies, Columbia University, New York. Cited in: Sir Denis Wright, *Britain and Iran, 1790–1980*, The Iran Society, London, 2003, p. 49.
37 Ibid.
38 For the transcript of the speech, see: Hawley, *Trucial States*, p. 324.
39 *Islands and Maritime Boundaries*, Vol. IV, p. 362.
40 Ibid. p. 243.
41 Ibid.
42 *Persian Gulf Historical Summaries*, Vol. IV, p. 68.
43 Ibid. p. 74.
44 Memorandum by H. S. Barnes (Foreign Secretary, India, 1900–03), 24 February 1901. Cited in Busch, *Britain and the Persian Gulf*, p. 244.
45 *Islands and Maritime Boundaries*, Vol. IV, p. 3.
46 Ibid. p. 272.
47 *Persian Gulf Historical Summaries*, Vol. IV, p. 73.
48 Ibid. p. 73.
49 *Islands and Maritime Boundaries,* Vol. IV, p. 3.
50 *Persian Gulf Historical Summaries*, Vol. I, p. 109.

51 *Islands and Maritime Boundaries*, Vol. IV, p. 245.
52 *Persian Gulf Historical Summaries*, Vol. I., p. 110.
53 *Islands and Maritime Boundaries*, Vol. IV, p. 246.
54 *Gozideh-e Asnad-e Khaleej Fars* (*Selected Persian Gulf Documents*), Institute for International and Political Studies (IIPS), Tehran, 1989, p. 537.
55 Ibid. p. 528.
56 Hardinge's letter to Marquess of Lansdowne, No. 123, dated 2 July 1904, in *Islands and Maritime Boundaries*, Vol. IV, p. 21.
57 *Islands and Maritime Boundaries*, Vol. IV, p. 35.
58 Ibid. p. 67.
59 *Iran Political Diaries, 1881–1965*, Vol. 2, edited by R. M. Burrell, Archive Editions, Slough, 1997, p. 745.
60 Ibid. p. 737.
61 *Islands and Maritime Boundaries*, Vol. IV, p. 57.
62 *Iran Political Diaries*, Vol. 2, p. 708.
63 *Islands and Maritime Boundaries*, Vol. IV, p. 81.
64 Ibid.
65 Ibid. p. 108.
66 *Lower Gulf Islands*, p. 346.
67 *Islands and Maritime Boundaries*, Vol. IV, p. 392.
68 Ibid. p. 387.
69 *Persian Gulf Historical Summaries*, Vol. I, p. 104.
70 *Lower Gulf Islands*, p. 350.
71 These letters are later briefly discussed.
72 *Lower Gulf Islands*, pp. 364–7.
73 Hawley, *Trucial States*, p. 162.
74 *Islands and Maritime Boundaries*, Vol. IV, p. 375, and *Persian Gulf Historical Summaries*, Vol. I, p. 100.
75 *Islands and Maritime Boundaries*, Vol. IV, p. 376.
76 Communication No. 174, dated 23 April 1904, from Foreign Affairs to India Affairs. Cited in: *Islands and Maritime Boundaries*, Vol. IV, p. 376.
77 Communication No. 10, dated 4 May 1904, from India Office to Foreign Office. Cited in: *Islands and Maritime Boundaries*, Vol. IV, p. 376.
78 Foreign Office to India Office, 23 April 1904; India Office to Foreign Office, 4 May 1904, p. 2559/04. Cited in: *Persian Gulf Historical Summaries*, Vol. IV, p. 100.
79 14 June 1904, p. 2904/04. Cited in: *Persian Gulf Historical Summaries*, Vol. I, p. 101.
80 From Hardinge to Foreign Secretary, Enclosure 1 in No. 25 dated 14 June 1904. Cited in: *Islands and Maritime Boundaries*, Vol. IV, p. 386.
81 Ibid. p. 386. Enclosure 2.
82 *Islands and Maritime Boundaries*, Vol. IV, p. 386.
83 Ibid. p. 388.
84 Nonetheless, the patrimonial and decadent nature of Qajar rule should be blamed for the lack of a systematic and forward-looking administration of the country. As a result, local notables could enjoy various degrees of autonomy and discretionary power in their fiefs. Constantly threatened by conspiracies and intrigues, they could easily fall prey to foreigners seeking to advance their influence in Iran.
85 Letter dated 28 June 1904, in: *Islands and Maritime Boundaries*, Vol. IV, p. 393.
86 *Persian Gulf Historical Summaries*, Vol. IV, p. 76

87	J. G. Lorimer, *Gazetteer of the Persian Gulf, Oman, and Central Arabia*, Vol. I, Part II, Superintendent Government Printing, Calcutta, 1915, p. 2138.
88	*Islands and Maritime Boundaries*, Vol. IV, p. 393.
89	Ibid. p. 384.
90	Political Resident to Government of India, 15 April 1904. Cited in: *Persian Gulf Historical Summaries*, Vol. I, p. 97.
91	*Islands and Maritime Boundaries*, Vol. IV, p. 383.
92	Telegram from Viceroy to Secretary of State for India, 24 November 1908, p. 2111/68. Cited in: *Persian Gulf Historical Summaries*, Vol. I, p. 97.
93	*Lower Gulf Islands*, p. 145.
94	Ibid. p. 146.
95	Enclosure in No. 78, dated 23 October 1908, in: Ibid. p. 148.
96	*Lower Gulf Islands*, p. 149.
97	*Persian Gulf Historical Summaries*, Vol. II, p. 153.
98	J. G. Lorimer, Volume I, 2138. Cited in: *Persian Gulf Historical Summaries*, Vol. I, p. 101.
99	*Persian Gulf Historical Summaries;* Vol. I, p. 101.
100	Telegram from Political Resident to Minister, 23 February 1913, p. 18 19/13. Cited in: *Persian Gulf Historical Summaries*, Vol. I, p. 102.
101	F. O. telegram 88, 1 May 1923. Cited in: *Persian Gulf Historical Summaries*, Vol. I, p. 102.
102	Dispatch 258 to F. O., 31 May 1923, p. 2243/26. Cited in: *Persian Gulf Historical Summaries*, Vol. I, p. 103.
103	*Persian Gulf Historical Summaries*, Vol. II, p. 145.
104	Ibid. p. 146.
105	Ibid. p. 98.
106	Mr. Reilly's Correspondence and Memoranda, Persia and Arab States, Order in Consular Jurisdiction 1857 to 1882, part II, Further Correspondence Respecting Consular Jurisdiction in Persia 1874–76, FO 60/451, p. 19. Cited in: P. Mojtahedzadeh, 'Arab–Iranian Territorial Disputes: Cooperation in the Region not Confrontation', in: Khair El-Din Haseeb, *Arab-Iranian Relations*, Center for Arab Unity Studies, Beirut, 1998, p. 297.
107	*Persian Gulf Historical Summaries*, Vol. I, p. 103.
108	Ibid. p. 99.
109	*Iran Political Diaries*, Vol. 2, p. 482.
110	*Persian Gulf Historical Summaries*, Vol. I, p. 100.
111	Ibid p.104.
112	*Islands and Maritime Boundaries*, Vol. IV, p. 392.
113	Ibid. p. 392.
114	Ibid. p. 393.
115	Ibid. p. 387.
116	Ibid. p. 393.
117	J. G. Lorimer, Volume I, 2138. Cited in: *Persian Gulf Historical Summaries*, Vol. I, p. 101.
118	Secretary of State for India to Viceroy, 13 May 1908, p. 3168. Cited in: *Persian Gulf Historical Summaries,* Vol. I, p. 101.
119	Tehran to F.O., Telegram 306, 23 April 1909, p. 3301/09. Cited in: *Persian Gulf Historical Summaries*, Vol. I, p. 101.
120	The full texts of these three documents are reproduced in: *Lower Gulf Islands,* pp. 495–9.
121	Ibid. Vol. II, pp. 473–4.
122	*Islands and Maritime Boundaries*, Vol. III, p. 659.

194 *Notes*

123 Ibid.
124 Ibid.
125 'Farming' was a system in which a powerful individual 'leased' from a despotic central government the entire tax revenues of a region, province or city in return for support and/or a fixed annual amount of cash. The leased area was then left to the unchecked rapacity of the tax-farmer.
126 Extract from Sir Edward Beckett's memorandum, dated 12 March 1932, FO 371/18901. Cited in: Mojtahed-zadeh, 'Arab–Iranian Territorial Disputes', pp. 298–9.
127 Telegram from Political Resident to the Secretary of State for India, T. 234, 22 August, 1928. Cited in: Mojtahed-zadeh, 'Arab–Iranian Territorial Disputes', p. 98.
128 For a copy of the original letter and an English translation, see: Mojtahed-zadeh, 'Arab–Iranian Territorial Disputes', p. 299.
129 See note 106.
130 Document No. 53, in: *Gozideh-e Asnad-e Khaleej Fars (Selected Persian Gulf Documents)*, Institute for International and Political Studies (IIPS), Tehran, 1989, pp. 168–9. Cited in: Mojtahed-zadeh, 'Arab–Iranian Territorial Disputes', p. 298.
131 *Islands and Maritime Boundaries*, Vol. I, p. 527.
132 Enclosure 2 in letter No. 25, dated 15 June 1904, in: *Islands and Maritime Boundaries*, Vol. IV, p. 386.
133 *Iran Political Diaries*, p. 482.
134 J. B. Kelly, *Eastern Arabian Frontiers*, Faber & Faber, London, 1964, p. 18.
135 John Bulloch, *The Persian Gulf Unveiled*, Congdom & Weed, New York, 1984, p. 47.
136 *Persian Gulf Historical Summaries,* Vol. II, p. 153.
137 *Islands and Maritime and Maritime Boundaries*, Vol. V, p. 89.
138 Ibid. p. 95.
139 Ibid. pp. 98–9.
140 Ibid. p. 100.
141 Ibid. p. 101.
142 Enclosure 1 in No. 1, dated 12 Nov. 1914, in: Ibid. p. 105.
143 Enclosure 2 in No. 1, dated 12 Nov. 1914, in: Ibid. p. 106.
144 Ibid. p. 104.
145 Ibid. p. 105.
146 *Islands and Maritime Boundaries*, Vol. IV, p. 362.
147 Ibid. p. 273.
148 Ibid. p. 241.
149 Ibid. p. 244.
150 Ibid. p. 278.
151 See: Memorandum by Colonel Cox 'British Relations with Turkey in the Persian Gulf', dated 1 December 1910. Cited in: *Islands and Maritime Boundaries*, Vol. V, pp. 317–22.
152 Memorandum by Mr E. C. Blech, cited in: *Islands and Maritime Boundaries*, Vol. V, pp. 216–17.
153 *Islands and Maritime Boundaries*, Vol. V, pp. 157–66.
154 Rosemarie Said Zahlan, *The Making of the Modern Gulf States, Kuwait, Bahrain, Qatar, the UAE and Oman*, Garnet Publishing, London, 1998, p. 116
155 Bulloch, *Persian Gulf Unveiled*, p. 47–51.

156 Ibid.
157 Anthony H. Cordesman, *The Gulf and the Search for Strategic Stability*, Westview Press, Boulder, CO, p. 416. For more information on Buraimi, see: Keesing's Contemporary Archives, Keesing's Ltd [1931–1986], vol. 9, p. 12890, and vol. 10, p. 14534.
158 Bulloch, *Persian Gulf Unveiled*, pp. 62–3.
159 *Persian Gulf Historical Summaries*, Vol. IV, pp. 2–3.
160 Landen, *Oman since 1856*, p. 176.
161 Hawley, *Trucial States*, pp. 170–1.
162 Ibid. p. 173.
163 Despatch 47 (EA 1017/3) of 2 April 1951, cited in: *Persian Gulf Historical Summaries*, Vol. II, p. 148.
164 Hawley, *Trucial States*, pp. 173 and 177–8.
165 Ibid. pp. 173–4.
166 Wright, 'George Nathaniel Curzon, 1859–1925', in Wright, *Britain and Iran*, p. 50–1.
167 Ibid. p. 50.
168 *Persian Gulf Historical Summaries*, Vol. I, p. 30.
169 Wright, 'George Nathaniel Curzon, 1859–1925', in Wright, *Britain and Iran*, p. 51.
170 The British flag at Basidu was hauled down on 31 July 1933 by officers of the Imperial Persian Navy. See British *note verbale* to the Iranian Foreign Ministry, No. 480, dated 23 September 1933, *Gozideh-e Asnad-e Khaleej Fars* (*Selected Persian Gulf Documents*), p. 408.
171 Memorandum of negotiation, dated 16 Aban 1312 (8 October 1933), *Gozideh-e Asnad-e Khaleej Fars* (*Selected Persian Gulf Documents*), p. 442.
172 *Gozideh-e Asnad-e Khaleej Fars* (*Selected Persian Gulf Documents*), p. 547.
173 Ibid. p. 558.
174 Hossein H. Moghaddam, 'Anglo-Iranian Relations over the Disputed Islands in the Persian Gulf', in Vanessa Martin, (ed.), *Anglo-Iranian Relations since 1800*, Routledge, London, 2005, p. 150.
175 Ali Banuazizi and Myron Weiner (eds), *The State, Religion, and Ethnic Politics: Afghanistan, Iran, and Pakistan*, Syracuse University Press, Syracuse, NY, 1986, pp. 205–11. Iran could only reclaim its natural role in the Persian Gulf in the 1970s, in the wake of the British withdrawal from the area and the massive acquisition of weaponry from the United States. It could also then for the first time be self-reliant in terms of defending its interests in the Gulf, as its foreign policy could then be effectively supported by its military.
176 Tehran Telegram to Foreign Office 267, dated 31 August 1928, p. 4770. Cited in: *Persian Gulf Historical Summaries*, Vol. I, p. 91.
177 F.O. Telegram 186, 4 September 1928. Cited in: *Persian Gulf Historical Summaries*, Vol. I, p. 91.
178 Telegram 278, p. 5139. Cited in: *Persian Gulf Historical Summaries*, Vol. I, p. 91.
179 The third-power policy could be traced to the Qajar period. It was to serve the overriding objective of politico-economic emancipation of Iran from the traditional influence of Russia and Britain and to act as a counterweight against them.
180 For more information, see: Rouhollah K. Ramazani, *The Foreign Policy of Iran: A Developing Nation in World Affairs, 1500–1941*, University Press of Virginia, Charlottesville, 1966, pp. 277–89.

196 *Notes*

181 Nasrollah Saifpour Fatemi, *Oil Diplomacy: Powder Keg in Iran*, Whittier Books, New York, 1954, p. 162.
182 Ibid. pp. 165–6.
183 Ibid. pp. 166–8. For this episode also see: Mostafa Elm, *Oil, Power and Principle; Iran's Oil Nationalization and its Aftermath,* Syracuse University Press, Syracuse, NY, 1992, pp. 32–3.
184 Saifpour Fatemi, *Oil Diplomacy*, p. 179.
185 *Persian Gulf Historical Summaries*, Vol. I, p. 92.

3 The restoration of Persian Gulf autonomy and the issue of the three islands

1 For the full details of Britain's large cuts in pubic expenditure, see: *Keesing's Contemporary Archives, Weekly Diary of World Events, 1967–1968*, Keesing's Ltd, London, pp. 22489–97.
2 For details of the British economic and financial crisis, see: David Childs, *Britain since 1945: A Political History,* Ernest Benn, London, 1979, pp. 164–5 and 194–6.
3 *Keesing's, 1967–1968*, p. 22494.
4 *Islands and Maritime Boundaries of the Gulf, 1798–1835*, Vol. I, edited by Richard Schofield, Archive Editions, Slough, 1990, p. 530.
5 As described in Chapter 1, the British assumed the role of policeman in the Gulf by the virtue of the peace treaty, and British warships patrolled the Persian Gulf in a bid to prevent fighting among Arab tribes. Therefore, the concept of the Persian Gulf having a 'policeman' was not alien to the locals.
6 Trevor Mostyn, *Major Political Events in Iran, Iraq and the Arabian Peninsula; 1945–1990*, Facts on File, New York, 1991, p. 73.
7 Asadollah Alam, *The Shah and I: The Confidential Diary of Iran's Royal Court Minister, 1969–1977,* I. B. Tauris, London, 1991, p. 199.
8 Anthony Sampson, *The Seven Sisters*, Hodder and Stoughton, London, pp. 225–6.
9 Alvin J. Cottrell, 'Iran's Armed Forces under the Pahlavi Dynasty', in George Lenczowski (ed.), *Iran under the Pahlavis*, Hoover Institution Press, Stanford University, Palo Alto, CA, 1978, p. 401.
10 John Bulloch and Harvey Morris, *Saddam's War*, Faber & Faber, London, 1991, p. 80.
11 Ibid. p. 80.
12 Anthony H. Cordesman, *The Gulf and the Search for Strategic Stability*, Westview Press, Boulder, CO, p. 492.
13 Ibid. p. 174.
14 International Institute for Strategic Studies, *Strategic Survey 1971*, IISS, London, 1971, p. 45.
15 Douglas Hurd, who accompanied Edward Heath, the leader of the British opposition and the future prime minister, in a fact-finding trip to the Persian Gulf countries, including Iran, recorded his impression to this effect in his book *An End to Promises: Sketch of a Government, 1970–1974*, Collins, London, 1970, p. 41.
16 Mostyn, *Major Political Events*, p. 122.
17 Alam, *Shah and I*, p. 46.
18 Ibid. p. 47.
19 Ibid. p. 34.

Notes   197

20 Rosemarie Said Zahlan, *The Making of the Modern Gulf States, Kuwait, Bahrain, Qatar, the UAE and Oman*, Garnet Publishing, London, 1998, p. 166.
21 *Foreign Relations of the United States, 1964–1968; Vol. XXI, Near East Region; Arabian Peninsula* (FRUS 1964–68 XX), edited by N. D. Howland, US Government Printing Office, Washington, DC, 2000, pp. 608–9.
22 Ibid. p. 610.
23 Ibid. pp. 280–1.
24 Ibid. p. 280.
25 Ibid. p. 270.
26 *Keesing's, 1967–1968*, p. 22494.
27 FRUS 1964–68 XXI, pp. 268–9.
28 For details see: Cecil V. Crabb, Jr, *The Doctrines of American Foreign Policy*, Louisiana State University Press, Baton Rouge, pp. 278–328.
29 Faisal bin Salman al-Saud, *Iran, Saudi Arabia and the Gulf: Power Politics in Transition 1968–1971*, I. B. Tauris, London, 2003, p. 66.
30 UN Security Council S/PV-1610 of 9 December 1971.
31 See: al-Saud, *Iran, Saudi Arabia and the Gulf*, pp. 29–45.
32 FBIS, Tehran Domestic Service in Persian, 14 January 1969.
33 Sir Denis Wright, 'Ten Years in Iran: Some Highlights', *Asian Affairs*, Vol. 22, October 1991, p. 268.
34 See: Hussein al-Baharna, 'The Fact Finding of the United Nations Secretary-General and the Settlement of the Bahrain–Iran Dispute, May 1970', *International and Comparative Law Quarterly*, Vol. 22, July 1973, p. 546.
35 UN Security Council S/PV-1610 of 9 December 1971.
36 Saudi Arabia refused to sanction it unless its claim to most of Abu Dhabi's territory was met. See: Glen Balfour-Paul, *End of Empire in the Middle East: Britain's Relinquishment of Power in Her Last Three Years*, Cambridge University Press, Cambridge, p. 126.
37 Wright, 'Ten Years in Iran', p. 267.
38 al-Saud, *Iran, Saudi Arabia and the Gulf*, p. 45.
39 S. Chubin, and S. Zabih, *The Foreign Relations of Iran*, University of California Press, Berkeley, 1974, p. 216.
40 Ibid. p. 217.
41 Wright, 'Ten Years in Iran', p. 267.
42 al-Saud, *Iran, Saudi Arabia and the Gulf*, p. 90.
43 UN Security Council S/PV-1610 of 9 December 1971.
44 Alam, *Shah and I*, p. 70.
45 Ibid. pp. 163–4.
46 Wright, 'Ten Years in Iran', p. 269.
47 Chubin and Zabih, *Foreign Relations of Iran*, pp. 224–5.
48 *Ettelaat* (Tehran), 27 June 1971.
49 Chubin and Zabih, *Foreign Relations of Iran*, p. 225.
50 *Ettelaat* (Tehran), 27 June 1971.
51 Chubin and Zabih, *Foreign Relations of Iran*, p. 225.
52 Alam, *Shah and I*, p. 153.
53 Ibid.
54 Interview with Sir John Coles, 11 March 1997, in al-Saud, *Iran, Saudi Arabia and the Gulf*, p. 100.

198 *Notes*

55 Middle East Economic Survey (MEES), 5 June 1970, cited in al-Saud, *Iran, Saudi Arabia and the Gulf*, p. 100.
56 Chubin and Zabih, *Foreign Relations of Iran*, p. 225.
57 UN Security Council Document, S/PV-1610, 9 December 1971, p. 13.
58 J. B. Kelly, *Arabia, the Gulf, and the West*, Basic Books, New York, 1980, p. 93.
59 *Guardian*, 3 November 1971.
60 Balfour-Paul, *End of Empire*, p. 118.
61 Alam, *Shah and I*, p. 101.
62 Ibid. p. 34.
63 Ibid. p. 154.
64 Ibid. p. 43.
65 Hossein H. Moghaddam, 'Anglo-Iranian Relations over the Disputed Islands in the Persian Gulf', in Vanessa Martin, (ed.), *Anglo-Iranian Relations since 1800*, Routledge, London, 2005, p. 159, and al-Saud, *Iran, Saudi Arabia and the Gulf*, p. 97.
66 al-Saud, *Iran, Saudi Arabia and the Gulf*, p. 85.
67 Ibid. p. 95.
68 PRO/FO, 8/1307, from Sir Denis Wright to Mr. Drace-Francis, 4 March 1970. Cited in al-Saud, *Iran, Saudi Arabia and the Gulf*, p. 97.
69 Alam, *Shah and I*, p. 34.
70 Ibid. pp. 44–5.
71 Balfour-Paul, *End of Empire*, p. 128.
72 PRO/CAB, 128/17, Cabinet Meeting 23 July 1970. Cited in: al-Saud, *Iran, Saudi Arabia and the Gulf*, pp. 95–6.
73 Wright, 'Ten Years in Iran', p. 269.
74 Kelly, *Arabia, the Gulf, and the West*, p. 94.
75 Jasim M. Abdulghani, *Iraq and Iran: The Years of Crisis*, Johns Hopkins University Press, Baltimore, 1984, p. 104.
76 Balfour-Paul, *End of Empire*, p. 133.
77 Telegram from US ambassador in Tehran to Dean Rusk, 14 December 1968. Cited in al-Saud, *Iran, Saudi Arabia and the Gulf*, p. 49.
78 For details of the proposal see: al-Saud, *Iran, Saudi Arabia and the Gulf*, p. 110.
79 Alam, *Shah and I*, p. 113.
80 Ibid. p. 114.
81 For the full text of the MoU and the confirmation letters, see: H. Amirahmadi (ed.), *Small Islands, Big Politics*, St. Martin's Press, New York, 1996, pp. 162–5.
82 al-Baharna, 'Fact Finding of the United Nations Secretary-General', p 31.
83 *Times* (London), 1 December 1971.
84 Wright's unpublished memoir, cited in: al-Saud, *Iran, Saudi Arabia and the Gulf*, p. 107.
85 Interview with Ramsbotham, cited in: al-Saud, *Iran, Saudi Arabia and the Gulf*, p. 120 and PRO/CAB, 128/49/70987, Cabinet meeting, 8 November 1971, cited in: al-Saud, *Iran, Saudi Arabia and the Gulf*, pp. 20–1.
86 al-Saud, *Iran, Saudi Arabia and the Gulf*, pp. 20–1.
87 Bulloch, *Persian Gulf Unveiled*, p. 54.
88 John Duke Anthony, *Arab States of the Lower Gulf: People, Politics, Petroleum*, Middle East Institute, Washington, DC, 1975, p. 203.
89 Mostyn, *Major Political Events*, p. 120.
90 Balfour-Paul, *End of Empire*, p. 134.

Notes 199

91 Mostyn, *Major Political Events*, pp. 120–1.
92 J. B. Kelly, *Arabia, the Gulf, and the West*, pp. 87–97.
93 *New York Times*, 8 December 1971.
94 GRD, minutes of meeting with Sir William Luce, 7 September 1971. Cited in: al-Saud, *Iran, Saudi Arabia and the Gulf*, p. 113.
95 Mostyn, *Major Political Events*, p. 121.
96 Alam, *The Shah and I*, p. 161.
97 al-Saud, *Iran, Saudi Arabia and the Gulf*, p. 115.
98 Cordesman, *Gulf and the Search*, p. 417.
99 Anthony H. Cordesman, *Bahrain, Oman, Qatar and the UAE: Challenges of Security*, Westview Press, Boulder, CO, 1997, pp. 293–4.
100 Balfour-Paul, *End of Empire*, p. 133.
101 Ibid. pp. 133–4.
102 Said Zahlan, *Making of the Modern Gulf States*, p.120.
103 Kelly, *Arabia, the Gulf, and the West*, p. 90.
104 Cited in: Abdulghani, *Iraq and Iran*, p. 91.
105 Amirahmadi, *Small Islands, Big Politics*, p. 72.
106 Cordesman, *Gulf and the Search*, p. 424.
107 Ibid. p. 418.
108 Unpublished memoirs cited in: al-Saud, *Iran, Saudi Arabia and the Gulf*, p. 111.
109 *Al-Anwar*, 30 November 1971, cited in: al-Saud, *Iran, Saudi Arabia and the Gulf*, pp. 116–17.
110 UN Security Council S/PV-1610 of 9 December 1971.
111 The statement by the UAE in 1992 to the effect that the MoU had been imposed under duress cannot not have any merit. On 30 November 1971, Sharjah and Ras al-Khaimah were under British protection, and Iran was not in a position to impose anything on Britain, which was a major global power. A reverse argument would be more plausible.
112 For both documents, see: Amirahmadi, *Small Islands, Big Politics*, p. 72.
113 Rouhollah Ramazani, *The Persian Gulf: Iran's Role*, Appendix D, University Press of Virginia, Charlottesville, 1972, pp. 142–3.
114 *Kayhan International* (Tehran), 29 January 1972.
115 Chubin and Zabih, *Foreign Relations of Iran*, p. 228.
116 The occasional unfriendly relations and/or disputes between Iran and the Arabs are a fundamentally new development, mostly a product of contemporary controversies and legacies of the1958 coup in Iraq and Nasserism in Egypt.
117 Omar Ali, *Crisis in the Arabian Gulf: An Independent Iraqi View*, Praeger, Westport, CT, 1993, p. 12.
118 Political Report Adopted by the Eighth Regional Congress of the Arab Ba'ath Socialist Party, cited in: Abdulghani, *Iraq and Iran*, p. 77.
119 Cordesman, *Gulf and the Search*, pp. 417–18.
120 Mostyn, *Major Political Events*, p. 120.
121 Ibid. p. 121.
122 Ibid. p. 121.
123 Ibid. p. 121.
124 Ibid. p. 122.
125 Haim Shemesh, *Soviet–Iraqi Relations, 1968–1988*, Lynne Rienner Publishers, Boulder, CO, 1992, p. 60.
126 The Political Report of the Eighth Congress of the Arab Ba'ath Socialist Party in

200 *Notes*

Iraq in January 1974, cited in: Tareq Y. Ismael, *Iraq and Iran: Roots of Conflict*, Syracuse University Press, NY, 1982, p. 29.
127 Ismael, *Iraq and Iran*, p. 86.
128 *Al-Thawrah*, May 1980, cited in: Ibid. pp. 90–1.
129 UN Document S/10409 of 3 December 1971.
130 Letter by the representative of Iraq to the Secretary-General, UN Document S/10434 of 7 December 1971.
131 The Exclusive Treaties allowed the Trucial states to enter into agreement with other powers, albeit only with British consent. The British themselves facilitated the conclusion of the MoU between Iran and Sharjah.
132 UN Security Council S/PV-1610 of 9 December 1971.
133 Ibid, p. 12.
134 Ibid.
135 Ibid. p. 22.
136 Ibid. p. 23.
137 UN General Assembly Official Records, 26th Session, A/PV/.2007 of 9 December 1971, p. 1.
138 Ibid. pp. 1–2.
139 Ibid. p. 5.
140 UN Security Council Document S/10740 of 18 July 1972.
141 UN Security Council Document S/10756 of 7 August 1972.
142 See: the UAE statements at the UNGA on 27 September 1972, UN General Assembly Official Records, 27th Session, A/PV/.2043, pp. 14–15, and 28th Session, A/PV/.2135, pp. 8–9
143 See: UN General Assembly Official Records, 27th Session, A/PV/.2055, of 5 October 1972, p. 3, and 28th Session, A/PV/.2055, of 1 October 1973, p. 8.
144 *Arab Report and Record* (London), December 1–15, 1971, p. 622.
145 For details, see: Anthony, *Arab States of the Lower Gulf*, pp. 115–18.
146 Mostyn, *Major Political Events*, pp. 122–3.
147 Ibid. p. 123.
148 Ibid.
149 Shemesh, *Soviet–Iraqi Relations*, p. 61.
150 Ibid. p. 60.
151 Ibid. p. 61.
152 Ibid. p. 63.
153 Ibid. p. 64. For details of Iraqi attempts to insert language on Iran, see: Ibid. p. 65.
154 Dilip Hiro, *The Longest War: The Iran–Iraq Military Conflict*, Routledge, New York, 1991, p .15.
155 Abdulghani, *Iraq and Iran*, p. 98.
156 Cordesman, *Gulf and the Search*, pp. 403–5.
157 Fred Holiday, 'The Gulf in International Affairs: Independence and After', in B. R. Pridham (ed.), *The Arab Gulf and the Arab World*, Croom Helm, London, 1988, p. 106.
158 Mostyn, *Major Political Events*, p. 139.
159 Ibid. p. 168
160 Ibid. p. 140.
161 Ibid.
162 Cordesman, *Gulf and the Search*, p. 397.
163 Holiday, 'Gulf in International Affairs', p. 100.

Notes 201

164 Ibid. 101.
165 Abdulghani, *Iraq and Iran*, p. 158.

4 Transitional period

1 Jasim M. Abdulghani, *Iraq and Iran: The Years of Crisis*, Johns Hopkins University Press, Baltimore, 1984, p. 194.
2 Ayatollah Sadegh Rouhani's call for annexation of Bahrain in June 1979 and once more in September the same year denounced the 1970 agreement on the status of Bahrain and claimed that Bahrain was an Iranian province. The Iranian authorities, including Deputy Prime Minister Sadeq Tabataba'i and Iran's ambassador to Kuwait, stated that Iran had no territorial ambitions on Bahrain and that Rouhani's remarks were his personal opinion. See: Christin Marschall, *Iran's Persian Gulf Policy: From Khomeini to Khatami*, RoutledgeCurzon, London, 2003, pp. 27–35.
3 John Nielsen, 'Saudi Arabia: A Shaky US Pillar of Security', *Newsweek*, 3 March 1980.
4 Abdulghani, *Iraq and Iran*, pp. 194–6.
5 Dilip Hiro, *The Longest War: The Iran–Iraq Military Conflict*, Routledge, New York, 1991, p. 76.
6 Ibid. p. 7
7 Rosemarie Said Zahlan, *The Making of the Modern Gulf States, Kuwait, Bahrain, Qatar, the UAE and Oman*, Garnet Publishing, London, 1998, p. 171.
8 Hiro, *Longest War*, pp. 76–7.
9 Said Zahlan, *Making of the Modern Gulf States*, p. 177.
10 Ibid. p. 178.
11 M. E. Ahrari, 'Iran, GCC and the Security Dimensions in the Persian Gulf', in H. Amirahmadi and Nader Entessar, (eds), *Reconstruction and Regional Diplomacy in the Persian Gulf*, Routledge, London, 1992, p. 203.
12 Anoush Ehteshami, 'Wheels within Wheels: Iran Foreign Policy towards the Arab World', in H. Amirahmadi and Nader Entessar (eds), *Reconstruction and Regional Diplomacy in the Persian Gulf*, Routledge, London, 1992, p. 168.
13 Associated Press, 30 May 1982.
14 Shahram Chubin and Charles Tripp, *Iran and Iraq at War*, Westview Press, Boulder, CO, 1988, pp. 28–9.
15 K. McLachlan, *Analyses of the Risks of War: Iran–Iraq Discord, 1979–1980*, in Farhang Rajaee (ed.), *The Iran–Iraq War*, University Press of Florida, Gainesville, 1993, pp. 25–9.
16 Abdulghani, *Iraq and Iran*, p. 199.
17 Ibid. p. 200.
18 Ibid. p. 199.
19 BBC Summary of World Broadcasts, 19 June 1979.
20 BBC Summary of World Broadcasts, 21 August 1979.
21 Farhang Rajaee (ed.), *The Iran–Iraq War*, University Press of Florida, Gainesville, 1993, p. 18; Trevor Mostyn, *Major Political Events in Iran, Iraq and the Arabian Peninsula; 1945–1990*, Facts on File, New York, 1991, p. 169; and Associated Press, 8 November 1979. See also: Jonathon C. Randal, 'Iraq Moves to Sever 1975 Border Accord with Iran', *Washington Post*, 1 November 1979.
22 See also: BBC Summary of World Broadcasts, 2 November 1979.
23 The Iraqi media reported this letter on 5 April 1980. See: 'Iraq Demands Iran Withdraw from Three Persian Gulf Islands', Associated Press, 6 April 1980. However, as described later, the letter circulated as a document of the UN Security Council was dated 30 April 1980.
24 'Saddam Hussein's 15th April Speech in Nineveh', BBC Summary of World Broadcasts, 18 April 1980.

Notes

25. Rajaee, *Iran–Iraq War*, pp. 18–19.
26. 'Iraqi Envoy to USSR on Relations with Iran', BBC Summary of World Broadcasts, 14 May 1980.
27. Rajaee, *Iran–Iraq War*, p. 21.
28. Marschall, *Iran's Persian Gulf Policy*, p. 67.
29. 'The Three Islands in the Gulf and Arafat', BBC Summary of World Broadcasts, 6 December 1979.
30. Facts on File World News Digest, 10 October 1980.
31. Hiro, *Longest War*, pp. 77–8.
32. John Duke Anthony, *Regional and Worldwide Implications of the Gulf War*, in M. S. El-Azhary (ed.), *Iran–Iraq War: A Historical, Economic and Political Analysis*, Indian edition, D. K. Agencies, 1984, p. 106.
33. Anthony H. Cordesman, *The Gulf and the Search for Strategic Stability*, Westview Press, Boulder, CO, p. 61.
34. Ibid, p. 397.
35. UN Security Council Document S/13918 of 30 April 1980.
36. Iran's response to Iraq drew a reaction from the UAE that will be reviewed later. What is important to note here is the fact that Iraq succeeded in bringing the issue back to the United Nations after an eight-year interval.
37. UN Security Council Document S/ 14117 of 21 August 1980.
38. UN General Assembly, A/35/PV.1-33 of 10 September–10 October 1980.
39. Ibid.
40. UN General Assembly, A/36/PV.1-33 of 25 September 1981.
41. John Kifner, 'Oil Sites In Iran and Iraq Bombed as Baghdad Troops Cross Border', *New York Times*, 24 September 1980.
42. Ibid.
43. Ibid.
44. Jim Hoagland, '*A Carter Doctrine for Mideast Oil?*', *Washington Post*, 3 June 1979.
45. George C. Wilson, 'Marines to Form Rapid Reaction Force', *Washington Post*, 6 December 1979.
46. Transcript of the State of the Union Address, Facts on File World News Digest, 25 January 1980.
47. In the words of Energy Secretary James Schlesinger, the curtailment of oil supplies from Iran loomed as 'prospectively more serious' to the United States than the Middle East oil embargo of 1973–74. See: Herman Nickel, 'The U.S. Failure In Iran', *Fortune*, 12 March 1979.
48. Daniel Beegan, 'Rapid Deployment Will Deter Soviets, Marine Officer Says', Associated Press, 16 August 1980.
49. Michael Getler, 'Persian Gulf: Little Debate on Build-up; U.S. Moving Fast to Build Up Military Forces in Persian Gulf', *Washington Post*, 10 August 1980.
50. Michael Getler, 'US Sending Ground Radar to Saudi Arabia', *Washington Post*, 6 October 1980.
51. Daniel Beegan, 'US Will Bolster Neutral Persian Gulf Nations', Associated Press, 8 October 1980.
52. Facts on File World News Digest, 10 October 1980.
53. Philip Shabecoff, 'Brown Discloses U.S. Sends Saudis Ground Radar and 100 Personnel', *New York Times*, 6 October 1980.
54. David B. Ottaway, 'Fear of Iran Nudges Wary Persian Gulf States to Closer US Ties', *Washington Post*, 24 February 1982.
55. Hiro, *Longest War*, p. 78.
56. John Duke Anthony, *A Darkling Plan: US View of Gulf Security*, in B. R. Pridham, *The Arab Gulf and the West*, St. Martin's Press, New York, 1985, p. 137.

57 John K. Cooley, 'Defending Oil: No Easy Task, No Rush to Help', *Christian Science Monitor*, 31 January 1980.
58 David B. Ottaway, 'Fear of Iran Nudges Wary Persian Gulf States to Closer US Ties', *Washington Post*, 24 February 1982.
59 Ehteshami, 'Wheels within Wheels', p. 156.
60 Jonathan C. Randal, 'PLO Chief, in Iran, Hails Shah's Fall', *Washington Post*, 19 February 1979.
61 Helena Cobban, 'Iraq Bids for Arab Leadership', *Christian Science Monitor*, 10 April 1980.
62 Edward Cody, 'Iraq Advances Slowly toward the Gulf; Syria Criticizes Iraq for Gulf Hostilities', *Washington Post*, 8 October 1980.
63 Hiro, *Longest War*, p. 80–1.
64 Henry Tanner, 'Libyans Back Iran; Ask Saudis to Expel U.S. Radar Aircraft', *New York Times*, 11 October 1980.
65 Hiro, *Longest War*, p. 79.
66 In fact, in the aftermath of the Algiers Agreement, Iraq's economic relations with the West witnessed a phenomenal growth and expansion, while those with Moscow began to lessen. Relations extended to the military field, too, but were very slow on the diplomatic front. See: Abdulghani, *Iraq and Iran*, pp. 160–3.
67 William Chapman and John M. Goshko, 'US Lifts Curbs on Certain Sales to South Africa', *Washington Post*, 27 February 1982.
68 Anthony, *Darkling Plan*, p. 120.
69 Hiro, *Longest War*, p. 73.
70 Ibid. p.79.
71 BBC Summary of World Broadcasts, 18 September 1979.
72 'Shaikh Saqr on Iranian Control of Islands in Hormuz Strait', BBC Summary of World Broadcasts, 4 April 1980.
73 As stated earlier, the Iranian letter was in response to the Iraqi letter dated 29 April 1980, in which Iraq's 'non-recognition of Iran's illegal occupation of the three Arab islands' belonging to 'the Arab nation' was stated.
74 UN Security Council Document S/13987 of 6 June 1980.
75 UN Security Council Document S/14111 of 18 August 1980.
76 UN Security Council Document S/14274 of 28 November 1980.
77 'Iraq on UAA "Official Statement" about Gulf Islands', BBC Summary of World Broadcasts, 6 December 1980. Note that the paper carefully refrained from referring to any particular country as the owner of the islands.
78 'The Greater and Lesser Tunbs and Abu Musa in the Gulf', BBC Summary of World Broadcasts, 22 September 1980.
79 UN Security Council Document S/ 14290,of 9 December 1980.
80 UN General Assembly, A/35/PV.1-33 of October 1980.
81 FBIS MEA, 19 January 1981, p. C7; cited in Abdulghani, *Iraq and Iran*, p. 199.
82 Ahmad Razavi, *Continental Shelf Delimitation and Related Maritime Issues in the Persian Gulf*, Martinus Publishers, The Hague, 1996, p. 246.
83 Said Zahlan, *Making of the Modern Gulf States*, p.181.
84 Marschall, *Iran's Persian Gulf Policy*, pp. 80–1.
85 Ibid. pp. 172–3.
86 Said Zahlan, *Making of the Modern Gulf States*, pp. 154–5.
87 Marschall, *Iran's Persian Gulf Policy*, p. 81.
88 'Iran Launches Diplomatic Offensive', United Press International, 12 September 1987.
89 Marschall, *Iran's Persian Gulf Policy*, p. 93.
90 *The Emirate News*, 31 Dec 1987, cited in: Marschall, *Iran's Persian Gulf Policy*, p. 94.

91 *Arab News*, 11 January 1988, cited in: Marschall, *Iran's Persian Gulf Policy*, p. 95.
92 Said Zahlan, *Making of the Modern Gulf States*, p. 155.
93 Ibid. p. 181.
94 Anthony H. Cordesman, *Bahrain, Oman, Qatar and the UAE: Challenges of Security*, Westview Press, Boulder, CO, 1997, p. 298.
95 Anthony H. Cordesman, *The Iran–Iraq War and Western Security, 1984–87*, Jane's, London, 1987, p. 107.
96 Jonathan Broder, 'Iran Fortifies 3 Gulf Islands, Presents New Danger for US', *Chicago Tribune*, 8 July 1987.
97 Ibid.
98 Ibid.
99 Ibid.
100 'US Prepares for Gulf Escort', *The Chicago Tribune*, 14 July 1987.
101 Michael Ross, 'US Discovers Mines in New Area of Gulf', *Los Angeles Times*, 29 September 1987.

5 Confrontational phase

1 Richard Haass, 'A Troubling Era Dawns in the Middle East', *Financial Times*, 17 October 2006. Haass asserts that this era came to an end mostly because the US invasion of Iraq.
2 'Rafsanjani on Desire to Improve Relations with Gulf States', BBC Summary of World Broadcasts, 11 January 1989.
3 'Rafsanjani's News Conference; Announces Candidacy for Presidency, Comments on Future Policy', BBC Summary of World Broadcasts, June 10, 1989.
4 Anoush Ehteshami, 'Wheels within Wheels: Iran Foreign Policy towards the Arab World', in H. Amirahmadi and Nader Entessar (eds), *Reconstruction and Regional Diplomacy in the Persian Gulf*, Routledge, London, 1992, p. 176.
5 Christin Marschall, *Iran's Persian Gulf Policy: From Khomeini to Khatami*, RoutledgeCurzon, London, 2003, p. 100.
6 Lara Marlowe, 'Crisis in the Gulf: Iran Offer to Small Countries', *Financial Times*, 13 August 1990.
7 Aly Mahmoud, 'Gulf Arabs and Iran Move Closer, but Some Skeptical', Associated Press, 29 December 1990.
8 Ehteshami, 'Wheels within Wheels', p. 176.
9 'Fears of Iran-Iraq Alliance Revived', *Financial Times*, 13 September 1990.
10 UN document S/RES/598 (1987), 20 July 1987.
11 Marschall, *Iran's Persian Gulf Policy*, p. 107.
12 Mahmoud, Gulf Arabs and Iran Move Closer'.
13 Kathy Evans, 'Gulf Leadership Looks to Future Security in Region', *Guardian*, 24 December 1990.
14 BBC Summary of World Broadcasts, 3 October 1990.
15 'Final Communiqué of GCC Supreme Council Meeting in Doha', BBC Summary of World Broadcasts, 29 December 1990.
16 BBC Summary of World Broadcasts, 7 May 1991.
17 BBC Summary of World Broadcasts, 4 March 1991.
18 Liz Thurgood, 'Peace in the Gulf: Tehran Attacks Saddam's Rule', *Guardian*, 2 March 1991.
19 Quoted in: Marschall, *Iran's Persian Gulf Policy*, p. 155.
20 Ibid. p. 109.

Notes 205

21 BBC Summary of World Broadcasts, 18 February 1991.
22 BBC Summary of World Broadcasts, 7 March 1991.
23 Robert Graham, 'The Gulf; Arab Ministers to Hold Security Talks with Baker', *Financial Times*, 8 March 1991.
24 Cited in: Thomas L. Friedman, 'After the War: Diplomacy; 8 Arab Countries Back Bush's Plan on Mideast Peace', *New York Times*, 11 March 1991.
25 Ibid.
26 Reuters, 11 March 1991.
27 Friedman, 'After the War'.
28 'Iran to Resume Ties with Saudi Arabia', Associated Press, 17 March 1991.
29 Caryle Murphy, 'Egypt's Pullout Signals Discord with Gulf; Measure Establishing 'New Arab Order' Appears on Brink of Collapse', *Washington Post*, 11 May 1991.
30 Ibid.
31 'Iraqi Planes Bomb Offshore Oil Fields in Abu Dhabi', United Press International, 25 November 1986.
32 For details see: Anthony H. Cordesman, *Bahrain, Oman, Qatar and the UAE: Challenges of Security*, Westview Press, Boulder, CO, 1997, p. 298.
33 Tim Ahern, 'Trio of Navy Warships Begins Escorting Reflagged Kuwaiti Tankers', Associated Press, 22 July 1987.
34 Marschall, *Iran's Persian Gulf Policy*, pp. 37–9.
35 M. E. Ahrari, 'Iran, GCC and the Security Dimensions in the Persian Gulf', in H. Amirahmadi and Nader Entessar, (eds), *Reconstruction and Regional Diplomacy in the Persian Gulf*, Routledge, London, 1992, p. 197.
36 US policy on the three islands in the 1990s is discussed later in this chapter.
37 David K. Shipler, 'Superpowers and the Gulf', *New York Times*, 29 December 1987.
38 Cordesman, *Bahrain, Oman, Qatar and the UAE*, p. 299.
39 Geoffrey Kemp and Robert E. Harkavy, *Strategic Geography and the Changing Middle East*, Carnegie Endowment/Brookings, Washington, DC, 1997, p. 252.
40 Dan Balz, 'Bush Praises Gulf Forces, Calls for Mideast Peace', *Washington Post*, 7 March 1991.
41 Caryle Murphy, 'Egypt's Pullout Signals Discord With Gulf; Measure Establishing "New Arab Order" Appears on Brink of Collapse', *Washington Post*, 11 May 1991.
42 Susanne M. Schafer, 'Pentagon: Pact with Kuwait First in Postwar Era', Associated Press, 5 September 1991.
43 Susanne M. Schafer, 'Perry Wraps Up Six-Day Visit with Pre-positioning Agreements', Associated Press, 23 March 1995.
44 Dana Priest and John Lancaster, 'Slimming Elsewhere, US Builds Muscle in Gulf', *Washington Post*, 18 November 1995.
45 Ibid.
46 Lachlan Carmichael, 'Breakdown of US Forces within Striking Range of Iraq', Agence France Presse, 1 September 1996.
47 Priest and Lancaster, 'Slimming Elsewhere'.
48 Ibid.
49 Stephen Dagget and Gary J. Pagliano, 'The Persian Gulf War: US Costs and Allied Financial Contribution', Congressional Research Service IB91019, 21 September 1992, pp. 11–13, cited in: Cordesman, *Bahrain, Oman, Qatar and the UAE*, p. 378. The war against Iraq cost around $61 billion – more than $54 billion was paid by

50 Cordesman, *Bahrain, Oman, Qatar and the UAE*, p. 378.
51 Sean Foley, 'The UAE: Political Issues and Security Dilemmas', *Middle East Review of International Affairs (MERIA)*, Vol. 3, No. 1 March 1999, p. 33.
52 Anthony H. Cordesman, *US Forces in the Middle East*, Westview Press, Boulder, CO, 1997, pp. 76–7.
53 Anthony H. Cordesman, *Bahrain, Oman, Qatar and the UAE*, p. 378.
54 Douglas Jehl, 'US Seeks Ways to Isolate Iran; Describes Leaders as Dangerous', *New York Times*, 27 May 1993.
55 R. Jeffrey Smith and Daniel Williams, 'White House to Step Up Plans to Isolate Iran, Iraq', *Washington Post*, 23 May 1993.
56 Ibid.
57 'Clinton to Sign Iran Sanctions Bill', United Press International, 1 August 1996.
58 R. Jeffrey Smith, 'Gates Warns of Iranian Arms Drive; Tehran Buys $2 Billion in Weapons Annually, House Panel Is Told', *Washington Post*, 28 March 1992.
59 Rosemarie Said Zahlan, 'The Impact of the US Policy on the Stability of the Gulf States, in Joseph Keshishian, *Iran, Iraq and the Arab Gulf States*, Palgrave, New York, 2001, p. 357.
60 'Excerpts From Meeting in Jordan' *New York Times*, 12 November 1987.
61 Alan Cowell, 'At Long Last, Egypt Is Back in Arab Fold', *New York Times*, 22 May 1989.
62 Riad N. El-Rayyes, 'Arab Nationalism and the Gulf', in B. R. Pridham, *The Arab Gulf and the Arab World*, Croom Helm, London, 1988, pp. 77–9.
63 Fouad Ajami, 'Iran: The Impossible Revolution', *Foreign Affairs,* Winter 1988/1989, 128–43.
64 Anthony Cordesman, *The Gulf and the Search for Strategic Stability*, Westview Press, Boulder, CO, p. 78.
65 Ibid.
66 Marschall, *Iran's Persian Gulf Policy*, p. 120.
67 This cycle of activity came in contrast to the passive behaviour of the UAE in the 1970s and 1980s, when abundant media reports of Iran's activities on the three islands never brought UAE officials to lodge any protest.
68 Marschall, *Iran's Persian Gulf Policy*, p.121.
69 Ibid. p. 122.
70 Caryle Murphy, 'Iran Claims Sovereignty Over Small, Oil-Producing Gulf Island', *Washington Post*, 25 September 1992.
71 Marschall, *Iran's Persian Gulf Policy*, p. 124.
72 'Gulf Countries Try to Contain UAE–Iran Dispute over Islands', Associated Press, 16 April 1992.
73 'Iranians Evict UAE Nationals from Gulf Island', Insight/Middle East Newsfile, 15 April 1992.
74 Two major news articles on this subject are also worth mentioning: Youssef M. Ibrahim, 'Iran Is Said to Expel Arabs From Gulf Island', *New York Times*, 16 April 1992; and Christopher Walker, 'Border Squabbles Fuel Gulf Tension', *Times* (London) 21 April 1992.
75 'Gulf Countries Try to Contain UAE–Iran Dispute over Islands', Associated Press, 16 April 1992.

Notes   207

76   'Iranian Foreign Minister Discusses Iran's Foreign Policy, Gulf Security', BBC Summary of World Broadcasts, 22 April 1992.
77   'Velayati Denies Iran Intends to Expel Arab Residents of Abu Musa Island', BBC Summary of World Broadcasts, 24 April 1992.
78   'Iran Deputy Foreign Minister on Relations with Gulf States, Abu Musa Island', BBC Summary of World Broadcasts, 23 April 1992.
79   'President's Friday Prayers Sermons on International Issues Including Gulf Islands, BBC Summary of World Broadcasts, 21 September 1992.
80   'Iran Says Agenda for Further Talks Mostly Agreed, Tunb Islands Non-Negotiable', BBC Summary of World Broadcasts 30 September 1992.
81   'Iran Refuses to Let Ship Dock at Abu Musa Island', Associated Press, 25 August 1992.
82   'Iran Reportedly Refuses to Allow Ship from UAE to Dock at Abu Musa Island, BBC Summary of World Broadcasts, 26 August 1992.
83   'Alleged Maltreatment of Passengers on Ship from UAE Denied by Official', BBC Summary of World Broadcasts, 27 August 1992.
84   UN document A/47/441 and S/24559 of 15 September 1992.
85   UN document A/47/449 – S/24566 of 16 September 1992.
86   UN document S/24609 of 2 October 1992.
87   UN document A/47/516 of 12 October 1992.
88   'UAE Envoy to UN Briefs Boutros-Ghali on Islands Issue', *Khaleej Times*, 9 October 1992.
89   'UAE Takes Dispute with Iran to UN', Agence France Presse, 29 November 1992.
90   'UAE Cancels Negotiations on Island Dispute with Iran', Agence France Presse, 10 September 1993.
91   'Opinion: UAE's Experiment with the Saddam Brand of Logic', *Tehran Times*, 30 September 1992.
92   Caryle Murphy, 'Iran, UAE Break Off Talks over Disputed Island,' *Washington Post*, 29 September 1992.
93   'Iran Says Agenda for Further Talks Mostly Agreed, Tunb Islands Non-Negotiable', BBC Summary of World Broadcasts, 30 September 1992.
94   'UAE Statement Blames Iran for Failure of Talks on Gulf', BBC Summary of World Broadcasts, 30 September 1992.
95   'Foreign Ministry Official Returns from Abu Musa, Says Arab Schools Have Reopened', BBC Summary of World Broadcasts, 17 November 1992.
96   'Iran Claims Possession of Disputed Abu Musa Island', Associated Press, 10 September 1992.
97   'National Security Council Says Security on Abu Musa is an Internal Matter', BBC Summary of World Broadcasts, 15 September 1992.
98   'President's Friday Prayers Sermons on International Issues Including Gulf Islands', BBC Summary of World Broadcasts, 21 September 1992.
99   Christopher Walker, 'Tehran Threatens to Shoot Down Aircraft Over Disputed Islands', *Times* (London), 22 September 1992.
100 'Khamenei Blasts West over Abu Musa', Agence France Presse, 15 September 1992.
101 'Iranian President Warns Gulf Arab States against Move on Islands', Agence France Presse, 25 December 1992.
102 US ambassador Armin Meyer's favourable attitude towards the Iranian position on the three islands is referred to in Chapter 3.

103 Murphy, 'Iran Claims Sovereignty'.
104 Warren Strobel, 'Syrian Official Sees "Total Peace"; Pledges May Nudge Mideast Talks', *The Washington Times*, 24 September 1992.
105 'Remarks of Edward Djerejian, Assistant Secretary of State for Near Eastern and South Asian Affairs, to the National Association of Arab Americans 20th Anniversary Conference, the Mayflower Hotel, Washington, DC', Federal News Service, 11 September 1992.
106 Chris Hedges, 'Iran Is Riling Its Gulf Neighbors, Pressing Claim to 3 Disputed Isles', *New York Times*, 13 September 1992.
107 Christopher Walker, 'Rifkind Pledges West's Aid against Iranian Aggression', *Times* (London), 24 September 1992.
108 Murphy, 'Iran Claims Sovereignty'.
109 Marschall, *Iran's Persian Gulf Policy*, p. 127.
110 'Iraq In Brief', BBC Summary of World Broadcasts, 20 April 1992.
111 Note that Iraq always in the past referred to the three islands as belonging to the Arab nation, and not specifically to the UAE.
112 'Defence Ministry Newspaper Questions Iranian Intentions in the Gulf', BBC Summary of World Broadcasts, 3 September 1992.
113 Abdullah Al-Shayeji, 'Dangerous Perceptions: Gulf Views of the US Role in the Region,' *Middle Eastern Policy*, September 1997, pp. 3–4.
114 Jeffrey Gardner, 'Kofi Annan Clinches UN Peace Deal with Saddam', *Financial Times*, 23 February 1998; and Aziz Abu-Hamad, 'Gulf State No-Shows', *Washington Post*, 20 March 1998.
115 'Gulf Rulers in Troubled Waters over Iraq', *Financial Times*, 7 March 1998.
116 'Emirates Condemns Gulf States for Rapprochement with Iran', Associated Press, 6 June 1999.
117 Robin Allen, 'Iran Sidesteps Pressure over Islands', *Financial Times*, 6 March 1998.

Bibliography

Documents

Lower Gulf Islands: Abu Musa and the Tunbs, Vols 1 and 2, edited by P. L. Toyes, Arabian Geopolitics 2, Regional Documentary Studies, ed. Richard Schofield, Archive Editions, Slough, 1993.

Foreign Relations of the United States, 1964–1968; Vol. XX: the Near East Region; Arabian Peninsula (FRUS 1964–68 XX), edited by N. D. Howland, US Government Printing Office, Washington, DC, 2000.

Gozideh-e Asnad-e Khaleej Fars, (Selected Persian Gulf Documents), Institute for International and Political Studies (IIPS), Ministry of Foreign Affairs, Tehran, 1989.

Iran Political Diaries, 1881–1965, Vols 1–14, edited by R. M. Burrell, Archive Editions, Slough, 1997.

Islands and Maritime Boundaries of the Gulf, 1798–1935, Vols I–V, edited by Richard Schofield, Archive Editions, Slough, 1990.

The Persian Gulf Historical Summaries, 1907–1953; Vols I–V (PG 13), Archive Editions, Gerrards Cross, 1987.

Political Diaries of the Persian Gulf, edited by Archive Editions and R. Jarman, Archive Editions, Slough, 1990.

United Nations Security Council and General Assembly documents.

Books and articles

Abdulghani, Jasim M., *Iraq and Iran: The Years of Crisis*, Johna Hopkins University Press, Baltimore, 1984.

Ahmirahmadi, Hooshang, *Small Islands, Big Politics,* St. Martin's Press, New York, 1996.

Amirahmadi, Hooshang, and Entessar, Nader (eds), *Reconstruction and Regional Diplomacy in the Persian Gulf*, Routledge, London, 1992.

Alam, Asadollah, *The Shah and I: The Confidential Diary of Iran's Royal Court Minister, 1969–1977*, ed. Alinaghi Alikani, I. B. Taurus, London, 1991.

Ali, Omar, *Crisis in the Arabian Gulf: An Independent Iraqi View*, Praeger, Westport, CT, 1993.

Anthony, John Duke, *Arab States of the Lower Gulf: People, Politics, Petroleum*, Middle East Institute, Washington, DC, 1975.

Balfour-Paul, Glen, *The End of Empire in the Middle East: Britain's Relinquishment of Power in Her Last Three Years*, Cambridge University Press, Cambridge, 1991.

Bibliography

Banuazizi, Ali, and Weiner, Myron (eds), *The State, Religion, and Ethnic Politics: Afghanistan, Iran, and Pakistan*, Syracuse University Press, Syracuse, NY, 1986.

Bulloch, John, *The Persian Gulf Unveiled*, Congdom & Weed, London, 1884.

Bulloch, John, and Morris, Harvey, *Saddam's War*, Faber & Faber, London, 1991.

Childs, David, *Britain since 1945: A Political History*, Ernest Benn, London, 1979.

Chubin, Shahram, *Security in the Persian Gulf; The Role of Outside Powers*, IISS, Gower Publishing, Montclair, NJ, 1980.

Chubin, Shahram, and Tripp, Charles. *Iran and Iraq at War*. Westview Press, Boulder, CO, 1988.

Chubin, Shahram, and Zabih, S., *The Foreign Relations of Iran*, University of California Press, Berkeley, 1974.

Cooper Busch, Briton, *Britain and the Persian Gulf, 1894–1914*, University of California Press, Berkeley, 1967.

Cordesman, Anthony H., *Bahrain, Oman, Qatar and the UAE: Challenges of Security*, Westview Press, Boulder, CO, 1997.

Cordesman, Anthony H., *The Gulf and the Search for Strategic Stability*, Westview Press, Boulder, CO, 1984.

Cordesman, Anthony H., *The Iran–Iraq War and Western Security, 1984–87: Strategic Implications and Policy Options*, Jane's, London, 1987.

Cordesman, Anthony H., *US Forces in the Middle East*. Westview Press, Boulder, CO, 1997.

Cordesman, Anthony H., and Wagner, Abraham R. *The Lessons of Modern War: The Gulf War*, Westview Press, Boulder, CO, 1996.

Cottrell, Alvin J., 'Iran's Armed Forces under the Pahlavi Dynasty', in Lenczowski, George (ed.), *Iran under the Pahlavis*, Hoover Institution Press, Stanford University, Palo Alto, CA, 1978.

Crabb, Cecil V., Jr, *The Doctrines of American Foreign Policy*, Louisiana State University Press, Baton Rouge, 1982.

Curzon, George N., *Persia and the Persian Question*, Vols. I–IV, Frank Cass, London, 1966.

Ehteshami, Anoush, Nonneman, Gerd, and Tripp, Charles, *War and Peace in the Gulf: Domestic Politics and Regional Relations into the 1990s*, Ithaca Press, Reading, 1991.

El-Azhary, M. S. (ed.), *Iran–Iraq War: A Historical, Economic and Political Analysis*, Indian edition, D. K. Agencies, 1984.

El-Issa, Shimlan, 'The Dispute between the UAE and Iran over Three Islands', in Haseeb, Khair El-din (ed.), *Arab–Iranian Relations*, Center for Arab Unity Studies, Beirut, 1998.

Elm, Mostafa, *Oil, Power and Principle: Iran's Oil Nationalization and Its Aftermath*, Syracuse University Press, NY, 1992.

Geran Landen, Robert, *Oman since 1856: Disruptive Modernization in a Traditional Arab Society*, Princeton University Press, NJ, 1967.

Haseeb, Khair El-Din (ed.), *Arab–Iranian Relations*, Center for Arab Unity Studies, Beirut, 1998.

Hawley, Donald, *The Trucial States*, George Allen & Unwin, London, 1970.

Hiro, Dilip, *The Longest War: The Iran–Iraq Military Conflict*, Routledge, New York, 1991.

Holiday, Fred, 'The Gulf in International Affairs: Independence and After', in Pridham, B. R., *The Arab Gulf and the Arab World*, Center for Arab Gulf Studies, Croom Helm, London, 1988.

Hurd, Douglas, *An End to Promises: Sketch of a Government, 1970–1974*, Collins, London, 1970.
International Institute for Strategic Studies, *Strategic Survey 1971*, IISS, London, 1971.
Ismael, Tareq Y., *Iraq and Iran: Roots of Conflict*, Syracuse University Press, NY, 1982.
Kashani-sabet, Firouzeh, *Frontier Fictions: Shaping the Iranian Nation, 1904–1946*, Princeton University Press, NJ, 1999.
Kelly, J. B., *Arabia, the Gulf, and the West*, Basic Books, New York, 1980.
Kelly, J. B., *Britain and the Persian Gulf, 1795–1880*, Clarendon Press, Oxford, 1968.
Kemp, Geoffrey and Harkavy, Robert E., *Strategic Geography and the Changing Middle East*, Carnegie Endowment/Brookings, Washington, DC, 1997.
Keshishian, Joseph, *Iran, Iraq and the Arab Gulf States*, Palgrave, New York, 2001.
Kodmani, Bassm (ed.), *Quelle Sécurité pour le Golfe?*, Institut Français des Relations Internationales, Paris, 1984.
Lorimer, J. G. *Gazetteer of the Persian Gulf, Oman, and Central Arabia*, Superintendent Government Printing, Calcutta, 1915.
Marschall, Christin, *Iran's Persian Gulf Policy: From Khomeini to Khatami*, Routledge-Curzon, London, 2003.
Martin, Vanessa (ed.), *Anglo-Iranian Relations since 1800*, Routledge, London, 2005.
Mehr, Farhang, *A Colonial Legacy: The Dispute over the Islands of Abu Musa and the Greater and Lesser Tunbs*, University Press of America, New York, 1997.
Mojtahed-zadeh, Pirouz, *The Small Players of the Great Game: The Settlement of Iran's Eastern Borderlands and the Creation of Afghanistan*, Routledge, London, 2004.
Momtaz, Djamshid, *Le Statut Juridique de Certaines Îles Éparses du Golfe Persique: Abou Moussa et la Petite et Grande Tumb*, Collection espaces et ressources maritimes, No. 8 (Paris), 1994.
Mostyn, Trevor, *Major Political Events in Iran, Iraq and the Arabian Peninsula, 1945–1990*, Facts on File, New York, 1991.
Peterson, J. E., 'The Historical Pattern of Gulf Security', in Potter, Lawrence G. and Sick, Gary (eds), *Security in the Persian Gulf: Origin, Obstacle, and the Search for Consensus*, Palgrave, New York, 2002.
Pridham, B. R. *The Arab Gulf and the Arab World*, Croom Helm, London, 1988.
Pridham, B.R. (ed.), *The Arab Gulf and the West*, St. Martin's Press, New York, 1985.
Rajaee, Farhang (ed.), *The Iran–Iraq War*, University Press of Florida, Gainesville, 1993.
Ramazani, Rouhollah K., *The Foreign Policy of Iran: A Developing Nation in World Affairs, 1500–1941*, University Press of Virginia, Charlottesville, 1966.
Ramazani, Rouhollah K, *The Persian Gulf: Iran's Role*, Appendix D, University Press of Virginia, Charlottesville, 1972.
Razavi, Ahmad, *Continental Shelf Delimitation and Related Maritime Issues in the Persian Gulf*, Martinus Nijhoff Publishers, The Hague, 1996.
Said Zahlan, Rosemarie, *The Making of the Modern Gulf States, Kuwait, Bahrain, Qatar, the UAE and Oman*, Garnet, London, 1998.
Saifpour Fatemi, Nasrollah, *Oil Diplomacy; Powder Keg in Iran*, Whittier Books, New York, 1954.
Saivetz, Carol R., *The Soviet Union and the Persian Gulf in the 1980s*, Westview Press, London, 1989.
Sampson, Anthony, *The Seven Sisters: The Great Oil Companies & the World They Shaped*, Hodder and Stoughton, London, 1975.
al-Saud, Faisal bin Salman, *Iran, Saudi Arabia and the Gulf: Power Politics in Transition, 1968–1971*, I. B. Tauris, London, 2003.

Shemesh, Haim, *Soviet–Iraqi Relations, 1968–1988*, Lynne Rienner Publishers, Boulder, CO, 1992.
Standish, John F., *Persia and the Gulf: Retrospect and Prospect*, Curzon Press, Richmond, 1998.
al-Suwaidi, Jamal, *Iran and the Gulf: A Search for Stability*, Emirate Center for Strategic Studies and Research, Abu Dhabi, 1996.
Sykes, Sir Percy, *A History of Persia*, Vol. II, 3rd edition, Macmillan, London, 1958.
Tadjbakhche, G. R., *La Question des Iles de Bahrein*, Editions A. Pedone, Paris, 1960.
Vadiei, K., *Joghrafiya-ie Ensani-e Iran (The Human Geography of Iran)*, Tehran University Press, 1974.
Wright, Sir Denis, *Britain and Iran, 1790–1980*, Iran Society, London, 2003.

News agencies, newspapers and periodicals

Agence France Presse
Ath-Thawrah (Baghdad)
America and the World (New York)
Asian Affairs (Hong Kong)
Associated Press
BBC Summary of World Broadcasts (Reading)
Chicago Tribune
Christian Science Monitor (Boston)
Ettelaat (Tehran)
Facts on File World News Digest (New York)
Federal News Service (Washington)
Financial Times (London)
Foreign Broadcast Information Service (FBIS) (Washington)
Fortune
Guardian (London)
International and Comparative Law Quarterly (Oxford)
Islamic Republic New Agency (Tehran)
Journal of Commerce (Newark, NJ)
Kayhan (Tehran)
Kayhan International (Tehran)
Keesing's Contemporary Archives, Weekly Diary of World Events (Harlow)
Khaleej Times (Dubai)
Los Angeles Times
Middle Eastern Policy (Washington)
New Statesman (London)
New York Times
Newsweek (New York)
Times (London)
United Press International (Washington)
Washington Post

Index

Abadan 71; first oil shipment from 39
Abbas I, Shah of Persia 13
Abd-al-Baqi, Foreign Minister of Iraq 108, 110
Abdallah, Foreign Minister Rashed 170
Abdel-Aziz, Sheikh of Sharjah 142–3
Abdulghani, Jasim M. 92
Abdullah, Rashid, UAE Foreign Minister 138, 140, 178
Abdullah, Sheikh of Bahrain 21–3
Abu Dhabi 9, 36, 37, 65–6, 75, 95, 158, 173, 176, 177; Iran–Iraq War, backing for Iraq in 119; oil wealth of 97, 142; Palestinian settlement in 162; Sheikh of 37; US and, cooperation between 152–3, 158
Abu Musa 41, 56–7; activity on, renewal of 163–78; approach to issue of Tunbs and 1–3; April and August 1992 incidents 164–8; Arab Federation, linkage with 85–6; Bahrain, linkage with 84; British arguments on, review of 56–61; British dispute with Iran over 45–51, 56–61, 180–1; contention between Iran and Arab world, prolonged issue of 176–8; double capacity argument of Britain concerning 57–9; factor of prescription for Britain 61; failure of Iraq on issue of 128–43; geopolitics and role of major powers in issue of 179–85; half-solution option from Britain on 89–96; importance of issue of 179; international forums, UAE raising issue at 169–70; international reaction to UAE hard line on 174–6; Iranian determination to recover 83–4, 86–8; Iranian reaction to UAE hard line on 172–3; Iranian sovereignty over, issue of 98–9; Iraqi plan to attack and seize 124–5; Iraqi raising issue at United Nations of 125–7; Iraqi shelving issue at United Nations of 127–8; letters concerning Arab title to 59–60; negotiations, UAE breaking off 171–2; preconditions, UAE subjecting negotiations to 170–1; regional forums, UAE raising issue at 169–70; revival of Iraqi interest in 122–4; UAE and GCC activity concerning, renewal of 163–78; UAE and issue in 1980s of 137–43; UAE hard-line position on 168–72
Achaemenian era in Persia 76
Afghanistan 1, 5, 25–6, 27, 71, 80, 116, 118, 120, 129–30, 132, 135, 162, 180
Africa 1, 80, 116
Afshar, Amir Khosrow 96, 97, 106
'age of imperialism' 32–3
Agence France Presse 170
Aghassi, Hadji Mirza 24
Ahmad ad-Duri, Abd ar-Rahman 124
Ahmad Khan, Sartip Haji 33–4, 36, 37
the Ain-ed-Dowleh, Prime Minister of Persia 49
Akhir Sa'ah 124
Al-Anwar 98
Al Ba'ath 134
Al-Baharna, Hussein 94
Al-Bakr, Ahmad Hassan, President of Iraq 108–9
Al-Dawlah, Vusuq 68
Al Dowleh, Mushir 45, 48
Al-Fajr 139
Al-Hadaf 138
Al-Hayat 170
Al-Jumhuriyah 123

214 Index

Al-Khalifa family 22–3
Al-Khalij 141
Al-Khater, Mubarak 147
Al-Merree, Khalifa Shaheen 148
Al-Nahar 123
Al-Nahayan, Foreign Minister Sheikh Hamdan ibn Zayed 170
Al-Qadisayah 176
Al-Qasimi, Sheikh Said bin Hamad 65
Al-Ra'y al-Amm 85
Al-Sabah, Foreign Minister Sheikh Nasser Mohammed 147
Al-Sadat, Anwar, President of Egypt 111, 162
Al-Suwaidi, Foreign Minister Ahmad 113
Al-Thawrah 109, 123, 139, 176
Al-Zawawi, Minister Qais Abd-Moneim 112
Alam, Court Minister Asadollah 78, 79, 86, 87, 90–1, 93
Algiers Agreement (1975) 100, 113, 121, 123, 139, 203n66
Amanullah Khan, King of Afghanistan 71
Amin-us-Sultan, Foreign Minister of Iran 57, 63
Anglo-Iranian oil concession 69, 71
Anglo-Iranian War (1857) 48, 49
Anthony, John Duke 125, 136
Arab League 77, 95, 96, 106, 136, 142, 144, 160–1, 169, 176–7, 185
Arab radicalism 99–110; international and regional repercussions to Iraqi radicalism 108–10; moves against Britain and Iran 101–3; weakening of 160–1
Arab world 77, 85, 96, 167, 174, 184; anti-Americanism in 131; Arab–Israeli conflict 131; conservative nature of 108, 144, 185; Damascus Declaration (1991) 149; financial aid to 119; fragmentation of 134, 136; Iran's relationship with, *rapprochement* in 111–14; Iraq and leadership of 127–8, 154; pan-Arabism 4, 77, 81, 100, 119, 122, 136, 139, 149, 151, 161, 176, 183; radicalism in 99–103, 164; realignment and shift in 160–3; three islands as prolonged issue of contention between Iran and 176–8
Arafat, Yasir 124
ARAMCO 84, 153
Argyll, George Cambell, Duke of 14–15
Arthur, Sir Geoffrey 95
Atkinson-Willes, Admiral 39

AWACS (Airborne Warning and Control Systems) 131, 135
Aziz, Tariq 103, 123

Bahrain 15, 31, 36, 53, 60, 69, 72, 76, 79, 95, 107–8, 176, 180, 181; British claim on 21–5; British Political Resident in 88; exclusive agreement with Britain (1892) 10–12, 37, 70; Iran and 85, 87–8, 89–90, 92–3, 111–14, 137, 146, 165; Iraq and 122, 125; linkage with three islands 84; regional realignment 117–18; Sheikh of 60, 64; US cooperation with 156–7, 165
Baker, Secretary of State James 149, 150
Balfour, Arthur James, Lord 38
Balfour-Paul, Glen 90, 97
Baluchistan 38; British interest in 27–8
Bander Abbas 18, 62
Bani Sadr, President of Iran A. H. 126, 127, 138, 140
Beckett, Sir Edward 59
Benjedid, President Chadli of Algeria 134
Besharati, Foreign Minister Ali Muhammad 141, 166
Bishara, Abdullah 147
Boer War in South Africa 37, 38
Bosanquet, Rear-Admiral 41
Boutros-Ghali, Boutros 169, 170
Britain: Abu Musa, arguments on, review of 56–61; Abu Musa, disputed with Iran 45–51, 56–61, 180–1; Abu Musa, double capacity argument concerning 57–9; Abu Musa, factor of prescription 61; Abu Musa, letters concerning Arab title to 59–60; 'age of imperialism', high point for 32–3; Anglo-Iranian oil concession 69, 71; Anglo-Persian relations, difficulties post-First World War in 68–72; Anglo-Persian relations, settling outstanding issues post-British withdrawal 83–99, 181–4; Arab radicals' moves against 101–3; Bahrain, claim on 21–5; Bahrain, exclusive agreement with (1892) 10–12, 37, 70; Baluchistan, interest in 27–8; Bubiyan Island, hold over 64–5; Buraimi Oasis, dispute over 65–6; Cape Musandim, hold over 63–4; challenges in Gulf area for 31–7; consolidation of position in Gulf area 40–5; de-Persianization policy 187n26; encroachment on eastern Iran 25–30; end of *Pax Britannica* 74–5; expansion

Index   215

of control, general policy of 63–6;
First World War and aftermath 66–72;
General Treaty (1820) 9; Greater Tunb,
arguments on, review of 56–61; Greater
Tunb, disputed with Iran 45–51,
56–61, 180–1; Greater Tunb, double
capacity argument concerning 57–9;
Greater Tunb, factor of prescription 61;
Greater Tunb, letters concerning Arab
title to 59–60; Greater Tunb, priority-
in-occupation argument 60–1; Gulf
Arabs, growing domination over 66–8;
Henjam Island as target for 15, 16, 18,
25, 31, 35, 40, 41, 42–5, 51, 62, 181;
Herat, Anglo-Persian War 25–7; India,
security at expense of Iran for 14, 15;
international environment, dealing
with 79–83; Iranian defiance of 68–72;
Kharg Island as target for 7, 14, 15,
16, 26–7; Khuzistan, interest in 28–30;
Kishm Island and British authorities
3, 10, 15–21, 22, 25, 34, 35, 37, 40–2,
53, 60, 61–2, 76, 181; Kolba Island,
territorial engineering over 65; Kuwait,
treaty of friendship with 66; Lesser
Tunb, arguments on, review of 56–61;
Lesser Tunb, disputed with Iran 51–5,
56–61, 180–1; Lesser Tunb, double
capacity argument concerning 57–9;
Lesser Tunb, factor of prescription
61; Lesser Tunb, letters concerning
Arab title to 59–60; Lesser Tunb,
priority-in-occupation argument 60–1;
Makran, interest in 27–8; 'Monroe
Doctrine', implementation by 38, 54;
Pax Britannica 10, 11, 73, 74–5, 92,
110, 180, 181; Perpetual Maritime
Truce (1853) 9–10; Persian Gulf,
assertiveness of Iran in 33–7; Persian
Gulf, communications hub 33; Persian
Gulf, growing importance of 31–7;
policy towards Iran 12–30; Political
Resident of 187n16; reaction to UAE
action on three islands issue 174–6;
relationship with Iran, strained nature
of 12–15; rising star of 6–12; Seistan,
interest in 27; Sirri Island, double
capacity argument 57–9; Sirri Island,
revival of controversy with Iran 55–7;
Strait of Hormuz, lease or purchase of
islands in 61–3; strategic innovation in
Gulf area 37–63, 180–1; subjugation of
Arab sheikhs 8; treaty-based relations
with Arab tribes 8–9; Trucial states,
exclusive agreement with (1892)
10–12, 37, 70; Verba Island, hold over
64–5; withdrawal from 'east of Suez'
4, 15, 73, 74, 89, 113, 128, 180, 181;
Zakhnuniyeh Island, disputes over 64
Brown, Defense Secretary Harold 130, 131
Bruce, William 19, 22
Bubiyan Island, British hold over 64–5
Bulloch, John 95
Buraimi Oasis, dispute over 65–6
Bush, President George 150, 155

Cape Musandim 37; British hold over
63–4
Carter, President Jimmy 130; Carter
doctrine 129–30
CENTCOM (US Central Command) 130,
131
CENTO (Central Treaty Organization) 77,
102, 127
Cheney, Defense Secretary (later Vice
President) Dick 155–6
China 108, 109, 159
Christopher, Warren 131, 159
Chubin, S. and Tripp, C. 122
Clinton, President William J. 159
Cold War 3, 74, 80, 81, 144, 154, 157, 182,
183, 184
Cole, John 88
Cordesman, Anthony H. 96–7, 112, 125,
162
Cox, Major (later Sir) Percy 43–4, 46, 49,
50, 51, 52, 55, 64, 65, 68
Crawford, Sir Stewart 88
Crowe, Colin 105, 182
Cuellar, Javier Pérez de 142, 147, 148
Curzon of Kedleston, George N, Lord 4, 5,
10, 14, 15, 16, 20, 26, 27, 31–72, 181
Cyprus 71

Dane, L.W. 47
Dhofar 78, 111, 112, 113
Djerejian, Edward 174–5
Douglas-Home, Foreign Secretary (later
Prime Minister) Sir Alec 92, 98–9
Dubai 6, 9, 67, 85–6, 88, 95, 97, 111, 119,
126, 141, 143, 158, 177; Palestinian
settlement in 162; Sheikh of 35, 36, 70
Duff, Grant 44–5

Eagleburger, Lawrence S. 174
Egypt 7, 74, 77, 100, 107, 109, 111–12,
115, 136, 149–51, 155, 160–1,
165–6, 175–6; Israeli–Egyptian peace

216 Index

agreement 115, 118, 120, 121, 133, 134, 162
Ehteshami, Anoush 133
Ellis, Henry 26
Elphinstone, Sir Monstuart 19
El-Shibib, Talib 104

Fahd, Crown Prince (later King) of Saudi Arabia 117, 143
Faisal bin Abd al-Aziz, King of Saudi Arabia 82
Faisal bin Salman al-Saud 106
Farish, J. 23
Farrant, Colonel 24
Fars, Prince of 19
Fath Ali, Shah of Iran 7, 8, 20, 24
First World War: Anglo-Persian relations after 68–72; British policy in aftermath of 66–8
France 6, 7, 16, 31, 33, 37, 41, 108, 158, 186n9
Frank C. Strick and Co. 51, 52
Fumani-Ha'eri, Mostafa 167

Gates, Robert M. 160
GCC (Gulf Cooperation Council) 120–1, 144, 147–8, 149, 151–2, 156, 160–1; attempts at normalization of ties with Iran 145–6; reaction to UAE action on three islands issue 174–6; and UAE in new cycle of activity on three islands issue 163–78
General Treaty of Peace (1820) 9, 23
Germany 11, 31, 33, 36, 37, 69, 71
Ghotbzadeh, Foreign Minister Sadegh 138
Goldsmid, General Frederic 27
Grechko, Defence Minister Andrei 109
Greene, C. 35, 57, 58
Grey, Sir Edward 52
The Guardian 90

Haig, General Alexander 162
Hamilton, George, Lord 38, 41
Hammadi, Foreign Minister Sadoon 107, 125, 126
Hardinge, Sir Arthur 43–4, 46, 48–9, 51, 55, 60
Hasan, Sheikh 41
Hassan, Abdul-Hussein Moslem 123
Hawley, Donald 5–6, 37
Henjam Island: British abandonment of 69–70; British target 15, 16, 18, 25, 31, 35, 40, 41, 42–5, 51, 62, 181; Sheikh of, expulsion of 70

Herat, Anglo-Persian War 25–7
Hertslet, E. 22, 23, 24, 25
Hiro, Dilip 125
Hogg, Captain Tony 175
Hormuz Island 7, 40, 41, 62, 181
Hoveida, Prime Minister A. A. 87
Hunt, Lieutenant 41
Hussein, King of Jordan 134
Hussein, Saddam 4, 102, 109, 118, 121–2, 124, 125, 127, 134, 136, 139, 146, 154, 158, 160–1, 173

IISS (International Institute for Strategic Studies) 78
India 37, 38, 39; Russian threat to 38, 40–1, 47; security of 15
Indyk, Martin S. 159
international environment, dealing with 79–83
international forums, UAE raising three islands issue at 169–70
international reaction to UAE hard line on three islands 174–6
Iran: Abu Musa, determination to recover 83–4, 86–8; Anglo-Persian relations, difficulties post-First World War in 68–72; Anglo-Persian relations, settling outstanding issues post-British withdrawal 83–99; Arab Federation–three islands linkage 85–6; Arab–Iranian controversies over Tunb Islands 96–8; Arab littoral, establishment of closer ties with 36–7; Arab radicals' moves against 101–3; Arab world and, three islands as prolonged issue of contention between 176–8; ascendancy in Persian Gulf of 110–14; Bahrain–three islands linkage 84–; British early policy towards 12–30; British relationship with, strained nature of 12–15; Constitutional Revolution (1905–6) 68; defiance of Britain 68–72; diplomatic overtures of 145–51; encroachment by Britain on east of 25–30; GCC, attempts at normalization of ties with 145–6; Greater Tunb, determination to recover 83–4, 86–8; half-solution option from Britain on three islands 89–96; historic position of 75–6; importance of three islands issue for 179; inherent position of 75–6; international environment, dealing with 79–83; Iran-Iraq War 101, 116, 118–19, 120, 122, 125, 130–1,

143, 145, 152, 163–4; Iranian–Arab relations, deterioration in 76–7; Iranian Revolution 116, 120, 134, 137, 138; Iraqi radicalism and, international and regional repercussions 108–10; Lesser Tunb, determination to recover 83–4, 86–8; Majlis in 68, 99; military build-up 78; nationalism of 13; naval force in Gulf 36; oil and gas, growth in importance of 77–8; power and interests, growth of 76–9; reaction to UAE hard line on three islands 172–3; reclaim of 'natural position' 75–83; regional autonomy, emphasis on 78–9; Russian loans for 35; Russo-Persian Wars 13–14; sovereignty over islands, issue of 98–9; territorial control, strengthening of 34–6; 'third-power policy' of 71, 195n179; Trans-Persian Railway 39, 61–2

Iraq: conservative sheikhs, moves against 107–8; failure on three islands issue 128–43; Iran–Iraq War 101, 116, 118–19, 120, 122, 125, 130–1, 143, 145, 152, 163–4; national ambitions of 121–2; plan to attack and seize three islands 124–5; radicalism of, international and regional repercussions 108–10; raising three islands issue at United Nations 125–7; regional ambitions of 121–2; revival of interest in three islands 122–4; shelving three islands issue at United Nations 127–8; United Nations moves of 103–7

Iraq Petroleum Company 101

IRNA (Islamic Republic News Agency) 168, 172

Israel 77, 119, 130, 151, 162, 163, 183; Arab–Israeli conflict 77, 81, 109, 110, 111, 132, 162, 163; Egypt–Israeli peace agreement 115, 118, 120, 121, 133, 134, 162; Lebanon, invasion of 236

Jaloud, Major Abd al-Salam 102
Joasmis (Qawassim) 15, 16, 20, 186n10, 186n13
Johnson, Colonel Eric 66
Johnson, President Lyndon B. 80, 81, 82
Jones, Sir Harford 16
Jordan 107, 111, 119, 135

Karachi 27, 62
Kayhan 146

Kazimi, Bagher 20–1
Keir, General Sir William 8, 17
Kelly, J. B. 22, 61, 97
Kemball, Captain (later Colonel) C. A. 37, 45–6, 47, 51, 56
Kemp, T. W. 64
Khalat, Khan of 28
Khalatbari, Foreign Minister A. A. 98–9
Khaled bin Muhammad al-Qasimi, Sheikh of Sharjah 92, 93, 94, 95, 98
Khalid, King of Saudi Arabia 135
Khalif, Salah (Abu Iyad) 131
Khamenei, Ayatollah Ali 146, 173
Kharbit, Abd al-Hamid 108
Kharg Island: British target 7, 14, 15, 16, 26–7; oil terminal on 77; periodic occupation of 181, 188n46
Kharrazi, Foreign Minister Kamal 148, 177
Khatami, Seyed Mohammad, President of Iran 177–8
Khaz'al, Khuzistan Sheikh 25, 28–9
Khoda Panahi, Foreign Minister M. K. 139
Khomeini, Imam (later Ayatollah) Ruhollah 117, 125
Khuzistan 25, 28–9, 39, 71, 77, 101, 122, 124
Kifner, John 127–8
Kishm Island 3, 10, 15–21, 22, 25, 34, 35, 37, 40–2, 53, 60, 61–2, 76, 181
Kissinger, Henry 112
Kolba Island, British territorial engineering over 65
Kosygin, Premier Alexei 109
Kuwait 10–11, 15, 76, 78, 81, 85, 89, 92, 100, 111, 118–19, 122; Berlin–Baghdad–Kuwait railway 31, 33; Bubiyan and Verba, claim on 64–5, 110, 113; crisis of (1991) 3, 4, 80, 128, 133, 146, 148–9, 156, 164–5, 184, 188n37; Iran and 70, 96, 105–7; Iraqi aggressiveness towards 111–13; Palestinian settlement in 162; Sheikh of 64–5; treaty of friendship with Britain 66; US protection for 156, 165

Lansdowne, Henry Charles, Lord 38, 42, 48, 190n3, 190n109
Larak Island 40, 61, 62, 181
Lesser Tunb 51–5; *see also* Tunb Islands, Greater and Lesser
Libya 96, 102, 103, 106, 107, 109, 134–6, 160–1, 183

218 *Index*

Loraine, P. 52
Lorimer, J. G. 18, 20, 50–1
Luce, Sir William 84, 87, 89, 92, 96, 97

Makran, British interest in 27–8
Maktum, UAE Vice-President 176
Malcolm, Sir John 14, 16, 17, 27
Malek-ut-Tujar 33
Marschall, Christin 141, 201n2
Meade, Lieutenant-Colonel 56, 58
Mesopotamia 28, 43, 66, 67
military build-up in Iran 78
Morley, John, Lord 52
Morocco 107, 135, 161
Mossadegh, Mohammed 71
Mubarak, President Hosni 151, 176
Mubarak, Sheikh of Kuwait 10–11
Musavi, Mir Hussean, Prime Minister of Iran 141
Muscat 6, 7, 15, 20, 24, 33, 42, 67, 141; Imam of 17, 19, 21, 22, 23, 60, 188n55; Sultan of 28, 36, 43

Nadir Shah, Emperor of Iran 25–6, 76
Napoleon Buonaparte 7
Nasir al-Din Shah, Emperor of Iran 27, 28
Nasser, Gamal Abdel, President of Egypt 77, 100, 111
national ambitions of Iraq 121–2
Naus, Joseph 35–6, 55–6
naval force of Iran in Gulf 36
New York Times 79, 127–8, 175
Nicholson, Harold 69
Nixon, President Richard M. 82, 109; Nixon doctrine 129
Norman, Herman 68
North Yemen 81, 107, 111, 113, 135, 136
Nouvel Observateur 140

oil and gas, growth in importance of 77–8
Oman 6, 18, 57, 59, 63–4, 97–8, 101, 107, 111–13, 116–17, 119–20, 126, 132; Gulf of 65, 76; Iraqi aggressiveness concerning three islands 123, 124, 125, 126; regional cooperation on security, call for 147; shipping safety, advocation of regional solution 141; Sultan of 5, 6, 18, 63, 125, 147, 150; Trucial Oman Levies 65, 68; UAE and, neutrality on Iran–Iraq conflict 141; US protection for 131, 156, 157
Ottoman Empire 6, 7, 10, 11, 13, 28, 31, 33, 64, 66–7, 100, 187
Oxy Oil 88

Pachachi, Adnan 85, 98, 105–6, 106–7
Pahlavi, Shah Mohammad Reza 74, 79, 81–2, 84–92, 94, 96–7, 103, 110, 117
Pahlavi, Shah Reza 4, 20, 29–30, 68, 70, 71
Palestine 1; effects on Persian Gulf 161–3; expatriates from 162; and Gulf, parallel between 102–3; Palestinian–Israeli peace process 163; pro-Palestinian orientation of Iran 117–18; question of, issues pertaining to 132, 134, 136, 149–50, 162–3, 168, 184; status of Palestinians 4; *see also* PLO (Palestine Liberation Organization)
pan-Arabism 4, 77, 81, 100, 119, 122, 136, 139, 149, 176, 183; defeat of 161; pan-Arab security arrangement 151
Pax Britannica 10, 11, 73, 74–5, 92, 110, 180, 181
Perpetual Maritime Truce (1853) 9–10
Perry, Defense Secretary William 156
Persian Gulf: activity on three islands, renewal of 163–78; Arab disarray in 133–7; Arab Federation–three islands linkage 85–6; Arab–Iranian controversies over Tunb Islands 96–8; Arab littoral, Iranian establishment of closer ties with 36–7; Arab radicalism 99–110; Arab radicalism, weakening of 160–1; Arab realignment, shift in 160–3; Arab world and Iran, three islands as prolonged issue of contention between 176–8; assertiveness of Iran in 33–7; autonomy of, strained but enduring 128–33; British Political Resident in 9, 11, 19, 22, 23, 35, 37, 45, 51–4, 56, 59–60, 68, 187n16; British strategic innovation in area 37–63, 180–1; British subjugation of Arab sheikhs 8; British treaty-based relations with Arab tribes 8–9; central position of 1; challenges in Gulf area for Britain 31–7; colonial past, consequences of 1–2; communications hub for Britain 33; conservative sheikhs, Iraqi moves against 107–8; consolidation of British position in 40–5; de-Persianization policy of Britain 187n26; diplomatic overtures by Iran 145–51; expansion of control, British general policy of 63–6; failure of Iraq on three islands issue 128–43; geopolitics and role of major powers in three islands issue 179–85; growing importance of Britain

in 31–7; Gulf Arabs, growing British domination over 66–8; half-solution option from Britain on three islands 89–96; importance of issue of three islands 179; India, importance for 1; Iranian ascendancy in 110–14; Iranian reclamation of 'natural position' in 75–83; Iranian regional autonomy, emphasis on 78–9; Iranian sovereignty over three islands, issue of 98–9; Iranian territorial control, strengthening of 34–6; Iraqi regional ambitions in 121–2; Iraqi revival of interest in three islands 122–4; last British Political Resident in 95; local autonomy in danger 152–60; Palestine, effects on 161–3; pan-Arabism, defeat of 161; regional realignment 116–21; regional security arrangement 146–9; 'Six plus Two' arrangement, failure of 149–51; threats to British omnipotence in 31; UAE and GCC activity on three islands, renewal of 163–78; UAE and three islands issue in 1980s 137–43; United Nations, Iraqi raising of three islands issue at 125–7; United Nations, Iraqi shelving three islands issue at 127–8; US global power, projection in 153–8; US military presence, growth of 152–3, 184–5; US policy of dual containment in 158–60, 185; *see also* Abu Musa; Dubai; Henjam Island; Larak Island; Oman; Sirri Island; Strait of Hormuz; Tunb Islands; UAE (United Arab Emirates)

The Persian Gulf Unveiled (Bulloch, J.) 95

PFLOAG (Popular Front for the Liberation of the Occupied Arab Gulf) 112

piracy: history of 186n13; in Persian Gulf 7, 8–9, 16–17, 24; 'Piratical Coast' 8, 10, 34, 180; slavery and 67

PLO (Palestine Liberation Organization) 119, 124, 131, 132, 134, 136, 163, 183, 184

Pravda 109

Qaboos bin Said, Sultan of Oman 125, 147, 150

El-Qaddafi, Colonel Muammar 135

Qajar Shahs of Persia 7, 13–14, 26, 28, 180, 186n9, 187n28, 192n84, 195n179

Qatar 10, 11, 15, 64, 70, 76, 85, 95, 107, 112, 119, 126, 141, 146, 169; Palestinian settlement in 162; US protection for 156, 165

Qawassim (Joasmis) 15, 16, 20, 186n10, 186n13

Rafsanjani, President Akbar Hashemi 145, 146, 148, 150, 165, 166–7, 171, 173, 177

Ramazani, Rouhollah 165

Ramsbotham, Peter 94

Ras al-Khaimah, Khaled bin Saqr, Sheikh of 96

Ras al-Khaimah, Saqr Bin Muhammad al-Qasimi, Sheikh of 53, 59–60, 70, 89, 90, 91, 92, 93, 94, 95–6, 97–8, 138, 139

Ras al-Khaimah, Sultan, Sheikh of 47, 53, 59–60, 94, 97

Rashid, Sheikh Katib bin 34, 35

RDJTF (Rapid Deployment Joint Task Force) 130, 131–2

Reagan, President Ronald, administration of 135, 153, 162

Reuters, J. B. 13

Rifkind, Defence Secretary Malcolm 175

Ross, Colonel Edward 34, 53, 60

Rostow, Walter 82

Rouhani, Ayatollah Sadegh 201n2

Rusk, Dean 80, 81, 92–3

Russia 6, 7, 13–14, 16, 25–6, 29, 31, 32, 37, 45, 50–1, 71; Anglo-Russian rivalry 32; Anglo-Russian Treaty (1907) 54; Constitutional Revolution in 14; Franco-Russian alliance 33; India, threat to 38, 40–1, 47; Russian Revolution and aftermath 54–5, 68–9; Russo-Persian Wars 13–14; strengthening Iranian territorial control 35–6, 180

Sad-ul-Mulk, Governor of Lingah 57–8

Sadeghi, Hossein 148–9

Safavid dynasty in Persia 13, 76

Said, Saif 141

Said bin Hamad al-Qasimi, Sheikh of Sharjah 65

Saiyid Sa'id, Imam of Muscat 15, 17, 18, 19, 20, 21, 22, 23, 60, 188n51

Salisbury, Robert Cecil, Lord 38, 54

Salman, Sheikh of Bahrain 21–3

Saqr ibn Muhammad, Sheikh of Sharjah 108

Sarmadi, Morteza 168, 172

Sassanian era in Persia 76

Satari, General Mansur 173
Saudi Arabia 76, 81–2, 92, 107, 110, 117, 163, 175, 177; Arab Federation, Iran and 85; Arab radicals, Iran, Britain and 103; Bahrain, Iran and 84; Buraimi Oasis 65–6; Damascus Declaration 149, 151; improved relations with Iraq 136; Iran–Iraq War and 118–19, 120, 121, 125–6; Iranian rapprochement with 146, 177–8; Libyan pressure on 135; material and logistics aid for Iraq from 135; Palestinian settlement in 162; US cooperation with 130, 131, 150, 154–7
Schofield, Richard 165
Seistan, British interest in 27
Shaikh Shuaib Island 62
Shargah, Jowasimi, Sheikh of 46–7, 48, 49, 51, 52, 53, 54, 55, 59, 60
Sharjah: *Al-Khalij* 142; Sheikhs of 49, 52, 59, 65, 88, 90, 91, 92, 93, 94, 95, 99, 104, 108, 142–3
Sheil, Colonel 23–4
Shiraz: annual tribute of 22; British threat of advance towards 27; Prince of 8; Treaty of 19, 23
Shuster, Morgan 68
Sirri Island 15, 21, 25, 34–5, 46–7, 49, 50–2, 54; as bargaining chip 40, 51, 181; double capacity argument 57–9; revival of controversy between Iran and Britain 55–7
'Six plus Two' arrangement, failure of 149–51
SNSC (Supreme national Security Council) of Iran 172–3
Somalia 106, 111, 136
South Africa 32, 37, 38
South Yemen 81, 95, 103, 106, 107, 109, 112–113, 118, 134, 183, 1235
Soviet Union 81–2, 97, 101, 108–9, 111, 112–13; Afghanistan, invasion of 79–80, 116, 128–9; China and 159; collapse of 154; international environment, dealing with 79–83; Iraq, relationship with 77; regional realignment 116
Stewart, Michael 86
Strait of Hormuz 6, 15, 16, 25, 40–1, 45, 54, 120, 125, 143, 178; British lease or purchase of islands in 61–3; strategic importance of 77, 104–5, 111–12, 125, 153, 158, 180
Straw, Jack 1

Suez: British withdrawal from 'east of Suez' 4, 15, 73, 74, 89, 113, 128, 180, 181; Suez War 74
Sultan ibn Muhammad, Sheikh of Sharjah 108, 142
Sykes, Sir Percy 5, 36
Syria 95, 107, 108, 110, 119, 134–6, 146, 149–51, 160–1, 162, 177

'third-power policy' of Iran 71, 195n179
Thoweymee, Sultan of Muscat 21
The Times 94, 97
Townley, Walter 61–2, 63
Trevor, Captain 44
Trucial states 15; exclusive agreement with Britain (1892) 10–12, 37, 70
Tunb Islands, Greater and Lesser 41, 56–7; activity on, renewal of 163–78; approach to issue of Abu Musa and 1–3; April and August 1992 incidents 164–8; Arab Federation, linkage with 85–6; Arab–Iranian controversies over 96–8; Bahrain, linkage with 84; British arguments on, review of 56–61; British double capacity argument concerning 57–9; British factor of prescription 61; contention between Iran and Arab world, prolonged issue of 176–8; disputed between Iran and Britain 45–51, 56–61, 180–1; failure of Iraq on issue of 128–43; geopolitics and role of major powers in issue of 179–85; half-solution option from Britain on 89–96; importance of issue of 179; international forums, UAE raising issue at 169–70; international reaction to UAE hard line on 174–6; Iranian determination to recover 83–4, 86–8; Iranian reaction to UAE hard line on 172–3; Iranian sovereignty over, issue of 98–9; Iraqi plan to attack and seize 124–5; Iraqi raising issue at United Nations of 125–7; Iraqi shelving issue at United Nations of 127–8; letters concerning Arab title to 59–60; negotiations, UAE breaking off 171–2; preconditions, UAE subjecting negotiations to 170–1; priority-in-occupation argument by Britain 60–1; regional forums, UAE raising issue at 169–70; revival of Iraqi interest in 122–4; UAE and GCC activity concerning, renewal of 163–78; UAE

and issue in 1980s of 137–43; UAE hard-line position on 168–72
Tunisia 107, 161

UAE (United Arab Emirates) 3, 4, 59, 66, 76, 85, 86, 92, 94, 95–6, 96–8, 104, 106–7, 113; breaking off negotiations on three islands 171–2; British reaction to action on three islands issue 174–6; and GCC activity concerning three islands, renewal of 163–78; hard-line position on three islands 168–72; Iranian reaction to hard line on three islands 172–3; and issue in 1980s of three islands 137–43; preconditions, subjecting negotiations on three islands to 170–1; raising issue of three islands in regional forums 169–70; US protection for 156
Ul-Mamalek, Mostufi, Prime Minister of Iran 63
Umm-ul-Kowain 37
United Nations: Iraqi moves at 103–7; Iraqi raising of three islands issue at 125–7; Iraqi shelving three islands issue at 127–8
United States: CENTCOM (US Central Command) 130, 131; global power, projection in Persian Gulf 153–8; international environment, dealing with 79–83; military presence in Gulf, growth of 152–3, 184–5; policy of dual containment in Persian Gulf 158–60, 185; reaction to UAE action on three islands issue 174–6

Velayati, Foreign Minister Ali Akbar 141, 146, 147, 150, 166
Verba Island, British hold over 64–5

Walker, Julian 61
WAM (Emirates News Agency) 167–8
Warden, F. 23
Willock, Sir Henry 18, 22
Wilson, Colonel F. A. 35, 56, 57–8
Wilson, Prime Minister Harold 74, 80, 89
Wright, Sir Denis 12, 39, 85, 86–7, 88, 90–1, 92, 94, 98

Yazdi, Ibrahim 124
Young Turks 13
Yusuf-bin-Mohamed, Sheikh 34, 58, 59

Zahedi, Foreign Minister A. 87
Zahlan, Rosemarie Said 97, 141, 142, 160
Zakhnuniyeh Island, disputes with Britain over 64
Zayed, Sheikh of Abu Dhabi 95, 97, 119, 141, 176